The Life and Times of
Martha Laurens Ramsay
1759–1811

The Life and Times of Martha Laurens Ramsay 1759–1811

Joanna Bowen Gillespie

UNIVERSITY OF SOUTH CAROLINA PRESS

UNIVERSITY OF SOUTH CAROLINA *BICENTENNIAL*

© 2001 University of South Carolina

Published in Columbia, South Carolina, by the
University of South Carolina Press

Manufactured in the United States of America

05 04 03 02 01   5 4 3 2 1

Library of Congress Cataloging-in-Publication Data

Gillespie, Joanna Bowen.
    The life and times of Martha Laurens Ramsay, 1759–1811 / Joanna Bowen
Gillespie.
        p. cm.
Includes bibliographical references and index.
    ISBN 1-57003-373-0 (alk. paper)
    1. Ramsay, Martha Laurens, 1759–1811. 2. Charleston (S.C.)—Biography.
3. Women—South Carolina—Charleston—Biography. 4. Upper class women—
South Carolina—Charleston—Biography. 5. Christian women—South
Carolina—Charleston—Biography. 6. Women—South Carolina—Charleston—
Religious life. 7. Charleston (S.C.)—Social life and customs. 8. Charleston
(S.C.)—History—1775–1865. 9. Christian biography—South Carolina
Charleston. I. Title.
F279.C453 R364 2001
975.7'91503'092—dc21   2001000742

Contents

Illustrations

Chronology of
Martha Laurens Ramsay
1759–1811

1759	Born in Charles Town, South Carolina; christened Martha Laurens (called Patsy).
1764	Next older sister, Eleanor (called Nelly), dies at age 8; family relocates to new mansion and gardens on East Bay Street.
1765	Father's enemies invade family's home at midnight because of Stamp Act; youngest living brother, James (Jemmy), born (nicknamed "Georgie Liberty").
1770	Mother dies after giving birth to Mary Eleanor (called Polly). Emotional devastation.
1771	Papa takes brothers to England; Uncle James (1728–1784) and wife move in to care for Martha and baby Polly; probable year of Martha's confirmation at St. Philip's.
1772	Martha's first cousin Mary Bremar (Molsy) involved in scandal.
1773	Martha's secret religious covenant created December 23.
1775	Uncle James' health poor; he and wife sail for England with Patsy and baby Polly. Papa elected president of the Continental Congress in Philadelphia.
1776	Beginnings of war; Martha suffers severe measles in England.
1777	Martha's first niece (John's daughter) born February 18 in England. Martha and Uncle James' household relocate from England to Nimes, France.
1779	Martha establishes local village school in Vigan. Henry Laurens appointed ambassador to Holland. Brother John proposes freeing and arming slaves to help fight England.
1780	En route to Holland, Henry Laurens captured by the British and held in Tower of London. Martha petitions John Adams and Benjamin Franklin for Henry's exchange or release.
1781	Henry Laurens released from the Tower of London 31 December in broken health.

1782	Henry Laurens appointed one of four U.S. commissioners for peace negotiations. Martha considers a marriage proposal from French merchant. John is killed in a South Carolina skirmish at end of the war.
1783	Martha travels to Bath, England, to care for her father; visits the countess of Huntingdon.
1784	Papa and Henry Laurens Jr. return to South Carolina; Uncle James dies and is buried in France.
1785	Martha, Aunt Mary, niece Frances Eleanor (Fanny, John's orphaned daughter), and sister Polly (Mary Eleanor) return to Charleston. Aunt Mary dies in July. Martha meets future husband, Dr. David Ramsay.
1787	Martha weds Dr. David Ramsay 28 January; Eleanor Henry Laurens Ramsay born in November.
1788	Martha's sister Polly weds Charles Pinckney; David Ramsay delivers address to the freemen of South Carolina on the federal Constitution.
1789	Martha Henry Laurens Ramsay born; David publishes *History of the American Revolution;* Papa Henry Laurens ill but recovers.
1790	Frances Henry Laurens Ramsay born; dies in infancy.
1791	Jane Montgomery born; dies in infancy. Martha begins secret diary. Celebrations honoring President Washington's visit to Charleston.
1792	Catherine Henry Laurens Ramsay born. Henry Laurens dies. David Ramsay, president of the South Carolina senate, casts tie-breaking vote to suspend slave importation for two years; also elected president of Santee Canal Company.
1793	Sabina Elliott Ramsay born.
1794	Martha's sister Mary Eleanor Pinckney dies after giving birth to her third child (Henry Laurens Pinckney); in addition to the newborn son, she leaves two daughters, ages three and five.
1795	Martha's first son, David Ramsay Jr., born; depression, "dismal dark night of trial"; surrenders dowry rights to two inherited properties; niece Fanny, aged eighteen, elopes.
1796	Martha recovers from "dark night of the soul"; a daughter, also named Jane Montgomery, born; David Jr. very ill but recovers.
1797	Baby Jane dies in July, age six months; investment in Santee Canal wipes out Martha's $25,000 legacy.
1798	James born; husband David Ramsay declares bankruptcy.

1800	David Ramsay publishes "Oration on the Death of Lt. Gen. George Washington."
1801	Nathaniel Ramsay born. David Ramsay publishes "A Review of Medicine in the Eighteenth Century."
1802	William Ramsay born.
1803	David Ramsay sued by Martha's brother Harry (Henry Laurens Jr.) for full amount of bonds owed.
1804	David Ramsay delivers oration on cession of Louisiana; Martha's stepson John Witherspoon Ramsay graduates from College of New Jersey and apprentices in medicine.
1806	Financial straits raise fears that household slaves must be sold.
1807	David Ramsay publishes a hagiographic life of George Washington.
1808	Terrible fire in downtown Charleston; Ramsay neighborhood threatened.
1809	David Ramsay publishes the first *History of South Carolina* (two volumes bound in one) with Martha's help.
1810	Miss Futurell returns to England. David Jr. goes to College of New Jersey at Princeton. Martha becomes ill in August with unnamed "severe affliction."
1811	Martha dies June 10. *Memoirs of the Life of Martha Laurens Ramsay* registered on 15 July in South Carolina by her four daughters.
1812	Second edition of *Memoirs of the Life of Martha Laurens Ramsay* published; also one in Philadelphia.
1813	Armstrong's first edition of *Memoirs* published in Boston.
1814	Armstrong's second edition of *Memoirs* published.
1815	David Ramsay fatally shot by escaped mentally ill patient.

Family Birth Order

Henry Laurens (1724–1792) and
Eleanor Ball (1731–1770), married 1750

Eleanor	1751–1751
Ann Elizabeth	1752–1752
Henry	1753–1758
John	1754–1782
Eleanor	1758–1764
infant	1757–1757
Elias	1758–1758
Martha	1759–1811
Henry Jr.	1763–1821
James	1765–1775
Samuel	1767–1767
infant girl	1768–1768
Mary Eleanor	1770–1794

David Ramsay (1749–1815) and
Martha Laurens (1759–1811), married 1787

Eleanor Henry Laurens Ramsay	1787–1857
Martha Henry Laurens Ramsay	1789–1844
Frances Henry Laurens Ramsay	1790–1791?
Jane Montgomery Ramsay	1791–1791
Catherine Henry Laurens Ramsay	1792–1876
Sabina Elliott Ramsay	1793–1853
David Ramsay Jr.	1795–1826
Jane Montgomery Ramsay	1796–1797
James Ramsay	1798–1832
Nathaniel Ramsay	1801–1882
William Ramsay	1802–1847

❦ | # Preface

CHARLESTON, SOUTH CAROLINA—visited by thousands of tourists annually for its garden and arts festivals, palmettos and oaks, elegant modern shops, bricked sidewalks, historic buildings, and racial-rainbow citizenry—may seem a surprising setting for the story of an eighteenth-century woman's struggle to be an exemplary Christian. Despite the geographic location plainly named on the title page of *Memoirs of the Life of Martha Laurens Ramsay* (1814), anyone today picking up a copy of that little antiquarian volume might easily assume it was one of the many pious memoirs once plentiful on New England library shelves. Undoubtedly that is the very impression its editor wished to convey in 1811 when he first submitted it for publication. The Charleston of his time was no more associated in the public mind with serious intellectual and religious literature than it is in today's media-diffused stereotype. Dr. David Ramsay, husband of the title character and the editor of her *Memoirs*, invoked the New England literary pattern for his wife's print memorial as a way of ensuring that this tribute to her would be seriously viewed by educated Americans up and down the Atlantic coast as well as in her native city.

Because Martha actually lived in the South, an expectation of regional allusions and distinctively southern themes is logical. Except for the topics of yellow fever epidemics and mosquitoes, however, much specific local color is startling in its absence. The large African population is also stunningly absent. With religion the intellectual and emotional centerpiece of most women's memoirs, denominational antagonism or competition—invigorating conflict between Anglicans and Dissenters, or upstart evangelical itinerant Quakers, Baptists, and Methodists—might also have been expected. But reference to religious rivalry is similarly minimal, genteel, and high-minded in what it omits. By the time Martha came on the scene in Charles Town's history, spiritual contention may have become more civilized than in the early part of the century, or solid institutional establishments such as St. Philip's and the "French Church" of Huguenot settlers had lowered the tension volume. The expansive commerce of this seaport metropolis during the mid-1800s—supposedly the most sophisticated American city in which to shop during the pre-Revolutionary period—might also have been expected to feature in the writings of a merchant's daughter, but that topic, crucial in her actual experience, remained part of the unnamed background in Martha's recordings.

Early critics of the lavish lifestyle among eighteenth-century Charles Town oligarchs enjoyed labeling Charles Town immoral—a hedonistic, self-indulgent culture that dismayed upright New Englanders. Even the first Church of England clergyman appointed to St. Philip's in 1708 was not welcomed by the already independent Anglicans in that parish, although his artist wife, Henrietta Johnston, was an immediate and contrasting hit. The self-styled gentry were eager to celebrate their economic eminence by keeping a talented portraitist occupied and relatively well paid. Henrietta's husband, the Rev. Gideon Johnston, outraged by the ignorance flourishing in the city, attempted to establish "a Free School" to raise the city's moral tone. His successor in the 1730s, the Rev. Alexander Garden, a more popular representative of English governance, remained rector of St. Philip's for some thirty years. The city itself expanded its streets and bridges, even becoming the second town in the American colonies to purchase "a water engine" for fighting the fires so continually devastating to buildings constructed of cypress and mahogany.[1]

But the greater menace always lurking in white Charles Town residents' consciousness, never explicitly noted by Martha, was the threat implicit in the city's disproportionately large Afro-American population. The first serious slave conspiracy was reported and punished as early as the 1720s. The driving motive of business prosperity could allow no brakes on importing slave labor, however. Slavery was considered essential to the cultivation of fortunes, as well as of the main cash crop, rice, and other standard items of trade, such as tar, pitch, turpentine, leather, corn, beef, and pork. The *South Carolina Gazette*, established in 1732, always carried advertisements for runaway slaves as a standard news component. The city's "paupers, vagrants, and beggars" were a concern only for churchmen associated with St. Philip's, like the father of Martha. A public workhouse and hospital, as well as a public burying ground, were established by the 1740s. Taverns with names like the Tea Kettle and Lamp, or Sign of the Bacchus abounded, though in Martha's genteel words there is no mention of anything as tawdry as public drunkenness or rioting. A letter in that local newspaper may have registered one of the first public condemnations—in Charles Town if not in the American colonies generally—of the sexual double standard in Martha's lifetime: "Then equal Laws let Custom Find, / And neither Sex oppress: / More Freedom give to Womankind, / Or to Mankind give less."[2] Yet none of this insouciant worldliness colors the

published *Memoirs*. Hurricanes, epidemics, the erection of a Jewish syna-
gogue, war with Indians, pirates, and the French, slave atrocities such as
"the detestable crime" of poisoning white owners, devastating economic
depression, and the triumphant building of a new state house—all such
events in Martha Laurens Ramsay's external world were never mentioned
in her writings, however indisputably present in her setting.

Why *place* is such a pivotal element in this study is that it single-handedly
demonstrates the universality of the Anglo-American religious culture in
which Martha Laurens Ramsay participated. The pattern in which she
wrote her private spiritual meditations and diary entries was shared by
educated, literarily competent women in the Anglo-Protestant world on
both sides of the Atlantic and had been for several centuries. Martha would
have shaped her letters and diary in the same way had she been born in
Waltham, Massachusetts, grown up in Elizabeth, New Jersey, or lived her
married life in Boston or Philadelphia. Thanks to the home into which she
was born, the religious consciousness of her parents, and the books and
journals to which she was exposed, she could align herself consciously and
unconsciously with other highly educated and cosmopolitan women who
chose to pour their spiritual and moral woes into diary-keeping and letter-
writing formats.[3] Among the published memoirs of eighteenth-century
American women, Martha's appear to be unique because she was from
Charles Town, South Carolina—emerging from Anglican spiritual roots
and a southern ethos permeated by regional issues like slavery. On the
other hand, her memoirs were indeed universal in tone and genre, deliberately designed to be part of this universal feminine religious "mainstream."

The difficult task of reinhabiting a long-vanished era like Charles
Town, South Carolina (known as Charleston after 1783), in the latter half of
the 1700s, is to avoid a simplistic slant on the title-subject's world as her preserved texts or manuscripts present it. No person's life and times has ever
been as straightforward, linear, and uncomplex as readers today may be led
to assume from a first reading of Martha Laurens Ramsay's preserved
words. Our culturally cultivated dependence on literal "fact" is the trap; if
something is not explicitly stated, we assume that such a fact cannot have
existed. Or, since it cannot be visibly documented, it has to be overlooked,
irrelevant. Literal dependence on historically preserved texts is both pleas-
urable and burdensome: a delight because the actual words, persisting
through the centuries, are our window into the actual thoughts of a Martha
Laurens Ramsay. It becomes a burden because those religious words and
the mindset they express were of course produced by a bewildering array

of forces and relationships, the vast majority of which can never have been explicitly named or mentioned. Just as some of the household implements Martha used every day and took for granted have long since become outmoded and are thus unknown to us, many of the people she saw at concerts or in church, whose ideas and language she absorbed, were never documented in her text but are nevertheless part of her story. The majority of white Carolinians Martha would have known and greeted remain without description; even the teachers that were obviously important in her development remain mostly outside her documented existence.

Readers themselves have the task of keeping in mind the complexity of her Charles Town backdrop. If the other major British American cities Martha knew were Boston, New York, and Philadelphia, her own was "richest" in the number of African-background pedestrians on the streets. She and her family knew the primary circle of the few wealthy, ambitious white merchants in that city, but they probably knew very few of the rowdy frontier-type stragglers scratching out an existence in the heartless seaport. Awesome public structures fronted grimy, stench-filled alleyways, and the caressing moist sea breezes were always suspected of bearing deadly disease. Other American cities also had harbors teeming with ships, imports, and immigrants, but none were as closely linked with the West Indies plantation economy and culture—and attitudes encouraging quick personal riches but little concern for public services like sanitation and civic regulation.

Thanks to Walter Fraser's unique "biography" of her city, *Charleston! Charleston!*, the actualities of Martha's life and times can become a lively part of her story. Nevertheless, the religiously expressed self-focus dominating the *Memoirs* turns out to be not the refrain of her life story but the stanzas themselves—the entire focus of her self-presentation as preserved and published.

Yet Martha Laurens Ramsay may in fact be a pioneer in the accumulating field of women's history, if not in dimensions we currently associate with that term. She was indeed one of the rare American women whose record reveals a conscious determination to shape her life around a formal religious covenant. That spirit—creating a personal written life plan—made her a hero and pioneer to nineteenth-century Christian women successors. For students today, that kind of radicalism (no radicalism of any kind was associated with most women in that era) can be seen as a unique expression of individualism for an eighteenth-century woman. In what we today would consider an unbelievably cramped set of possibilities, Martha Laurens Ramsay's act of writing, signing, dating, preserving, and cherishing a religious covenant she intended as the touchstone of the rest of her life was a remarkable act for a woman. The qualifying phrase "for women" is not merely tedious repetition but hugely significant, underscoring as it does the narrow limitations circumscribing all females in her time and place. Its impact on a strong-minded female like Martha can scarcely be imagined today.

This present biographical study was deduced primarily from the information found in her writings, some two hundred print pages in a slender 3½" x 6" leather-bound volume titled "Memoirs of the Life of Martha Laurens Ramsay." These were compiled and edited within weeks after her death by her grieving but adoring husband, Dr. David Ramsay. This primary publication, reprinted and excerpted frequently in the nineteenth century, offers today's suspicious reader no hint of current radicalism, while its language and ardent spiritual (we today add psychological) self-analysis mesmerizes and puzzles. What we might hope to see as the "real" person remains largely concealed beneath eloquent verbiage. Even further constricting present-day access to the presentation of her authentic voice and viewpoint were her own mental constraints about what kinds of self-expression belonged in a secret diary, in personal letters, or in meditations—plus a husband's editorial opinion about the kind of memoirs he wanted to compile.

Bringing the "lived" Martha out of family and Revolutionary War shadows onto center stage—the biographic challenge—required reconstructing her culture and context. Her sophisticated use of religious concepts for coping with her own interior and external anxieties produced writings that were not intended so much for autobiographical self-disclosure—as we today expect of memoirs—but rather to demonstrate her mental capabilities in applying theological language to everyday acts and decisions. Her dialogues with God illustrate what she thought crucial and important enough to record; they have nothing to do with favorite recipes or local gossip, only with her culture's view of sin. Her soul efforts were cloaked in high theological terms because that was the way in which the male devotional writers she admired and wanted to imitate expressed themselves.

It is particularly puzzling that she does not mention a historic event like the once-in-a-lifetime Charleston extravaganza that welcomed President George Washington in 1791. Her hero-brother John had been General Washington's intrepid, daring aide-de-camp during some of the dark days of the Revolutionary War. Naturally Martha would want to greet the great visitor and receive the accolades he would tender the Laurens name. The

president undoubtedly also complimented her aging and ill father's service
to the nation's birth process as diplomatic prisoner of war in the Tower of
London and later negotiator of the Peace Treaty. But if Martha went to that
gala, what she wore or said or how she felt about such a glamorous occasion was not recorded in her secret diary or in any letter her editor included
in the *Memoirs*. She would have deemed that public information; soul
work, for her, was intensely private. The kind of immortality she wanted
was spiritual, not literary.

Deciphering her "lived" life from what was preserved in the *Memoirs*,
then, required extensive contextual information, first and foremost from
the lives and writings of the men who shaped the course of her life, and
thus her attitudes and her writings. These were found primarily in the published volumes of *Papers of Henry Laurens*, edited by Philip Hamer et al.
(Columbia: University of South Carolina Press, 1968–), and the biography
of her husband, *To Be an American: David Ramsay and the Making of the
American Consciousness*, by Arthur Shaffer (Columbia: University of South
Carolina Press, 1991). Dr. Ramsay logically decided to pad his tribute to her
with any other of her writings he could readily collect. He amended the
limited amount of prose he chose to extract from her diary (sixty-seven
pages out of a completed memoir of more than two hundred pages) with
several long footnotes, one of which illustrated her technique of self-
education: a comprehensive abridgement of a British preacher's treatise on
"heart religion," which she made in outline form. Tutoring one's self
through taking notes and outlining an author's published work was
the eighteenth-century autodidact's method—more often used by men
than women it would appear. Dr. Ramsay supplemented the core of her
memoirs—excerpts from the diary, labeled appendix 5—with five other
appendices and a forty-seven-page biographical introduction of laudatory
anecdotes commending her intellectual range, skilled household management, mindful curriculum planning for her family "school," and careful
programming of a beautiful death scene. The memoir itself was arranged
chronologically and in every respect followed the standard New England
pattern established by preachers, daughters, and friends of eminently pious
women. Other cultural artifacts of her era—newspapers, novels, textbooks,
neighbors' letters, Charleston reminiscences—yielded small but illuminat-
ing nuggets of information that helped evoke her physical reality.

Martha's prose was cast in the two verbal forms available to all literate
women in her time: diary and letters. Epistolary communication was as
natural as breathing for her, and in her father's agenda for his children it

was equally important. Still, however necessary the ability to compose intelligent, elegant letters, diaries were assumed to connote a deeper level of introspection; as such, they were accorded greater cultural significance by both the diary keeper and the memoir reader. A diary was viewed as a safe place in which to consign one's fears, hopes, and dreams to language, to pour one's deepest self into words on paper. The act of writing one's self into being, ostensibly for the writer's eyes only, suggests a harvest of compelling insight into the writer's pivotal issues of identity and location, since the major quest of diary examination is always the writer's autobiographic query: "Where do I fit in all this?" For the episodic entries and fragments of discontent in a compiled memoir like Ramsay's, that framework provides the necessary subtext of coherence. Dr. Ramsay's major justification for transforming his wife's prose into a published memoir lay in that cultural view of the significance of diaries. Letters were assumed to be less significant, in a way, if more chatty; unfortunately, in Martha's case only a very small number of letters had been preserved, in contrast with the marvelously human and witty lifetime correspondence of her contemporary Abigail Adams.

Martha Laurens Ramsay may well have been reaching for a bit of earthly immortality when she confided, in the last days of her life on earth, where her secret writings had been hidden and requested that they be preserved "as a common book" for the family. Whether or not the dying middle-aged woman recalled her youthful vow to "do honor to that last finishing scene . . . with my expiring breath," the mournful watchers at her bedside believed that the way she had patterned the last hours of her life fulfilled perfectly the Christian memoirist's ideal. In the pattern of many learned females whose memoirs she had read and admired, her final gestures provided the deathbed imprimatur for turning her previously unknown and secret writings "toward a more enlarged sphere of usefulness," the possibility of influencing others through their publication.

Since the originals of Ramsay's diary and most of her letters have apparently disappeared, the experience of seeing her handwriting (during the Revolutionary War) in the microfilmed collections of first American diplomats in Europe, Benjamin Franklin and John Adams, makes an almost visceral impact. Young Miss Martha Laurens herself had petitioned them directly in an effort to obtain her father's release from the Tower of London. An audacious step for even an upper-class woman, those well-written, politely demanding letters are a first concrete evidence of her independence and practicality. Someone in the family had to do it, and her older brother was in the American army and her uncle was too ill. Mrs. Ramsay's hand—at that time still Miss Laurens—like her father's and brother's, was bold, legible, almost masculine in style, in marked contrast with her husband, David's, erratic physician scrawl. It was clearly a product of her father's belief that penmanship indicated character, breeding, and social responsibility.

No flouter of boundaries in any case, Martha was the kind of woman wise enough to wrap herself in them—both as a means of preventing herself from offending the cultural ideals she aimed to embody and as giving herself an impeccable exterior that would allow her own mental agenda to develop behind it. She disdained celebrity in any field other than religion as unworthy and became one of its American exemplars in nineteenth-century Protestantism. The memoirs were cited after her death in a variety of popular religious literature, most notably Sarah Josepha Hale's *Woman's Record; or Sketches of All Distinguished Women from "The Beginning" till a.d. 1850* (New York: Harper & Brothers, 1853). Interestingly, the excerpts most often reprinted were drawn from the soul-searching miseries of her diary, testimony to the universal language of women's spiritual agonies and to the uneven cultural weight assigned the more casual discourse of letters. For nineteenth-century editors, formal religious language and psalmodic intensity were the telling theological qualities.[4]

The larger contextualized picture of Martha Laurens Ramsay is of a woman who set out to exemplify the patriarchal expectations of female Christians in her era and class—dutiful daughter and respectfully submissive wife. The *Memoirs* valorized her skill in that accomplishment while unwittingly revealing the disjunction between her willed patterning of self (to fit those unspoken boundaries) and her striving individual spirit. Since all her writings are subjectively religious in language, imagery, and psychology, that disjunction has in the past been glossed as "evangelical." A more recent interpretation suggests that pietism, in the broad meaning of inward and subjective spiritual emphasis, is a more evocative description of her religiosity.[5] For many readers, the diary's emotional intensity and self-criticism overshadow the more accessible human glimpsed in her notes and letters, since authentic "religious experience" in our culture has usually been measured in relation to Wesleyan revivalism—an ecstatic emotional state seen as the mark of "true religion."[6] The predominance of self-analysis in the *Memoirs* make it the palimpsest for her total prose legacy, allowing her image to be treated as one-dimensional and "evangelical." In spite of all the constraints imposed on Martha Laurens Ramsay and her efforts to "surrender" her will, a striving spirit that cannot keep from breaking through is what makes her interesting. We expect flaws rather than goodness in our heroes, even a woman whose goal in life is to achieve "the heroism becoming a woman of an honest and a pious heart," her father's commission to her in the fateful year 1776.[7] The strains of that impossibly demanding self-image reveal her humanity and evoke our empathy.

Today we admire Martha Ramsay for choosing to employ the only psychologically analytic language available to her, making religion a high-minded template for writing herself into being. If that overall life story is somehow disappointing, it is because we have insufficiently reentered her world—her mindset, her dreams, her ambitions, her self-perceptions. Including Martha Laurens Ramsay in the pantheon of early American women prose writers gives us the soul and sensibility of an elite white southern woman in early America who struggled through and survived turbulent national, financial, and familial times—a personal window into our national beginnings.

Acknowledgments

I FIRST NOTICED Martha Laurens Ramsay's *Memoirs* while browsing a secondhand San Francisco bookstore in the mid-1980s, early in my awakening to the excitement of the "new" American history to be found through women's perspective on events in their own times and in their own voices. I had discovered the only "biographies" available for eighteenth-century women were their so-called memoirs, that were nothing as personally autobiographical or revelatory as we expect today. Even so, I was avidly reading all I could find. When it came to Martha's memoirs, however, it wasn't easy. I was uneducated in southern revolutionary history, unaware of the significance of her illustrious family in the revolutionary era and of her ringside seat to the writing and ratification of the U.S. Constitution. In her own words, her "participation" in those heady events was nil. But the passion in her religious language remained magnetic, making me return again to try to figure it out. In and of itself, her religiosity was not off-putting since I was involved in my own midlife version of it; however, the way she described hers made little connection with any I knew at the time. As an independent scholar, I was heavily dependent on friends and colleagues at the Stanford Institute for Research on Women and Gender and many California libraries, including the resources of the Huntington Library in southern California.

A senior NEH fellowship at the Omohundro Institute of Early American History and Culture in Williamsburg, Virginia, and long immersion in the vast literature of British and American women's pious memoirs helped me begin to uncover the rich layers of South Carolina history, theology, and the developing slave economy that had shaped Martha's life and times. My own deepening experience as a late-twentieth-century Anglican brought me within range of her soul struggles and a fascination with understanding her touch of mysticism. The most valuable reinhabiting of her life and times came from acting like a "subscriber" to the *Columbian Magazine* from 1787 to 1792 in the Reading Room of the John Carter Brown Library in Providence, Rhode Island. Like Martha and David Ramsay, I pored over each successive issue, being naturally drawn into their times and mindsets. I made firsthand acquaintance with the books, authors, viewpoints, events, and humor (as it seemed to them) crammed into that early magazine's infinitesimally tiny print and yellowing pages—scarcity of paper a probable explanation for such near-blinding frugality. Afterwards, as I left the library, Martha's world surrounded me in a figurative sense: the eighteenth-century cobblestones in a few streets of old Providence were still there, evocative of a very different "walk" underfoot and one present-ing mortal danger in today's shoes. Seeing houses that her contemporaries lived in or visited, trees that were young when she was alive in another part of the early nation, and furniture like that she herself may have dusted (or admired on her travels)—all helped loosen my late-twentieth-century mental horizon. During that period I benefited greatly from the interest of John Carter Brown Library director Norman Fiering and the excellent staff of that wonderful collection; I was also a fortunate participant in its weekly discussions with scholars exploring widely varied aspects of the same men-tal and physical world. My neighbor and mentor, the late Nancy Lyman Roelker, a retired professor of early modern French history, was important in my self-education, and her sister, Helen Roelker Kessler, then a research historian with the Sibley's Harvard Graduates project at the Massachusetts Historical Society, was a valued colleague offering an extra pair of eyes.

Linda Wagner-Martin (*Telling Women's Lives: The New Biography*, 1994) recommends obtaining "more background and more insight than the subject herself may ever have had" to re-create a life lived two centuries earlier—advice that has sent me to the Rare Book Collection of the Swem Library at College of William and Mary; the Omohundro Institute of Early American History and Culture Library; the John Carter Brown Library and the John Hay Library in Providence; the Rhode Island Historical Society, Providence; the Columbiana Library in Columbia and the South Carolina Historical Society in Charleston; the Southern Collection at the University of North Carolina, Chapel Hill; the Massachusetts Historical Society in Boston; and the manuscript collection of the New York Public Library, New York City. Plus I have had numerous telephone conversations with museums, offices, scholars, and history departments.

I can never adequately thank the many individuals who have assisted and enlightened me, sometimes more by providence than by my ability to frame questions. Mary Beth Norton loaned me a picaresque fantasy-type novel Martha had owned (about which I would never have known or even guessed). Nina Dayton gave me advice on compiling a biography of a sub-ject whose writings are minimal. The late Dr. George C. Rogers provided unfailing encouragement and suggested that this could (and should) be an "insider" family history, an emotional mirror for a distinguished early

American family in amazing, painful times, with a focus that studies of her male relatives would not produce. Many colleagues sent me snippets of reference to Martha and the Laurens family they had come across while working on their own projects—especially Edith Gelles, biographer of Abigail Adams and colleague from Stanford University's Center for Research on Women and Gender; Jean B. Lee, now at University of Wisconsin; and Peggy Clark, my "inside link" to the Laurens Papers editorial office.

For editing and pruning my overenthusiastic prose (likely one of the reasons I understood David Ramsay as well as I did), I am grateful to many gimlet-eyed editors over the years: first, Michael McGiffert at the *William and Mary Quarterly,* Phil Gura at *Early American Literature,* and a host of collegial women historians, many more than can possibly be named. In the manuscript's final version, Ruth Herndon provided fine logic and instinct based on what her students would find useful, and Phyllis Bolton, a multi-talented artist, patiently helped weed out the contextual welter. Ruth Kaufman, formerly of Yale University Press, and neighbor and poet Joan Landis were both helpful. I am indebted to Alexander Moore at the University of South Carolina Press and his two anonymous readers, who readily grasped the significance of Martha's story and pushed me toward clarity.

I'm also forever indebted to David Gillespie, my husband and resident computer expert, for countless gifts of disentanglement and formatting, plus for sticking with me and Martha through the years.

Friends have asked how I managed to live with Martha's self-castigating, sin-berating persona. Do I like her? My answer, after long acquaintance, is that I have come to see that aspect of her personality as only one part of the total human woman. Because it *is* the primary part of her that remains visible, it has been overemphasized as *the* authoritative voice. But the woman who loved, wept, gritted her teeth, and aimed high was also a friend I might well have known. Someone recently asked what would happen should the long-lost original of the diary turn up, throwing new light on my interpretations and assumptions. Because I care that Martha Laurens Ramsay should "have her say" historically and take her place in the Laurens family pantheon, I could, to use her words, only "rejoice at being proven wrong." If that pipe dream of every biographer should miraculously occur, knowing more about her life and times would only enrich us.

An experienced British historical biographer, Victoria Glendenning, gave me a summary in a *New York Times* interview: "There is no such thing as a definitive biography. All versions . . . from the gossip and Chinese Whispers of . . . contemporaries, to the wilder flights of speculative fancy and the sober gleanings of scholarship and historical research" contribute. But, even if writers do their "utmost," they are never able to state conclusively exactly what "*was* . . . . The living, breathing, joking, suffering [subject] remains a lost original" (29 June 1999, B8). Insofar as I have succeeded, Martha Laurens Ramsay here begins to live and speak with us, for herself.

The Life and Times of
Martha Laurens Ramsay
1759–1811

Introduction

WHEN NEWBORN MARTHA LAURENS first opened her brown eyes on 3 November 1759, one of the smiling faces peering into her cradle, alongside her beaming parents, may well have been a slave nurse. This privileged South Carolina infant would grow up in a loving family unusually indulged in all the graces—books and music, art and religion—a life whose every dimension was made possible, undergirded and supported by slave labor, the basic unacknowledged element in her record. At the beginning of the twenty-first century, her life may be read solely as a narrative of elite advantage in her time and place, or it may be read as a cautionary tale about the spiritual and psychological costs of slaveholding while striving to be an exemplary Christian—a strain likely to have contributed to her adult diary entries cataloging a war within her soul.[1] Her actual life story, reconstructed, is that of a woman attempting to be the best person she knew how to be in her times—one who fulfilled her place in the scheme of things and achieved the highest self-realization possible.

Martha, usually called Patsy within her childhood family, came into the world of the booming pre-Revolutionary Charles Town slave economy. The War of Independence from Britain, 1776–1782, was the dramatic backdrop of her adolescent and young adult years. The men defining her life as a Laurens were major players in those world-changing scenes. Her father was one of the major slave importers in the Carolinas and a central figure in the Revolution.[2] He was president of the Continental Congress, then a diplomatic prisoner of war in the Tower of London, and finally, in 1782, one of four official negotiators of the peace treaty that concluded the war. The brother to whom she was closest was an aide to Gen. George Washington in the Revolutionary Army and tragically killed in one of the war's last skirmishes. Martha, living in her uncle's household after her mother died,[3] spent the decade that encompassed the war (1775–1785) in Europe, deeply affected by it vicariously but never in real physical danger.

After the war, when adult Martha Laurens returned to Charleston and became Mrs. David Ramsay in 1787, her life unfolded in sharp financial and cultural contrast with her fortunate girlhood. As the wife of a professional physician and historian, and with a family of four boys and four girls to rear and educate in urbanizing Charleston, her sphere of privilege narrowed.

Dr. David Ramsay's income, like that of many physicians in that era, was chancy: patients seemed to "rely on God to pay their doctors' fees."[4] The doctor brought a certain flair to his involvement in the city's political, religious, and civic affairs and early established himself in the wider community of the new nation's literati. Martha was similarly well known in the sphere to which educated, illustrious wives were restricted: no woman of Charleston could be called exemplary in public print until her eulogy. She died of a lingering illness at age fifty-one, 13 June 1811, leaving a devoted husband and eight living children. That same year, David honored her by collecting her writings into *Memoirs of the Life of Martha Laurens Ramsay,* a production consciously fashioned after the hagiographic voice and tone of traditional women's "pious memoirs." His act established Martha posthumously on the new nation's literary scene,[5] his print memorial to her being the first of its kind to venerate a woman from the South in the style of a New England literary genre, so far as is presently known.

Locating Martha Laurens Ramsay's biographical skeleton within the epochal issues of her times requires first and foremost an acknowledgment of the institution and realities of slavery—from the child watching her mother organize the cutting of "Negro Cloths" out of huge bolts of fabric to the adult reading tracts and sermons circulated by the emerging network of antislavery societies in the late 1780s.[6] In fact, the man she married was a distributor of the tracts, known for his antipathy toward slavery. A second invisible but powerful current was endemic to those revolutionary and constitution-crafting times, an excitement that deeply involved both the Laurens and Ramsay families. As girl and woman she imbibed the heady ethos of nation-building, the dynamic evolution of a way of thinking about one's national identity, and the invigorating horizon of new personal possibilities—all of which had to find expression within approved boundaries for white female aristocratic daughters. Third, intrinsic to her mental, emotional, and spiritual evolution, and shaping her relationship with both slavery and the new American patriotism, was the religious ethos from which her ideals, imagination, and vocabulary derived. Her actual church experience started in the Church of England in Charles Town and developed in her husband's Circular Church, a denominational hybrid he idealized as an "ecclesiastical democracy."[7] The religious language Martha used in her writing was the highest form of intellectual culture available to her; in her mental world, religion was synonymous with education and a demonstration of women's capacity for rational thought, that concept just emerging as a major source of pride for modern women. Religion was her message as well as her medium; its mediator, after her death, was her editor-husband, David Ramsay.

I

To engage first with Martha Laurens Ramsay's most visible and inclusive major theme, religion and its language—including two concepts largely outmoded in twentieth-century diaries, reason and providence—necessarily introduces her first biographer, David Ramsay. An enthusiastic word-smith himself, he was a creature of the optimism generated by the nation's struggle for independence that allowed Americans to "think, speak and act far beyond that to which they had been accustomed." Fired by a burning desire to be important to his times, he had successively married the daughters of important men: Sabina Ellis, the daughter of a rich Charleston merchant; Frances, a daughter of John Witherspoon, president of the College of New Jersey at Princeton; and Martha.[8] The same instinct that led him to convert Martha's "literary remains" into a published volume inspired him to include her famous father's wartime letters to her in the memoir.[9]

For readers idealizing the virtue and self-sacrifice recently demonstrated by Revolutionary War heroes like Generals George Washington or Nathanael Greene, David Ramsay's literary portrait of the Good Wife was audacious and timely. His active theme in books and orations was "American cultural nationalism"—trumpeting American models of achievement and their superiority over those inherited from England and Europe.[10] In addition, heroes of virtue and of military skill were an educational model he and his wife approved, one already demonstrated by his friend Jeremy Belknap's *American Biography* (Boston, 1794). But no one on the national scene had yet thought to offer a female model.

Martha kept her small cache of writings a secret from everyone, including her husband, until three days before she died. At that time, she revealed their hiding place and requested that they be presented as a "common book of the family." Thus David was given his historical mandate. Always looking for ways to instruct and inspire on the grandest possible scale, he perceived that his editorial labors on her *Memoirs* could be a triple service: matrimonial, religious, and public. He arranged and titled her materials in the following sequence, proportion, and pagination: a preface, pages iii–viii; a biographical introduction by the editor, 9–47; and six appendixes: appendix 1, "Letters from Henry Laurens to Martha Laurens" (his famous "war letters" written in 1776), 47–54; appendix 2, "Religious

Exercises," specifically her self-dedication and solemn covenant with God, 54–62; appendix 3, "Supplication for a Beloved Relative," 62–66; appendix 4, "Devout Meditations" (written between ages sixteen and nineteen), 56–98; appendix 5, "Extracts from Mrs. Ramsay's Diary," 99–166; and appendix 6, "Letters from Mrs. Ramsay," 166–99, a final section of which was subtitled "Letters to her Son (David Ramsay Jr. at Princeton College, 1810–11)," 199–219.[11] The appendixes present various facets of her life without much connective tissue.

Women's memoirs as a genre had long been the accepted pattern for an assemblage of female spiritually analytic musings.[12] Editors or compilers of memoirs—usually a clergyman, daughter, friend, or, rarely, a husband—viewed a diary as the ultimate repository of authentic self-revelation, especially sorrows and discontents. They were also a form of self-tutorial in the art of scrutinizing one's inner being. If the diary contained relatively little religious material—if it were more a budget record or domestic calendar—it would likely have been deemed unworthy of preservation in a memoir. A remarkable example of that miscalculation today is the formerly ignored, mundane diary record of an eighteenth-century Maine midwife, Martha Ballard, recently transformed into newly potent social and community history by Laurel Ulrich.[13] A few British diarists of this era, such as Hester Thrale and Fanny Burney, published written records of secular everyday life in order to give themselves some significance.[14] But the majority of women who sat down to written spiritual introspection in Martha's time treated their diaries as places for soul work rather than mere chronicle or calendar keeping.

Because of that religious preoccupation, Martha's editor believed that her diary and letters would be helpful to others who "walk[ed] in fear and darkness, for want of knowing how others have been affected in scenes of trial like their own." His primary contribution was a fulsome biographical introduction. In the preface he confessed that his first intention had been to let her words speak for themselves. But his second thought was for the reader: "Without some [contextual] knowledge, many reflections of the writer would be comparatively uninteresting, if not unintelligible." His intention was "to throw light on their contents,"[15] not tamper with their inherent sensibility. He thus stamped her major print archive with the intractable issue of two voices and two agendas, his and hers.

As presented in the *Memoirs,* Martha's written words are self-evidently her own—yet edited, annotated, and sometimes interpreted by her husband's footnotes. As far as we presently know, the original sheets of paper and journals covered with her bold, distinctive handwriting have long since disappeared. The compiled literary amalgam that became her memoir thus preserved an authentic voice of a real and thoughtful female who documented her pressing religious concerns as if the world of fact and event outside her heart did not exist—or required no explicit descriptions. Editor Ramsay imposed section titles and freely excerpted both letters and diary. Internal evidence weighs strongly against his having inserted his own words into what he selected of hers; editorial omissions, yes, but editorial intrusion only in self-labeled interpretive footnotes. Still, two authors of this governing source in the life and times of Martha Ramsay illuminate, for late-twentieth-century historians, the vexing problem of voice: who is really speaking? That quandary is further compounded by the disproportionate weight accorded anything quotable from an earlier era: words preserved on paper are presumed to constitute fact. However admiring and faithful the editor, a dual-voiced memoir mandates that today's reader bring a speculative, expansive approach to what in this case is presented as "history."

However, without David Ramsay's biographical framework and its minimal inclusion of concrete events (his writing also being more generous with rhetoric than particulars), Martha Ramsay's writings would be even more disembodied. Because her reporting of deaths and prayers for the bereaved were usually dated, they provide a partial chronological anchor in the diary. Most of her pages, however, are filled with agonizing internal dialogues addressed to God about inner unworthiness and a failing she calls "my easily besetting sin."[16] Today's readers see these written struggles as an obsession with the relational dimension of autobiography, "Where do I fit in all this?" rather than the autobiographical question "Who am I?" She was born to be clear about that.[17]

As preserved, the diary contained no rejoicing over any of her eleven births—inexplicable by today's standards. Neither did she record pleasure over complimentary reviews of her husband's books or his widely hailed speeches on major public occasions like the Fourth of July or the Louisiana Purchase.[18] Even her thanksgivings were confined to matters of life and death, literally and figuratively: for example, baby Sabina's safe deliverance from "the dangerous time of weaning." Actual, concrete information about setting was rarely recorded by any diarist of Martha's times. Where did she sit to write, and when? Who was watching the children? Which household demand was tugging at her? What was she worried about? Such questions are the historian's magnetic field, and minefield: few eighteenth-century memoirists make it easy for twentieth-century readers.

Martha's personal letters present a different but related problem. Most of those selected for publication in her memoirs were theological in content, most often a heavily religious condolence for a loved one's death. Their tone is somber, their style evocative of belles-lettres. In contrast, the very few notes to her two closest nieces are tantalizing. Martha's only sister, Mary Eleanor Pinckney, died young (1794), leaving three small children with whom their Aunt Martha had almost daily exchanges, editor Ramsay explained. To those little girls, Martha was spontaneous, playful, and bubbling with affection. "My darling niece [Frances Henrietta Pinckney] . . . how happy I am in daughters, both at home and a little way off." Her own daughters' stopover with their Pinckney cousins, en route elsewhere, would be "a *fly* or a *long teasing mosquito* of a visit." And self-caricature: "I have just dismissed my scholars and feel like a tired old schoolmaster!"[19] Even motherly pride in her youngest son's ability to recite stories of the Greek myths was conveyed in a letter, not the diary. Nevertheless, because the overall content of both letters and diary was restricted to religion and the state of her "heart," the mood of the *Memoirs* is ponderous despite its passionate vocabulary. The sense of personal revelation that often characterizes a diary is present here largely as unspecified spiritual regrets. Gradually it emerges that the villain in her diary must be her own impossibly high standard of religious achievement; ultimately, it appears that she was "discontented with nothing but her heart."[20] Apparently the only material worthy of her diary drew from the psychic battleground of her own "heart" and will. "When shall I advance in the spiritual life," she would sigh, no longer "wound[ing] my peace, and disgrac[ing] my profession?"[21] That self-accusatory tone galvanized her husband's editorial intrusion on several occasions.

To mitigate the diary's burden of guilt, editor Ramsay was impelled to intervene early in the diary section. "[Her] self-abasements and condemnations may appear to some to be extravagant," he wrote in a lengthy footnote; actually they were merely examples from the Bible or "descriptions of human depravity in holy writ."[22] Holiness and knowledge are alike, he editorialized, in that "he who knows most is most sensible of the defects of his knowledge . . . The serious Christian [like Mrs. Ramsay] is apt to think worse of himself [*sic*] than of any other person." Religious diaries also require more "intelligence" (introspection) than other types of writing, he warned: those who are "unacquainted with the workings of their own minds" or are "strangers to heart religion" could never be "competent judges" of self-writing like Martha's. The insensitive or ignorant reader would tend to dismiss her written prayers as "weakness, rant, or enthusiasm."[23]

David's need to protect his wife from those three negative labels was a direct statement of the Ramsays' social and religious self-image. In the 1790s a new element had appeared in some Anglo-cultural religious groups—emotional forms of worship such as revivalism and exuberant prayer meetings—which is what he meant by "weakness." "Enthusiasm" was his code for the practice of speaking in tongues at Methodist camp meetings; "rant" inferred a lack of decorum and pastoral restraint in the hellfire rhetoric of an evangelist's sermons. David Ramsay wanted to portray Martha serene and dignified among her books, safe from such distasteful associations.[24]

But he knew that rational persuasion, a method high on the Ramsays' scale of values, was insufficient. The only way to validate Martha's language of self-struggle had to be existential: "Take the same pains to acquire self knowledge," Dr. Ramsay instructed her readers; study the same books with the same application, "underlining with a pencil." Only then would they be equipped to judge whether "the language in the diary was that of a weak, enthusiastic person" or, as he saw it, "the genuine expressions of real, unaffected humility grounded on self knowledge." Certainly any behavior justifying her diary "self-abasements" had been "totally unseen by any human being while she lived," as he could attest.[25]

The religious worldview shaping Martha's writings was a theology both broad and elite. Her father's Huguenot Protestant habits of mind and expectations structured her upbringing—the substance of chapter 2, from her father's letters and a few family legends included in the biographical introduction to the *Memoirs*. The Laurenses were the unusual Charles Town family who regularly attended church, St. Philip's worshippers who read elegantly worded formal prayers and liturgy that communicated both liberality of doctrine and stability of custom. It induced a sense of toleration "for all sorts and conditions of men," as well as enjoyment of the world's pleasures, in moderation.[26] Her father's own self-image—that he always "wore a little mantle of religion" about himself—was her inherited Laurens family pattern.[27] Confirmed at St. Philip's around the age of twelve, Martha knew the importance of church attendance and viewed books as teachers and friends. She absorbed the bestsellers of her time—sermons and devotional books of English poets and clergy. These were the inspiration for and source of the solemn covenant with God she secretly created amid all the upheavals afflicting the Laurenses during the crucial year she turned fifteen—her life-directing "pinch of destiny,"[28] described in chapter 3.

Martha's decision to write a "contract" with God, not out of character for a serious Christian in her era, was her response to family scandal and national anxieties over impending war. Today's teenage diary resolutions vowing self-improvement and more disciplined habits are echoes of that impulse in a similar life stage. In her time, written covenants or constitutions were an idealized but also standard instrument—used by church bodies, women's charitable groups, and ambitious young men who wanted to form a book exchange or debating society. Apparently considerably more rare among young female individuals, Martha's choosing a model on which to create her own covenant revealed both her capacity for independent action and a desire to name (and claim for herself) authority in her life. Perhaps instinctively she sought religious strategies of self-control, concrete ways of generating the discourse and character toward which she yearned. Having a verbal map that directed her longings, decisions, and actions toward an idealized adult self at such a troubled time in her own physical and emotional development must have represented profound emotional and spiritual security. Martha would have experienced relief and a great sense of purpose in committing to paper an authorized life plan that surrendered to, or located ultimate responsibility in, the almighty God, the only true surety in a frightening, exciting world.

During Martha's exile in Europe as a young adult (chapter 4), she was exposed to new cultures and customs; in religion she touched the evangelical currents challenging traditional practices of the established church that had implanted her childhood Anglicanism. If she had not realized it before, she could hear preaching that developed the new denominational movement in England and later in the United States known as Methodism. Her intellectual horizons were similarly expanded by the writings of educated, scholarly British women—later called bluestockings. When she married Dr. David Ramsay in 1787, after the war, and joined his Independent (or Circular) Church, its forward-looking stance, articulated by Princeton-trained clergy, combined the freedom of Congregational church organization or polity with Presbyterian theology. (He himself had joined it during the Revolution as a British prisoner of war.)[29] Throughout Martha's life, religion allowed her to continue to educate herself and obtain spiritual nourishment. In chapter 5, we learn about the Ramsays' "republican marriage" as they idealized it.

During Martha's childhood, bright girls in privileged families were expected to achieve intellectually, like their brothers—if only to exercise their talents in and through female roles defined by the patriarch. Martha's written struggles, adolescent and adult, within that constriction testify to the excitement with which eager, intelligent young females grasped the ideal of reason and rationality—the dawning awareness that they were as capable in that arena as their brothers. She found instinctive agreement with the modern rationalistic Calvinism of English divines in poets like Edward Young—for whom religion was not compartmentalized or separated from "the secular" and Nature, but holistic, all-encompassing, and thrilled with the rational capacities of man (and woman).

What Martha understood as "reasonableness" was the ability to trust her own processes of ratiocination—the capacity to think for herself, to throw off former mental boundaries, superstitions, folk beliefs.[30] Women like her, educated with their brothers, were encouraged to think and write not only in diaries and journals but also in the new magazines welcoming "the fair sex" as readers (and writers under pseudonym).[31] Immense pride in a female rationality equal to that of men was the subtext of many American epistolary novels she read, such as *The Hapless Orphan* (1793), by an anonymous "Boston Lady." Female rationality was openly celebrated in the published essays of her New England contemporary Judith Sargent Murray. Martha expressed hers in religious terms: "I desire now to try myself, to search my spirit . . . [in] self-examination and devotion." She justified being absorbed in her own mental processes by the need to hold her "mind in such a state as to regard every occurrence in a Christian view."[32] Adult advice to her daughters interlaced intellectual and spiritual concerns: "I could wish you . . . to read Priestley's *Lectures* [on history]. Profit by his science while you lament his error in divinity"; or "If you are not acquainted with . . . Taylor's *Holy Living and Dying* which I send you, [it] will be pleasing to your intelligent and pious mind."[33] Today Martha's mental capacities and intellectual interests would find her writing for a scholarly journal like *Signs* or *Religion and American Culture*. Religion located her on the cutting-edge of female modernity in her times, within and in spite of the patriarchal and social class barriers that constrained the possibility of employing her gift of reason beyond the domestic sphere.

Martha's religious framework undergirded everything from child rearing to household management and was in fact her understanding of women's "citizenship"—the focus of chapter 6. As an adult her satisfaction came from fulfilling rather than resisting the structures ordering her culture—its theological and ethical assumptions, its parental and matrimonial patterns. She created her own system for the "home schooling" of her children and a few boarders, analytically and thoughtfully selecting materials and educational theories. In her own personal, strictly local way, Martha Laurens Ramsay embodied the same systematizing *mentalité* that in Enlightenment Europe was producing Linnaeus' botanical classifications, Hoyle's rules for parlor games, Telemann and Bach's musical rules for the composition of the fugue. She was not born with the imagination of a novelist or the poetic vocation of Annis Boudinot Stockton—or the drive to be "an AMERICAN AUTHOR" like Judith Sargent Murray, the rare American contemporary who admitted a goal of "stand[ing] well in the opinion of the world" through her written publications.[34] Martha's intellect, like her father's, inclined to the practical and scientific; for example, she produced the first floor plan drawing for the new Circular Church building to incorporate antihierarchical, democratic ideals in its physical design.[35] A logical, point-to-point reasoning process characterized the recordings in her diary of warfare in and with her "heart." Paradoxically, however, her heart was also the only theme about which she allowed a mystical sensibility to surface—during the crisis she survived in 1795, for example (see chapter 8). By and large, her musings reveal what her contemporaries called "seriousness" of intent and intelligence; spiritual (today also psychological) introspection provided the vehicle. Religious language itself was both substance and structure.[36]

Indeed, religion, unlike politics or business, was the acceptable discourse for women in Martha's lifetime, the only legitimate topic of intellectual exchange in which an educated female could speak out beyond the family parlor. It formed the substance of Martha's commission from her father during the fateful summer of 1776: she must embody "the heroism becoming a Woman of an honest & a pious Heart." Both of them understood that to be the highest possible ideal: he would rather see her "a wise and virtuous woman . . . than a fine lady" who is "too often deficient in both wisdom and virtue."[37] Women of her standing must express opinions about governmental (men's) affairs only *en famille,* even if their father was a prominent leader in establishing the new America.[38] The very language of affection between this father and daughter (and his other children) was filled with homely proverbs, hectoring cautions, and religious adjurations. Letters to Martha's eldest son at Princeton from 1809 to 1811 imitate the same mix of preachment and overarching parental affection that then epitomized the modern American parent (chapter 9).

Martha the social being was sophisticated, well traveled, unusually well-read, and admired for intellect and perspicacity—in contrast with Martha the diary writer, who appears to be virtually monochrome. She was

also well-married: how many devoted husbands published memorials of *Reason*
their wives? Diary reflection on the "state of one's heart" was her rationale
for the application of Reason to her spiritual discipline: she had made a
rational commitment to "let *nothing* pass without some holy reflection [or]
pious meditation."[39]

In addition to reason, a second religious concept employed in her *Providence*
diary was "Providence," which superimposed biblical associations or overtones on real events. It functioned to help ordinary Anglo-American Christians reconcile the emerging scientific understanding of nature with the
unlikely coincidence or natural phenomenon such as a lightning strike.
Providence became a useful explanatory trope among Protestants—the
theme of countless theological volumes and sermons, and a popular *deus
ex machina* in early fiction. Sometimes it also gave respectable cover to folk
beliefs—like nailing a horseshoe over an entrance—that persisted quietly
in the culture.[40]

For Martha, Providence was the specific lens that made everything fit
into her religious mind-set, her way of constituting meaning. Providence
helped her cope with trauma; for example: "My dear little Patty fell into the
parlor fire, but by God's good providence I was enabled to snatch her out
and smother the flame before any . . . considerable injury." Or: "Mrs. Petrie
died of a six days illness, [wed] only twelve days. God grant that no such
awful and awakening providence . . . pass without serious [attention]."[41] In
her carefully loyal references to spiritual submission, compromise and surrender were ennobled: "I often enjoy inexpressible rapture in the contradiction of my own will"; "My outward affairs can only be helped by thy
providence, my spiritual troubles by thy grace."[42] Male theologians in the
Age of Reason refrained from writing about, or may not have seen, the
"correspondences" between their experience and the scriptural images fur-
nishing women's mental landscape.[43]

At one level, Martha's use of the concept of Providence was a verbal
reference to divine presence. At another, in the face of adult crises, it signaled her surrender of logic to functional truths about God. Philosophers
and poets, most often male, grappled with huge ideas like Truth in Nature;
women like Martha who were coping with life and death, disappointment
and pride, invoked the balm of Providence for transposing otherwise
unbearable pain into a religious abstraction, from the unselfconscious
authority of their own "bleeding footsteps."[44] Despite the internal and
genre limitations in a memoir focused almost exclusively on the state of
one's "heart," Martha's little book becomes its own testament to women's

rational abilities as clearly as any man's event-driven history, or the travel geographies then popular, which demonstrated a male author's powers of deduction and reasoning. The primary difference between these gendered literary forms was the terrain each covered: in a woman's memoir that ground was interior, usually secret (at least at the time of its composition), and most often sacred.[45] *Memoirs* traces Martha's life trajectory from her youthful spiritual warfare toward adult acceptance of life's insoluble complexities and the need for God's grace in dealing with them. Writing her Self into being through her diary and letters with their interrelated discussions of religion, education, and citizenship, she embodied the learned woman's "fervent religious piety" of her time and place.[46]

II

The two other major themes in Martha's cultural biography, crucial to her actual lived experience—slavery and the patriotic ethos of her era—must be largely inferred rather than translated, the case with her religious language. Slavery was the most difficult to discern, although it was neither a "curious abnormality" nor a marginal feature of her times but an established, thoroughly American institution providing the service of unfree labor to those who could afford it.[47] In her *Memoirs* there are less than a dozen actual references to slaves. The institution itself became visible only when extreme financial stringency threatened the Ramsays with selling their last convertible assets—slaves. Where the complexities of slavery for owner and owned were prominent and visible was in her father's business correspondence. By age eight or nine, Martha must have absorbed her culture's social and mental denigration of slaves as subhuman beings—a realization that did not tally with the real individuals she knew who cradled her in comforting arms or sang her to sleep. The commercial Carolina empire her father was building, symbolized by the diligent clerks she saw everyday in his countinghouse, and its unstated dependence on slavery, was as unquestioned in her childhood as church bells tolling the hour from the steeples of St. Philip's and St. Michael's. So were lessons, the coming and going of guests, businessmen, clergy, many cousins, illness, the weather, and ever-present death. Without explicit instruction, she and her siblings silently grasped the lesson that slaves per se were not to be given much conscious attention or comment, and that they were certainly not a topic of polite conversation.

Attitudes about slavery in adult Martha's life were marginally more visible, thanks to the tension evident in the increasingly available antislavery publications during the 1780s—and the tacit suppression of any public comment about slaves or slavery whatsoever. The Ramsays' segment of the South Carolina elite complied with that unspoken consensus, writing about it only in intrafamily letters and only occasionally allowing it to be mentioned in their daily existence. Sorting out the layers of Martha's silence—hers or her editor's—is the problematic task of chapter 7 two centuries later. Among the conflicting influences visible in her record are the impact of her hero-brother John's proposal during the war to free and arm slaves for fighting the Britons; her admiring relationship with a British aristocrat whose ardent religiosity was unmarred by awareness of the moral ambiguities of slaveowning; the model of religious concern for slaves represented in the much-respected senior pastor of their Circular Church; and her own father's lifelong ambivalence toward slaveowning and management, contrasted with her invalid Uncle James' abhorrence of it. A revolution of the black Haitian population in 1792, until then held in subservience by brute force, abruptly silenced any emerging abolitionism by the fear it generated among white Charlestonians. Her husband's own ambivalence was continually irradiated by the unambivalent antislavery words of his lifelong best friend, Dr. Benjamin Rush of Philadelphia. And Martha Ramsay's psychological makeup profoundly intermeshed her dominant religious principles with these varying and contradictory pulls.

What are the layers of intention beneath the single longest diary entry mentioning slaves (in *Memoirs*), written in 1806—a thanksgiving "that the servants whom we feared to lose, and who feared to lose us, are still in our possession"? The harsh truth behind Martha's prayer was not moral revulsion at the institution of slavery but the deplorable state of the Ramsay finances, which raised the possibility of "losing" their slaves. Martha was a just mistress in her time, and her slaves might well have dreaded a less reasonable owner; at the same time, manumission was not an unknown topic in her household. Exploring the various strands of abolitionism and theological challenge to slaveowning that assailed Martha's inherited sympathies in the late 1780s and early 1790s raises the question for today's reader of whether *Memoirs'* silence on the issue was editorial rather than self-censorship. Through her musings, readers may glean a view of the separate yet wholly interrelated lives of slaves and masters in a high-minded southern family after the Revolution. Beneath that enforced intimacy lie the barest hints of the true reality of daily interactions between owner and owned. The only other published letters of a female South Carolinian slaveowner in this era, Eliza Lucas Pinckney (1739–1762), contain vintage references to slavery in the abstract when discussing labor accomplished; for example, "she" was "cultivating" her plantation, not her workers; she reported "harvesting" her indigo crop.[48] Martha's diary monologues had to portray a picture of domestic harmony, predictable order, and reciprocity in her world, even as her intelligence and conscience could not help but register theological and ethical concerns about its slave underpinnings.

The Ramsays lived the uncomfortable contradiction between lip service to the revolutionary and the Christian ideal of liberty, and its racially exclusive application in their locale and generation. Without naming slavery as an explicit blot on the nation's glory, Dr. Ramsay lamented his country's decline in the self-interested 1790s, from the exalted time when "the world turned upside down" and there was "more patriotism in a single village" than existed in all thirteen states.[49] Many New England and southern Anglican sermons similarly lamented moral, religious, and patriotic "declension" at the turn of the new century, but very few openly linked it with slavery. One who did was a Congregational pastor with a distinguished family name, Jonathan Edwards Jr., his name a message to those with similar inheritance, like Henry Laurens' daughter. "Domestic slavery in a free government is a perfect solecism in human affairs,"[50] he pronounced as part of his warning against the "self-interest" that was replacing "disinterestedness," the Lockean principle sacred to the founding generation's self-identity.[51] Whether Martha pondered slavery as a solecism or not, she also lamented a "declension" that was a falling short of spiritual goals. Edwards' high-toned aphorism combined economic, political, and theological judgment, a broad-scope indictment familiar to the Ramsays; yet his culminating prediction struck a very American belief in possible progress. Thirty years earlier, he wrote, "scarcely a man in this country thought the slave trade or the slavery of Negroes to be wrong." But now at the beginning of the nineteenth century, many were openly "plead[ing] the right of humanity"—the new humanitarian language of rights the Ramsays themselves employed. Within the next fifty years, Edwards Jr. pronounced, holding a Negro slave would become "as shameful" in terms of personal guilt as "common robbery or theft."[52] The heart and mind of a striving Christian like Martha would have found that image both troubling and visionary.

Martha's own few words acknowledging the existence of slavery reveal nothing of her true feelings, either about the institution itself or individual personal slaves—an almost unbelievable silence from a woman as highly self-analytic and conscientious on every other moral and ethical issue of the times. Whether her preserved record indicates unthinking acceptance of the most encompassing institution on her horizon, therefore warranting no comment, or whether her writings had contained words her husband decided to omit as too incendiary in their Charleston setting, remains a matter of speculation. On this issue she constituted one angle of a family triangle, between a father for whom slavery ("black gold") had been the most profitable enterprise of his commercial career despite his later misgivings, and a husband who condemned it on principle while living and participating in a society where it was intrinsic. Because her passionate religious language as preserved is silent on the topic of slavery, her adult soul's unease lets us glimpse the struggle of living as a Christian of conscience in the unquestioning, monolithic slaveowning society of her times; even then, her words as printed convey such hints only in theological code.

III

Finally, the third world-changing current that made a major impact on Martha Laurens Ramsay's life and times in countless invisible ways was the colonies' separation from England, war, and "Americanization." Martha's letters reveal her patriotic evolution: in a few letters to her longtime Carolinian friend, Elizabeth Brailsford, also in a boarding school in England, she alludes to her strenuous adjustment in a foreign culture and unfamiliar social world during her own early months in England; and in 1782, we can see in letters from her father that Martha strained filial bonds to the breaking point, a prototypical American daughter-versus-father struggle. Unfortunately, Martha's letters to him are lost.

All wishes for a detailed epistolary documentation of her thought processes are doomed to remain unfilled.[53] The family drama over a father's authority in her choice of suitor produced Henry Laurens' admiring but weighted description of Martha—a "true American woman"—after their crisis resolved in his favor; the phrase itself illuminated the change in their relationship and the distance it had traversed. As a well-brought-up, dutiful Charles Town daughter in a pro-British home and culture, Martha Laurens' circumscribed horizon was split asunder when she, a colonial outsider, arrived in England at the beginning of the war. Those years abroad, an ocean away from her home ground, were the catalyst requiring her to develop the successive layers of ego strength that finally allowed an independent American female to become visible (through posthumous print).

Her father's Americanism had been wrenched from his earlier proud loyalty to England: she, the motherland, had betrayed his faith. Writing from Carolina on 27 February 1776 to a British partner, he confessed: "I . . . weep for Great Britain . . . but alas I perceive that I am to be separated from her & that my Children are to be called by some [illegible] new name."[54] In August 1776, shortly after he learned of the first shots in Concord, Massachusetts, he wrote his son John in England, "I am not a rebel . . . I love the people of England. I love England. But . . . our brethren [there] have suffered mischievous and ill-informed men to force America into measures which have produced [not only] bloodshed but a <u>political</u> separation."[55] That same August he wrote his brother James, whose household by then had resettled in England with Henry's daughters, "I can perceive . . . that the name of American may be abominable to many men [there]," and that you and my daughters "will be exposed not only to ordinary insults but . . . to the heaviest calamities."[56] That same month, for the first time in family correspondence, he employed the new label for their country: "these now United free and independant States."[57] In those early months of the conflict, Henry Laurens can be seen reluctantly extracting his mental and religious roots from European soil by trying out the new language. If Martha at first felt peripheral to that change, as was expected of females, there was no avoiding the new vocabulary in all their round-robin letters. It became part and parcel of the powerful bonds defining, enabling, and constraining her.

Certainly the decade she resided in Europe understood "Americanness" as stereotypically symbolized by the Laurenses' fellow countryman Dr. Benjamin Franklin, whose "Paintings, Busto's, Medals & Prints" rendered his "visage almost as well known as that of the Moon."[58] Like many white Carolinians, the Laurenses considered themselves culturally British—home furnishings, china, books, and decor mostly imported. At the end of the century, when Martha, once again back in Carolina, read the new nation's authors, American characters were already portrayed positively in contrast with European characters, who were effete, world-weary, and insincere. By the 1790s the adjective "American" connoted to its own authors a person with "naturally good understanding" and virtues "implanted in [the] heart with a liberal hand." It even signified the physical attractiveness of Nordic or Germanic coloring and stereotypical "good sense": good nature, benevolence, and unbounded energy.[59] Martha's assimilation of that view was visible primarily in her modern approach to education, discussed in chapter 6.

Beyond Martha's evolving "American" sensibility, the two other cultural systems that constrained all her choices were the family claims on any child of oligarch Henry Laurens, and patriarchy, the comprehensive system of assumptions and expectations for all female children born to any Anglo-European family anywhere at that time. Young Miss Martha Laurens developed a strong sense of selfhood out of the ways she worked within, resisted, and elasticized those embedded claims of patriarch and family. Everything constituting her true American womanhood had to be forged within those bounds. Although travel and her own studies indeed gave her a kind of finishing school, even those broadening experiences were still circumscribed by daughterhood. Yet within those systems, writing itself—a comfort and release, as well as spiritual duty—actually constructed more internal strength of soul and ego than the submissiveness (to fate, father, and God) for which her written words continually pleaded. "It is not easy to fight the ego in a diary," Thomas Mallon has pithily observed; "whenever one attempts it, one is fighting on the opponent's home ground."[60] Fortunately, her private literature (letters, prayers, and meditations) illuminates what would otherwise be a latent and invisible process of character development and identity formation; the comprehensive Laurens' family correspondence offers up the formatting of their new identity. Those thirsting for women's history in Martha's specific record must follow a path that is introspective and biographical,[61] a trajectory only rarely turned outward to comment on events in the "real world," and then often only by implication.[62] Today we are likely to think that biography lifts the subject out of her family context in order to reveal her uniqueness as an individual, a personality. However, and paradoxically, the only way Martha Laurens Ramsay's religiously encoded life and times can become comprehensible is by locating her firmly within family narratives: the spiritual, social, and intellectual map imprinted on her as a child in the household of Henry Laurens, and her experience of wifehood and motherhood with David Ramsay—the period in the new republic when the diary became her confidant.

Martha Laurens Ramsay's triumph has to be located in her mere act of surviving; her own consciousness has to be the platform for her drama, on which she lived out the fate into which she was born (with no realistic possibilities of changing it). Today we identify more readily with the woman who was an overt critic of the late-eighteenth-century constrictions encasing her; in the nineteenth century, women striving for political voice and vote, and against religious repression, are the heroes. Martha's story is about its own kind of heroism, the exercise of choice within the confines of her circumstances. Her inner determination "to be somebody" led her to keep a diary as a way of making sense of "God's dealing with my soul."[63] While previous historiography has confined Martha's life and memoirs to anthology and encyclopedia entries, treating her only as auxiliary to her father's and husband's biographies, here—as much as is historically possible—she finally speaks for herself.

| "Gladdening the Heart
of a Father"

MARTHA LAURENS, GROWING UP in a slaveowning society and a
family important enough in that era and region to merit more than the
usual historical attention, in terms of the record, was a cherished child.[1]
War with and independence from England, followed by nation building,
were the external currents that shaped her and her times; the more immediate factors were those of Charles Town's eighteenth-century elite white
world. Her father, Henry Laurens, was an entrepreneurial success story, a
living example of the prowess and pleasure to be found in a merchant's
career.[2] Martha's childhood unfolded against a daily backdrop of of his
many civic and commercial activities, a household of constantly shifting
numbers, many types of lessons, and ever-present death.

Henry Laurens (1724–1792) and his siblings James and Mary were heirs
of John (Jean) Laurens (1696–1747), a second-generation Huguenot merchant who was already a skilled saddler when he migrated from New York
to South Carolina.[3] There Martha's grandfather Laurens established himself as a successful importer in Charles Town, his shop near the juncture
of Meeting and Broad Streets—where the Fireproof Building stands today.
That first Carolina Laurens, along with other Huguenots and Swiss, German, and Dutch settlers eager to align themselves with the elite of the city,
had become Episcopalian. The Laurens' church of choice was St. Philip's,
the oldest Church of England parish south of Virginia. Its doctrine of
"civil utility"—church and state separate but still mutually supportive—
understandably appealed to diligent, ambitious immigrants. An engraving
of this "most complete structure" on the raw colonial landscape was featured in the midcentury British *Gentleman's Magazine.*[4]

Along with Anglican religious identity and a leadership role in St.
Philip's congregation, Martha's father, Henry, inherited material emblems
of the achieved Laurens status when his father died in 1747. Grandfather
Laurens' inventory indicated his prosperity: chairs, beds, and blankets,
table "linnens," "Pewter measures and basons," thirteen brass candlesticks
and snuffers, an eight-day clock, and five slaves—a mother, Flora, and her

daughter, Chloe; a mother, Jenny, and her daughter, Lucy; plus "a Negro Man (Colonel)," to be divided (according to the will) among the heirs after their widowed mother chose her two.[5] During the 1740s John Laurens had marketed a wide range of goods, from women's "glaz'd Lamb Gloves" and Oznaburg fabrics for Negro clothes, to dimity, lawn, and "searsuckers," beads, buttons, and gun "shott," as well as elixirs, spices, and toyboxes.[6]

The eldest son, Henry, combined inherited commercial propensity and Huguenot practicality and was a natural in the world of business. Like his father, Henry steadily ascended in the Carolina merchant oligarchy after training in Richard Oswald's London firm in the 1740s.[7] Henry Laurens launched his own commercial enterprise with partner George Austin in 1749 in the relatively new social world of Charles Town (the name itself remained two words until 1783), aristocratic in aspiration and highly British in its taste. By 1757, two years before Martha's arrival in the family, Henry had acquired enough stature and wealth to be elected to the Commons House of Assembly and elevate the Laurens name into the colony's roster of pre-Revolutionary elite—along with Gadsden, Lowndes, Pinckney, and Rutledge. Such rapid social mobility for successful businessmen was heady. A caustic Anglican clergyman observed in 1771: "Pray look back to your own Origin and draw the curtain up but for one and twenty years only. It is a strange succession of fortuitous Causes that has lifted up many of your heads . . . At the beginning of this century, what was Carolina? What Charles Town?"[8]

Henry Laurens, for one, found mid-eighteenth-century opportunities invigorating. Charles Town harbor's shoreline, with its public wharves and docks, proved hospitable to international shipping. In the 1730s, rice, a cash crop ideally suited to Carolina's geography, was established; in the 1740s a second cash crop, indigo, had been introduced by the celebrated Mrs. Eliza Lucas Pinckney. Swampy land fully engaged in producing exportable goods created a major demand for a slave labor force, which in turn became a means of rapid wealth accumulation. Laurens' firm, Austin, Laurens & Appleby was among the leading importers of slaves and goods during this period.[9] In fact, some sixty-one slave galleys owned by his firm unloaded their African cargo in Charles Town between 1751 and 1761.[10]

Successful merchants like Martha's father were also beginning to identify themselves, consciously and unconsciously, by the reputation of their countinghouses and by what they wore, how their houses looked, and what toys they purchased for their children. Confronted with unprecedented variety of choice for consumers, the act of buying itself became a statement of cultural identity in a setting like Charles Town that was bursting with new material goods.[11]

Business with British partners—importing and selling English goods as well as slaves— was making Henry Laurens a very rich man. Unlike some of his New England counterparts, Henry wasted no criticism on imports considered extravagant or self-indulgent by some; he was content in the selling. In fact, choosing china patterns and wall coverings gave him visceral satisfaction. "Every shop here imports its own goods, from Oznaburg to Lawn [fabrics], from an Anchor to a Minikin Pin [all sizes of steel pins]," he boasted to a would-be competitor. His own orders leaned to the practical, however; for example, blankets for slaves rather than luxury items like waistcoats. He preferred English rather than French goods, despite his French Protestant bloodlines, and enjoyed his shrewd, significant role in the new consumerism—both for the status his wealth could demonstrate and for his own skill in the gamesmanship of commerce.[12]

The household into which Martha was born had been established in 1750, when Henry Laurens married Eleanor Ball (1731–1770) at Comingtee, one of the Ball family plantations on the Cooper River.[13] Eleanor Laurens was the fifth of six Elias Ball children by his second wife and was the flower of his old age. (Her much older sister, Ann, was married to Henry Laurens' business partner, George Austin.) By the time little Martha arrived in 1759, if not long before, an imported cradle was a central fixture in the parental bedroom, which was also equipped with necessaries such as a candle stand, a warming pan, and a bedpan passed along from grandfather Laurens. Because Henry and his wife, Eleanor, anticipated extensive use for that nursery item, the cradle was probably one that rocked, featuring a "gauze pavilion" with turned posts at its four corners to support mosquito netting. Any cradle her Papa chose must be durable as well as stylish. Charles Town elite houses were beginning to enjoy British bedroom furnishings and the new, immensely popular printed fabric known as "chints" for window curtains and bedspreads. Floor coverings also were increasingly stylish and elegant; by 1766 "nothing [was] so common as Turkey or Wilton Carpetts."[14]

The most adoring face above infant Martha's cradle, alongside that of her exhausted young mother, would have been her father's, beaming at this addition to his accumulating tribe of descendants. In the closing salutation of his business letters during this period, he routinely referred to his children as his "riches in a family." Probably his pleasure in enumerating them was related to having lost three infants to death before 1754. He had not always enjoyed such riches.

A daughter, Eleanor, was born in 1751, the year after Henry and Eleanor wed, but died shortly;[15] another child died right after birth in 1752; and in 1753 a child named Henry lived only until 1758. However, John, born in 1754, survived to become the favored eldest son. When Henry Laurens finally had three living children, he would treat his correspondents with tender references to his "little people": "Affection draws me toward them," "a true picture of my heart," "that little flock in which you so kindly wish me comfort," and "those dear little Connections." A phrase from the psalms, "the apple of a father's eye," was his verbal embrace for Martha.[16]

Henry Laurens reveled in fatherhood. After John, a second infant also named Eleanor (Nelly), after her mother, brightened their lives in 1755. In 1758 another newborn, Elias (after Eleanor Laurens' father) did not survive. Then came the second baby girl, Martha, who in southern fashion was called Patsy. Those three living children—John, Nelly, and Patsy—represented many hopes raised and dashed in the short period of nine years. The toll on Eleanor Laurens' body can scarcely be imagined: calcium leeched from her bones and teeth, her uterus prolapsed. Only after twelve years could Henry Laurens finally employ the poignant phrase "my riches in a family," the same riches that ultimately ended his wife's life.[17]

During her first year, infant Martha's brush with eternity entered the family legend. Describing her escape from inevitable death after smallpox, her husband-biographer (writing in 1811 after her death) clothed the incident in the supernatural—a standard eighteenth-century means of conferring divine purpose on the individual being honored. Baby Martha had been so ill she was thought to have died and "was actually laid out preparatory to her funeral." As it happened, while the room was being cleaned and straightened, her tiny body was placed to one side—under an open window. "Probably recalled to life by the fresh air of the open window," she showed a slight movement. Dr. Moultrie, the family's physician, entered the room at that moment and affirmed her survival; otherwise, she would "shortly have been buried," as was the custom in a plague year of "extensive mortality." (Dr. Ramsay, a progressive physician in his time, reminded readers of his deceased wife's memoirs that the former "absurd mode of treating the small pox in 1760" required a totally airless, "close" room for the stricken victim.) His interpretation of that incident proclaimed: "A valuable life was thus providentially saved for future usefulness."[18]

The shallow presumption of some twentieth-century historians that an eighteenth-century family experiencing annual births and deaths suffered less than would a present-day nuclear family can only be seen as scholarly arrogance. The shield of supposed scientific objectivity is necessary for assuming that numerous (rather than few) children from a mother's womb, only some of which survive, evoke a lesser attachment from their parents than children in today's numerically limited families. Henry Laurens' letters exude the preciousness of each child, even in death, and his intense emotional investment in his offspring, while the mother's emotions are left to our imagination. A 1763 letter expressed his deep satisfaction and thanksgiving in a fond, avuncular complaint: "Mrs. Laurens and my three little ones are well and now playing in the Back room. Their noise which would disturb any body else lightens my labors now by candlelight."[19]

The Laurenses' "matrimonial partnership," Martha's diary description of her parents' bond, clearly viewed sex as primary. Eight births in nine years, and five deaths: primary indeed. The bodily task of producing offspring was central but unmentioned in Henry's letters until the partnership's second decade. Perhaps by then his business was established enough to allow that luxury, or maybe he had begun to see his features in his daughter's face, his wife's mannerism in his little son. For whatever reasons, in his middle years Henry began to pour the emotional language of family into his correspondence.

Matrimonial partnership also included a wider network of extended family and community interests. Letters between members of the Laurens household and various nieces reveal the Laurenses' involvement in family affairs. Shouldn't a daughter who had eloped with Henry's dashing military colleague (from the Indian expeditions of 1760–1761) be forgiven and embraced by her father? Another time they bemoaned the terrible health problems of Eleanor's Bampfield cousins. Henry's letters offer casual glimpses of Martha and the next baby brother being taken to visit Ball cousins and of Ball nieces visiting their Aunt Eleanor. Henry often consoled male friends over the death of infants: "Mrs. Laurens and I very heartily sympathize with you and the poor afflicted Mother on the loss of your Dear little [son]. These are subjects that soften one too much to dwell long upon ... I can only say that it is our duty in all circumstances to be resign'd & thankful."[20]

South Carolina's swampy geography around Charles Town was the setting for little Martha's childhood. The heat could be appalling, the miasmic summer encouraging rampant epidemics of disease. Storms were sudden and fierce. When Martha was only two, a waterspout played macabre tricks on the city. Her parents' friend Mrs. Manigault recorded on a cloudy, windy Monday in May 1761 that "the scud [was] flying very fast." By two o'clock in the afternoon, "an unusual noise, not unlike the rattling of many coachwheels on a rough pavement" forced everyone to stare up at the sky. What they saw was "a stupendous thick pillar of clouds, about 30–35 degrees high and seemingly 250 yards broad . . . the clouds in view flying with great velocity from all points as if attracted into the vortex." The tide became capricious and deadly in this typhoon—"retir[ing] . . . in so extraordinary a manner" that a ship floating at the wharf was suddenly beached. Then returning just as suddenly, numbers of vessels were swamped and streams overflowed, depositing "the leaves of bushes and trees" on a ship five miles out from Sullivan's Island.[21]

In Martha's earliest consciousness, surviving midday heat was an item of Huguenot virtue. Her vigorous Papa insisted that keeping busy between 9:00 a.m. and 3:00 p.m. was the only and best defense, a motto she carried into adulthood. Carolina summertime could be "almost intolerable," an itinerant Anglican clergyman declared; he could "hardly bear the weight of my Whig and Gown during [church] service." His own misery did not make him tolerant of women in his country congregation who attended worship in shockingly scanty dress—a practice not appropriate for urban children. Fierce heat and wilting humidity were the probable source of a Hessian soldier's astonished observation, during the 1780 Siege of Charleston, of the number of slaves more or less constantly occupied with cleanliness— boiling laundry, washing, scrubbing, and polishing. Children like Martha and her older sister, Nelly, of course, hardly gave a second thought to dirtying their clothes by splashing in the fish pond or the horses' drinking trough. The city markets, "picturesque but full of smells," with their hovering turkey buzzards, were undoubted magnets for curious children, no matter how torrid the temperature.[22] Her father worried that his wife's gardening in the heat put extra strain on her health, although he did not seem to worry that annual pregnancies were similarly "injurious and sometimes destructive to our good women."[23]

In 1764 five-year-old Martha experienced her first major relocation: from her first home in St. Michael's Alley, south of Broad Street, to her father's new Ansonboro mansion in the same neighborhood where merchants Lynch and Pinckney had also built elegant houses. Her Papa negotiated for more than a year to purchase land with its own wharf and creek, four acres that included a green called Laurens Square, and bounded by Pitt, East Bay, Centurion, and Anson Streets.[24] Martha's parents had planned the move for March, but it was delayed until June because of workmen's deadlines, Henry's business demands and his accidental fall from a horse, which incapacitated him for a time, and—worst of all—the sudden, totally unexpected death of oldest daughter, Nelly, in April.[25]

Papa Henry's pleasure in the new house glowed in his letters. "Mahogany is the thing by all means for your Stair case. You would agree in opinion with me if you saw mine." Though the darker wood was costly, "in time it becomes abundantly cheaper as it is firm, durable, and gains beauty whether you will or not, with age, whereas Cedar is brittle, splintery and without an excess of rubbing and waxing fades and loses its colour in a very few years." He enjoyed careful oversight of every step. "Cypress is the best and cheapest wood for wainscot, but your [English] oak in my judgment is infinitely preferable. I have painted one room in my house Wainscoat color and pattern upon a coat of brown Plaister. It stands very well and is much admired."[26] His use of the magisterial "I" meant, of course, that he supervised the task, not actually performed it.

Henry Laurens wanted their new home on East Bay Street to be "worthy . . . to be occupied by a merchant," to reflect his cosmopolitan horizons. Spacious, roomy, and open rather than ornate, and somewhat unimaginative externally, the house was a "plain barn-like building" of brick, almost "square to the winds," 38 and ½ ft. x 60 ½ ft.—pretentious not in ornamentation or iron grillwork but in acreage and gardens, "with a wall all upon the front of my garden [Wall Street]." Henry had purchased a "Mulatto" slave bricklayer, Samuel, that spring especially to create elegant garden paths around the house. One feature visible from those bricked walks was a jerkin-head roof—a hipped roof cutting flat angles at the corners of the house.[27]

Inside, the house from cellar to roof featured heavy-hewn timbers. Two floors had four large rooms each, downstairs and upstairs, plus several small "apartments"—rooms topped by a "spacious attic" with room for wine storage in the hipped-roof corners. Near the front door was a small hallway, "little more than a vestibule" on the south side of the structure, and a stairway on the left led to the upper story while a door on the right opened into the library. (Surprisingly, Henry Laurens had omitted the wide central hall great Charles Town houses usually featured in hopes of luring every possible breeze.) But the library was a huge room (18′ 8″ x 17′ 2″) with two hundred running feet of shelves, and the books were protected by beautiful decorative glass doors embossed with geometric shapes—octagons, squares, and triangles. Behind the library was an equally hospitable dining room (17 ½′ x 17 ½′) with a paneled ten-foot-wide chimney all the way to the ceiling. Immediately above, on the second floor, was the same size ballroom. Some of the fireplace mantels were marble, others elegantly carved wood—all in the highest tone of simplicity and dignity. The mantels were undoubtedly imported from England, like the ones Henry had ordered for the house of his neighbor Charles Pinckney.[28]

The dining room, with fancy mirrors and a very large "chimney glass," boasted sconces on the wall, handsome pewter serving dishes, silver tureens, a brass warming pan, and a tinned Japanned waiter—to say nothing of elegant china for entertaining (family meals were served on earthenware). Martha's father knew his merchandise: he ordered mirrors "truly elegant and worthy of a place in a Dining Room occupied by a merchant." But he returned the first ones: "their fault was their fineness. They are too fine, I will rather say too large for my dining room." Unfortunately, in the shipping from England to Charles Town, faulty packing had damaged some of the gilded ornamentation and scraped some of the "Quick Silvering." "The packer or workman ought really to be answerable," he demanded. Upstairs in the drawing room, a harpsichord for Martha's arpeggios and sonatinas held a place of honor, flanked by elbow chairs, a card table, a tea table, settees, and portraits.[29] To five-year-old Martha, the new home was a palace.

Since the locale and climate of Charles Town allowed a twice-yearly harvest, vegetables and many exotic trees—peach, apricot, mulberry, walnut, chestnut, fig, bitter orange, and pomegranate—flourished. British gardener John Watson was employed to cultivate the new Laurens acres into a charming botanical cornucopia. Henry and Eleanor wanted the kind of beautifully laid out English garden that was rare in the colonies, a display of the useful and ornamental plants that Carolina produced or that Henry could import. In that sense, landscaping was a more overt statement of the Laurenses' affluence and sophistication than the house itself. Neighbors like Eliza Pinckney, who also prided herself on gardening, noted that "only 2 squares from her house, the rich merchant HL was filling his extensive grounds with every rare plant and shrub his numerous connections enabled him to collect." Little sisters Nelly and Patsy and their numerous cousins could fashion snapdragon dolls and chant the evocative flower names "foxglove," "sweet alyssum," and "periwinkle" as their mother instructed.[30]

Philadelphia garden historian John Bartram, named royal botanist by the king in 1765, came for a visit the year after the Laurenses moved in. He noted a remarkable "grape vine 7 ½ inches in circumference" at the new home "of Col Laurance [*sic*] in Charles Town." It "bore 216 clusters of grapes, one almost 11 in. long and over 16″ in circumference, the grapes large "and as close set in the bunch as they could possibly grow." In addition, he admired "a fine young olive tree 15 ft. high, luxuriant." By contrast with this luxuriant green, Charleston streets were deep and dusty at a child's eye level. Laid out in regular, unpaved, and widely spaced design to allow breezes to reach the buildings from all sides, the soft sand made its choking way into noses and eyelids. Narrow paths at each side would one day become sidewalks, but not yet.[31]

Early on, Martha would see St. Michael's Church looming on the horizon near Market Street—one of the two huge structures where public meetings occurred (the other was her parents' church, St. Philip's). Her ears and eyes would recognize these buildings, thanks to the bells in their towers that punctuated the daily routine. The original St. Michael's clock (an Ainswirth-Thwaites imported from England in 1764) had a ring of eight bells but only an hour hand, its tower featuring a "strong 30 hour clock [showing] the hour in four different directions." Public bell tolling carried its messages, secular and religious, a great distance—up to five or six miles. The Laurens household and the church bells expressed the modern approach to timekeeping. More like New England Protestants than his southern compatriots in this regard, Henry Laurens exemplified daily scheduling, planning, and diligence. "An Industrious Man may gain near 12 Mo. in a Year over the bulk of his contemporaries," Henry could admonish a correspondent. "How much Time is lost in what is commonly stiled Pleasure." Even sleep was an indulgence, absorbing too much time for the "Sons & Votaries of Pleasure." Responsible "husbanding of time" was an early watchword learned by the Laurens young.[32]

The year after Martha's parents married, St. Michael's (built in 1751, an "offspring" of St. Philip's) was named the "most elegant Religious Edifice in British America." St. Michael's pews were made of the local cedar Martha's father denounced as splintery. The pulpit, a double deck arrangement with reading desk, located high and central, competed visually with the altar; behind it was a massive sounding board supported by two Corinthian columns. In 1768, when Martha was nine, a real pipe organ had arrived from London. The church she sat in every Sunday, St. Philip's, was also wide, "one hundred feet in breadth" and tall, "a cupola of fifty feet" that featured two bells and a clock. It, too, had a great organ and rich ecclesiastical hangings for its altar, pulpit, and lectern. "Divine Service [was] perform'd with Great Decency and Order: both on Holidays and Week Days." Outside there were wide porches on three sides—the west, north, and south; inside, steps led up to an elevated altar, on which a little girl could just glimpse "a very large Service of Plate"—silver communion vessels called chalice and patten for the holy meal.[33]

To Martha's mind, "church" signified awe—a building where huge, solemn civic gatherings were held, and, more personally, a pew where she knelt between her parents as sonorous Elizabethan-style prayers resonated in the arches. Henry Laurens' children were among those Charles Town residents reared in the habit of regular Sunday attendance at worship, as well as daily devotions at home—in contrast to many more typical, nominal churchgoers. Henry's correspondence continually acknowledged his grounding in Huguenot religious roots—for example, congratulating a friend on the birth of a new son. "You see I can't help carrying a little mantle of Religion about me, indeed I will not be laughed out of it [because it is] the only source [of] vital warmth" against the "cold hand of Death."[34] He was one Carolina oligarch known for much more than material success; for him, the "language of improvement" encompassed religion and culture as well as a financial fortune.[35]

Behind the big front door on Bay Street, little Martha was the kind of child who tagged after her brother, eager to play with his toys and imitate his games. Their grandfather Laurens' inventory had listed a large box of "Tea Toys," including a miniature tea set and imported doll furniture, but they also enjoyed games like nine-men's morris or dibstones, using pebbles or sheep's knucklebones. Privileged children like these could pore over picture books and Aesop's fables, play board games such as fox and geese, and pull a stuffed toy horse on a rolling platform with tiny wheels.[36] Fortunately, their father and mother held the enlightened view that early intellect developed best when unforced—the new, progressive Lockean belief in learning through play. If "children are taught ABC by T Totum [a four–sided disk with letters of the alphabet on each]," he would later remind his son John, "epistolary intercourse [between a] papa and his son" should easily produce both written eloquence and the "necessary rules" for transmitting "the most important intelligence."[37]

Not surprisingly, little Martha (Patsy) displayed "a great capacity and eagerness for learning." Striving to keep pace with her older sibling, she was automatically "cozen'd into a Knowledge of the Letters without perceiving it to be anything but a Sport, playing into that which others [must be] whipp'd for."[38] In many eighteenth-century narratives, precocity in reading was a standard attribute of the bright child and the child saint, whether that meant the mere recognition of alphabet letters or the actual combining of print letters into words. Family legend credited Martha with the latter by age three: she could "readily read any book," and go one better by reading upside down—holding the volume "in an inverted position." Literal or apochryphal, that item of family lore testified that Martha Laurens' budding intellect was immersed in the print transmission of ideas and concepts from her earliest days.[39]

Further, she had an aptitude with numbers and arithmetic (later geometry and mathematical science) rarely cultivated in a female child. Among the self-made aristocrats of Carolina, Henry Laurens was unusual in emphasizing the importance of arithmetic skill as well as geography and history—testament to his inborn Huguenot practicality and business acumen. Further, in a locale where men's conversation often limited itself to the acquisition of land, slaves, and crops, girls' education was scarcely mentioned; very few daughters were taught numeracy. But Martha escaped that disadvantage. "After writing, the next necessary step toward qualifying a Person for Business is Understanding that truly laudable and most excellent Accomplishment, the noble Science of Arithmetic, a knowledge so necessary in all the Parts of Life and Business that scarce anything is done without it," the American instructor George W. Fisher pronounced in mid-century.[40]

In Martha's life, print and numbers were as ubiquitous and consequential as the moist Carolina air. Besides her father's collection of books in his elegant new library, her Uncle James was in the business of importing religious books—merchandise for both commercial and religious markets. To help spread the Word of his faith, he was willing "to sell [imported books] very cheap." For the vast majority of white children in mid-1700s Carolina, print was a relatively rare and precious commodity; little Martha could not guess how exceptional was her situation. As an example, in 1754 her father paid for the printing and distribution of his friend Dr. Alexander Garden's farewell sermon. This public gesture honored the man who had been Rector of St. Philip's during much of Henry's life—Garden offered thirty-four years of ecclesiastical leadership in this important colonial city—and demonstrated Henry's appreciation of print as a means of symbolic and historical memorializing. His generosity preserved for posterity a landmark event in the life of his parish and provided fellow parishioners with a material keepsake. Print gave Henry's gesture permanence and cultural weight, a highly appropriate tribute to the last of the colonial commissaries sent out to the province of South Carolina by the Church of

England. Martha, Nelly, and John were among those privileged children who took print for granted. Even so, the number of books specifically aimed at children in their era was little more than a publisher's footnote in comparison with the quantity that would become available to Martha's own children a generation later.[41]

Along with other literate children, Martha undoubtedly read James Janeway's *Token for Children,* a compendium of salutary stories about pious children's last illness and death that were intended to "make" its readers good. Another ubiquitous book was Thomas White's *A Little Book for Little Children,* a child's abridgment of the massively influential *Foxe's Book of Martyrs.* Such real-life stories glorified standing on principle and conscience to the point of gory martyrdom. However, the most popular author for children, Dr. Isaac Watts, carried a less dolorous and judgmental tone, and young Martha loved his poems so much that she would speak of hoping to meet him in heaven. Passing on her own treasured childhood experiences, Martha reemployed his *Divine and Moral Songs for Children* (1715) with her own children.

Watts, a clergyman inspired by Locke's progressive theories of education, cast his religious messages in a child-friendly form. "What is learnt in verse is longer retained in memory," his preface explained; "the like sounds and the like number of syllables exceedingly assist the remembrance." Repetition was one key element in learning, the special emotional weight carried by the closing or summary stanza another. From the hymn whose first line read, "Happy's the child whose youngest years," his typical last verse promised comfort and security rather than threat:

> *Let the sweet work of prayer and praise*
> *Employ my youngest breath;*
> *Thus I'm prepar'd for longer days,*
> *Or fit for early death.*

Watts represented enlightened religiosity in his time, a desire to not "bludgeon [children] into belief" or treat his poems as "a metrical cat-o-nine tails." Moral tales and tracts, just beginning to fill a new niche in religious publishing, chose story form—"entertainment"—as a means of ethical instruction. Martha Laurens and her siblings were the beneficiaries of these updated trends and of parents who sprinkled conversation and letters with many literary references. Quotes from Shakespeare and the Bible flowed from Henry's mind to his pen; for example, the image of a smile on the face of a judge masking "murther" in the heart, from *The Life of King*

Henry the Fifth.[42] Martha would echo that stylistic habit in her adult letters and diary entries.

Henry Laurens specifically addressed Martha's education in female morals and virtuous behavior, along with his expectations of her mastering numbers and letters. In 1771 he heartily thanked Uncle James, with whom adolescent Martha was then living: "The good account which you give me of Patsy fills my Heart with Joy. And I am particularly pleased to hear that She is an acceptable Companion to her Aunt. I shall love her for that." Worried that the "wretched State of female Virtue, at this very time, in England" was far worse than he remembered from his previous time there, he fumed: "Chastity is certainly out of Fashion . . . And women talk another Language than that in which modesty was best understood twenty years ago."[43]

At the end of the 1760s, Martha, nearly ten years old, was definitely "forward in her learning," her father bragged to his British partner and relative George Appleby. "She reads well & begins to write prettily, is not dull in the french Grammar and Plays a little on the Harpsichord." Her music teacher may well have been the organist at St. Philip's or George Hartley, who played at St. Michael's until his pro-British sympathies made him persona non grata during the war. French and writing tutors Andrew Ellient, Thomas Delaland, Oliver Wilson, William Gordon, and Thomas Pike instructed Martha along with her older brother. Henry was as proud of her female accomplishments as he was of her intellectual ones. "Better than all, she handles her needles in all the useful branches & some of the most refined parts of Women's work, & promises me to learn to make minced Pies and to dress a Beef Steak."[44] In addition to the basic production of Negro clothes, the "useful" needlework Patsy's fingers were expected to execute included many refinements. Though no particular instructor was mentioned, an accomplished slave seamstress or Martha's mother taught such skills as petit point, embroidery, lacework, waxwork, and shellwork. Most girls of Martha's social background usually had to be content with needlework, music, and reading, but Martha's schooling was much broader. In 1771 her father "promised to give Patsy an Opportunity of Learning to Draw," arranging for a tutor in botany or "drawing from nature," at her request.[45]

For all of Henry Laurens' children, handwriting was *the* prime indicator of mental development and character—putting one's best hand forward, so to speak. Their father's business records—impeccable handwritten accounts and exact copies of correspondence made by skilled, paid clerks—were the model. To him, a good hand symbolized children's evolving intellect and self-discipline, so he often emphasized its singular importance. Since every experience contained an opportunity to learn, Henry had his children put as many as possible in writing. On any journey, he instructed his children to "mark down at least the Cities, Rivers, Canals, Hotels & other gross objects which fall" along their path. A junior version of that plan could be taught to even the littlest pupil: mapping the neighborhood from front gate to the Green, to the Market, and back. Every action deserved a record—preserved in writing and thus assimilated. Uncle James was expected to ensure that Martha recorded her first impressions of England during their 1775 relocation.[46]

Henry explicitly chided his son John about this. "Had you been nearer," he wrote across the ocean in 1774, "the *last letter* would have been returned for recopying." Invoking the Laurens standard of excellence, Henry Laurens warned: "You should not expose yourself to . . . censures of your friends by such scribbled blotted performances," a product "disrespectful to them and disreputable to yourself." Such bad habits would clearly impede future honor as well as profit. Henry scorned those bereft of legible handwriting, criticizing the deluded posturings from "a [careless] Merchants' Clerk" or "a hackney Amanuensis . . . Believe me Jack tis all affectation or the effect of Idleness or idle hurry. You can write a fine hand, quick & with accuracy. To [perfect that] will be a particular advantage to you, will always command praise[,] and never be disgraceful to a first rate Scholar of Independent fortune." Interestingly, while polite correspondence among the Carolina gentry avoided ethical topics like slavery, the moral and cultural weight given to self-presentation through penmanship was plentiful, expressing the classist assumption that penmanship defined the man (and woman). A few years later, Dr. Benjamin Rush recorded his version of that article of faith: incorrect handwriting and bad grammar could ruin one's reputation as a scholar and a gentleman, for life.[47]

Martha's own adult handwriting was startlingly masculine in its regularity and boldness, a surprise compared with her husband's execrable physician scrawl.[48] (As an adult, Martha's penmanship was "very fast and at same time a round distinct legible hand." Her father said she was the best clerk, of many very good ones, he ever had).[49] Henry's lectures on cultivated penmanship were most often addressed to one or another of his sons, yet she was the child who eagerly delighted in meeting his standards. In general, Henry Laurens' parental oversight was typified by minute instructions, such as recommending a specific abridged history from which the children could memorize the character and order of English kings and queens. His letters to them usually closed with a parting proverb: "remember [my advice] and profit from the friendly hint."[50]

Perhaps because she was determined to share her brother John's tutors and mental world, Martha early developed skill at mental and spatial organization along with "the useful and ornamental parts of female education." She enjoyed the grammatical structures of the French and English languages and a "considerable acquaintance with geometry and mathematical science"; she relished the new subject of geography and maps, nourished by an indulgent Papa who purchased "a pair of globes" from England because she requested them. He penned an avuncular boast to John about Martha's unusual solicitation: "You see what learned folks we are all to be. I hope she can [also] make a good Plumb Pudding," he summarized, "& in that hope, I'll send her both worlds [a pair of terrestrial and celestial globes]." Henry followed that with a written caution to Martha herself: her inquiry would be honored with "a pair of the best 18 inch [globes], with caps and a book of directions" and the bonus of "a dozen Middleton's best pencils marked [with her initials] ML." All she need do by way of thanking him was to remember "when you measure the surface of this world, . . . that you are to act a part on it, and think of a plumb pudding and other domestic duties."[51]

Beneath his fatherly concern for basic, foundational education, his primary epistolary lectures addressed the children's religious development. He urged "daily read[ing] the Bible" and regular repeating of "the Catechism of the Church of England [so] as to get it perfectly by Heart." Never one to omit the summarizing precept, Papa would add, for the nth time, that if his children should "hereafter depart from its [catechetical] principles," deep habituation will have made them "well acquainted with the Tenets of the Profession from which [they] dissent." He often added a signature benediction, the verbal equivalent of crossing himself: "Gracious God, Paul may Plant, Apollos May Water, but thou alone can'st give the Increase. Thy will be done." During the mid 1770s, as war threatened his vast landholdings and the slaves that comprised his fortune, Henry Laurens would reiterate again and again that education might turn out to be their most precious inheritance. "Virtuous liberal Educations to my Children may be the only Estates with which kind Providence will permit me to endow them." His ethics themselves were practical and briskly summarized: love Truth; hate deceit and unfair dealings even with those of your own age; do justice; be kind and merciful; be diligent and frugal so you will always have something to give the poor; and govern your passions. Such rules are the only way to have "invaluable Riches and intrinsic Honour in a conscience free from guilt & a contented mind."[52]

Henry Laurens' educational strictures and evaluations were intended to school Martha in company with brother, John, and in the same subjects. She must have a vigorous foundation of "English, Reading, Writing and Cyphering." But for all his reliance on mottoes, Papa had no patience with instructional pedantry for its own sake—such as "Latin masters" who insisted on "cypher[ing] *before* . . . grammar." He disdained lawyers who had to learn to "keep accounts *after* appearing at the bar," and "many a Divine and many a Physician" who lacked the "common and inferior parts of school learning." First master the essential basics, he intoned, then—if appropriate to one's future occupation—the classics. His own educational credo, paraphrased, was this: "The Foundation which I shall have laid will bear all a child's later Superstructure." The ultimate criterion was usefulness: each must become "an useful Member of Community. This is the Summit of my desire when I meditate upon the future well being of my own Children in this Life."[53]

Whether or not Henry's brother James Laurens imported anti–Roman Catholic tracts—lurid popular novellas filled with villainous Roman Catholic priests—is unclear. In one such popular novel, *The French Convert,* the agent of conversion was a literate if unsophisticated man, the humble, Bible-reading gardener on a large French estate; his convert was the noble Christian woman, wife of his employer who was away at war, being misled by sinister priestly authority. Stereotypically, the falsity and trickeries of the ancient church were presented in contrast with the honesty, modernity, and uprightness of Protestant reformers. In the Huguenot tradition, anti-Catholicism was an inherited ethos. The Laurens family stories started with her father's grandfather's flight from France after the Revocation of Nantes in 1685. Their own trail—from France to England to New York to Charles Town—had to have been the substance of many family gatherings.[54] Their grandfather's ethnic independence, joining the Church of England rather than the Charles Town "French Church" established in 1686, undoubtedly launched the Carolina Laurens in a pro-British mindset.[55]

Among the experiences of Martha's childhood was a tale she later told her own children. They thought it important enough to insert into a mid-nineteenth-century reprint of Martha's memoirs, adding it to their father's biographical introduction to preserve a teaching point they believed their mother had embodied: exemplary manners as a mark of respect for others.[56] Martha and a little cousin had been walking in a public park outside the new Laurens gardens when the two youngsters came to "a wet place which was too wide for them to jump over." Charleston's low-lying streets were prone to flooding and could quickly become impassable. As the little girls pondered what to do, daunted yet thrilled at the adventure, "a sailor appeared." For eighteenth-century children, Jack Tar personified the bogeyman of the seven seas, a fearsome image enlarged through tales of innocent boys snatched from the streets and "impressed" into brute labor on a navy ship. With this frightening lore in their heads, Martha and her cousin felt "not a little alarmed" to look up and see a sailor near them. Without ado, the formidable stranger "very kindly took Martha up and carried her quietly across the wet place, for which service she curtsied and thanked him." He then went back for the other little girl, but before she was halfway across," she became hysterical. She "cried and struggled with so much violence that the sailor took her back and left her" where she first stood. The two little girls stared at each other from opposite sides of the water barrier, one "lamenting her folly until help arrived," the other safe across and calm.[57] Illustrating the lesson of good manners, this story presented a small female child who survived an adventure with a scary adult and substantiated the Laurenses' family legend (reported in her husband's biographical introduction) that Martha was something of a tomboy in childhood, unusually adventurous for a girl. "In youth, her vivacity and spirits were exuberant," he had been told. "Feats of activity, though attended with personal danger, were to her familiar; great exertions of unusual poise and a feisty spirit, bodily labor; romantic projects; excesses of the wildest play" were what delighted her.[58]

Martha experienced her first inexplicable grief when her sister, Nelly, died after only two days' illness in 1764. Just as the family prepared to move into their grand new home, that chastening event plunged them to the depths. "An accident, melancholy enough to us who are nearly concerned, in my family, the sudden & unlooked-for death of my eldest daughter on the 18th Inst, filled my mind with so much grief & concern & employed me so much to compose & quiet her distressed Mother, upon whose health the Life of another [in utero] child greatly depended, that I must acknowledge all business was for some days put out of my head as if I had been altogether unconnected with trade," Henry wrote to a business friend.[59]

A month later a father's helplessness against death was still pitiably visible. "I have indeed been shocked & almost ready to murmur [against

Providence] at the Death of some very promising Children, particularly an improved Boy of nearly Six [the first Henry Jr.] and a clever Girl of Eight Years old [Nelly]," he wrote another friend. These blows to one "who may be called a fond Parent proved almost insurmountable. But thank God I have two Sons remaining [John and Henry Jr., known as Harry] . . . and a lively Girl [Martha] in her fifth Year." The blow of Nelly's death had caused a grieving father to "retreat . . . by graduate Steps from that bustle & hurry that . . . commerce . . . had led me into." Even Laurens' hospitality had suffered "when my Wife and I were in distress under the loss of our eldest Daughter."[60]

Nelly's death appeared in many succeeding letters. "Mrs. Laurens, Jacky, Patty and Harry are well, my once Dear Nelly is no more mine, but I must forbear," he concluded a letter in late August. Grief occasioned business slipups. "Several accidents in my family conspir[ed] to make me more remiss in business than ever I was wont to be . . . the severest stroke of all was the sudden death of my dear Little improved Girl Nelly, but thank God I have pretty well recover'd my former health & vigor, and my family are once more in a state of order and tranquility." At the end of that year, Papa congratulated partner George Appleby on *his* "Jubilee Year" but countered with a recital of his own woes. "To me it has proved a Year of affliction," he wrote, "a Dead eldest daughter, a Sick summer, a Sick and dying Wife [another pregnancy, plus the standard fevers and dysentery], a dying Captain Courtin [one of his employees who was a ship's captain], and a dead John Coming Ball [his wife's brother], my best friend and best Overseer."[61]

As the eldest daughter, Nelly would have been drawn into her mother's household sphere, allowing Martha room and time to indulge her tomboy propensities. When death made Martha the eldest daughter, she had to become the apprentice in those duties that fell to the female head of household: administering hospitality to a constantly varying number of family and guests; cooking and kitchen management of slaves, recipes, and food preserving; making and sending wedding gifts and baby presents; sewing slave clothing for the various Laurens plantations; caring physically for the household's medical needs; and organizing the family's religious observance and charities.

The Laurenses' social and cultural affiliations were by no means limited to kin or business associates, but Martha's girlhood produced no preserved record of any glittering social events. Though she watched her mother and cousins dress up for the occasional ball or musicale, Henry's correspondence is bare of descriptions of any such female rituals. Reading the Laurens household record strictly through the father's letters suggests an aspect of religious and characterological seriousness that was almost Puritan amid the gregarious and glamorous ethos of the 1760s Charles Town elite.[62]

Another incident from Martha's childhood, also later inserted into the 1845 edition of *Memoirs,* happened at the dame school she attended after her older sister's death and involved her favorite doll. Just before the move to their new mansion, a clergy widow named Mrs. Stokes opened a boarding school for girls in order to support herself and her daughter.[63] At its inception on 1 January 1763, Henry, wanting to be helpful, immediately enrolled Nelly, who attended there until her death in April 1764. Martha, nearing her sixth birthday, was enrolled in the same school and had brought a doll with her for comfort. The teacher, "an ill-natured, waspish person," according to the story, turned on her "in a moment of irritation," snatched the doll from the little girl's arms, and "threw it out the window." Bewildered, Martha wept copiously. The remembrance of that injustice had been so hurtful that for a long while she "could not go near the woman or even hear her name without crying," Martha recalled to her daughters.[64]

Even at that tender age, Martha knew that weeping over a doll was too babyish a reason for crying at school—or anywhere outside the shelter of home. So she impulsively offered an explanation for her tears that grownups would have to respect: the death of her sister. "I'm crying because sister Nelly's dead," she had sobbed. To her later dismay, that phrase proved so useful that it "grew into a proverb among her playmates. Whenever she seemed not to know why she was weeping, they would say, 'She's crying for sister Nelly.'"[65] Martha as a mother instructed her children against lying by interpreting that blurted response as the kind of cover-up to which children resort when they are too embarrassed to admit the truth—a harsh self-judgment of that six-year-old's grief that allowed no room for psychological vulnerability.

The parable encompassing the insult to little Martha by an insensitive teacher suggests grief instead of dishonesty; its major learning for a child was that death was the unexceptionable rationale for tears—"crying for sister Nelly." The lesson drawn from that memory by adult Martha was a foreshadowing of what would create her middle-aged "dark night of the soul" in 1795, when her spiritual ambitions demanded too much of her psyche and literally overwhelmed her capacity to live up to her high standards of righteousness.

Henry Laurens was indeed distinguished for more than economic accomplishment— accumulation of slaves, land, and money. During the first decade of Martha's life, he was an officer in the Charles Town Library Society, a founding member of an ecumenical literary or reading group, a commissary of the work house (where slaveowners could maintain public order by having their slaves disciplined without doing it themselves) and of the market. He was prominent enough to become the object of envy, and when his reputation was attacked, he had to respond. The outrage was a double taxation, levied by a Crown-appointed Admiralty judge, on one of his ships moving materials from his plantations to Charles Town. "Never was I in a law suit before, never wronged Caesar of his dues, always discountenanced smuggling and illicit trade," he fumed in August 1767. To clear himself—a technicality over filing papers—he whose commercial success was founded on integrity would have had to falsify a departure time. "Every merchant ought to be a Man of strict Honour" was his watchword.[66]

The enemy behind this public humiliation was British placeman Sir Egerton Leigh, the Admiralty court judge who was married to his niece; its tool was a jealous merchant, Daniel Moore. Despite resolving strenuously to maintain his dignity, Henry Laurens found himself suddenly, irresistibly reaching out to "twist his [Moore's] nose" as the two men faced each other in court. It was an unmistakable aggression, a gesture equivalent to calling the man a liar in front of witnesses.[67] However gratifying to indulge the impulse, her father mourned, the act "really humbles me, instead of making me proud and vain. It keeps me more at home & makes me shun the croud in every appearance, except the Church and State . . . I go to Church & come home again, to the House of Assembly and return . . . avoiding all disputes about tenets, refin'd politics & party." Henry's peers generally sided with him against the court's manipulation, but he himself felt degraded by the incident. Corruptible court appointees like Leigh would turn out to be "the most likely instrument to effect a disunion between the Mother Country and her American Offspring," Henry prophesied after his run-in.[68]

Martha was raised in the midst of unarticulated but clear boundaries between white and black people within and outside the home; for example, slaves were allowed to sleep only on the floor in her room or outside its door. Walking along sandy Broad Street in the 1760s, she would have seen an almost equal number of white and black pedestrians, intermixed yet totally separate. Thirty years earlier a startled European visitor had commented, "Carolina looks more like a Negro Country than life in a Country settled by white people."[69] By age eight or nine, Martha would recognize that general attitudes about slaves and slavery were different from her experience with the real individuals she knew, her experience of being rocked and sung to after a bath or singing in the kitchen. Exactly what she absorbed of her father's business has to be a matter of speculation, although she was too acute not to have received deep impressions. The actual work of slaves in their owners' households, even something as fundamental as the care of a newborn child, remains uniformly invisible in polite literature, including family letters. Slaves were primarily visible in the amazingly exact and complete business accounts kept by Martha's merchant father.

From Henry Laurens' first sale of a slave cargo eight years before her birth and throughout her childhood, his satisfaction in the techniques of conducting business and his exuberance at mastering them was palpable. After five years, he had learned that the youthfulness of his human imports was the commercial key: "people are . . . very delicate in what they buy [as slave property], over the age of twenty." He learned that at certain times of the year, "sales [were] a good deal duller" than others, and that slaves "from Callabar" were "quite out of repute" with local buyers because they were too prone to "destroying themselves" and thus their owners' profit. He became expert at calculating the cost of provisions for a slave labor force. What young Martha clearly recognized about her Papa's business was his pleasure in it.[70]

In the same good news/bad news year of 1764, amid their move into the new house and the paralyzing grief over sister Nelly's death, Martha's father recorded an example of his assessment of slave qualities for a potential buyer. Summarizing a man he'd owned for twelve years, Henry compiled a clearly detailed balance sheet of slave Abram's strengths and weaknesses—the negatives being his overfondness for females and therefore distractibility, his bent for pilfering trifles, and his skill at "warding off whipping."[71] While a little girl could not understand her father's business calculations, her emotional world rested squarely on her father's confidence in his own judgment. The respect with which the clerks in his own countinghouse greeted him assured her that the family universe was on solid ground.

A sharp-eared child necessarily assimilated her father's views of such things as the qualities of a good overseer and the comparative worth of slaves born in America: "such Negroes—for their ability in making Negro Clothes, attending sick people & a hundred things which new or Shipd

Negroes cannot perform—are invaluable." Martha was old enough in 1767 to note, without grasping its significance, her parents' good-natured banter over a particular female slave. "Nanny is a breeding woman and in ten Years time may have doubled her worth in her own children. Mrs. Laurens had a great covetousness for her when I first bought her, but knowing her value I would not convert the property." Like most power interactions in slaveowning households, nothing substantive was preserved in writing about that kind of jockeying.[72]

By the time Martha was four, however, her father was already beginning to acknowledge the deleterious effects of slavery on the white children in a slaveowning society. Urging a Moravian pastor, Jacob Ettwein, to settle his white congregation in South Carolina, he found himself admitting that physical labor—field cultivation, for example—was demeaned in a society where only blacks were supposed to do it, thus giving white youth a false view of honest work. His admiration for Moravians and other pious citizens like the Quakers made him deeply regretful that he couldn't lure more such white settlers to Carolina: "what pity," he wrote, "that all Quakers are not Church [of England] Men and all Church Men not Quakers." Much of his letter argued the congruency of Henry's religious principles with those espoused by the Moravians—yet on this point he was too honest to deny the problems created by a slave labor system, about which Pastor Ettwein had specifically questioned him.[73]

And other reservations, qualified and cautious, occasionally appeared in Henry Laurens' letters during the first decade of Martha's life. Pleasure in his commercial success had drawn him further into the business— "insensibly . . . by means and circumstances quite adventitious"—than he originally intended. Rationalizing, he added, "However, the reflection is comfortable that my Servants are as happy as Slavery will admit of, none run away, [and] the greatest punishment to a defaulter is to sell him." By November of 1759, the year of Martha's birth, he found it useful to compare the degrees of cruelty endured by black slaves with that experienced by Irish indentured servants. He had considered giving up the huge profits in the slave trade "because of many acts from the Masters . . . toward the wretched Negroes, from the time of purchasing to that of selling them again" that offended his deepest moral instincts. He nevertheless repeated the regional self-justification that many slaves were "uncontroulable," and then declared: "I never saw an instance of cruelty in 10–12 years in . . . the African Trade . . . equal to the Cruelty exercised upon those poor Irish . . . crowded in ships, [enduring a] terrible voyage . . . with little provisions, misled by fancy ads in Ireland." Concern for "poor white wretches" gave him misplaced empathy, one of the few times Henry identified skin color as a factor in favoring one exploited population over another.[74]

Martha grew up under the beneficent shadow of her father's Carolina business empire and civic reputation. An appreciative northern visitor penned an idealization of it in the mid 1780s: Mr. Laurens' plantation Mepkin "displayed the beauties and advantages of nature no less than the ingenious improvements of its owner," this observer noted. "He is a rare instance of method, whereby his plantation raises itself above those of this [region of the] country [where] everything is done *immethodically*, by the round-about means of force & Labour." Henry Laurens was that rare plantation owner innovative enough and organized enough to employ the new "machinery & the contrivances of art" that helped make him extraordinarily successful.[75]

Long before Martha could appreciate outsiders' admiration of her beloved Papa, however, a frightening nighttime intrusion into the Laurenses' own domestic space taught her that some outsiders were unexpectedly dangerous. In an early local contretemps over the Stamp Act near the end of October 1765, Martha's father took the unpopular public stand of defending the agents assigned to collect that vastly resented British tax. His refusal to engage in vitriolic denouncement of the "stamped paper" brought a political nightmare into the household and drove her beloved mother, again pregnant, into hysteria. Henry's notarized report to Joseph Brown, justice of the peace, described it at length.

At about midnight on 23 October 1765 the Laurenses' house was startled awake by "a most violent thumping and the chants of Liberty! Liberty!" and "Stamp Paper!" The attackers were "chiefly in disguise" and demanded to search the house. "No fair words would pacify them," even when Henry shouted that he had *no* "stamped paper nor any connection with stamps" and accused them of "cruelty to a poor sick woman far gone with child." His wife was beside herself with fear; their approach—"to attack a single Man in such a multitude"—was cowardly.[76]

His terrified family huddled at the top of the stairs, six-year-old Martha and two-year-old Henry Jr. clinging to their mother's nightgown. Eleven-year-old John probably longed to rush down and join his Papa's defense. Back in mid-September, two Charles Town newspaper owners, Peter Timothy and Robert Wells, had reluctantly announced that they would indeed pay the extra stamp duty on their newspapers despite fervent local opposition to it. (Timothy wrote Benjamin Franklin that his announcement had made him "the most unpopular Man in the province, by taking upon me a place in the Post Office . . . and declining to . . . engage in the most violent Opposition.")[77] Even though Henry Laurens had *not* agreed to pay the outrageous tax, his enemies chose to believe he would.

"Conscious of my Innocence," his statement continued, "I was pausing," deciding whether to refuse all demands or to open the door. "Mrs Laurens' condition and her cries prompted me to open the door which in two minutes more they would have beat through." The ruffian group poured in, pressed him into a chair with a "brace of Cutlasses across my breast," and called for lights. Some of them pretended to carry out a search—a "superficial search indeed, or rather no search at all, in my House, Counting House, Cellar & Stable." Under their disguises of "soot, Sailors habits, slouch hats & etc.," Henry recognized some of them and called them by name. If Martha was able to see the scene from her upstairs perch, it would certainly have reinforced the sailor-as-bogeyman fear. Finding no stamped paper and realizing their advantage was slipping, the invaders tried to force Henry to take a "Bible Oath" that none was concealed anywhere. Henry refused in "language which I only had learned from them"—employing "damns of equal weight with their own."[78]

From the darkened stairway where the weeping mother and the three children cringed, the noise and glint of swords in lamplight would have appeared like a bad dream. "My sentiments of the Stamp Act were well known," Papa Henry recalled; "I had openly declared myself an Enemy to it & would give & do a great deal to procure its annihilation, but . . . I could not think they pursued a right method to obtain a repeal." Increasingly mollified, the intruders reduced their demand to a peripheral issue: that he should not "hold way" or be a friend to "one Governor Grant," an official from the east Florida province. That revealed the prime instigator to be newspaperman Peter Timothy, who was offended both by Henry Laurens' cool reasonableness in this farce and his longtime relationship with Grant.

Emboldened by the change in tone, Henry said he "corresponded with Gov. Grant & esteem'd him as a Gentleman." He "knew nothing in [Grant's] conduct or principles as a Gentleman" that was disgraceful, and in the unlikely event that the governor had "criminal schemes or projects," he would have been "too prudent to trust *me* with his secrets." Switching to flattery, Henry then said: "I am in your power. You are very strong & may if you please Barbicue me. I can but die, but you shall not by any force or means whatsoever compel me to renounce my friendship or to speak ill of Men that I think well of, or to say or do a mean thing." His moral victory complete, the masked ruffians then abashedly raised "three Cheers, God bless," and "hope the poor Lady will do well, etc.," and left. The invasion lasted an hour and fifteen minutes. Henry was proud to report not "one penny damage to my Garden—not even to walk over a [flower] Bed and nor do 15 c/ damage to my Fence, Gate, or House." The only real damage, he feared, was the trauma to his wife and children.

After that nightmare, Henry wrote, Eleanor was "very ill indeed, but today I have great hopes that she will go out her expected time of four or five weeks longer [before giving birth]."[79] How many succeeding nights Martha's dreams were filled with disguised demons and real swords was never noted, but six weeks later her father and his friends joked about the incident. They called her healthy newborn brother "Georgie Liberty" to commemorate the masked men's midnight invasion—something about which Martha and her mother probably were never quite as amused.

In an odd twist of circumstance, the very next year, 1766, the same Governor Grant whom Henry defended at sword's point became a lengthy guest in their home when he was struck with a virulent illness. His travels had brought him to "rest himself on one of my Beds & there has been resting ever since," Henry reported in a letter, "sometimes promising to make an eternal rest of it, nor is he quite out of danger yet." His poor wife, Eleanor, was still weak at that time and worrisome. "She frets a little under this very hot weather," the burden of "a very sick unexpected guest," and the "trouble which naturally arises every day in a large family."[80]

In September of 1766, Henry reported, "Thank God my family has been unusually healthy, only Patsy [Martha] with a little fever confin'd three or four days but is now better; little Liberty, alias Jemmy, is a fine fellow at Nine months." Of course Martha's mother was again pregnant. The following September, Henry recorded the opposite kind of news: "I have had a very sick Wife & buried a Young Child within three Weeks past, which—added to some other affairs that have taken my attention from the Counting House—has not allow'd me time to examine your accounts."[81]

Three years later, the household experienced its ultimate tragedy. Martha's beautiful, universally loved mother was pregnant for what would be the last time. She died on 22 May, only thirty-nine years old. For nearly a month before, Henry's letters revealed dark forebodings. "I await an event in my family. When that is over *and well over* I shall have the pleasure of seeing you," he wrote. The cautious repetition "and well over" symbolized a mental crossing of his fingers against fate. In late April his worst fears were realized. "My heart is full, my mind embarrassed. Mrs. L was delivered

Yesterday of a daughter—they say a child likely to live, but the Dr. and the women around her . . . report the bare possibility of the Mother's surviving 7 days. This gloomy prospect distresses me beyond description, and in such a manner as you cannot feel." He had been "waiting a happy issue of her late circumstance" before taking John to England for schooling; those plans were based on having "a tender watchful Mother . . . and a faithful friend in all respects to me," who would care for the other four children. "In an instant the scene is shifted; clouds rise thick before me and darken my path." The possible dispersal of his children after her death haunted his dreams.[82]

At age eleven, Martha was all too familiar with the reality of sickbeds, and perhaps somewhat aware of the many things that could go wrong when women gave birth. She knew the finality of death because of Sister Nelly. But no child her age was prepared for the agony overwhelming her brave Papa. "The prospect of losing a good Friend in such a Wife and of having five Children upon hand"—once his greatest joy—"melts my Heart and fills my Mind with Anxieties," Henry wrote in May as he awaited the end. No matter how fiercely he attempted to "submit" to "the Decrees of Providence . . . [that] we cannot stay nor controul," his profound gloom would not lift. "This is at least an ingenuous Confession of the weak State of my own breast."[83]

Several letters written on 10 May 1770 detail the agonies of lingering death: nearly a month for Martha's dwindling mother and her survivors. A letter begun on 15 May, a week before Eleanor actually died, was finally finished after the funeral. "It was really out of my power to command myself—this is the first letter to anyone in England, and the first day since [the funeral] I have been able to sit down to any business." Henry attempted to marshal his thoughts. "Thank God the Storm begins to abate, my Dear little Children all of whom you know except the little Female added 27th April, call upon me to attend them, to inspect their education, to cultivate their Manners, to train them in the manner they should go. Affection draws me toward them, Reason demands to resume her Seat."[84] In his letter of 1 June he wrote that "Virtue has lost a Friend" in her death, but that his own unbearable pain was still comprehended by God. "A hearty Submission to Gods Will and even Thankfulness for many undeserved past and present Mercies are intermixed with my Complaints." In utter helplessness, he added, "I look round upon my Children. I lament their Loss. I weep for my own. I bless God that I have such Children and that I have Bread for them, & yet I weep. This is Human and it is a true picture of my heart."[85] To another friend, he wrote, "I feel this stubborn Heart of mine violently agitated between contrary passions and Affections which alternately claim Supremacy. But Grief still seems predominant & I feel as if something which constituted my Happiness was torn from me. Every Thing else therefore . . . wears the Aspect of Gloom and uncertainty."[86]

For the next five years, Henry Laurens would demonstrate a remarkable preoccupation with the responsibilities of his domestic life. During the summer of 1770, after Eleanor's death, this suffering husband poured his pain into words. Letters written 12, 21, 25 June and 1, 25 August rehearsed the same grievous litany: his wife's thankfully serene death, his desolation, and his anxieties over "the sole Charge of five Children." In one he even recognized the children's trauma: "those dear little Connections will not allow me to leave my habitation even for a day."[87]

Ten letters in September 1770 began to indicate that his interest in business was trying to "emerg[e]." In a tone somewhat more reminiscent of his former self, he wrote John Holman that he would indeed make an effort to sell any slaves sent to him, or see to their profitable marketing—only "send me young ones." Then came a qualifying afterthought: "I don't mean Children." That same day he responded to old friend Richard Oswald's letter of condolence by evoking the image of "me surrounded by five children bewailing the Loss of one of the best of Mothers and of Wives . . . an Event [that] drew my Thoughts within a narrow Sphere" and made him "wholly inattentive to everything beyond my Domestic Circle."[88]

As his grief took on written form, his memories cataloged Eleanor's goodness. "[She] never *once*, not once during 20 years most intimate Connection, threw the Stumbling Block of Opposition or Controversy in my way, to whom in that great Part of our short Span of Existence I never had Cause to impute any other Fault than that of an Excess of Goodness, Condescension & Charity, which took from my Children, a Mother indeed! from the Poor a chearful & liberal Benefactress, and from Virtue a Friend." Her death was "a Blow which staggerd me almost to the Gates of Death, the Weight of which still lays heavy on me and which I feel most sensibly, upon every such Recital as this, and in all my Hours of Retirement."

His children's loss was almost as heavy on his heart. "My Children are now around me five in Number, all apparently sound in Body and Mind, they have large Demands upon me, they Hang upon my Breast and my Knees, and look up with eager Cravings for Education and for that tender Care in domestic Life which they have always experienced in their dear Mother."[89] The absence of his beloved friend left him bereft of anyone "to participate of that Joy . . . of their Improvements, None to impart my Sorrow unto, nor to consult with if Evil at any Time shall betide them." But there was no question about his sense of priority regarding them. In a handwritten sigh, the aching father struggled to accept this "Stroke of Providence" as best he could.[90]

He added a profound spiritual interpretation that only a fellow Christian could share. "If I had not been a Witness of that absolute Resignation in which my Dear wife expired without a sigh, repeating in full Assurance of Bliss 'Father, thy will be done,' I should believe really—from my own rebellious Feelings—that [even] the most Perfect Submission among us poor Mortals is constrained [partial]." Anger at her premature death made him want to protest "the Decrees of him to whom Omnipotence and Omniscience is to be ascribed & whose tender Mercies are over all his Works." But in atonement for a rebellious heart, he reminded himself that God was just in "all his Dispensations." He ended the sentence with the usual phrases of benediction—"to whom be Glory, Honour, & Thanksgiving For Ever & Ever."[91]

Henry meanwhile had quietly explored one possible scenario: "looking for a discreet Woman to keep my House, to take off Part of the Trouble which Children always create, but without Success tho several have offered." Obviously his plantation supervision would also have to be curtailed. "In that Quarter I [also] stand in great need of a Friend." A month later, he again enumerated his multiple roles: "I am Father, Mother, Nurse, Tutor & Companion to 4 Children and must often visit & pass an hour with a 5th. Thank God it is a pleasing and delightful charge, and I receive my reward in the Discharge of my Duty."[92]

He was nearing a more critical decision. In a letter of sympathy to John Poulson, he wrote: "You have lost a good Wife, a Loss which [in this life] may be retrieved. Many good Women remain in the world." Henry's own loss, however, was irreplaceable. "But I have lost a Mother, a tender and good Mother to my five Children, 4 of whom stand in the utmost need of such a Mother. How shall I repair this Loss? It is not to be done. I might soon get a wife, but it is impossible for me to obtain a Mother for those Infants." This announcement was a turning point and presaged his recovery. "I must therefore not barely submit to the Stroke of Providence, but I must also suppress as much as possible every Rising of Grief . . . I am and must be for a while longer, confined in the delightful domestic Task which Providence has been pleased to assign me."[93] With these words Henry Laurens moved to open up his life once again.

The following winter, as might be expected after such total emotional debility, his entire household succumbed to physical illness. Early in 1771, poor little Jemmy nearly choked to death on a piece of "plumstone" in his windpipe. Before "[his] Amendment could quiet the Apprehensions of my Mind, Jacky was laid down by epidemic Sore Throat and Fever—then Harry—then Patsy—together with four of my Negroes." Finally, inevitably, "myself—so that my House has been a hospital . . . The Alteration of my Family Affairs from the late melancholy Loss . . . . must for a while claim the Indulgence of my Friends."[94] In this bleak scene the tears and misery of eleven-year-old Martha remained an unwritten, possibly even unnoticed, footnote.

Because Papa Henry needed to travel, it was decided that his brother James and his wife, Mary, should move into Henry's mansion on East Bay Street, bringing with them the baby, Mary Eleanor (Polly), for whom they were caring. Maintaining Martha in her own setting was the major consideration in this plan. She would not have to be uprooted and could enjoy the companionship of a loving aunt to supervise her studies. In addition, she would enjoy her baby sister. Uncle James' own newly purchased house in the center of Charles Town was nearly ready for occupancy, but it would be rented. He would supervise Papa's business in the countinghouse to the best of his abilities, despite his apprehension over that responsibility. Henry, preparing to take the two older boys to England, warned friends they should not expect his former buoyant conversation and energy. "Don't recommend me to . . . Folks that are very gay . . . I am not sour, nor displeased with the Taste and Fashion of the present Age, but I find myself less & less qualified, or more & more indisposed to take part in them. In short . . . I can't recover yet from the Shock which the Loss of last Year gave to my Mind."[95]

Papa Henry's commitment to being the comprehensive parent required a decision about schooling. "In my present State of Family, having 3 Sons and two Daughters and no Mother to them, and the present State of our Charles Town Schools, public and private under worse Direction than ever," he saw no alternative to London. He faced the necessity of "part[ing] with some of them," Martha and infant Polly, for the benefit of their brothers' education.[96] Definitely enrolling the older two boys in English schools, he would also take Jemmy, "Please God he lives" after his "inoculation for Small Pox." His letters record the torment and grief over his "two girls left [behind], one of 11 yrs old, the other about 18 mo."[97] The most terrible cost of his wife's death was the "hastening on a separation between me and my Children . . . One of them (Harry) is already gone from me" to England.[98]

Surrendering daily custody of his oldest daughter, even to a brother, was anguishing, no matter how loving the second family.

Schooling at dame school and at home by tutors helped occupy Martha's active mind after her father and brothers departed. Uncle James' continuous supply of imported books was a literary cupboard in which a girl could lose herself. But nothing could replace the aching emptiness of a mother's absence. The sentiments her father wrote to one of her Ball cousins surely described Martha's own mourning: "Many attempts did I make to write . . . upon the subject of [your] Dear Aunt's Death, but those always around me can bear Witness that I was never able to go through a Letter. Even at this distance of Time, the bare Mention of the Name hurries reflexions upon my mind which betray a weakness [tears] that I can not yet conquer."[99]

During the first months of Martha's geographic separation from her Papa, nature vented some capricious violence on their new East Bay home. A late November hurricane sweeping in from the sea struck their house with a mighty gust of thunder and lightning at about 9:30 one evening, according to the newspaper account. The gale knocked off the "westerly Funnel of the north Chimney" and viciously scattered bricks more than fifty yards distant. Inside the house, at the foot of the chimney, a "great deal of Earthen Ware was brok to pieces and Pewter turned black or melted." Near the ceiling of the second floor, likely at the place where the exploded chimney joined the wall, gushing streams of rain "went through the floors so [powerfully] the Boards were forced upwards." Considerable damage occurred in the two north rooms, above and below. Three large looking glasses shattered, one small looking glass was "beaten all to Shivers," the "silver handles of cutlery melted, and two Setts of China in a Closet were . . . as if pounded by a Mortar." A great portion of furniture, glass, and pictures was destroyed, "yet the harpsichord received no damage." The wind's force drove pieces of wood straight into the partitions and walls. The fourteen-pound weight in the grandfather clock standing in the south- east corner came unfastened, though securely attached with an inch-and- a-half screw. Open grillwork on both sides of the clock case was "beat inwards," but the clockworks themselves were not "put out of adjustment." The newspaper report concluded by noting that ten people lived in that household under the care of Mr. Henry Laurens' brother James and his wife, Mary Laurens, the littlest girl (Polly) in a baby bed (the number apparently included slaves), yet not one person was injured.[100] When Henry Laurens finally read of this near-disaster from across the Atlantic Ocean, he filled pages with tearful thanksgivings for their deliverance from his most dire imaginings.

What Martha thought about this freakish visitation has to be imagined. If she remained a fairly confident girl, this assault of nature on her daily world could have been an interesting adventure, an event about which to write or boast a little to cousins. If she was still feeling abandoned by her dearest and closest relations, father and brothers, and emotionally fragile over her mother's death, the hurricane's tumult could have strengthened the deep sense that fate was ominous—that life was going to be more fearful than hopeful and exciting.

Unfortunately, any actual words Martha might have written in the crucial years when she was twelve and thirteen were burned by her before the uncle's household removed to England.[101] Her father's letters, meanwhile, begin to record more humanitarian thoughts about his slaves. Undoubtedly softened by his own experience of loss, he was able, perhaps for the first time, to articulate the grim realities endured by his slaves: "How much do I pity those poor unhappy Men, Women & Children to whose Distresses and Starving condition the Rice Planter is indebted for the vast Advance of Price for his Produce. Have I any Cause to complain? when I reflect one moment upon their miserable Circumstances and compare my own with theirs."

In early 1772 he sounded as if he were actively backing away from further trade in slaves. He wrote Uncle James: "these Branches, the most profitable, I have quitted to people more eager for them. You know I have given up many Thousands of Pounds by so doing." Referring obliquely to Uncle James' responsibility for his most precious possessions, his daughters, he added: "But let me not be robbed of my little Ewe Lamb[s]." He could direct outrage at an overseer who defrauded him by starving his horses and withholding provisions for the slaves—also for sleeping with a slave (Mary). In early 1773 he finally fired the man. Henry was clear about the connection between overseer Gambrell's lack of humane supervision and the "vast Desertion of nine slaves," runaways. "If he makes less Rice with more hands but treats my Negroes with Humanity I would rather have him . . . than . . . one who should make twice as much . . . and exercises any degree of Cruelty toward those poor Creatures who look up to their Master as their Father, Guardian & Protector."[102] Being a plantation master stirred complex, conflicting emotions.

Two years after his wife's death, Martha's father was again finally in full charge of all his family concerns, deeply involved in the mounting political turmoil with Britain, and managing his extensive financial empire. What should be the choice of career for John? "Physick" or law? Henry's younger son, Harry, needed to settle down. In addition, his daughters were in danger of becoming more a part of his brother's life than his. These long thoughts constituted the subtext of a letter to fellow Huguenot John Gervais, a former employee and now young partner who had married at the end of 1773. His wedding party included young Martha among its bridesmaids, perhaps out of respect for her absent father, but also to offer the motherless girl a kind of celebration on entering her teens.

Henry's heartstrings were tugged at the thought of a daughter he still fancied his little girl being suddenly old enough to participate in a wedding. And when he read that the groom had assumed the seigniorial claim to a dance with her, as well as a grownup kiss, Henry Laurens, far away in England, had to strive for jocularity without success. "So you made my Patsy one of the Bride's Maids & anticipated my own expected pleasures in mimicking the poor little Orphan." That sentence contained a torrent of emotion, but the word *orphan* stopped him. "Ah that Term! Why did it drop from my Pen—a Tear Accompanies it and interrupts the Subject. There. I have given Vent but must not return."[103]

As he envisioned his teenage Martha now so grown up and so far away, the absence of his loved companion and his own geographic helplessness must have dumbfounded him. In his mind to that point, Patsy had remained the clever, affectionate girl-child who kissed him good-bye. Being so distant from his daughter as she became a young woman undoubtedly made a tender father feel totally overcome.

3 | "A Wandering Sheep, a Prodigal Daughter"

A FAMILY SCANDAL THAT OCCURRED in Martha Laurens' early teens initiated an adolescent rite of passage for her and inaugurated a pattern of spiritual attunement she would refer to throughout the rest of her life as "heart-work." Though the actual disgrace that led her to label herself a "prodigal daughter" belonged to her first cousin Molly Bremar rather than to Martha herself, its impact on the family and on adolescent Martha—who had to watch helplessly during the family's trauma—became a major factor in the way she thought and lived from then on. Of course there is rarely a single cause or interpretation of a specific turning point in any individual's life, a sole explanation that rules out all others. Undoubtedly the taint of public disgrace and fear of a similar weakness in herself heightened the crisis for Martha, at a time of overweening self-absorption when her external world was also in tumult. Obviously, a combination of motives, conscious and unconscious, propelled this budding girl to seek what she hoped was spiritual armor. The print record, as preserved, states only that she set out to construct a written compact with God—the most impregnable inner shield that she could envision.

The actual precipitating event, near the end of 1772, was the birth of an out-of-wedlock child to Martha's eighteen-year-old cousin ("Molsy") on a ship in Charleston harbor that was about to sail for London. Public speculation about the father immediately centered on Sir Egerton Leigh, married for sixteen years to Molsy's older sister.[1] He was the same British appointee with whom Martha's Papa Henry had crossed ethical and economic swords in the 1767 Admiralty Court dispute, and he was widely known as the one who derided the Laurens family reputation for pious integrity. When Molsy's salacious news erupted, however, the Laurens family was dispersed; Martha's father was far distant in England and, as it must have felt to her, preoccupied with her brothers. Still grieving her mother's death, Martha had remained behind in their new Charles Town mansion with her second family—Uncle James, Aunt Mary, and baby sister Polly.

Worrisome cousin Molsy Bremar first surfaced in the uncles' transatlantic letters in late 1771. Henry Laurens, mentioning her name in "appropriately evil English weather," prophesied further "evils" from the Leigh-Bremar combination, but at that point it was only foreboding. Both brothers brought heavy hearts to their kinship duties for widowed sister Mary Bremar and her three unmarried grown children, the uncles having carried that troubling brood financially for years. "Our Niece has acted amiss on your Side [of the ocean] and . . . has run all Hazards to try her Fortune on this Side," Henry surmised. This news "embarrassed my Mind and forbid the Closing of my Eyes before Two O Clock this morning." Then Sir Egerton Leigh himself appeared in the text. "Mr. Leigh [is] with her. This may be what he calls treating her as his eldest Daughter"—the promise he'd made to her dying mother in Henry's presence—although his subsequent public fondness for her exceeded all definitions of stepfathering.[2] Henry's gloom issued in a gruff attempt at humor. "But I think it would be shewing the Child Mercy, to hire some Ruffian to expedite the Work which his Perfidy is carrying on by slow Degrees." What if this new "Act of his Villainy" turned out to be worse than anything else thus far?[3]

For almost the whole of 1772, the scandal that was indeed growing in Molsy's womb did not reappear in family letters. Then three days before Christmas, Uncle James took up the tale from Carolina. The previous Sunday evening a friend had come by with the news that his niece Molsy had been smuggled onto Captain White's ship, which was docked in the Rebellion Road wharf and ready to sail with the first wind. Uncle James instantly summoned the captain, who confessed, "She [Molly] was delivered Last Night of a Live Boy . . . and I would give 50 Guineas that I had never taken her on board my Ship." He apologized for withholding this information from the distinguished Laurens family but had been "strictly enjoyn'd to secrecy." His orders were to deliver Molsy to the lodging of a Mrs. Parsons in London, but he was clearly worried; her present state was pitiable, only "very scanty Stock [of food and drink] laid in for her" and "no assistance but a Negro Girl who waited on her."[4]

Uncle James' first response had been sympathy. "I can't express the Anxiety & Compassion I felt for the unhappy Girl," he wrote, "first ruined & then left to Perish by the most unnatural Children of the same Parents [her two ne'er-do-well older brothers] & [then] influenced by one [Egerton Leigh] who has been a curse to them all." Quickly dispatching supplies to the ship via some trusted friends, Uncle James included a "Kind letter" offering Molsy refuge and the hope she would seek "Amendment of Life"—Anglican prayer-book language for repentance. His messengers brought back the report of a brazen Molsy "sitting in her bed amazing hearty with her child by her." The foolish girl had returned her uncle's note, "accounting for her present Situation by such a Stupid improbable tale as never was heard of." Grimly counting back to the previous spring in London as the "time of her ruin," there could be no doubt about the progenitor of "that Cruel Act."[5]

Only at that point in his letter did Uncle James admit to Henry that he and Aunt Mary had often invited Molsy to the house during the preceding months as company for her cousin Martha. But Molsy, more enamored of the Leighs' social whirl than the staid household sheltering her motherless girl cousins, had always declined. As early as October, a friend had confided "that M.B. was with Child." At that point, Uncle James had already reached out to Molsy with "pity & Compassion," offering to "rescue her from Infamy, & find a retreat to hide her Guilt from the World."[6]

Molsy's denial had been so "artfully and rigidly dissembled" that Uncle James and his wife actually allowed themselves to believe her. "What a Complication of wickedness in so young a Creature," Uncle James now acknowledged. She had offered to swear her innocence on a Bible, she whose sins were as scarlet, serious affronts to God and to the Laurenses' moral standards. They included adultery and worse, "even a Murderous intention" of abortion, "for tis Little Less than a Miracle that all the Means she has used to destroy the Wretched Infant in the Womb did not affect it." At that point Uncle James, verbally throwing up his hands at his own ineffectiveness, appealed to his older brother: "If *you* can do any thing to Save her from destruction and persuade her to repent, I am sure you will."[7]

The females in the Laurens household on East Bay Street had to cope with such a gossip's feast as best they could, Aunt Mary becoming upset to the point of illness. No discussion about their other niece, Molsy's older sister who was married to the scoundrel Leigh, was recorded. As for Henry's favorite daughter? "Patsy knows nothing of it," Uncle James wrote somewhat disingenuously, though "naturally she is uneasy at Seeing her Aunt & me troubled." His final sentence acknowledged the inescapable truth: "But the matter I suppose is Public & everyone will hear it very soon."[8] At whatever point the scandal did register on Martha's youthful consciousness, her feelings must have been a jumble—embarrassment at the family's disgrace, anxiety for her humiliated elders, and curiosity about Molsy herself.

In January 1773, a very long epistle from Henry Laurens in Westminster, England, to Sir Egerton Leigh in Carolina, London, spelled out the case for legal action against him, point by point. First was Leigh's hypocritical promise to his wife's dying mother that adopted Molsy as his eldest daughter, second the disgraceful circumstances of the infant's birth in a cramped ship's cabin, third his manipulative deceit of the captain, and fourth—ultimately most damning—the death of the innocent child. Born "hearty and stout," the infant had "perished for want of care on the 5th or 6th day" because the young mother "had no milk and nothing proper to feed it," and its tiny jaws locked. According to Captain White, these lurid details were "notorious knowledge" even before the ship could set sail. In all, the letter detailed fifteen charges, including the preposterous explanation Molsy had been instructed to offer: that the previous March she was raped by an unknown assailant in a London park, her cries supposedly stifled by a kerchief in her mouth. According to Henry's letter, "Everyone" dismissed the fictional rapist in favor of Leigh himself.[9]

The list of accusations concluded with Molsy's own hysterical confession. Her London landlady had recently brought word to Henry that "a most Violent Agony" overwhelmed Molsy in the night, causing a "disburthen[ing of] her overloaded mind" severe enough to threaten her sanity. Henry inscribed the loathsome words she screamed out: "her Sister's Husband Mr. Leigh . . . who had solemnly promised in the presence of God & the Spirit of her deceased Mother to adopt her, Molsy, as his Eldest Daughter, had debauched her, promised to Marry her after the death of her sister," an occasion he implied would be soon, "composed the Fable of the Rape and the Park, bid her stand firm to the Story, and at the peril of her Life never to betray him."[10]

Henry's proffered olive branch, if Leigh was man enough to confess and make amends, would spare Leigh's own wife and children "the Infamy." Leigh's absolute worst blasphemy, in Henry's view, was *pretense:* daring to be "a partaker of the Holy Sacrament of the Body & Blood of Christ" when he should be on his knees for the "uncommon Pains . . . [brought upon] the Grey Hairs of two Mothers with Sorrow to the Grave . . . and Ruin [to] two whole Families."[11] Leigh's sister in England had added to the list of his misdeeds the defrauding of his own mother's legacy. "Good God, which is the blackest of his numerous Crimes?" Henry raged in another letter, "or is all the Turpitude of which Human Nature is capable, centered in that One Man."[12]

Earlier relating the outrageous story to his son John, who with his younger brother, Harry, was studying in Geneva, Henry Laurens sighed: "My Pen will drop from my hand if I attempt to tell you particulars . . . The scene is black . . . My Tears continue flowing & . . . I have scarcely taken food or rest for 5 days past." But his note changed tone abruptly as he summoned a comforting image: "Patsy writes a pretty Letter of 16 December and earnestly intreats her Dear Brother to correspond with her."[13] In the midst of horrendous news about Cousin Molsy, his sister was yearning for contact with the brother she adored. During the entire year of 1773, letters between members of the Laurens family alternated between despair over Molsy's dreadful situation, fury at her despoiler, mundane plantation business, and comforting evocations of fatherly affection.

In one letter to his brother, Martha's father brutally worded his worst fears about Molsy. What if she should "become a comon Prostitute, end her days full of disease, Crying Matches or Sprats [for sale in the streets]?" What if Molsy should "starve upon her earnings, and Die in a Ditch?" Worse, what if "with her latest Breath, [she should] Curse her Mother's Brothers whose disertion of her might be dated from this time, and appear to be more Cruel than the treachery of her Foster Father?"[14] Young Martha could not help but see that both uncles felt besieged as well as aggrieved.

On top of worries about Molsy's soul and body, Uncle James' letters from Carolina revealed mounting anxiety over his having to manage Henry's commercial affairs. Henry Laurens repeated to John his uncle's "distress of . . . mind," the result of "a Ruined Niece—a Leigh—an undutiful ungrateful Bremar [Molsy's brother, their errant nephew, proving untrustworthy in James' employ]—and a hundred other perplexities, just at a Season . . . when he sought for retirement, Peace and Quietness."[15] Martha and her Uncle James were each disconsolate in their own ways, waiting months for letters between London and Charles Town, in the midst of gossip and scandal, longing for a brother or father to be in charge. The uncles' letter exchanges fell into accusation—James that Henry wasn't giving him sufficient direction, Henry that James' many demands were stretching him too thin. In February, a dreadful attack of gout reduced Martha's poor Papa in England to bedridden agony, "confined 26 days, in perfect health but wholly [without] the use of my left leg."[16]

By April 1773,[17] Henry had decided to deposit Molsy in an Ursuline convent in France, en route to Geneva to visit his sons. There he hoped she would be safe from the temptations in London and employ the time to redirect her life. He described their parting at the convent doors as indeed portentous, Molsy as tearful as if leaving "a tender long Loved Parent." Henry himself wept. "A Conversation through the Medium of double Iron Grates was quite a new scene to Miss Bremar."[18] His rationale for this severe plan was long schooling in disappointment: "At present she wears the Aspect in her countenance, her words, & her Manners of a true Penitent."

However, he knew from the past that "dangerous & very sudden alterations [might be] wrought again in my absence," which led him to try to establish "the foundation of [her] future prosperity" with a period of incarceration in a foreign holy setting.[19]

What meanings and fears Martha read into this flurry of anxious letters can only be imagined. Being a Laurens herself, she undoubtedly longed to do *something,* whatever a girl who was not fully grown and powerless in the real world could in fact *do.* All she could think of was to try very hard herself to please her grownups—father, uncle, aunt, and God. Perhaps her strenuous efforts at goodness would make them all relieved and smiling once again. Such a vague goal may have seemed sufficient at that point, even if Martha's father had transmitted directly to her at least some of his concerns. According to the Henry Laurens letterbook of 1773, "a Long letter" to daughter Martha on March 17 was cited, "with extract Letters" to her brother John, but no surviving copy has been found. Again on April 8, a letter to her was listed, but no copy.[20] What would an overstressed, gout-suffering father have chosen to convey to the distant fourteen-year-old apple of his eye? The fact that her father chose to write directly to Martha while his outrage at Molsy and her debaucher were at their peak must speak for itself. A clue, however, may be found in another letter on a related subject from this period.

On that April 1773 trip to the convent and then on to Geneva, Henry Laurens chanced to stop at the same inn as his son John's former Charles Town tutor, the Rev. Henry B. Himeli. What had befallen this once-promising man in the person of an abominated female left Papa Laurens stuttering with horror. "The Love & friendship of Good Men . . . and the prospect of Glory and future good Days, All, All," had been sacrificed by Himeli's "falling on his knees to a little Freckled Faced ordinary Wench." Patriarchal outrage singled out the female as villain for not preserving her virtue and saving this man from ruin. Himeli's "Trumpery Woman," of "doubtful quality," had breached the social order by passing herself off as his wife. There was nothing glamorous about her, Henry sniffed, rather the opposite: she was only a punishment to poor Monsieur Himeli. She alone constituted the "bar to [his] Honest Fame and peace of mind, the Work and Hopes of Parents, the Labour & Laudable Ambition of all the years in Youth"—all of which were now "tumbled down by a Baggage of no Value."[21] His concern for morality and propriety included all the children, but Martha may have felt its fullest impact in light of Molsy.

While Henry Laurens consistently showered his children with mottoes, comments on sexual conduct per se were rare enough that their impact on his children had to be awesome. Today historians at least admit the existence of backstairs racial mixing in slaveowning society (the word *miscegenation* had not yet come into use),[22] although her father's strong Huguenot sense of duty would have militated against it, as against all self-indulgence. Sexual liaisons with slaves were a sign of general untrustworthiness in his view, in a class with sexual infidelity. Henry would employ sexual innuendo to denounce an American double agent in 1777: "I never will believe a Man very chaste who delights in private meetings with harlots & debauchers[,] should he produce a thousand witnesses of his constant repetition of the 7th Commandment at the regular striking hours of a Town Clock."[23] But after the death of his beloved wife, Eleanor, sex for Martha's upright father appears primarily as a figure of speech in his letters; for example, equating unbridled female "gust" with the same kind of anarchy potential he associated with free blacks—another vivid caution for Martha in 1774. Her psyche had to be deeply etched with his gender and race expectations.

There is no record of Martha's thoughts about Molsy's "punishment"—something that must have seemed more like a story in a gothic novella than anything actually involving her own cousin. Molsy, older and more headstrong than Martha, also had no mother to defend her, and she was locked away in a foreign convent where she did not speak the language and was supposed to repent her incest. How could it not sound like prison? Meanwhile Sir Egerton Leigh remained free and offensive, showing around South Carolina a letter, purportedly from Molsy, swearing that she'd been *forced* to accuse him—his way of implicating the ill-will of the Laurens brothers toward him.[24]

During this scandal, letters between Henry and James Laurens always concluded with pledges of greeting and affection to and from Henry's daughters. At the end of their pages filled with handwritten fury at Sir Egerton Leigh, the images of Patsy and baby Polly seemed a conscious attempt to mollify their frustration and angst. Sometime during the same period, Martha's private response to the trauma apparently tapped depths unsuspected by any of her concerned adults—James, Mary, or Papa. At her stage of life, any girl was subject to vacillations of mood and temper, even when no family trauma loomed. How could a person of her tender years and inexperience protect herself against the evils to which Molsy had succumbed? Martha must have searched the print world in her father's library for explanations, links, directions. By Thursday, 23 December 1773, she found what she had been seeking and was ready to act.

She found solace in chapter 17 of the manual appealingly titled *The Rise and Progress of Religion in the Soul* (1744), by dissenting British clergyman Philip Doddridge. The chapter's title, "A Self Dedication and Solemn Covenant with God," sounded suitably adult. It employed the elevated images and sweeping terminology that could entrance a sophisticated fourteen-year-old longing to make a powerful gesture. Martha had found and claimed a major artifact of domestic religion in the early modern era, a kind of devotional aid she personally could apply, a religious ritual to be performed in her own "closet."[25] On one level, Martha's writing such a covenant may have felt like forming her own secret society with God, an image that gratified an adolescent's need for drama. At another level, it was very adult: creating a concrete landmark of her personal enrollment in the ageless spiritual aspirations of the many pious women whose memoirs she had read. Fortunately, Doddridge's covenant was cast in a literary medium with which Martha already felt comfortable. It was written in first-person dialogue with the transcendent Being—conversational prayer.

The project of covenant-making between humans and God was eminently familiar to Martha from Bible stories she had heard during her childhood. After the Protestant Reformation in Europe, the idea of "covenant" took on new significance and functions, ultimately helping to create the political mind-set that idealized "the people's" participation in governing—the "consent of the governed."[26] Martha may well have read a covenant written earlier by British poet and mystic Elizabeth Singer Rowe called *Devout Exercises of the Heart* (1737); other devout Charles Town women knew and quoted that work,[27] and she herself would later use Rowe's poetic turns of phrase and images in her adult diary entries. Rowe, *the* influential English devotional writer in her era (1674–1737), distinguished herself from other eighteenth-century female writers by an interest in saints like Julian of Norwich or Teresa of Avila, another factor likely to appeal to a striving adolescent. Writing in a contemplative style, Rowe's tone differed from her activist contemporaries, British evangelical reformers like Lady Selina Huntingdon or Hannah More. Her intense, personal spiritual voice was exotic and sensuous in comparison with the formal, elevated rhetoric Martha was used to hearing on Sunday mornings at St. Philip's.

In Rowe's description, "covenant" signified reciprocity between God's promises and the commitment of one's soul in response. "A covenant with

God," section 4 of her *Devout Exercises,* was considerably shorter than the Doddridge model Martha chose but contained the same elements: apostrophe to an invisible God ("O Incomprehensible Being!"); self-abasement (divine powers beyond all human imagining); dedication ("I . . . bind myself to thee by a sacred and everlasting obligation"); many vows of service and submission; renunciation of the world's "glories"; pledge ("deny or give me what thou wilt"); and a concluding, almost legalistic statement of bond: "This is my deliberate, my free and sincere determination."[28]

All the intellectual currents in Martha's environment and mental training to that point had encouraged the practice of spiritual logic rather than spiritual ecstasies.[29] Her inherited predisposition was not particularly poetic, nor would her Huguenot temperament allow her to indulge in much mystical language, not until a shattering depression in her middle years. But in this first family crisis of her adolescence, she wanted to do something "serious." Martha instinctively chose the most exalted spiritual language she could find, willing herself into a spiritual sensibility quite different from what was usual among her contemporaries. She wanted to aim for the kind of life praised in sermons and theological books but rarely by lighthearted Carolina youth, one that idealized communion with God, hour by hour, day by day—a state of "continual prayer."[30]

Martha had begun to covet a "Serious" demeanor over the ethereal feminine languor for which Charles Town beauties were famous. "Serious" meant being attentive to a deep, interior response to messages found in the mysteries of creation—the hand of God in the minuscule detail of a feather or in a drop of water, the mental exploration of weighty philosophical quandaries. The diaries of Elizabeth Fry, an English Quaker one generation younger than Martha, describe a gradual discovery of religious seriousness as an inner state others might not even notice; it was the sense of "resting under the shadow of the wing of God," of glimpsing "which mountain [it is] that *I* have to climb."[31] Seriousness traced a deeply individualist path for a young girl. In Fry's case, attentiveness to serious spiritual matters made her lose interest in conventional pleasures like dancing and fancy clothes in favor of plain Quaker dress. For Martha, external evidence of being serious was less important, since hers must remain secret. But she determined to cultivate an openness to divine messages she might previously have missed.

Elizabeth Fry feared confusing "being religious" with "being the quaker"—that she might fall into an extreme of observance and rule-keeping obsession instead of reflecting the true Spirit. In fact, Fry's serious gaze made her critical of the emotional display she saw in those Church of England reformers who called themselves Methodists: "Many say *that* leads to religion," she recorded in her journal at the same age as Martha when she created her covenant. "[Such display] may lead to the emotions of religion, but true religion appears to me to be in a deeper recess of the heart where no earthly passion should produce it." The phrases of this young English Quaker help portray the serious turn that characterized Martha Laurens' response to her family's troubles; they also illuminate some of the kind of perceptions that opened her soul to the appeal of Doddridge's model covenant, which Martha seized as her own holy grail.[32]

After reading the first sixteen chapters of Doddridge's book, which built up the case for a *written* contract with God, chapter 17 delivered into Martha's hand not one but two models of covenant, a veritable "sacrament."[33] Through her preparation for confirmation at St. Philip's, Martha knew that *sacrament* was more than a mere sign or symbol of something sacred: it was both instrument and symbol, an action actually conveying what it signified. Writing out the covenant was a sacrament Martha herself could perform—without any other earthly mediator. It took her far beyond the mechanical observance of form such as attending a Sunday service. It answered her need for emotional intensity with religious intensity and affirmed that she was her own person, standing alone before God.

The elaborate, precise dating and signing of her copy of the covenant, exactly as Doddridge recommended—"December 23, 1773, Being This Day Fourteen Years and Seven Weeks Old"—demonstrate her solemnity. Even if Martha was not entirely sure what she hoped from this secret sacrament, the desire to see herself in a special, historically elite religious fellowship, part of something much bigger than herself, was implicit. Yet there was also a parallel and contradictory desire in it: to see herself as utterly unique in God's eyes, her own independent Self.

Martha's choice of gesture and text are clues about the person she would aspire to become, as the document's careful preservation through all her future travels testified. Perhaps she had spent many long hours during those eleventh, twelfth, and thirteenth years after her mother's death thinking deeply about the imponderables: family, Molsy's scandal, the adult world she both dreaded and longed to enter. After her mother's death, the refuge of her father's library probably allowed her a place in which she could quietly bemoan another act of abandonment: how often did letters from her distant, preoccupied father ask her to "accept her Papa's love through [Uncle James] for the present," due to the press of his business?[34]

Private library hours undoubtedly became a precious routine. More than just a place where a young girl could explore books and thought on her own, it could be her private "corner," her own place of refuge. With no living mother to confide in, Martha yearned for wisdom about many mysteries in the life she was entering, her own physical changes, and her cousin's. How could Molsy let that dreadful old man fondle her? Martha, approaching fifteen, was only a few years younger; some of her girlfriends were already marrying. What could she think about a man who was supposed to be Molsy's protector and had done the deed that produced a child?

Martha's secret library browsings would have uncovered many catechetical books, not just about religion but also questions and answers about nature and other "scientific" topics. Catechism was the eighteenth-century means for efficient transmitting of information, and little children often memorized its form before they acquired the skill of reading. In a childhood like Martha's, reading and the book as its precious container were indistinguishably linked with spirituality; reading "religion" was the same as learning to read.[35] Martha had also discovered that she could apply whatever type of discourse she was reading to her own need and situation. In a patriarchal world, the possibility of discerning one's own meanings, even in serious religious books, gave her reading a dynamic purpose.[36] The many texts available to a privileged Laurens daughter were the indispensable building blocks of her religious precocity.[37] Books were teachers, companions, and friends to her, not ornaments on library shelves.

And private devotional reading—metaphorically retiring to one's closet for meditating and praying—meant time secluded from play or tasks, focused expressly on heavenly interests. Uncle James and Aunt Mary would have encouraged Martha's retreat to the library as her "closet time," preparing her soul for heaven. One of the earliest children's books, considered a necessity for religiously well-educated Americans and imported by booksellers like Uncle James, was Janeway's *Token for Children* (1680), originally published in England and reprinted many times in the colonies. Many similar funereal warnings for young people were intended to lead a child's thoughts away from earthly preoccupation, toward "serious impressions." One of her father's colleagues in the Charles Town reading club, the Presbyterian minister John Joachim Zubly, had published such a collection called *Real Christians Hope in Death* (1756); it was endorsed by his interdenominational friends, including Henry Laurens. Closet observance was seen as a supplement to Sunday worship and encouraged the production of a special devotional literature—part advice or admonition, part scriptural illustration, part written prayers.[38] (That was the purpose for which Martha's own posthumously published memoirs would be reprinted again and again in the nineteenth century.) Doddridge's volume, filled with didactic, sequential instruction in spiritual living and embellished with graceful belletristic expressions, was to Martha the very highest example of closet literature she knew at that important time in her life.[39]

Already well exposed to the spiritual grandeur of Anglican funerals for sister Nelly and her mother, Martha was not afraid of large subjects like death, sin, and punishment. Perhaps the act of putting such topics into a covenant was awe-inspiring, letting her see herself as a responsible child of God even at her age. Those adults she wanted most to please were accustomed to citing Scripture and invoking religion at crucial times; Martha wanted a way of taking her place beside them, joining the long, historical procession of spiritual giants she read and dreamed about.

At Martha's stage of physical development, the hormonal changes of puberty undoubtedly immersed her in fantasies—about sin, about romance, about heroism in God's name. Thanks to Molsy, those images had opened new territory. By the age of twelve Martha had begun "to be the subject of serious religious impressions," according to what she had told her husband (reported in the *Memoirs* introduction years later). Confirmation, the religious coming-of-age ritual for Church of England children, required her to master the catechism from the *Book of Common Prayer*,[40] the rite of passage essential for admission to "the fellowship of the Lord's Table"—receiving the bread and wine of Holy Communion. Its theological counterpart was being "well instructed in the great gospel mystery of salvation," as her biographer-husband wrote. By the time Martha entered the "years of discretion," Anglican euphemism for adolescence, she and her siblings would have long since memorized the Offices of Instruction, a child-sized version of the adult catechism designed to aid a child's grasp of weighty sacred concepts.

The Offices of Instruction were themselves a simplified translation of the vows promised in her name when she was christened 9 February 1760.[41] Customarily such events were attended not just by her godparents but also the physician who attended her birth, neighbors, aunts and uncles, even slave caretakers. Her adult sponsors—parents and godparents—would have ritually promised that she, infant Martha, "would renounce the devil and all his works, the pomps and vanity of this wicked world, and all the sinful lusts of the flesh" at age twelve or thirteen, when she was confirmed.

The second and third vows were preparation for that confirmation: she must "believe all the Articles of the Christian Faith" and "keep God's holy will and commandments, walking in the same all the days of her life." The Apostles' Creed, the Lord's Prayer, and the Ten Commandments constituted the articles of faith that were sentence-by-sentence training for Martha and her siblings—memorized at home and recited at special Sunday examinations. Under the firm Anglican regime of her father and mother, her memorization would have been checked by the Rt. Rev. Robert Smith (also bishop of the new diocese of South Carolina), St. Philip's chief pastor from the year of her birth until well into her adulthood (1801). This training was specified in the Prayer Book rubric: "Only when a child could say 'the Articles of their faith, the Lord's Prayer and the Ten Commandments' was [she] to be presented to the Bishop for Confirmation."[42]

In the course of that training, the child's version of the seventh commandment contained language intended to help young girls understand Molsy's fall from grace. The words forbidding adultery advised, somewhat abstrusely, "keep[ing] my body in temperance, soberness, and chastity." In contrast, the child's version of "thou shalt not steal" was plain enough for even little brother Jemmy: "to keep my hands from picking and stealing, and to be true and just in all my dealings." The commandment about adultery was less clear: did keeping one's body in temperance and soberness mean not gorging on sweets? not laughing too loudly in adult company? Adults' use of "chastity" of course included physicality: "purity from unlawful sexual intercourse."[43] Still, was it Molsy's being unwed to the man who fathered her unfortunate infant that made it a sin?[44] Any girl of elite Carolina society would have grasped the serious connotations of female chastity contained in veiled (or crude) allusion to legal property ownership. The famous British lexicographer Dr. Samuel Johnson summarized the prevailing mind-set in a typical aphorism: "Upon [female chastity], all the property in the world depends. We hang a thief for stealing a sheep; but the unchastity of a woman transfers sheep, and farm, and all, from the rightful owner."[45] That understanding had surely fired up her father's epistolary venom over the trumpery woman who ruined Pastor Himeli.

When Martha finally pulled Doddridge's *Rise and Progress* from the shelf, she may have felt something like a "pinch of destiny."[46] Everything about it seemed an answer to her quest, including the preface assuring her that this "guide to self-improvement" was written at the inspiration of his friend Isaac Watts—Martha's own beloved poet from childhood. And Doddridge himself even provided an option "for the sake of those who may think the preceding [long form of covenant] too long to be transcribed, as it is probable many will": a second, abbreviated form only four paragraphs long. However, Martha's choice signaled her seriousness: she wanted the most complete coverage possible, the full six-page pattern that could encompass her entire life.[47]

Martha envisioned much wider consequences from her covenant than its mere writing. Having it exist physically, on paper and in her own private keeping, would remind her forever that God was present to her in a very specific way on a specific day in 1773—a visitation that may have been more significant to her inner need at that moment than even her first experience of the sacrament of Holy Communion. Clearly she knew a transcendent moment when she saw it. Doddridge's instructions—the warning not to say (or write) anything rash in God's presence—confirmed her instincts. Everything about the covenant—the choice of it, the text she copied, the ritual of its inscription—took on the highest, most solemn importance. Martha's way of guaranteeing its authenticity was to follow the author's exact wording, except for the filial change of "son" to "daughter." She would indeed make her "whole heart consent to it," as Doddridge commended, not by altering the covenant (except in that particular) but her self. Such literalism that today might suggest self-censorship was for her a declaration that she would live by all his prescriptions, not just some of them.

Like Elizabeth Singer Rowe's covenant, Doddridge's pattern began with elaborate apostrophe—addressing almighty God in the most exalted phrases the human mind could articulate. He employed the large descriptors—"eternal, unchangeable, above all heavenly and earthly beings"—usually reserved for public worship rather than the intimate address Martha knew from Isaac Watts' prayers for children. Obligatory self-abasement, "I, a sinful worm," had to be followed with awe at the idea of a mere human being actually contracting with the King of Kings and audaciously asking for a *guarantee* of "righteousness and grace." To a self-dramatizing youth, images that sound extravagant today, like "sins so vast they reach up to heaven," and the generous use of exclamation points, probably only added to its drama and appeal. The next images—"a wandering sheep, a prodigal *daughter*, a backsliding child"—named trials well beyond Martha's sheltered experience to this point, but they would cover any future adventures.[48]

"Hear Oh heavens! and give ear O earth! . . . record it in the book of thy remembrance, that henceforth I am thine, entirely thine." The emotional heft of the archaic form of the word *vow* was gratifying: "I *avouch* and declare myself this day to be one of his covenant people." Doddridge's vocabulary epitomized the spiritual ideal of the age: *fervent rational piety*. "Fervency" expressed a religious state capturing "the whole frame of my nature, all the faculties of my mind, all the members of my body"—a rational and reasonable comprehensiveness that comforted Martha with its combination of Enlightenment vocabulary and deep piety. What could be more satisfying to an eager young female than total absorption (including one's physical being) in the highest ideals known to the world in that time? Even possessions were included in that dedicated "all": she must surrender not only *self* but *"all* that I can call mine." Whatever treasures and mementos she could mentally enumerate helped enlarge the sense of obeisance. To Martha, the covenant's language of unworthiness represented willing self-effacement in a grand cause, not castigation or martyrdom.

The paragraph pledging "all, all to God" projected Martha far into the future, a "resolve that all others, so far as I can rationally and properly influence them, shall [also] serve the Lord." Becoming an influential role model was the ideal image in which to pour youthful dreams of glory. Urgent petitions toward that goal filled the next paragraph. From this day forward she hoped to be numbered among "God's peculiar people," no longer a "stranger and foreigner but a *fellow-citizen with the saints* and *with the household of God.*" Martha's contract made her forever an insider—"one of God's covenant people."

The Doddridge pattern ended by restating God's part in the agreement. The natural rights language pervading her mental world had schooled Martha to view a "covenant" as a legal bond between two parties, each with its own responsibility and also interdependent.[49] The wonderful blessing encapsulated in the Doddridge model was that this written covenant—the completed and signed document—was her guarantee that whatever might go wrong in her lifetime would be righted and redeemed at its ending. In case of a death without sufficient warning, like her sister Nelly's, that was crucial. God himself was obligated under contract, by this very document, to cast "a pitying eye" on his "languishing, dying child," Martha, whatever her age and spiritual stage. The covenant committed God to reserve her a place in "the embraces of thy everlasting love."

Images of transfigured dying were a rich, hallowed scene to be visited often in her secret imagination. The covenant's earthly partner herself was given a touching final request: "If this solemn memorial should chance to fall into the hands of any surviving friends, may it be the means of making serious impressions on their minds." That sentence captured Martha's human longing to be important in a great cause, to be a star leading others to heavenly heights. Mere physical death would not quell Martha Laurens' desire for importance, for special attention in the spiritual realm. Doddridge's words provided one way she could count on some earthly immortality.

This document, the most portentous action she had ever undertaken, carried spiritual gravity far beyond its literal words. Martha's own final summary, after Doddridge's ending, incorporated a self-benediction: "Henceforth I am not mine but God's forever." Then, as if she couldn't stop, she appended one more verse, a redundancy perhaps from a favorite Watts hymn. The former child Martha seemed to join the aspiring young girl Martha on her chosen path: "Lord I am thine, forever thine,/ My soul doth cleave to thee;/My dearest Lord, be ever mine,/ I'll have no love but thee." Deep satisfaction from this dedicatory sacrament would remain her life-long secret, along with the covenant itself, but readers of her posthumous *Memoirs* see its shadow in her writings and prayers at crisis points throughout her life.

The family's Molsy troubles lasted through 1774. That long, degrading affair, Henry wrote Uncle James, "is so far concluded as to give me hopes it will be . . . no further talked of." The two antagonists, Leigh and Laurens, had met in London, where, after "some struggles, [Leigh] fully confessed his Guilt, earnestly begged pardon of both you [James] and me, repeatedly declared his Contrition," and with a "flood of Tears, shewed every mark of the deepest Sorrow." Their ultimate focus was Molsy, the third point of the triangle: Leigh agreed to "600 guineas pecuniary restoration" in return for her surrender of all accusatory documents. Leigh had followed that meeting with a letter confirming all these arrangements, in a tone "such . . . as would make Some Men proud," Henry recorded modestly (17 September 1774).[50]

Molsy, by her own overreaching machinations, was the one who ruptured the continuing sense of obligation the uncles still held for her. Returned to London from the French convent, she almost immediately enlisted her London landlady in a scheme to extort "a thousand Guineas" from Uncle Henry. Confronted with this new evidence that Molsy was unregenerate, Henry Laurens washed his hands of her. He wrote the landlady, Mrs. Parsons, with terrible finality: "I call God & the Spirit of my Dear Sister her Mother to witness; I have acted the part of an Uncle, of a parent, toward her. She shall not wallow in frolic & Idleness at expence of my own Children." Though his own severest financial constraints were still in the future, the niece had pushed him too far this one last time. "If she will behave herself as becometh her Station and circumstance I will continue her Uncle, her friend, her father, if not, she must apply to those . . . whom she most studies to please. I will not be amused nor fooled by any of them. Adieu the Subject."[51] And it was indeed adieu for the "discontented and flighty" Molsy, who died in December 1777. According to speculation among the family, her premature end may have been hastened by an addiction to laudanum.[52]

Martha's covenant, the most direct response to her cousin's ruin that she could produce and an extraordinary spiritual gesture for a girl at any period in history, would remain a secret but profound element in her life until her death in 1811. Already twice touched by death—the enemy that had stolen the two closest females of her life, mother and sister—Martha viewed her covenant as a bulwark against the existential fragility in the truncated life and premature death of poor Molsy. Thanks to Doddridge's model speaking in clarion tones to those inner fears, she was armed with a means to fend off such self-destruction. The Anglican sense of destiny implanted in Martha's childhood allowed her to welcome the vision of a self that could be God's *co*-worker, no matter how life might unfold before her—an outsize ambition she never admitted to another human being.

Given the high stakes Martha set for herself, in the next years she had to record several shortfalls of that covenant standard. Three such confessions were noted on the document itself. The first came two years later, when "these solemn covenant engagements" were so totally abrogated that they required rededication on Christmas 1775. The second came a year later, 7 April 1776, after she attended Holy Communion at St. Werbrough's (in England), perhaps in response to the spiritual drama of that English church liturgy. The last, reprinted in her *Memoirs*—who knows how many others were not recorded—came on 26 May 1776, "more solemnly and with more affecting circumstances than ever." No helpful background explanations accompanied these dates.

The impact of family scandal launched Martha Laurens into young adulthood and led her to stake out the future territory that she must master in her secret document. As an adult, after she had lived abroad for the decade spanning the Revolutionary War, her covenant mentality would attract her to other "serious" citizens who were concerned with the administration of poor relief in her hometown—as her father had been when he was younger and a warden of St. Philip's. And she would increasingly expect active "good works" from herself. The covenant also gave her her lifelong permission to study the leading religious thinkers of her time and create her own program of continuing self-education.

Sometime in her late teen years she memorized long sections of *Night Thoughts,* the elegiac, fatalistic tone-poem by the renowned British scholar Dr. Edward Young; her husband recorded that she knew "nearly the whole of [it] by heart." *Night Thoughts,* celebrating nature, reason, and piety, was acclaimed as the emblematic treatise of an age that idealized the combining of rationality and spirituality; it was praised, discussed, and quoted in the company Martha aspired to join. One of its stanzas might even have become a motto for her, so closely did it trace the emotional landscape of her covenant-making.[53] After the Molsy debacle and in the face of approaching war, Martha's soul must have resonated to Young's exclamation:

> *Religion! Providence! an After-state!*
> *Here is firm footing; here is solid rock,*
> *This can support us; all is sea besides;*
> *Sinks under us; bestorms & then devours."*[54]

Edward Young's grand assertion would have been awe-inspiring as well as a comfort to young Martha Laurens in its vehement certainty. It offered the type of confidence for which she would strive—always expecting more of herself religiously than was humanly attainable—for the rest of her life.

4 | "Grown Quite a Woman," a "True American Woman"

Early in 1775, Henry Laurens wrote to son Henry Jr. (Harry), at his school in England, that the oldest sister, Martha, whom he would soon see again, was now considerably changed: "Sister Patsy is grown quite a woman."[1] Martha, aged sixteen, would shortly arrive on English shores with Uncle James and Aunt Mary Laurens, little Polly, and an unspecified number of servants. Her father, returned to Charles Town after establishing her brothers at school in England, had been immediately elected to the city and state government, and the South Carolina Committee of Safety that was already preparing for confrontation with Britain. Martha may have been ambivalent at being uprooted but had to be excited at the prospect of traveling and tasting foreign scenes such as her brothers and Papa Henry described in their letters.

The idea of England certainly represented the broadening and exposure to new horizons that travel alone could provide at that time. Martha could not have anticipated the dark times she would also see: how prophetic her father's financial alarms would soon become and how much family responsibility she would find herself assuming in those displaced circumstances. From the perspective of an elite white merchant's daughter in the small world of Charles Town, she could not imagine that an order given by her Papa for the Council of Safety—to have the local military seize a camp of unarmed runaway slaves on Sullivan's Island—was in fact the first step toward revolution in her home state.[2] Nor within the family circle could she have guessed the critical greeting John would arrange for her. ("Martha Laurens was received in England by her elder brother John Laurens from whom she had been for some years separated," was her husband's bland sentence about it in the biographical pages of her posthumous *Memoirs*.) A number of things Martha wrote during those early months abroad reveal the two overarching themes of her continental adventure: first, she was determined to make religion her arena of self-development and striving; and second, family could turn out to be at least as puzzling, hurtful, and constraining as it was supportive.

Those coded reports of her adolescent experience in strange settings were of course embedded in and shaped by the larger cultural system of assumptions and expectations for all girl-children born to any Anglo-European family anywhere in that era—patriarchy. Adrienne Rich defines patriarchy as an invisible force that impinges on the mental and physical world of all women, as "the power of the fathers: a familial-social, ideological, political system in which men, through force, direct pressure, or through ritual, tradition, law, language, customs, etiquette, education, and the division of labor, determine what part women shall or shall not play, and in which the female is everywhere subsumed under the male." This did not mean that women had no power at all, but that even where men and women had certain largely equal powers, very different things were assumed according to gender.[3] The arrangements governing Martha's life until 1782, the year concluding this chapter, were made by her father with little or no consulting of her inclinations—in fact, in the assumption that she would *want* to comply with his choices. Patriarchy was clearly the basic factor in the defining differences between eldest Laurens daughter, Martha, and eldest Laurens son, John.

Fortunately, the extensive intrafamily correspondence provides instructive contrast between the internal scripts ingrained in a daughter and a son within that same family. John was inculcated with high expectations of duty, responsibility for his relatives abroad, and living up to his potential for public leadership (in many ways a huge burden for a youth not yet twenty). But as the eldest son of the eldest Laurens brother, he was also the family's prince regent, and he did what males of his social position and privilege did in those years: he read all the newspapers, debated in coffeehouses the tensions between England and the colonies, visited with his friends while pursuing his studies less than vigorously, and picked up liberating ideas about the institution of slavery. In sum, John had a role on the public stage of thought and action, as was expected of him.[4] Martha at sixteen was embarking on an equally strenuous time of self-exploration and identity formation; but hers was expected to take place within the requirements of Uncle James' domestic circle and, even more restrictedly, within her own heart and mind. In this important period of coming to maturity, young Martha Laurens already planned to pursue the pattern of religious self-determination on which she had embarked. She would also craft what would become a new "American" sensibility, while she developed, elasticized, and resisted the claims of patriarch and family.

Nothing about adolescence is ever uncomplicated, but the years in England and then France that ushered Martha through the rest of her adolescence and into early adulthood were filled with extraordinary challenges in the world around her. Who would have imagined living with her uncle and aunt instead of at home? When her father had returned to Charles Town and local business, Martha believed she was old enough to serve as his hostess in their handsome house.[5] She was already "an excellent translator of French," and he thought her "very notable and clever" when she helped Papa entertain a friend at dinner. But she saw herself more ready for a public role in her father's life than he was ready to accept.[6] And suddenly Uncle James' health turned desperate; by May 1775 all his household, including Henry's daughters, were en route to England—a sea voyage being the only thing anyone knew that might extend his life.

In June, on shipboard, any future Martha tried to imagine was built around nursing dear Uncle James, tutoring her darling little sister Polly, and being handmaid-companion to Aunt Mary—all in a strange setting. She was very far from home, cut off from girlfriends and social routines, and learning that the physical burdens of sea travel entailed a new kind of indignity. The one corner of her previous identity she had smuggled with her was her solemn *Covenant with God* (1773).[7] That written contract was to be her toehold on the life of mental and spiritual self-organization she intended to conduct no matter where she was—a religiously sanctioned path she hoped would see her through all the unknown changes of geographic and emotional displacement. To her way of thinking, the act of writing and signing her covenant had been the sign that she was putting away childish things—the scriptural phrase for becoming a grownup. By treating her contradictory moods and impulses religiously, under the imprimatur of spiritual discipline, she was (she hoped) consciously engaged in creating the kind of personality strong and dramatic enough to meet her times.[8] Martha needed to consign her choices and fears, anxieties and dreams to a divine system of control—a plan that assured her she was exercising personal management over them. Following her internal map of spiritual guideposts and rational mental steps, Martha would attempt to tailor her written musings while abroad into patterns she already admired. The memoirs she had read and would find in England—of learned, devout French and English men and women writing in a style of thought and self-examination they called Christian philosophy—were to be her mentors and companions in print.

However, from the moment of disembarking in England on 12 July 1775, Martha found herself once again in the physical orbit of her adored brother John—a dutiful moon circling his magnetic planet. At first, geographic reunion seemed the answer to a sister's prayer. But almost immediately, proximity to the Laurens paragon taught her it might also be one of the trials she would have to bear. As older brothers will, John appointed himself judge and monitor of his sister's prowess, a duty their father Henry had specifically commended to him, though probably not in the lordly manner John chose to deploy it. In his newly acquired sophistication, John had devised a rather mean test to find out whether or not his sister was still "the same Spartan girl he had left" several years before. He wanted to prove to his own satisfaction that she remained more daring than most other girls—"superior to the common accidents of life and the groundless fears of her sex." Accordingly, he had bribed the postillion driver to force the team of horses at terrifying speed over the hilly, rocky-cliff roads that were totally unlike the "low, flat, stoneless country of Carolina." During that hair-raising ride, John openly studied his sister Martha's face for evidence of "womanish fears."[9] Fortunately, Martha had already grasped the value of an external social mask and could meet his exacting standards—likely admitting to herself, through clenched teeth, that this brother she had longed to see once again could be nemesis as well as idol.

A short month later, the Laurens family on both sides of the Atlantic was once again stunned by death. Ten-year-old Jemmy, the youngest brother, died from an accident (a slip leading to a ten-foot fall and skull concussion) while playing at the English home where he boarded between school terms.[10] When Henry finally received the sad news across the ocean, his heartbreaking letter expressed for all of them their distraught encounter with more grief, more loss. "In the depth of my lamentations for a Son gone before, I recollect that I [still] have 2 Sons and 2 Daughters who by God's grace may remain long after me . . . o my Child, my dear, my favorite Child! but I submit—he is [now] happier than his distressed father." Some of his bereaved thoughts were too black to be committed to paper, he acknowledged, but then added: "I will not give up myself a prey to melancholy, I will as soon as nature permits me, turn my Eyes from [Jemmy's] bloody Corse . . . and withdraw the arms of affection from grasping a shadow." Thanking God for English friends who comforted his loved ones there, as he physically could not, Henry wrote: "If I cannot repay them personally my gratitude to them shall be paid in Acts of kindness to mankind at large."[11]

Martha had many reasons to be shaken, emotionally dazed. At this vulnerable period in her life she lived in a strange place; her little brother was cruelly snatched by death; and the oldest brother, from whom she always craved approval, viewed her in a critical, distant way—adding to her sense of forlornness in the cosmopolitan London scene. She felt isolated on the edges of a new social and churchly milieu in which she had to find her place. And family duty dictated that ill uncle James must receive her first attention and loyalties, including the disposal of her time.

Uncle James himself was worrisome. Henry Laurens' younger brother, for whom Martha was nurse, secretary, and intellectual companion into the foreseeable future, had in his own right accumulated "a handsome fortune"; but untoward happenings were reducing him to "worse than mere poverty"—they were reducing him to debt, Henry's worst abhorrence. Because of all that he and his business partnership owed, James was "in arrears no inconsiderable sum." Perhaps the sudden decline in his health that led to the sea voyage was related: the onset of James' depression was so severe he had become "unwilling to rise from bed" and thought mostly about dying. Henry had put his whole fortune on the line as guarantee against James' creditors (Hawkins Petrie & Co.): "I could not do less to serve such a brother," Henry wrote in explanation to John and Martha, "but now [we must live with financial] discretion!"[12]

Meanwhile, the younger generation had its own interpretation of Uncle James' ill health. John thought that "if he would renounce Tobacco and could be tempted to use proper Exercise of Body, together with an abstemious Diet, he would do better." Youthfulness made John unsympathetic: Uncle "flatters himself that walking backwards and forward in his Parlour is sufficient Exercise," whereas John decried the fetid household air and "monotony." They induced a "lassitude of mind" that Uncle called "fatigue of Body," when what he really needed was "the free Air" to "invigorate and enliven" his nature.[13] Poor Uncle James was his own worst enemy, nephew John summarized loftily. Martha's view, shaped by the same robust standards, may have made her similarly impatient with her uncle, but a courteous niece would not express such a critical opinion, even in a letter. Fortunately she was already practicing written dialogue with God and learning in her constriction its steadying powers.

Paradoxically, a literal reading of Martha Laurens' words reveals little of her inner turmoil. Docility and conformity were the virtues she had been taught to wear, the demeanor for which she was expected to strive. Rebellion was not a conscious possibility, making any vocabulary for it irrelevant to Martha. Females had no language other than Scripture for the independence of self and action central to modern readers. Especially, she could not imagine her life apart from her father's and uncle's plans and needs, any more than she could consciously dispute her secondary status in relationship to John. From her childhood as a bright tomboy whose doting parents encouraged her to explore every interest, Martha thus far had had no reason to try envisioning life outside the parameters of family authority and direction. At the same time, by age twelve or so she had deeply absorbed the gendered expectation that her big brother would be the child to live out her father's dreams of civic leadership. As oldest daughter, her life was directed exactly opposite. She was expected to unfold in, and remain in, the private sphere—the patriarchal location for females' role and vocation. Martha was destined to do her excelling in "relative duties," the symbolic phrase that defined the religiously circumscribed domestic function of well-reared females with her social and educational lineage.[14]

Undergirding these foreordained oldest-son and oldest-daughter paths was the language of Protestant Calvinist theology and the cultural mores visible in their father's oft-invoked pieties. Perhaps naturally but not inevitably, Martha, in her ambition to make something of herself, seized religion as her territory. She would not be content with the passive repetition of childhood religious habits; she had already secretly taken a step that lifted her consciousness to a different level of discourse and analysis. Like the males in her family, Martha took pride in her own ability to think and reason, albeit within family parameters. Her brother John made the same psychological transformation, in a sense, when he expanded the boundaries of "liberty" that were generally accepted by his father's generation. In the near future, John's defining gesture would be the startling proposal (for a southern son of a slaveowner) to free and arm some of his own slaves for the conflict with Britain—the national struggle being something he already imagined as his public destiny ("and the military fame that may be incidental to it," he fondly hoped).[15] Females like Martha could, without censure and, in her case, with paternal approval, pursue mental as well as spiritual growth under the canopy of religion. Yet her close identification with family heroes, brother and father, could not fail to have made her willing to shoulder—of course vicariously—their public political goals as well. Though she could not use their words, she inherited the same drive toward achievement as John had: she wanted to offer her talents—to be useful—in a grand, noble cause that was also self-enlarging. For Miss Laurens, the internal process of religious self-monitoring would turn out to be the means of cultivating the new, more independent "American" personality, all (of course) within family bonds.

Martha's first response to England was to withdraw a bit from her father. Perhaps bewildered by the strangeness and unused to the new routines of life in England, Martha gave Henry the impression she had retreated into total self-absorption. From 20 August 1775, when Uncle James' entourage landed, until mid-December 1777—fifteen long months— she did not respond to her father's plea for a letter. Henry Laurens had eagerly anticipated hearing her "first ideas of England, and the journey, [with]in a month." Beginning with his specific commission 16 August 1776 (the outbreak of war impelling his "war letter" to her, discussed below), he appended pleading queries to those letters addressed to son John and brother James: 3 February 1777: "not a syllable yet from my dear eldest daughter;" 28 March 1777: "why will not my dear Patty write to me?"[16] From the meditations posthumously received by her husband (for publication in her *Memoirs*), it is clear that Martha was indeed writing: but to herself, a girlfriend, and God.

By the end of 1777 Martha had survived over a year in a place far from her homeland. She had recovered from a dreadful siege of measles, far more physically debilitating to her than her little sister. And the James Laurens' household was planning another move, this time to the Protestant section of southern France. The advantage of Vigan, a village "13 leagues from Nismes in the Cevenne Mountains," was a "perfectly temperate climate, & free from Musquitto & buggs (which . . . with the excessive heat & uncommon drought have rendered both Nismes & Montpellier intolerable & very sickly)." There they could live more cheaply and in more friendly surroundings, among "polite, Civil inhabitants from whom we receive much courtesy . . . a great happiness that we fell in with this retreat."[17] In France, Martha would not have to hear her father, by now elected president of the Continental Congress, "calumniated" as a "fomenter of the disputes between Britain and her colonies" and denigrated as an "ambitious man wishing to rise to consequence at every hazard"—the slander repeated by his English enemies. Only when Uncle James' household was finally settled in its new location would Martha, for the first time since they had parted, append a loving note to her father— a postscript on a letter Uncle James had dictated to her. Finally she felt prepared, perhaps, to resume written connection with the person sure to pepper her with advice and opinions—his language of affection and control. Her brief message conveyed daughterly affection and a promise to write soon. Its most pointed request, however, was for news of John (by now back in America and in the army) rather than her father: she solicited "Intelligence" about *her brother's* "Health and Safety from Papa, if not direct from [John]."[18]

Establishing a footing on English soil during that first exile year must have required all Martha's energy; an absent father's vast public burdens could easily slip to second or third place in her daily concerns. Any miseries her father might witness, any responsibilities he had as president of the Provincial Congress and then of the Continental Congress in Philadelphia (after June 1777) seemed remote and disengaging, not able to elicit the contact her father wanted. John, studying law at the Temple in London, had, in his own way, also been somewhat self-absorbed—impatient to return home, join the patriot army, seek the glory of war. The letters from Carolina described her hometown under siege: "our very doors and window-shutters . . . taken from the house . . . sashes beaten out; furniture demolished, goods carried off; beds ripped up."[19] Militia may have been chopping wood on the polished floors of mansions, the British may have been seducing slaves with false promises of freedom—these topics consumed the adults at her uncle's dinner table, but Martha had apparently remained lost in her own thoughts.

Unbeknownst to anyone else during those English months of feeling like a displaced person, she was steadily "trying on" this or that aspect of adult behavior, as young people do, to protect herself from dire news about Charles Town, to distract herself from the physical limitations of nursing and tutoring. During this period Martha wrote some twenty undated "religious exercises" (which were later preserved through a friend's care) that her husband would label Devout Meditations when he included them in her *Memoirs.*[20] Their focus and method was self-examination, so he captioned them, in the language of the times, "Pleasures of Communion with God." In one, Martha chastised herself: "I hate all company, all amusements, all business that diverts my mind from spiritual things." Another time she ticked off the pointless rituals of an English tea: "they examine laces, dresses, ornaments and finery," and speak only of "this agreeable party, that set, the other amusement." A verse from her newfound poet Edward Young *(Night Thoughts)* contained a gratifyingly baleful view of such lightheartedness. One stanza pronounced:

A land of levity is a land of guilt.
A serious mind is the native soil of

Virtue and the single characteristic
That does true honor to mankind.[21]

Another meditation voiced her longing to escape the "circle of worldly delights" that intimidate any self-conscious youth. She recorded a dramatic disdain for her reaction: "Earth is a tiresome place, I am quite sick of it." Tensions in an invalid's household undoubtedly played some part in this soul work: "I am the most ungrateful creature in the whole house," she described herself. In retrospect her bad temper was so embarrassing that she ought to hurl herself "at the foot of the cross, under droppings of the blood of Jesus."[22] Her uncle described Martha in that same period: "my Dear Niece who has it now in her power by many tender offices to repay her Aunt for her past Care & Attention to her, as well as assist in watching over & Instructing her Little Sister, will be of our party (moving to South of France) and is altogether agreable to herself & I have no doubt will be so to you."[23]

The subtext of Martha's written pleadings for divine help was a longing to surrender those personal needs and desires that kept her from being peaceful and content. One paragraph recorded what she called her willfulness and her efforts to contain it. Then, reflecting fulsomely on God's mercy, she declared: "Lord, I love trials, I love crosses, for they send me near to thee." Her language, burning with the intensity and overreaching of youth, drew many images from her literary grounding in Scripture: "God is ingenious at making crosses for us . . . of what we love best . . . [but] crosses laid on us bring their own grace and comfort, the Hand of God, with them."[24] Martha had rightly assimilated the message that one way to achieve spiritual significance—and to *prove* herself in terms that were clear to her Protestant mind-set—was to employ the vehement spiritual vocabulary of "crosses." Why not plumb the dramatic power to be found in that ultimate symbol of martyrdom?

The meditation "Preparation for an Hour of Trial" addressed the anxious moments suffered by any female before going out to a party. Martha dreaded "gay, worldly, profane company." She begged God to help her embody poise and inner assurance, to "let religion tincture every word and action" so that "nothing but holiness [should] proceed out of my mouth." Underneath her stern religious language was an insecure girl heading into unknown social waters. What if she were dressed all wrong, looked the pitiful colonial? What if no one spoke to her or even came to stand near her? Would her "fear of singularity" turn her into "a babbler?" Dear God, she prayed, if I can't supply "an innocent or useful part in the conversation, keep me silent."[25]

Another reflection followed a visit to an art gallery, obviously a stunning visual encounter that opened a rich channel in Martha's imagination. She summoned the most dramatic words she could muster to evoke the impact of the "mangled body and blood of Jesus" on her "bodily eyes," trying to transfer them to the "eyes of the Mind" by her recording. Such experience of her senses should become an "overpowering force" able to "melt the rock" of her heart. Her pleasure in solemnizing these reactions was palpable: she vowed to have her "mind in such a state" as "to see *every* occurrence in a Christian view, [to] let *nothing* pass without some holy reflection . . . some pious meditation."[26] Never halfhearted about anything, young Martha took step after step to assimilate ("read, mark, and inwardly digest" the words of Scripture) new perspectives during those first months in England and later in France. She could not have guessed that such intense self-analysis was actually constructing psychic independence and would lead her far beyond the limitations of the female role with which she was trying to make her peace.

Another day, she wrote defensively, "I expect temptations and reproach." A poignant revelation of girlish loneliness came when she admitted that "love of creatures" was painfully important to her; naturally she had to upbraid herself for that. What did she, Martha Laurens, living in a Christian household, know about real trials of faith—she who was "applauded for pious resolution and encouraged in devotion" by an uncle and aunt who themselves were "patterns of piety?" With merciless self-interrogation she pondered whether she could bear to be laughed at for her "preciseness," ridiculed for her American rigidities. Could she remain righteous where she heard nothing but "gay, fashionable" talk? She saw herself as overly susceptible to doing in Rome whatever the Romans were doing: "the world is too apt to engross my thoughts."[27] What she was actually doing, unconsciously, was constructing interior layers of ego strength.

At this stage of life Martha enjoyed accusing herself of apostasy—a heavy theological lash to punish longings as normal (and merely human) as finding herself ill at ease among strangers or desiring to find a way to conform. According to the standards in her secret covenant, that would be called "backsliding." She enjoyed enumerating negative acts of self-indulgence: "Too much time spent on sleep, meals, outward adornings, visits, unprofitable conversations, idle curiosity, and ten thousand other trifles." In her pages of self-scrutiny, she was guilty of two "flagrant crimes"—"shocking levity, and trifling idleness and deceit."[28] Again these were weighty condemnations of a need to be taken seriously, to be viewed as an adult instead of merely seventeen years old. Martha's adult use of theological language was its own youthful exaggeration. Her relative inexperience of the larger world—both in the new social context where she strove to "find" herself and in the verbal persona she was creating through letters and meditations—is evidenced by the jarring juxtaposition of her written language with her actual daily life. During these same years, John was hurling himself toward adulthood and the new American army, similarly trying on new language styles and persona. However, what was appropriate for an eldest son had to be translated into religious terms and onto interior religious ground for an eldest daughter.

The depth of Martha's adjustment trauma in England—being "foreign" in a country she had not expected to find unwelcoming—can be measured by the quantity of handwritten material she wanted to preserve from this period. Each time Martha moved to a new location during her lifetime, she destroyed her personal writings "to prevent their falling into unsympathetic hands." These devotional and psychologically revelatory thoughts, deposited for safekeeping with Elizabeth Brailsford, a girl from Charles Town also living in a boarding school near London, resurfaced after Martha's death for inclusion in her memoirs. But they were a minor part of the overall quantity of exchange within the universe of Laurens family papers during 1776 and 1777—a homely indication of the momentousness of those years. There was always uncertainty that any one piece of written communication would actually make it across the ocean and into the hands of the addressee. And much portentous action characterized the male Laurens in these crucial years—Henry Laurens' election to the presidency of the Continental Congress, John's military role as aide to Gen. George Washington, and the friendship of both father and son with the youthful Lafayette.[29]

Indeed the Revolutionary War in faraway Carolina became considerably more vivid in Martha's consciousness when she received her own "war letter" from her father in August 1776. If her written meditations to that point were Martha's spiritual analysis of her own life and emerging personhood, Papa's letter gave explicit direction in which she, a female, must deploy that spirituality and personhood in the face of war. Shortly after the war's beginnings, the prospect of losing most of his wealth, and fears of what lay ahead, led an anxious Henry Laurens to pour out to his children his major expectations for each of them. For the two eldest, Martha was to embody his deepest religious concerns, while John, of course, carried his concerns for leadership of the family as well as in the nation. Young Harry was to prepare himself for business.[30] Religious anxieties for sons were expressed but less dominant than in his commission to Martha; other concerns took precedence for boys.

Henry Laurens' letter to Martha (dated 16 August 1776) opened with his laments of not hearing from her in over a year and equally familiar forebodings about the horrors of war. "What difficulties, what anxieties does our unhappy national quarrel occasion to Individuals . . . When it will be ended, & what Streams of blood are to fill up the measure is beyond all conjecture."[31] Because of postage costs, all letters were circulated among the family, and John would have shared with her "a great deal of American News, and particularly of the escape we have had from Enemies who talked of nothing less than eating us up." But then Papa himself couldn't desist from retelling again the "boast" of Lord William Campbell: that British invaders aimed to sweep American soldiers aside, "Breakfast at Sullivant's Island[,] dine at Fort Johnson & Sup in Charlestown." Wishing that "more suitable amusement could be found for Lord William," and that he would lose the shrewd assistance of fugitive slave Sampson, Henry philosophized: "All the mischiefs which have happened & all that Shall Still happen . . . are to be charged to wicked & foolish Counsellors." He prayed for "wiser & better Men who may devise means for effecting a friendly intercourse between Great Britain & these now 'United free & Independant States.'"[32]

Having for the first time invoked the nation's new name to Martha, Papa Henry immediately cautioned her not to *do* anything unsuitable for a young woman. She was not to speak about politics or the twistedness of human motives: "I am persuaded you will not give offence to any body by interposing your opinions concerning these matters." He also warned her against quoting *his* opinions in order to avoid offending her new acquaintances in England. A father or an older brother could speak about political matters but not a daughter (and not a younger son, Henry Jr.). In fact, Henry Laurens had to rationalize discussing politics with her at all: "To relate to you what has happened cannot be amiss, which is all I mean." Argumentative women were a popular journalistic anathema;[33] Martha must be well enough informed to serve as his confidant and to understand men's political actions, but at the same time she must remain mannerly and feminine by eschewing public disputation. She, "in the Wise order of that Superintending Being who holds the Scales of Justice in his hand," must cultivate the demeanor of female submission. More explicitly, lest this beloved daughter disgrace her upbringing, "You will *in Silence* Submit the future progress & final determination [of the war and our family fortunes] to Him . . . who hath Set bounds to the bared Arm of the mightiest Monarch on Earth, as . . . to the Seemingly irresistible power of the Ocean."[34] The obligations of gender imposed clear limits, specific and unquestionable, on any participation from females in her type of family in this vital national conflict.

Henry did deliver a specific commission to Martha. "Your part will be to join with the Sons & daughters of piety and pray incessantly for peace: peace to all the world . . . to [that] country in which you reside," England, "and especially to that which you more particularly belong [the new United States]." It comforted her Papa to envision daily spiritual contact with her, through prayer. In his terms her commission was global and national, larger and more encompassing than a family obligation. She must "lament your father's unhappy lot to be engaged in War, Civil War, God's Severest Scourge upon Mankind."[35] Then affection gleamed through the strictures: "I anxiously wish to See you my Daughter, you are an object continually in my view—but when & where Shall I really See you? *the question* so immediately after the Declaration of 4th July in the face of 25,000 British and hireling Troops invading a Center Colony [New York City], and at the eve of a Second intended attack, *is impenetrable.*" He forced himself to add: "I must, I will with Submission & fortitude bear the Suspense, improve the present hour and hope time will come."[36]

On a more cheerful note, he relayed home-front news to the daughter who would in the future preside over his dinner table. Their domestic slaves remained loyal, in thankful contrast with those deluded by British promises of freedom. In fact, "all desire to be remembered to Miss patsy & Miss Polly." He evoked a specific scene: "My Servant James manages them extremely well, you would be much pleased to See my House kept in as good order & my Table, often for a great deal of Company, as well Spread as if there was a Lady in it." Aware of how such bachelor self-sufficiency might strike Martha, he corrected himself: "I Should have Said *almost* as well."[37]

Thoughts of the new nation's precarious state circled him back to property, and from there to dowry for a marriageable daughter. "I have no doubt, my Dear Daughter, but that you take every advantage which the Country you are in affords for *the improvement of your mind & your address.*" That phrase embraced the totality of her self-presentation: appearance, manner, bearing, competence. "Address is of more importance to a Lady than is Sometimes thought—to you in particular your friends [relatives] should recommend it." Warning her against the specter of future poverty, he added: "God knows through what Scenes you are to pass; if, instead of affluence, of which you had lately a prospect (& to which you have Still a just claim) Servitude is to be your portion, qualify yourself for an upper place." Even if reduced to the humblest standard of living, she must exhibit Laurens superiority. "Fear not Servitude, encounter it if it shall be necessary with a heroism becoming a Woman of an honest & a pious Heart."

Papa expected pride in being a Laurens to arm Martha for any and all circumstances. But concern for her future also made him probe the religiosity with which she cloaked herself, even now, within the family: was it genuine, not just role-playing or affectation? Only "a Woman who has not been affectedly nor fashionably Religious" would merit his laurels for "an honest and pious Heart." He reiterated their familial roles—his to warn, hers to listen and comply—as the reason for his badgering: "I See it my Duty to guard against every thing which may happen, & Sound repeated warning to those who are dearer to me, & of more value to the World, than my Life."[38]

His closing paragraph cited her role as kinkeeper, at which she already excelled. "You will take care of my Polly too. I need not tell you to be dutiful to your Uncle & Aunt, to Love & reverence them as tender parents, they may be reduced to very great Streights." The miseries again flooding his imagination stopped his pen. "There, my heart is most wrung, but I must forbear, the Subject overpowers me. God in whom I trust will protect you all." Intending to sign off, he wrote: "Adieu, dear daughter, write as oft as you can, & in some measure lessen that anxiety which arises from the uncertainty of your being restored to your faithful friend, your affectionate father."[39]

But he found he couldn't stop. He added a revealing postscript about Martha's self-presentation that inadvertently passed on a hurtful opinion of brother John's: skepticism about her present religiously exacting manner: "Your brother's letter [six months ago] says you were not well & ascribes your indisposition to confinement & want of exercise. You must, my dear, Avoid a Mopish Life. If you indulge it, the consequence will be HABIT, and loss of health both to your mind & Body." From the two most important men in her life, this criticism had to sting.

A domineering brother's observation could wither a sister even if transmitted through her father's loving concern. Six months earlier, Henry had in fact queried John, as acting head of the family in exile, about

Martha: "Does she wear off the too domestic habits?" All the men in her familial universe held contradictory expectations for her. Fastened by love and duty to an uncle's sickroom and governess to a little sister, Martha had few options that were not domestic. She was not free to travel about the countryside visiting her own friends, as her brother was; her social position required invitations first, then travel. Yet a patriarchal father and demanding brother expected her to display the pleasing, graceful bearing of one who had a great deal such experience.

John's fuller report to Henry Laurens back in South Carolina, the one to which Henry's postscript alluded, had blended brotherly condescension with concern. His sister, he judged, was indeed shy ("with a retired Disposition") and awkward ("deficient in that Grace of Deportment which gives Splendour to every Action and increases Respect for the Virtue which it accompanies"), but his own strong ego made him confident she would change to please him, would adjust herself to his prescription. And even if she did not, John had concluded, Martha would always "possess in an eminent degree those Qualities which will render her valuable in Society, & lead her to her Duty in all the relative Situations of Life"—his magnanimous summary. Since no one could deny her intelligence and character, she would always be valued by her relatives even if she was not particularly beautiful in the eyes of the world. His sister was too tentative to suit a man of the world; she lacked poise and charm. Her brother's patronizing conclusion: "She has good Sentiments and couches them in well-chosen words, but they frequently lose Effect by being conveyed in an undecided Tone."[40]

Growing up female in the Laurens family would have been strenuous at any time in history, without the added hardships of wartime and no mother. Being a resident alien in a country that "calumniated" both her nation and her father, and wounded by a brother's disparagement, Martha in her heart of hearts had plenty of cause to withdraw into the domestic circle and stay by herself.[41] Unspoken competition with the male darling of the dynasty, may have contributed to her shy and austere demeanor. Unacknowledged sibling rivalry could easily impel a younger sister to extremes, though the only extreme for a Laurens female would have to be religious.

"Your remarks respecting Miss Patsy are very good," Henry had responded to John's evaluation. "No doubt you, as often as possible, act the preceptor" since "You are happy in all the requisites for that friendly office, & your sister does not want docility." He soothed the siblings evenhandedly—approving John's assessment while trying to shield Martha from cruel clarity. "There is sometimes seen a species of pride, in the minds of people of good understanding," which certainly included his beloved daughter, "which leads them to censure those graces you speak of [the ones *you* say she lacks], under the harsh epithets of *vanity* & *affectation,* because they themselves are grown stiff in a homely gait & tone." Her father was privately admitting that, perhaps by the world's standards, Martha was not strikingly attractive and her maturing femininity was still somewhat awkward. When she felt like a gawky foreigner, why shouldn't she defend her lack of that social poise for which she secretly yearned by dismissing it as "vain" and "affected"? Martha's styling herself as an aloof purist was undoubtedly self-defense—her profile half-turned from others as she disdained their gossiping and social banter about the "hillocks of mortality."[42]

"If you perceive anything of this nature [in Martha]," father Henry had advised John, "you will aim gently at the root; the happy mean [between worldly poise and spiritual modesty] . . . is not to be acquired by everybody, & very seldom by those who do not frequent polite company." Martha's entrapment with sick relatives, as well as their wartime economies, ruled out much exposure to "polite company." As the American stranger, she felt unwelcome at balls and teas with English acquaintances, although dashing John had no trouble finding sympathizers with the American cause. She was distant from female contemporaries who might have tutored her wordlessly in the social graces, so naturally she spent her free time alone—reading. At that thought, her father rallied stoutly to her defense, quoting John's own words back to him. "Of the two extremes, give me the Daughter & you the Sister 'possessed in an eminent degree of qualities which will render her valuable in Society and fit her for her Duty in all relative situations of life,'" he exclaimed. Martha was to be valued and praised, even if she had not mastered that "Grace of deportment which gives splendor to every action" expected by her stylish big brother. No, the father in Carolina chided his son and heir in England, let us be glad she is *our* Martha "in preference to a simpering Toy!" Edging John toward *his* benign paternal view, Henry Laurens signed off: "Here I dare say we agree."[43]

Martha's meditations indicate the lines along which her budding "American-ness" was evolving. However special her education, mental acuity, and enlightened thinking, for a woman, she would always be seen primarily as a representative of the family by both world and family. She would always be expected to subordinate any interests of her own to that primary calling. She was expected to uphold the best of the nation's character in her Laurens heritage, in all roles and eventualities, while definitely remaining behind the scenes. Brother John's preoccupation with the army and its military battles awakened her to the realities of war and the new entity of "America," far more than her father's efforts for the fledgling nation. Before, that had seemed mainly an affair of the grownups. Then in October 1776, John confessed (first in a letter to Uncle James, not his father) that he had been "forced," out of "pity," because she was pregnant with his child, to marry Martha Manning, the youngest daughter of Henry Laurens' friend and business partner in England. In a subsequent letter to his father, filled with fiery words against the British occupation in homeland South Carolina, John inserted a tentative sentence about his fait accompli: "Will you forgive me Sir for adding a daughter-in-law to your family without first obtaining your consent?" Quickly, in the same sentence, he thanked Henry for permission, at long last, to "return to my Native Country."[44] John's impatience to fight England hadn't prevented him from seducing one of its gullible English schoolgirls. The gallant young father then rushed off to fight his wife's country at the side of General Washington, shortly before this first Laurens grandchild, Frances Eleanor Laurens, was baptized on 18 February 1777 in St. Andrew's Undershaft, London.[45]

At age eighteen, sister Patsy already knew John more deeply than he would ever know or understand her. Such a brother inspired and represented her own patriotism. Though she had to remain "retired" in the French countryside, utterly remote from urban news and war involvement, in her imagination she could follow at John's elbow and bask in thinking about his exciting part in the transatlantic drama. When Martha wrote of "boldness" in the "glory of the Lord," and *her* battles against "floods of conflict" and "seas of tribulation," she was figuratively aligning her inner self with her own family hero. Consciously, of course, her combative instincts were directed inward, onto her own battleground—the soul and her emerging selfhood.[46]

The mind of a young woman like Martha, "early imbued with sentiments that looked on the serious and important duties of life," demanded weighty, serious investment of her time and energies. While still in England she had dismissed the female role of social ornament as anathema.[47] Her husband's summary of the years constituting Martha's French exile described them as having been spent "usefully to her uncle, profitably to herself, and as pleasantly as straitened circumstances and anxiety for her friends and native country . . . would permit." Fortunately, given her intellectual appetite, "she had many opportunities of improving her mind by reading and conversation, which she diligently improved," and the modest provincial social life was deemed congenial to one of her disposition. "She and the family of her uncle received great civilities from the French, for the same reasons they had received slights from the English."[48]

David Ramsay's tribute to her sophisticated mental life listed only a handful of the ideas and authors Martha must have absorbed during her European stay, and only a few more were specifically named in family correspondence: Richardson, Goldsmith, Defoe, historians and biographers, popular religious texts by spiritually articulate contemporaries like Mrs. Sarah Trimmer (1741–1810) and Mme de Sevigné (1626–1696).[49] Phrases in her later diary writings demonstrate familiarity with the poetry of Elizabeth Singer Rowe and Edward Young. These in turn symbolize a broad acquaintance with other learned writers of the era such as Lady Elizabeth Montagu and Catherine Talbot. The memoir of one such scholar, Elizabeth Carter, would be recorded as the last "women's history" Martha read before dying in 1811. Her own letters demonstrate the significance of Philip Doddridge's *Rise and Progress of the Soul.*[50]

Martha also "improved her mind" (her husband's umbrella phrase) by assuming the authority to establish a village school in Vigan. Taking that educational initiative was a fairly typical action for eighteenth-century women who wanted to be religious entrepreneurs back in the colonies, as the many dame schools attest.[51] Though Martha was unusually competent in the French language, such initiative in a female was protected from being seen as too bold by its religious motives. Her temperament and genius was practical; she needed to do something concrete, like teaching children to read the Bible. Reading to children and enjoying their attention undoubtedly fulfilled the innate Laurens need for leadership—to "feel a tool in the hand of God." A similar outreach by young English Quaker Elizabeth Fry a generation later recorded the steps Martha would thus have undertaken: finding a suitable empty building for use as a schoolroom, training a few older children to help as preceptors, opening each day with prayers, teaching the alphabet, choosing texts for the little ones to memorize. Books, scarce and expensive, would have been a problem, but at one point her father gave Martha a gift of 500 guineas for Bibles to use as instructional texts—each Bible viewed as a library in itself by early female schoolkeepers.[52]

But Martha also expanded her mind and personality in dimensions unintended or at least unforeseen by her father when he penned that August 1776 letter of commission. He had surely not meant to encourage personal independence or autonomy in a daughter, yet that was one result of her "improvement" during the uncomfortable adjustment in England. She had been forced to develop confidence in her own ability to reason and to use Christian theological language for coping with her frustrations. She had learned how to be critical, how to stand apart and think for herself. With the eyes of a foreigner and stern self-manager, she had been able to reject those customs and standards that seemed superficial. Recognition that the English viewed her as "stiff" and "unnatural" forced her back on her own mental supports. The act of moralizing thus became the engine of her personhood; she had turned the individual decision about *each* action—attending church, nursing her aunt when she fell ill, writing a meditation—into an obligation about which she must make a separate moral decision, discern right or wrong, good or ill. Each decision, however inconsequential, had to be consciously rational, had to express stringent intentionality. Martha's mental-improvement years—writing, reading, evaluating, praying, thinking, teaching, negotiating and inevitably adding successive layers of ego—were *her* psychic participation in the emerging spirit of American independence.

Outside of the cities on the continent, the kind of sociability for which Martha hungered was probably available in few places. "Learned ladies" were a rarity not likely to be found in a French village. "Sensible and ingenious minds cannot subsist without a variety of rational entertainment," one learned Englishwoman (Mrs. Montague) wrote about another (Mrs. Vesey) to another (Elizabeth Carter) in 1765. Whether Martha knew this correspondence or not, its next sentence is a helpful summary of the means she used to survive mentally and even flourish during those years. "If a person is robust enough to bear *a course of hard study,*" the writer stated, "they may live in any place, with dull society sometimes, or in retirement without any society at all."[53] Martha knew that truism existentially if not from reading Mrs. Montague.

Though Martha meditated and prayed about becoming the approved model of humility and duty within her uncle's household and in the small world of Vigan, her own inner authority was unconsciously developing. Electing a principled, rational, and slightly counterpublic persona wherever she went positioned her somewhat apart from polite society. In the five years since she had signed her solemn covenant with God, her efforts to fulfill that contract inexorably expanded her internal independence and gave Martha permission to use moral self-evaluation as a tool of her own self-creation. She had undoubtedly begun to see herself as answerable to divine authority rather than just to other human beings.

And confident now of a *self,* she could credit her own competence within the family. Discovering how crucial she was to the functioning of her uncle's household strengthened her; her ability to deal with tradespeople and French neighbors was central to the James Laurenses' comfort. Finding a genuine outlet for self-expression in her village school and receiving credit for enriching the lives of local children with "keys to regions of the spirit" assured her she was transmitting the most important lesson of all—that their first and great object was to follow Christ.[54] If Martha met other women who created a similar local role of usefulness, it was not recorded. But her Laurens drive for achievement found gratification in her circumscribed life at Vigan, despite war worries about her father and brother.

One of the major patriarchal lessons Martha had to learn was "not to murmur at any disappointment," but rather find whatever good she could in whatever happened.[55] By 1780 she was ready, whether she recognized it consciously or not, to challenge the relationship with the father who had thus far arranged her life. No longer a girl mutely accepting role and custom, she assumed actions in the public sphere for the family that demonstrated the progress she had made toward autonomy and womanhood. When her father, en route to Europe on a diplomatic mission, was captured by the British and imprisoned in the Tower of London near the end of 1778, she was the family member who lobbied the American diplomats in Europe—Benjamin Franklin and John Adams—on his behalf. She herself wrote them letters, carefully couched in the customary rationale that this task had fallen to her because her uncle was too ill and her brother was in the army.[56] Martha consciously employed the leverage of moral obligation: if representatives of the new nation allowed disrespectful treatment to a man of Henry Laurens' stature and importance they were defaming that country. Back in the new United States, the war was forcing many women to petition for redress, to seek out a means of interacting with their government.[57] In that audacious action and in the arguments she employed, Martha entered a new personal and familial zone of independence with her patriarch.

In 1780 the Laurens family in France was in a fever of anxiety over Papa Henry's desperate conditions in the Tower of London: vindictive guards sometimes withheld food and clothing, allowed him protection against the cold only on impulse, and attempted, by manipulating his British friends, to trick him into betraying his country.[58] At that point Martha apparently took charge of petitioning for his welfare, putting her "American-ness" on a par with her brother John's by daring to act as family spokesman. John had earlier written Martha with great affection, "I love you the more for the patriotism that animates you when you speak of America . . . It is a consolation that I am serving our common mother, and that our friendship cannot be affected by time, place, or circumstance." But when she suggested traveling to England herself to ascertain their father's condition, his tone became a curt rebuke. He totally disapproved of her applying for the passport required for firsthand inquiry; he actually forbade her to proceed. "[Your visit] will have a very ill effect both in France and America, in a public point of view."[59] Bowing to his strong words, Martha desisted. Of course Henry himself tried to alert his government and refused to let physical hardship make him traitorous.

The next year, 1781, in response to hopes that her father might be released in a prisoner exchange, Martha received a chilling explanation: "they [the British] would keep Mr. L to hang him at the peace, if the War should end in their favor." That quid pro quo—diplomat Henry Laurens for General Burgoyne, captive of the Americans—revealed that the English "would have no objection to America recalling and hanging Burgoyne" if the war should go in the Americans' favor.[60] John had minimized his sister's enterprise, saying that such a high-stakes game was no place for females, although John himself was meanwhile brashly demanding the French court provide financial support for the Revolutionary army.[61] How could any woman effectively intercede for the "true representative of America," as John's colleague Lafayette referred to their father? (Lafayette particularly praised Henry Laurens' "noble, steady conduct" under "insulting" conditions in the tower during imprisonment that lasted from November 1780 to the last day of December 1781.)[62] The prisoner Laurens was allowed several precious visits with his English partner, Manning, who brought along his daughter Martha Manning Laurens (now Papa Henry's daughter-in-law) and the infant Mary Eleanor, his only grandchild. Martha learned that her father's every act in the Tower of London was minutely scrutinized— by the British for traitorous sentiments that justified their harsh treatment and by his American colleagues for betrayal or complicity with the English.[63] Some of his warders actually tried to be kind and friendly, Henry reported, but others were unpredictably strict; rent and food had to be paid for and medical attention was denied, among many vexations.[64]

Finally, however, on the first day of 1782, Henry Laurens was freed from prison. "Mr. Laurens Enlargement will not be . . . unconsequential. I am told he behaved with Firmness and came into no Conditions repugnant to the Honor and Independence of the United States," John Jay reported to Benjamin Franklin on 11 February 1782.[65] Sadly, Henry was immediately reimprisoned by the illness that crippled him for "near two months": their friend Lafayette once called her father's terrible sieges of gout "Mr. Laurens' [own] slavery."[66] Her father's May 1782 letter to Martha, their first exchange free of British inspection since late 1780, took up the question of their return to the States. He had been commanded to serve the new nation a little longer as a peace commissioner, and home itself was "still a land of Blood, the violent and vindictive Enemy has closely blockaded my land" in South Carolina. To move Uncle James to such a scene was unthinkable, he concluded reluctantly; they would have to wait for the "dawning of a general peace."[67] Would his brother and family in France consider settling in a healthful American location anywhere other than Charles Town? Henry's plans, running far ahead of present realities, instructed Martha to lead them in that direction.[68] But during the late summer of 1782, their letters were to be filled with a tension previously unknown in the family, that disrupted all plans for returning home.

Early in August 1782, Henry instructed Martha to purchase proper travel clothes for herself and sister Polly, to outfit themselves appropriately for entertaining important diplomats like Dr. Franklin and others in Paris. Martha might even "turn merchantess" and bring with her a hundred pairs of rare silk stockings, which could be resold there at considerable profit.[69] Departure for America was still his major long-term preoccupation when an unexpected harvest of conflicting property and patriarchal claims over Martha intervened. Uncle James, too ill to even attempt a voyage, announced by letter that he would never leave France alive; Henry, dismayed by resistance to his agenda, accused his brother for the first time of suborning the loyalty of "my eldest daughter." Martha had told Henry of her foster parents' pleas of helplessness if her competent, loving care were taken from them. And when her uncle died, what would become of Aunt Mary? Martha was their intermediary with the locals, established as a personage in Vigan village. One can imagine some secret satisfaction on her part as she wrote these resistant thoughts for Uncle James—presenting her father with evidence of her value and importance in eyes other than his. She was a woman of twenty-one, in charge of an increasingly dependent household in a foreign setting. Martha herself embodied the challenge: you, father, ordered my life to undertake this responsibility, can you now order me away from it without concern for my uncle's welfare?[70]

The letters of 6 and 7 August (1782) that jockeyed for Martha's services clothed brotherly affection in legal and business terminology. On the seventh, Henry wrote that James' determination to die in France made him, her father, "anxious for the situation of my eldest daughter." Earlier in the summer Henry had paid a visit to the household in Vigan and, en route back to the Paris peace negotiations, had "swooned" from another attack of gout and fevers that trapped him at Mrs. Babut's boardinghouse. He rallied enough to dictate a letter (to Henry Jr.) intended to put pressure on James: people back in America would wonder why his brother would "not return into the arms of his own country and among his friends?" The letter also announced that he, Henry, felt duty bound "to invite [my eldest daughter] *to come to me and return with me* to America." Having stated that decision, he began to act on it: he was sending son Harry back to fetch her. There could be no more indecision: Uncle James and Aunt Mary could keep young Polly with them, since they'd been her "parents" from infancy, but Martha was definitely coming with him and would be his hostess. He needed her; "the treaty for peace is going on slowly."[71]

With Harry dispatched to Vigan to collect Martha, Henry Laurens again wrote her about purchasing proper attire for Lyon and Paris and the rooming arrangement he had made in a French home for her and Polly. Since he expected Harry to arrive at Vigan by 21 or 22 August, he was stunned to receive a letter from Martha, written the same fateful day on which he had written her (6 August), that "dashed [his] happiness with grief." In his mind, Martha was already woven into his future plans and on her way with Harry to join him. But he had discounted his invalid brother's emotional hold on Martha's loyalty.

A second letter from her, dated 7 August, doubled his distress: "grief upon grief." Her father responded to both her letters in his own, dated 18 August. First he called her threat—to keep Harry there in southern France till Henry agreed to delaying *his* departure—a "very unwarrantable & pernicios design," mean punishment for an ill father who needed her and Harry. Worse, Martha's second letter had contained "more extraordinary and unexpected matters" than the first. The second letter in two days was the one that really staggered him. "As soon as I could a little recover from . . . the Imports of both . . . I sat down to the table & am now [trying] the best reply I am able." That no copies of these letters to her Papa survive, apparently, are the great deprivation of this study.

Martha's second letter seemed to double and triple the emotional ante. Papa Henry's 18 August letter all but sputtered as he attempted to face heretofore unimaginable topics. Why hadn't she, when he was with them in Vigan last June, intimated any resistance to returning to her "own Country"? He quoted her words back to her: "'My Dear Papa I am yours, I will do whatever you desire.'" Whether she had said them or not, her father thought she had, and that she had agreed to leave Vigan with Harry whenever her Papa sent for her. He reminded her that she had sat by his bedside during his visit there and assured him that she would not "attempt a deviation" from his plans. Henry Laurens had allowed himself to leave Vigan en route back to Paris "fully satisfied," believing that she actually "wished to join me."

With anger her weary father now regretted not having brought her back to Paris himself. Overconsideration of sick relatives and uncertainty about conditions in America had led him to promise a "respectful (four or five weeks) notification" before an actual departure. Now, in hindsight, Henry Laurens recalled "the last evening I was with [your uncle]," perceiving "a very long threat of design"—the hint that Martha's departure would hasten his death. Martha had soothingly interpreted that as "the effect of [an invalid's] weakness." "Here I must stifle my feelings and prohibit my Pen from tracing the sources of this new mortification," Papa wrote. Martha had suggested that she stay in Vigan until everything was over— Uncle James' and perhaps also Aunt Mary's lives. Then she would join him: surely her Papa was too generous to "leave [the ill couple] sick and dying in a strange land" by taking away "<u>our only comfort and support</u>" (his underlining, quoting their words to her). Henry had found himself psychologically trapped.

Wanting to view himself as generous "even to Enemies and Strangers," Henry Laurens struggled with his daughter for the upper hand. The "one trait that I am compelled to display upon the present occasion," he wrote, was to "hold submission to God's Will to be one of the *first* principles, the *grand* principle of religion . . . I submit." Arguing with himself, however, he added: "If it pleases God . . . to restrain me in pursuit of a measure . . . I thought would have promoted the happiness, the honor of my Eldest Daughter, my favorite Child, . . . 'Thy will be done.'" Henry's words of defeat in this exchange made him the sympathetic party, and since there are no written words of Martha's, except those her father quoted back to her in his letters, she today appears at a disadvantage. At the time, her letters must have been filled with inner conflict: wanting to sustain her dear uncle in his last days and also to placate and please a father who finally needed her, now that she was an adult.

Henry brushed away the suggestion that his need for her was simply for the care she would give him (although he believed he was nearer to dying than any of them wanted to think). "I should tell you to stay," he wrote, "but I cannot. You are already grown old by nursing and I wished to relieve you." For the first time in all those years, Papa Henry acknowledged the isolation and servitude of Martha's years in Uncle James' household. The next sentence could have been defensive if it had not been so transparent. Remember, he wrote, *I* focus on nothing but "my children's happiness, truth forbids it," while Uncle James and Aunt Mary are necessarily more needy because of their own tragic health. But the language of patriarchal duty bolstered his demand. Her father and brother needed her now, making *that* her first duty. Revealingly, he added: "You are not bound [to them] by ties of gratitude!"

In the same letter, Henry Laurens recalled the terms under which he had first consented to his brother's taking Martha, at sixteen, with him to England. "Well do I know the best part you have acted, you have been a faithful, a dutiful, a hospitable servant, you have (upon a fair reckoning) lost more than you have gained." His commercial language was perhaps intentionally grating: Martha may have owed something to Aunt Mary as her "second mother," but "they owe you more than you them." Then he pushed the metaphor too far. "If I had such a servant . . . at home in plenitude of fortune, I should have [thought myself] a gainer." Her skillful assistance, "my daughter, at twenty-two years of age," could be calculated at "wages of 100 guineas per annum." He added a touch of irony: "Far is it from my breast to envy your Uncle & Aunt the advantage [of your services], but there is a time when we should hold it incumbent upon to think a little for the benefit of [even] a faithful domestic."

To mitigate his employment of merchant vocabulary, her father next tried empathy. "I know the difficulties you have to struggle with," he wrote, "and most sincerely pity you." She must remain there with uncle and aunt, "dear child, until you shall find it in your heart to come to me," adding the manipulative phrase, "if I am still alive," and then cited his favorite piety: "Whatever God wills, will be best." Martha could show this letter to Uncle James or not, as she deemed best. "For you, my dear daughter, to whom *this* is addressed only, I feel at this moment, and have, from that in your last letter, and shall continue to feel for a darling child, LOST, sensations which you know have often tortured this heart in the course of my pilgrimage." Henry Laurens could not fully repress his feelings of being under emotional siege. In this letter's final sentence, he struck a martyred tone: family complications are "against me, they completely derange all my plans," succeeded by a verbal sigh: "Tis no matter what happens to me—the back is fitted to the burthen."[72]

Henry Laurens' full epistolary counterattack focused on the meanings of kinship. He was an aging, tired patriarch beset by a mountain of woes, including severe gout, once again. His country still demanded his services in negotiating peace, and his adored John, in the Revolutionary army in South Carolina, was a constant worry. These, however, were about to be topped by another "grief upon grief," a thrust deeper than any hitherto imagined, a "bitter disappointment" threatening to unseat all his "parental labors." In Martha's two letters of early August 1782, Papa Henry had learned that he was not vying for Martha's loyalty and companionship with Uncle James alone but also with another man—one who could offer her a separate and powerful motive for remaining in France.

Monsieur Caladon deVerne, a local fellow-Huguenot merchant, who was obviously well known to the James Laurens household and to his daughter, had dared discuss the topic of marriage with Martha without first obtaining his, her father's, permission. (Unlike John's independent act of sexual liaison and then hasty marriage without parental permission, Martha was accused of dishonoring and attacking the social order for even thinking of it.) Here was an unlooked-for betrayal by daughter, brother, and sister-in-law. All three nearest and dearest family members, those he trusted most in the world besides John, had conspired against him, had defrauded him of his rightful expectation that *he* was the disposer of Martha's life decisions.[73]

Naturally, a father's plans for an adult daughter included marriage, the goal of all patriarchs—although in a correspondence preoccupied with war, property loss, and health matters, that concern about Martha had received minimal priority. Any intelligent, dedicated Christian woman would aspire to marriage, "the highest form of friendship," one of her favorite authors, the Rev. Dr. Jeremy Taylor, pronounced. The prevailing mind-set among privileged, educated women was that "Marriage is the settlement in the world we should aim at." To attain one's own household was the only way upper-class females could "mak[e] ourselves of use to Society and rais[e] ourselves in this world."[74] With the element of potential marriage added to the father-daughter standoff, Henry intensified his emotional barrage, inadvertently solidifying Martha's independence. Since only Henry's side of the conflict has been preserved, the reality of his daughter's hopes and affections must be imagined—something her fond Papa steadfastly refused to do. Yet the Martha Laurens formed by reading, discussion, and spiritual self-improvement was not one to bestow her affections lightly or illogically. No matter how dim her suitor in the eyes of an outraged

Henry Laurens, M. deVerne's virtues and person had to have more to them than mere availability.

During the remaining months of 1782, correspondence between Martha and her father conveyed his deep unwillingness to recognize the powerful logic and appeal of matrimony for her and her refusal to simply fall in line with his wishes: he clearly recognized that he was facing the challenge of his life with her. In his emotional state, everything about the timing of this potential marriage was an unthinkable mistake, an unpatriotic surrender of loyalty to her new nation. That he might forever lose Martha to a life across the Atlantic Ocean was too grievous to put in words.

Henry had to unburden himself to someone, so he sent an urgent message (dated 20 August 1782) to intercept Henry Jr., who was, as mentioned, already en route to collect his sister. Debating whether or not Harry should continue on to Vigan—"a long and expensive Journey" that might prove "ineffectual for the purposes intended"—Henry at first urged him ahead so he could "expostulate with your elder Sister and if possible open her eyes." Enclosed in this letter, Harry would see a copy of the note Henry had written Martha about her "gentleman"—the word dripped scorn. Her suitor was obviously a scoundrel who "honors me by stripping me of my Daughter," hoping to benefit from "houses and fields acquired by *my* labor." The enclosed copy of Henry's fierce response to her "was writ immediately upon reading *her* letter, it will admit of much enlargement but I send it to you verbatim as it was penned in the first impulse." Then, to a fellow Laurens male, he loosed full patriarchal outrage: "Where is the Religion, Where is the Virtue, the common prudence, in a Woman's giving her affections without consulting her Father, her Brother, her Foster Father & Mother, to a person not worth a farthing of near-double-her-Age, who declares he is only or most affected to her Fortune?" A dark afterthought brought the Vigan uncle and aunt into focus: they must have encouraged this connivance. "Is there no ground to fear [this] error may be if not encouraged, a little winked at and soothed by one [James] who hopes thereby to keep her in servitude?"[75]

Two days later (22 August), having marshaled his grievances by "stretch[ing] my mind through a sleepless Night," Henry again unburdened himself to Harry on paper. Having reviewed "your sister's letters of the 6th and 7th . . . comparing the various parts with each other" and recalling her assurances when he had seen her at Vigan, Henry had convinced himself that daughter Martha was the innocent party—that "the poor Girl without perceiving the self-deception, has been made a Stalking Horse [toward] the ends of an 'attachment.'" Her actual motive, "piety to her Uncle and friendship or gratitude to her Aunt," was so virtuous that it deluded her as to their actual intentions. But to whom had Martha allowed herself to consider attachment? A person totally inappropriate in Henry's mind, unromantic, "whose age and experience have cooled his passions." Henry now recalled that Aunt Mary had whispered to him, during his last visit, that M. deVerne was thirty-nine, although Martha had written that his age was thirty-six. Whatever his age, Henry's embattled instincts believed M. deVerne's principle interest was mainly in "a fortune."

Unstopping, he tormented himself with the worst imaginable scenario: after a year or so, "the burthen of a Young Wife" would find the middle-aged merchant returning Martha to her father. Martha's assurances that M. deVerne was "religious" and "virtuous" earned the father's scoff—"I am sick of the sight and sound of these Garbs"—although in other circumstances these were in fact his own favorite adjectives. He wrote out the script a dutiful daughter ought to have followed with such a suitor, torturing himself further: "I will consult my Father, my Uncle, my Aunt. Their happiness is intimately connected." Rewriting her words as he wished they had been was exquisite pain.

Martha *could* have given a "more conclusive reply," he moaned, thanking M. deVerne "for the intended honor," and pointing out "the disparity between [her and his] respective Ages & other circumstances." That would "leave [her] with nothing to add but good wishes" for a "more suitable Match." She *should* have closed with: "I intreat you Sir to think no more of me." At that point in his rewrite, the father expostulated to Harry: Good God, can a woman "at her time of life" (as mature as she already is), with her gifts and wisdom, claim an attachment that "'nothing but Time and Religion can conquer'" (apparently her words) for a man so utterly unsuitable? Surely, clever as that daughter is, and believing in her utter "candor," surely her weak answer to deVerne (that disarranged her father's plans) represented only a "very foolish, half-imaginary, half forced 'attachment.'"

Earnestly enlisting Harry to promote the family claims, Papa Henry urged his "dear Son" to "detach your mind from all other engagements" and "think seriously on . . . the saving [of] a Sister who is worth saving." He invoked self-interest: Harry would protect his own future interests by helping sway Martha's determination. "An indiscreet step on her part in 1782 may not only work *her* ruin but sow the Seed of trouble and vexation . . . [that] even *you* may reap forty Years hence." Along with his sister's welfare, a brother must consider potential economic burdens. If she married "the

Man," she also married his "family, numeros & poor," who "for generations will all think themselves married to her family." The true American paterfamilias made no distinction between his love for Martha and the financial future of the entire family. "Do everything in your power to rescue your Sister, to save your Brother's, your Sister's, your own honor, and . . . relieve your [poor] father laboring under much distress of mind" that further weakens "a much enfeebled Body." He suspected his sister-in-law was the temptress behind Martha's imprudence: "For a woman of sense she has acted very indiscreetly," in "a pursuit which has neither honor nor happiness in prospect." While every father of Henry's social standing feared fortune hunters and warned all daughters against forming "any attachment in Europe," the emotional bedrock of the Laurens-deVerne contest was geographic and legal as well as familial. If she were married in France, Martha would be lost to the nation his forebears had chosen and to him by the ocean that separated them.[76]

Final instructions to Harry took several more pages. "If she continues to resist, speak to her very affectionately but pointedly" . . . "I shall hold [Uncle and Aunt] Criminal in preferring a little self convenience to the honor and happiness of my Daughter, of her Father, and her Brothers." They would do well to credit Henry with the "privilege of the Camel, to rise when I feel the burthen is enough, otherwise I may be provoked to throw off the whole!" If Harry absolutely could not "obtain . . . my Daughter's concurrence," he was to turn around and leave, "seeing she has cast us off." Warn "your Sister not to bring Strangers into our family," or any about whom *we* have not been consulted "nor they invited." If Uncle wants her to stay and marry the stranger, *he* may provide the dowry fortune. Henry concluded with a groan of helplessness: "My thought is too big for expression." But his last sentence gave Harry an ultimate threat to deploy: his sister was shortening her father's days: "Say finally you apprehend [that her resistance] will cost me a Winter's journey to Vigan, at the hazard of my Life and the risqué of my reputation at home."[77]

In the Laurens father-daughter contretemps, the prime offense was Martha's disregard for familial and hierarchical order. Someone other than a father (Uncle James) had given this paragon of a daughter her first real sense of value as an adult, and someone else (M. deVerne) had given concreteness to the longing for her own household. James and Mary had turned Henry's fraternal generosity into a nest of revolution. Henry's dear dead wife long ago had predicted that brother James might become jealous and competitive, "the worm at the root of my vine," he recalled. His brother's ungrateful accusation, that Henry wanted his daughter only "as a nurse" was ridiculous: money could easily buy him one. Considerably more baffling was the stance of his grown daughter: if it were really possible for Martha to find contentment with M. deVerne, something Henry could in no way comprehend, he would inevitably have to say, "Thy will be done."[78]

In his note to Harry about the villain deVerne, Henry Laurens' outrage was more directed at the suitor than at a daughter defying class, custom, and patriarch; M. deVerne's marriage offer had contained, as was the custom, the financial qualification of a dowry. To John, back in America fighting the British, their father stormed: what has deVerne to offer? "One who will think he honors me and you, by taking away my daughter, and a fortune to be prescribed by himself?"

Papa's late August letter warning M. deVerne away accompanied a separate one to Martha containing numbered stages of his paternal logic. "I refer you 1st to the Letters which I have lately written to you"; next, "to a recollection" of her former agreement with his plans when he had visited at Vigan; and third, to a review of her "August 6th and 7th letters." Surely the first assured her of her father's deep, devoted "Estimation" of his "Eldest Daughter"; if he were truly indifferent to her welfare, he would simply have advised her to "remain where you are." The second point addressed "an unsteadiness" in her conduct, the "source of that versatility which you yourself, unhappily self-entangled in a snare, had not perceived"—but which the eye of a distressed, affectionate, jealous father (his own adjectives) instantly penetrated. His third argument attacked her "with imputations of insincerity," naming "the shifting ground of your excuses" for "resist[ing] the advice and invitation of your father." He enumerated proofs of his love for her: "I would do great things, I would hazard my life and the fragment of my Estate to serve my Brother & Sister, but I dare not carelessly hazard the honor & happiness of my Eldest Daughter . . . for any consideration." How could his darling Patsy be so "very much out of the guard of prudence and discretion?" That she might have *chosen* to lower her guard and consider marrying M. deVerne was unthinkable.

Henry aligned himself with all "fathers I have known, disappointed in their prospects by the indiscretion of their daughters." He was *not,* like them, "disposed" to fall into "outrajeous & violent resentments" even if he knew similarly the "anxios days & sleepless Nights an Affectionate Parent [feels] when the sudden stroke of Death snatches from his embraces a darling Child." The intensity of his domestic struggle had totally distracted

Henry Laurens from his civic duties. "If I am to lose my Daughter by her own folly, her own self-deception," began his parting verbal thrust, and "by the unfaithful conduct of her Guardians [who] prefer self convenience . . . to our honor and happiness, Time and consideration may, I hope will, reconcile me to the event." He sounded a more oracular note: "I may submit to the loss, but I can never forget the Injury."

For a moment, his final paragraph actually saluted her independence. "I have not power to command. I have not inclination to compel nor to overawe. Dispose as you please of the admonitions of your affectionate Father, your faithful friend."[79] What he knew that Martha could not realize was the enormity of her stance—"dangerous to the peace and happiness of father and brother . . . whose health you wish to maintain." She had made a figurative pact with the devil by letting this "love" create yet another demand on her loyalties, even if her plan was doomed without a dowry. He again wielded his chief weapon: her proposed husband's disavowal if she brought no fortune. "My dear child, can a lady of your understanding talk of an attachment for such reasons, such inadequacy in every respect?" Finally, he named her actual crime: not placing everyone else's need and expectations ahead of her own. "You violate the advice of your own father."

That father, unused to competing for centrality in his eldest daughter's world, then lapsed into incoherence. Fragments of sentences and incomplete phrases filled the page: "If I am to lose a daughter by her own folly," he began, then broke off. "Indiscretion—sleepless nights—." Perhaps his reduction to primal cries allowed him, finally, to write words that Martha needed most to see: indications that her father was attempting to come to terms with her autonomy in this situation. He did not "mean to compel," he wrote; still he couldn't resist two parting shots intended to wound her as deeply as he was hurt. He questioned whose love for her was greater, the uncle and aunt to whom she was giving first loyalty or the father who had given her life itself? Then he asked whether *their* "love" was truly a specter of exploitation: "are they, by any chance, hoping to keep you in servitude?"[80]

On 28 August, the epistolary duel of wills ended: John Laurens, back in South Carolina in the army, was killed. Here indeed was "grief upon grief" for father and daughter. Years later, Martha reported to husband David Ramsay that she had sat up in bed one night, knowing John was dead. (At the time she prayed it was only a nightmare, but confirmation of her brother's end on that very date arrived several months later.) In October, M. deVerne, still unaware of Henry's profound hostility, submitted a formal written request for Martha's hand. In Henry Laurens' 13 November response—its tone magisterial, its diction icy—there was a single oblique reference to the death of his beloved son: this letter was concerned for the life of a *living* child. DeVerne had breached custom and etiquette by "clandestinely securing the affections of a young lady under guardianship." If indeed a "mutual attraction" existed between him and Martha, quoting deVerne's words, the father had a right to be outraged at its originating under the very roof of his brother. His daughter's "competence" was too high, her sense of duty too elevated for that. Angry as he was at Martha, familial pride made him exonerate her.

Henry cited his own courtship of Martha's mother, Eleanor Ball, in 1749 as the proper model. If M. deVerne were as sophisticated as he pretended, he would have known the accepted steps and maneuvers, the obligatory "discussion of some intermediate considerations." "Savages" might "dispose of their daughters" in "so unceremonious" a way, Henry wrote witheringly, but not a Laurens. "You deprive me of my dearest property by craft and subtlety, leaving me no option, *then* solicit my acquiescence." His words chilled: "How very cold, sir, is this compliment."

The closing stated: "I have *a right* to gratitude from my daughter, and want no claim on yours." Patriarchy carried the prerogative of exclusion as well as bestowal. If M. deVerne hoped to be "esteemed as a man of honor," he must relinquish any claim on Martha's affections "and restore them to her much distressed father." He must also remove "the reproach of indiscretion" from James and Mary Laurens "for insecurely guarding a most sacred trust."[81]

These lofty sentences manfully disguised Henry Laurens' agonies. Though at the apex of public service to his newborn nation, he was assaulted by ill health and fraternal conflict, and his son and heir had been sacrificed in the war for independence from Britain. Worse, the deepest challenge to his patronal self-image had emanated from the least expected domestic quarter—his eldest female descendant. At the very moment a shattered father most needed daughterly compliance and support, Martha had chosen to exercise her autonomy—the ultimate female sin in patriarchy.

Two days later, 15 November 1782, Henry sent a copy of his deVerne dismissal to brother James. The dying uncle must face its contents, no matter how ill he felt. In the covering note Henry Laurens made it clear that he expected Martha to read it aloud to her uncle, since the first thorn in it was directed to her. Henry wrote, "How deeply was I wounded by your ungracious, unaffectionate taunt, 'you have two sons, they are better than me,'" quoting James' words back to both of them. That thrust may have ruptured a lifelong tenderness between younger and older brothers. Or were those Martha's words, a clear-eyed summary of a daughter's subordinated status in comparison with the son and heir of her Laurens family? One or both of them, Martha or Uncle James, had cruelly dared to name the inequity of affection in a system that valued males over females. Whoever originated the charge, the next sentence was an arrow of justification plucked from his own bleeding heart: "I have but one son [Harry] and for aught I know, had but one in that evil moment when you excited forboding fears." That could apply to either daughter or brother.

Another taunt had to be returned. Uncle James had confronted Henry with Martha's profound grief over her brother John's death: "Whose sorrow can equal her sorrow?" Henry Laurens' rejoinder to that breathed fire. How dared "a complainer" who has "not felt the little-fingers' weight of eight years civil war," brother James himself, "who has been happily placed without the sight and sound of our country's calamities," mention sorrow to *him*—who was just released from prison and an unwilling eyewitness to British destruction of our properties? Henry instantly softened and attempted to contextualize their joint loss as one among thousands in the larger cosmos of war's destruction: "What are all our sorrows put together in comparison [with] those [of] our many compatriots and friends—a gravelsand to a mountain?"

This patriotic apotheosis was followed by an unequivocal command. "Read the enclosed, seal, and deliver it to M. Deverne," Henry ordered his brother, "sav[ing] me, if you can, from the sorrows which will result from the living death of another child." A kind of balance sheet then listed, by implication, everything that he, Henry Laurens, had done and borne for James and Mary Laurens and concluded with the claim on Martha's loyalty that *they* owed *him*. His sister-in-law "has been very faulty, her own convenience and interests have blinded her better understanding." After such unprecedented plain speaking, Henry resumed his standard role as shepherd of the Laurens family: "Still, she will always find a friend in me," he concluded.[82]

Fifteen days after this ultimatum, Henry Laurens was well enough to return to the diplomatic negotiations that still clamored for his attention; on 30 November 1782, he became one of the signatories of the preliminary Treaty of Paris between his new, "free and independant United States" and Great Britain. The intensity with which Henry defended his claims on Martha were undoubtedly aggravated by the larger helplessness he felt toward the many unknowns in his future. Were papers safe where he had hidden them back in Carolina? Were his furnishings and houses preserved? Or were his plantations uncultivated and slaves deserted? The one thing he had counted on—the powerful, sustaining bond of family relationships—now, also, was altered.

The agonizing year 1782 was not allowed to end without a few more aggrieved letters from father Henry to Martha and to his brother James: where else could he direct his pain? He accused his brother yet again of manipulating Martha's affections; he accused the entire household at Vigan of plotting and scheming; he tortured himself with the potential outcome of a "traduced" arrangement—his daughter's automatic loss of civil status in France as a Protestant, making any future offspring illegitimate. To Aunt Mary, his last communication of 1782 conveyed defeat: tell Martha I am silent in response to her letters not through anger but because there are no further words, no arguments or persuasions left. "I write only in tears, compassion, anguish."

By early January 1783, Uncle James' health was at such low ebb that Henry regretted their contentiousness. To Martha, he wrote once again that if any daughterly affection "subsisted in [her] bosom," the "indiscretion that had made [him] doubt it" could indeed be wiped away by a clean break with M. deVerne. He also penned the ageless parental acknowledgment of a "child" who was no longer his to direct: "But you are not lacking for advice." He reiterated his litany of loss: all those previous dead children, and now John, "the one I counted as prop of my declining years"; my daughters "deprived me for various causes"; my country "demanding my services." Uncle James? "Let me suffer, rather than him." Two days later, a genuinely despairing note had been added: "*More* than necessary has been laid on me." The thought most deeply rending his heart was "the unkind confidence [of brother and wife] that *I* could bear mountains"—that Henry Laurens was strong enough to bear *all,* even to "lose you my daughter, after also John."[83]

A month later, at the beginning of February 1783, Martha made her choice, cutting short the conflicting claims of father and uncle. She apparently traveled straight across France toward her father in Bath, England, with such dispatch that his agent in Paris had to apologize. "Her short stay in this city did not permit me to shew her such civilities as those that belong to you and have a right to from me. I regret that I had not the honour of making her acquaintance. She sent for 50 louis by Mnr. Vaughn which I paid."[84] On 15 February 1783, Henry Laurens wrote his South

Carolina colleague William Drayton, also in England: "I had heard of my daughter's arrival at Paris from the South of France and supposing she would be unhappy in a place strange to her . . . I determined either to meet her there or to send her brother [Harry] to conduct her to London. But neither was necessary. She had, with her maid, traveled upwards of 900 miles, like a true American woman, and reached London the evening I left Bath." Mlle Martha Laurens, instead of pausing for Parisian sociability with the wives of John Jay and John Adams (fellow peace commissioners with her father) or waiting until a male family escort arrived, had driven single-mindedly toward the next stage of her life. Her father was ill and needing her care.[85]

What heartbreak and emotions traveled with Martha were not documented. Perhaps her independent journey was not as daring as it seemed to her father. Perhaps his imagery and the new patriotic salute to her competence contained an implicit apology. Clearly it expressed gratitude, with scarcely a hint of triumph that she had resolved the familial conflict in his direction. Did he give the slightest thought to any regrets Martha would have to mask, feel any sympathy for her surrendered hopes of marriage and her own family one day? The silence about her inner turmoil constitutes its own bridge to readers' empathy, the absence of any actual words of loss and despair simultaneously implying their presence. Her father's new metaphor, "true American woman," captured the altered relationship between a father nearing sixty and a daughter, now a woman of twenty-four. It conveyed admiration, perhaps a little alarm, and implicit acknowledgment of her independence.

The American personality her father saluted matured almost out of nowhere. Though Martha Laurens had been conversing in French, reading French and English newspapers and books, conducting business with French tradespeople, listening to European sermons, absorbing European landscapes, and visiting European museums, what emerged was the sensibility her father implicitly christened "American."[86] In fact, both family letters and her husband's biographical sketch in the *Memoirs* credit that European displacement with heightening her determination to be a patriot American. Even considering the possibility of a marriage to a French citizen intensified her Americanization in the long run.

For the next two years (1783–1785) Martha served her father as clerk-secretary, hostess, strong right hand, nurse, and companion. The closing salutations of Henry's formal letters now included her as he had once included the greetings of her mother.[87] She and brother Harry remained with Henry during the peace negotiations in Paris and then in England, where his name and reputation involved him with old and new friends, including the renowned evangelical aristocrat the countess of Hunting-don.[88] Martha enjoyed her new centrality in the daily life of her important father and its tacit acknowledgment of her new role in the family. She had produced, through self-government and self-culture, her version of American independence by mastering and then triumphing over the sacrificial self-denial that epitomized female virtue in the new republic. This made her a "true American woman."

Since Martha was now mostly at her father's side, there were no long letter exchanges to document her thoughts or hopes.[89] In the cursory notes Henry Laurens wrote her from shipboard in the Bristol channel in 1784 as he and Harry waited for the right wind to sail, Papa addressed her as a respected compatriot and assistant more than as his once-rebellious daughter. After Henry and Harry departed for Charleston, she was the family chaperone delegated to wait in England until 1785, when Aunt Mary could join her (after burying Uncle James), Polly, and John's orphaned daughter, Fanny (who had become Henry Laurens' ward after the death of both her young mother and father), for the return to Carolina. Any evidence of Martha's adjustment to a life as her father's unmarried kinkeeper—however independent her spirit—was likely to remain invisible and keep her postwar existence in Charleston invisible.[90] Well-bred daughters knew what was expected of them, whether they had chosen it willingly or not.

1. *Portrait of Martha Laurens as a young girl (ca. 1767) by John Wollaston (fl. 1734–1767). (Private collection.)*

2. *Portrait of Henry Laurens at the apex of his governmental career (1782) by John Singleton Copley (1738–1815). Laurens' daughter Martha was twenty-one at the time. (Published by permission of the National Portrait Gallery, Smithsonian Institution, Washington, D.C.)*

3. *Portrait of Dr. David Ramsay by Rembrandt Peale (1778–1860), oil on can-
vas. Though one of Ramsay's eyes had been blinded in his youth by smallpox,
the artist corrected this facial feature in the painting. (Gibbes Museum of
Art/ Carolina Art Association, Charleston, S.C..)*

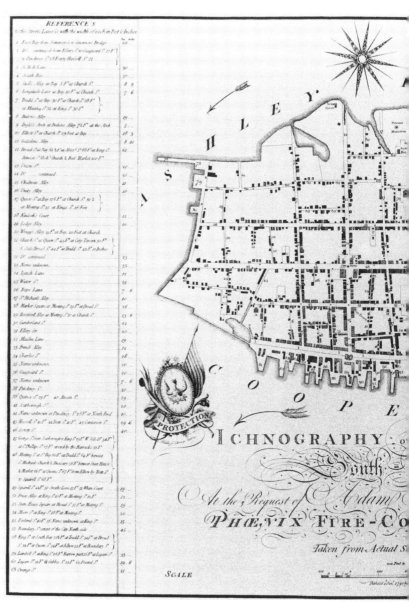

4. *Map of Charleston, 1788. Martha's childhood home and Laurens Wharf #98 (lower far right) are located on the edge of the open area, earlier known as Laurens Green but here renamed Federal Green by Henry Laurens in honor of the new U.S. constitution.*

To the Editor of the COLUMBIAN MAGAZINE.

S I R,

While you are amusing the public with engravings of various kinds, suppose you give the following *Circle of the social and benevolent Affections, in their usual Gradation and with their respective Names*, a place in your MAGAZINE.   From   A. B.

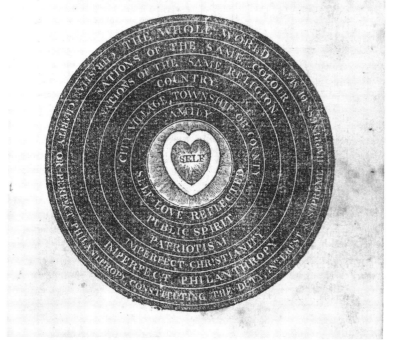

5. *Circle of Social and Benevolent Affections. This diagram of the ideal relationship between individual and society to be inculcated through parental instruction in the "social and benevolent affections" appeared in the* Columbian Magazine *for 3 February 1789 (p. 109). The text, circling outward from SELF in the center, reads:*

SELF
Family = Self Love Reflected;
City, Village, Township or County = Public Spirit;
third circle, *Country* = Patriotism;
fourth, *Nations of the Same Religion* = Imperfect Christianity;
fifth, *Nations of the Same Colour* = Imperfect Philanthropy;
outer circle, *The Whole World* = Christian Charity or Perfect Philanthropy,
Constituting the Duty, Interest, & Supreme Happiness of Man.

(Reproduction courtesy of John Carter Brown Library, Providence, R.I.)

6. *Ramsay House, 92 Broad Street, Charleston. Constructed before 1750, altered ca. 1816. According to Jonathan H.* Poston in The Buildings of Charleston *(Columbia: University of South Carolina Press, 1997), 172–73: "The first-floor plan is slightly asymmetrical with a rear stair hall and a front room . . . for [the doctor's] business. Upstairs is a front drawing room . . . much of the original woodwork survives, including several fully paneled rooms." David Ramsay purchased the house around 1784, and Martha, the third Mrs. Ramsay (1787–1811), spent the remainder of her life here. (Courtesy of the Historic Charleston Foundation. Photo taken in 1984 by P. Saunders.)*

7. *Staffordshire creamware jug, 9 ¼" high, circa 1800. This jug was among the type of household goods imported by Martha Laurens' father. The allegorical female holds a staff topped by the Liberty Cap. Transfer printed in black and inscribed "Rule Britannia for Britains [sic] Never Will Be Slaves"; verso "Bone and Flesh or John Bull in Moderate Condition." (William B. Goodwin Collection, Portland Museum of Art, Portland, Me. Photo by Gregory Welch.)*

MEMOIRS

OF

THE LIFE

OF

MARTHA LAURENS RAMSAY,

WHO DIED IN CHARLESTON, S. C.

ON THE 10th OF JUNE, 1811,

IN THE 52d YEAR OF HER AGE.

WITH AN APPENDIX,

CONTAINING EXTRACTS FROM HER DIARY, LETTERS, AND
OTHER PRIVATE PAPERS.

AND ALSO

FROM LETTERS WRITTEN TO HER, BY HER FATHER,
HENRY LAURENS, 1771—1776.

BY DAVID RAMSAY, M. D.

The experimental part of religion has generally a greater influence than its theory.
Mrs. Rowe's Posthumous Letter to Dr. Watts.

Fourth Edition....Armstrong's Second Edition.

BOSTON:
PRINTED BY SAMUEL T. ARMSTRONG,
AND SOLD AT HIS BOOKSTORE,
No. 50, CORNHILL.
1814.

8. Title page from the second New England edition of David Ramsay's print memorial to his wife, Memoirs of Martha Laurens Ramsay. The original was registered in Charleston 15 July 1811 by its proprietors, Martha's adult children—Eleanor Henry Laurens Ramsay, Martha Henry Laurens Ramsay, Catharine Henry Laurens Ramsay, and Sabina Elliott Ramsay—at the office of James Jervey, federal clerk, South Carolina District, in the "thirty-sixth year of the independence of the United States of America." (Courtesy South Caroliniana Library, University of South Carolina.)

moving sermon, from John xiv, 27. "Peace I leave with you, my peace I give unto you. Not as the world giveth, give I unto you. Let not your heart be troubled, neither let it be afraid."

January 29th, 1797. I no longer note the text, because my eldest daughter does, which I think a good means of fixing the Scriptures in her memory.

November 29th, 1797. Since the death of my dear little Jane, which happened the last day of July, after two months of anxiety and suspense, I have been in great weakness of body, and sadness of mind. During the last three weeks of her sickness, I was deeply exercised in soul. Some very especial sins and failures in duty, were set home on my conscience, and in her sickness I felt the rod due to my departures from God, and the unevenness of my walk. I endeavored to seek the Lord, by deep contrition, confession of sin, repentance, faith, and prayer. I sought the Lord by day, and spent almost every hour of the night, that I could spare from nursing, prostrate before him, taking hardly any bodily rest. I thought if the life of the child should be granted me, it would be an evidence, that the Lord, for Christ's sake, had forgiven me those things, which, with so many tears, and with such brokenness of spirit, I had bewailed before him; and there were appearances of her recovery; but, alas, how vain were my hopes. My child was taken, and I was plunged into the double sorrow of losing a most cherished and beloved infant, and of feeling the stroke, as a hiding of the Lord's face, and

9. *A page from the diary section of Martha Laurens Ramsay's* Memoirs. *(Courtesy South Caroliniana Library, University of South Carolina.)*

A Y E S.

Meſſrs. C. C. Pinckney, C. Gadſden, E. Rutledge, D. Ramſay, T. Heyward, jun. E. Dartel, I Motte, T. Gadſden, J. Mathews, E. Blake, T. Bee, D. Deſauſſure, T. Jones, J. F. Grimke, W. Johnſon, J. J. Pringle, J. Blake, D Stevens, D. Cannon, A. Toomer, H. Rutledge, J. Budd, F. Kinloch, W. Somerſall, M. Kalteiſen, R. Lulhington, N. Ruſſell, J. Smith, L. Morris, E. Lightwood, J. Edwards, C. Pinckney, J. Rutledge, A. Vanderhorſt, W. Read, J. Manigault, J. Reed, J. Toomer, H. Laurens, W. Montrie, H. Laurens, jun. G. Drayton, R. Hutſon, T. Fuller, J. Ladſon, R. Izard, jun. C. Drayton, W. Scott, J. Glaze, M. Waring, T. Waring, W. Poſtell, M. Hutchinſon, J. Dawſon, R. Izard, P. Smith, B. Smith, G. Manigault, W. Smith, J. Parker, jun. J. Deas, jun. J. Huger, T. Karwon, T. Screven, R. Daniel, L. Fogartie, I. Harleſton, I. Parker, P. Hamilton, G. Haig, J. Slann, R. P. Saunders, W. Waſhington, J. Lloyd, J. Crofkeys, J. Pettigrew J. Barnwell, I. Joyner, J. Kean, W. H. Wigg, R. Barnwell, W. Elliot, J. Stewart, I. Dubofe, L. Miles, S. Warren, R Withers, J. Mayrant, T. Horry, T. Waties, S. Smith, C. Kinloch, W. Allſton, jun. T. Allſton, D. Morral, W. Wilſon, A. Tweed, W. Frierſon, T. Legare, R. Muncreef, jun. D. Jenkins, H. Wilſon, I. Jenkins, E. Mikell, W. Smelie, J. Poſtell, J. Fenwick, J. Harleſtone, S. Stafford, H. Holcom, T. Hutſon, J. M'Pherſon, J. Maine, J. A. Cuthbert, J. Lightwood, J. Simmons, S. Deveaux, J. Palmer, H. Maham, S. Dubofe, J. Peyre, J. Cheſſut, J. Harris, S. Earle, L. J. Allſton, J. Thomas, jun. J. Miller, W. M'Caleb, H. Pendleton, J. Hunter, F. Cummins, W. Thompſon. P. Warley, L. Leſtarjette, J. Rumph, D. Bruce, L. Benton, W. Dewitt, C. Spencer, S. Taylor, R. Brownfield, B. Hicks, jun. S. Smith, W. Dunbar, J. Vince, W. Robiſon, J. Collins, J. Clark, T. Wadſworth.

N A Y S.

10. A list of South Carolinians voting for ratification of the federal constitution, including Martha's husband, David Ramsay (line 2), and brother Henry Laurens Jr. (line 14), in the Charleston City Gazette and Daily Advertiser, 28 May 1788. (Reproduced courtesy Charleston Library Society, Charleston, S.C.)

5 | Republican Marriage

The Politics of Matrimony (1787–1811)

In 1787 MARTHA LAURENS, already twenty-eight years old, married Dr. David Ramsay—a Charlestonian by adoption who was busy reestablishing his medical practice and political voice in postwar Charles Town—two years after her return from Europe.[1] That same year, the constitution for the new nation, which David vigorously supported, was being written, as well as his own first full-length published book, *History of the Revolution of South Carolina*. Martha had returned to Charleston, whether or not her heart still yearned for the potential marriage in France she had decided to forgo, and become her father's household manager. That meant, among other things, assuming responsibility for her sixteen-year-old sister, Polly, as well as her brother John's orphaned young daughter, Fanny (Frances Eleanor Laurens). Martha met the doctor while he was the attending physician to her Papa, whose health never really recovered from the damage inflicted during his incarceration in the Tower of London. His life-long diet undoubtedly helped make him hopelessly vulnerable to gout (the all-purpose diagnosis given for almost all of his illnesses).

Through the next twenty-four years of the Ramsays' "joint pilgrimage here on earth," Martha's diary-image for a remarkably companionate marriage in that era, her identity as Mrs. Ramsay involved surviving the "losses and crosses" of her husband's failed business ventures and other family tragedies. While her preserved writings never acknowledged inner needs that might imply a contradiction to her image of ideal wifehood, Martha's innate drive for self-development, spiritual autonomy, and efficient home management—all deeply entwined in nuptial standards of duty for women in her class and culture—had to be accommodated. And while there is little written indication of her own opinions, positive or negative, about any of her husband's civic or governmental works, a marital companion like Martha undoubtedly made her reactions known to him. Martha was able to assemble the "quilt pieces" of a wifely identity consonant with her intelligence, sense of self, and social, spiritual, and familial ideals in her own strong-minded way, all the while attempting to remain in the background, where she thought women belonged.[2]

The Ramsays' marriage may today be considered not only a "joint pilgrimage" but also a product of joint writing. Martha's life as a wife was enriched and intellectually deepened by her labors at copying David's letters and scholarly manuscripts; since his handwriting was the typical illegible physician's scrawl, her assistance must have been vital. And if there was an eighteenth-century husband who fully valued his wife as mental peer, she had him. Martha was sophisticated enough to read the scientific thought of the times and could thus assist David with searching his medical texts for symptoms and diagnoses.[3] At the end of Martha's life, with her permission and collaboration (in effect), David put himself in charge of *her* "text," his editorial skills shaping her written record in *Memoirs*.[4] David's appreciation of their intellectual and emotional mutuality was expressed in what appeared to have been a marriage motto among couples who similarly subscribed to a high-minded marital ideology. In a letter to his lifelong best friend, Benjamin Rush, thanking Rush's wife for her congratulations on his marrying Martha, David penned this graceful summarizing image: "Writing to you is the same as writing to her [Mrs. Rush] for I know you to be one."[5]

Inevitably, however, the biography of Martha he wrote to introduce *Memoirs* reveals "scenes of struggle between opposing tendencies" within the marriage and within Martha herself. In fact, today their partnership may be seen as a type of "act of linguistic domination," a literary phrase denoting the shaping of literary image to accord with a set scheme of interpretation. Perhaps consciously, perhaps unwittingly, Martha's mind-set and the vocabulary through which she expressed the few worries about her spouse that were allowed to stand in the preserved *Memoirs* convey a sense of carefully controlled words. And David Ramsay, out of his high intention to honor Martha through her own writings, apparently interpreted their marriage—the "primary political experience" of most adults—to fulfill his personal, authorial, and patriotic agenda that he believed she also shared.[6]

In *Parallel Lives,* a study of five nineteenth-century British couples, Phyllis Rose makes the trenchant observation that educated, cosmopolitan couples nearly always invoke the language of love when they are discussing transactions involving power.[7] From that angle of vision, some of Martha's prayerful observations about her spouse are a case in point; for example, "Oh be pleased to give my dear husband judgment, and steadiness of mind, in the duties of his profession, and preservation from the dangers of it."[8] The words Martha and David each used about their marriage suggest that the picture of the Ramsay marriage throughout *Memoirs* may well be an analogue of the shifting social order in the new republic—of the internal rule changes altering marital and parental discourse, and even citizenship itself. Marriage was *the* popular literary symbol for social and political rela- tions in the new republic, even if the institutions of family and state were not yet sharply differentiated into public and private arenas (as they would later become).

Already past twenty-five years of age when she met her father's physi- cian, Martha was thoroughly ready to respond to an established intellectual and professional suitor even if he was not handsome or wealthy; in fact, she might well have professed herself superior to such requirements. David was ten years her senior, already twice widowed, and he brought an infant son, John Witherspoon Ramsay (to whom his second wife, Frances Wither- spoon, had died giving birth in 1784), to their household. And he was var- iously involved in post-Revolutionary Charleston society—as a physician, historian, and (at that time) congressman. Having written Charles Willson Peale in November 1786 that he was courting the daughter of Henry Lau- rens, David received urgent admonition not to "lose a moment in attention to a Lady so worthy."[9] He followed that advice and they were married 23 January 1787; their first child, a daughter, was born in November 1787. One of her contemporaries remarked censoriously on Martha's undisguised pleasure at being pregnant and her announced goal of having many chil- dren "by the sweet Dr. Ramsay."[10] Ten more babies blessed their conjugal partnership, eight of whom survived Martha's own life.[11] "The *name* of the family always depends on the sons; *but its respectability, comfort and domes- tic happiness, . . .* on the daughters. . . . In Carolina where sickness and health, poverty and riches, frequently alternate in rapid succession, wives and daughters bear incredible fatigues and privations with exemplary for- titude and accommodating propriety," her husband would proclaim.[12]

David Ramsay wrote this uncommonly egalitarian tribute to the female population of South Carolina because of his wife, a woman who "adorned every relation she sustained, and filled with dignity and useful- ness every sphere of life in which she moved," according to an admiring clergy friend. This tone prefigured that of the *Memoirs,* his published tes- tament after her death in 1811.[13] Attributing family harmony a bit fulsomely to the female sphere of influence was David Ramsay's means of fulfilling his own political-idealist motives and registering the overall significance of women in the regional social order.

Dr. Ramsay could not openly acknowledge, if he articulated it to him- self, the oppressiveness of that culture for women like Martha, but he could endorse and emphasize the religious Self she had constructed—her "consolation under afflictions, disappointments and trials" that taught, more impressively than any precept, "the value of piety, and the comfort of submission to the will of God." Her text exists two centuries later because he viewed her life and writings in that light and welcomed an editorial task in relation to them. That it also reconstructed a specific domestic culture—the marriage of a busy professional couple in an urbanizing Charleston who lived into the first decade of the new nineteenth century—plus his wife's perception that kinkeeping and "relative duties" were her form of "citizenship," is an added benefit for today's readers. Turning from Laurens family letters as the primary source of cultural information about Martha, *Memoirs* and the doctor's own correspondence become the primary window to the interplay between the private, domestic lives of David and Martha Ramsay—their joint life and times.[14]

Marriage and its meanings for this Charlestonian couple make visible the strands of republicanism, marital ideology, and political perspective—the "politics of context." In his portrait of their marriage, David's Protestant Calvinist language logically emphasized the reigning cultural expectation that their marital compact must portray ideals of kinship, parenthood, and citizenship. For Martha these multiple strands, and the language in which they were expressed, were not separate but rather interlocking facets of the identity that she, an elite, educated wife, was expected to inhabit.[15]

The South Carolina locale of the Ramsay marriage contributed to their intrafamily dynamics more subtly than it would in nineteenth-century Charleston, when regional consciousness intensified through conflict with northern abolitionists. Born and educated in Pennsylvania and New Jersey, David had become a resident by choice and adoption after finishing his medical training in 1775—while Martha, though born in Carolina, was by temperament and Laurens' training impatient with the languor and self-indulgence often explained as a feature of the climate. For example, she believed that people suffered the "extremity of Carolina summers" far more if they were "listless, complaining and unemployed" than if they kept busy—having absorbed her father's brisk denial of the effects of weather on productivity.[16] Though their marriage undoubtedly evoked much soul-searching about slavery for Martha, and although David's known opposition to slave importing cost him an election in 1788 (amplified in chapter 7), *Memoirs* reveals only minimal reference to slavery in Martha's and David's own words—a social avoidance uniformly observed among most

white Christians of the times, north and south. In contrast, her father's letters, though his fortune had been built on the slave trade, leave a more visible trail of doubt and personal misery about its morality.[17]

Historians today know more about the evolution of the constitutional
document itself, phrase by phrase, than about the daily experience of families living under the Constitution that evolved. The microcosm of the
Ramsay marriage illuminates some of the changes and continuities that
people were experiencing in the new republic. One change saw the popu-
larity of the eighteenth-century rationalist mind-set begin to wane.
Upwardly mobile Americans like David, filled with a new, almost romantic sense of individual possibilities, seemed to overpower the elegancies and
balances of the Enlightenment worldview, producing a more practical
"didactic Enlightenment"—while females like Martha continued to exert
what psychic and spiritual balance they could on such emotional and commercial entrepreneurialism.[18] Another change affected the issue and locus
of authority—in personal and marital relationships, in educational prescription, in attitudes toward government, and in religion itself. The everyday experiences of a highly educated wife and mother in a period that was
more "revolutionary" in its effect on the white professional class in
Charleston than the war itself dramatize quiet but far-reaching existential
changes in internal and interpersonal rule structures in ways that political
rhetoric can only imply.[19]

One continuity amid such profound change was the symbolism of
marriage itself. An idealized view of male-female cooperation in marriage
was the standard; as historian Sheila Skemp notes in her biography of
another eighteenth-century woman, "in an otherwise egalitarian, indi-
vidualistic, and competitive society, marriage remained the single most
important institution [still] embracing the values of paternalism, self-
sacrifice, and deference." For men, personal happiness was part of republican citizenship, the expected, logical result of a good marriage; for women,
marriage gave political significance to the republican ideal of "disinterestedness." Wives were expected to embody that classical dimension of
virtue—self-dedication to a greater good.[20] Confident that he articulated
his wife's view as well as his own, David Ramsay exulted about the constitution in the first year of their marriage (1787), "I think it ought to be a
matter of joy *to every citizen* that so excellent a form of government has
passed the convention." Its "three necessary [structural] checks" . . . are "an
apt *illustration of the Trinity.* The whole power is from one source that is *the
people,* & yet that is diversified into three modifications with distinct per-

sonal properties to each." Among *the people* constituting the new nation, of course, wives were given no distinct public properties except in the customary closing salutation between close male friends, "With Mrs. Ramsay's best respects to Mrs. Rush."[21] Citizenship through one's male relatives remained the reality for women after the Revolution. Whatever their social or class background, or political sympathies, wives' republican idealism was refracted along "the fault line of gender."[22]

Martha Laurens Ramsay's marital republicanism held religion to be the indispensable medium for both the personal, familial aspects of marriage and the external political sphere. "Private" domestic virtue was still the fundamental ground of public virtue and thus of republicanism itself. And public virtue or "perfect disinterestedness"—a commitment to the ideal civil government that was intended to be informed and shaped by Anglo-Protestant religious ideals instead of private self-interest—was still credited philosophically by people like the Ramsays as the only adequate foundation for public leadership.[23]

These widely acclaimed religious-republican ideals were, of course, applied idiosyncratically, perhaps more as ideal than actuality. In the Ramsay marriage, for example, egalitarianism was an honored principle, except when the future of sons was the issue. David Jr. would never be able to become a businessman like his very wealthy grandfather Laurens—but, like his father, he was expected to "rank among the men of literary and public consequence." Similarly, the ambition to accumulate personal wealth and status was not appropriate to the new republican view of virtue, except if it should happen to be an incidental by-product of David Ramsay's own patriotic projects, like investing in a canal or the new experimental engines driven by steam. Not surprisingly, then as now, psychic and social differences between David and Martha as spouses were most visible around money, child rearing, and the marital relationship itself.[24]

Religion as the framework for a polemic on marriage and women's citizenship was not unusual when *Memoirs* was published, unlikely as it seems to twentieth-century readers. If Martha Laurens Ramsay had been less well read, less high-minded, and less conscious of her own internal standards for spiritual excellence, she might have felt freer to write her secret diary in a less formulaic style of self-expression. But being analytic and sophisticated, and determined to avoid the foolishness she abhorred (female babbling, as she had called it in her youthful meditations), there was no other option. In her mental world the language of elation was religious: "Lord how shall I praise thee? . . . my soul is filled with thankfulness and my mouth with praise."[25] The language of puzzlement was religious: "oh day, blackened with sin and spotted with transgression . . . when shall I advance in the spiritual life and not thus wound my peace?"[26] The language of suffering, pain, and despair was religious: "How lately hath thine afflictive Providence been wringing my heart, with a twofold anguish: the loss of my sweet baby, and the considerations of those sins which required this chastisement."[27] The language of marital anxiety was religious: "the conflict with affliction is great; my husband is under trials and straits, which make my heart ache for him, and for myself, as tenderly feeling and sharing in all his griefs."[28] Her understanding of "citizenship" (the term itself an anomaly for females) was religious: "[may I] watch against indolence, remembering that the Christian life is a warfare and that the kingdom of Heaven must be taken with a holy violence, and cannot be obtained by the slothful."[29] "Afflictive Providences [are salutary; they] force our consciences to a stand, make us examine and try our ways, and lift our hearts as well as hands to God in the heavens." Mrs. Ramsay was similar to a majority of Americans in her time, including less well-educated workers, shopkeepers, lawyers and merchants: republicanism as ideal and as a mode of life was inseparable from and contained within her Protestant Christian mind-set. Biblical religion was their major vein of imagery, analogy, and literary and political voice.[30]

Martha's "literary remains" demonstrate the depth, breadth, and complexity with which she employed religious language, concepts, and perceptions. "She daily brought before her Maker the cases of herself, family, friends, neighbors, and sometimes of strangers whose situation was known to be interesting," her husband recalled. The most revealing connection between religious diction and republican marital symbolism in the Ramsay text was the language of submission: "Lord, not my will but thine be done; only be pleased to give me the spirit of submission and humble waiting upon thee." Martha's willed self-sacrifice, which her husband praised as wifely subservience for a greater good, fulfilled the ideal of marital harmony. In *Memoirs* that language was the wife's, celebrated as a political (and nuptial) recommendation by the husband. His tone about her religion expressed his quintessential republican idealism.[31]

The relationship between citizenship and self-sacrifice or submission was, however, a subtext in Martha's written self-analysis. Men like David Ramsay and his contemporaries often used religious aphorism to make republican points, but unlike women they also had a political language— while terms like *power, representation,* and *checks and balances* appear rarely, if at all, in the writings of eighteenth-century women (with the brilliant exception of Abigail Adams' famous letter about taxes). David's justification for publishing Martha's writings posthumously lay in the way her language of submission exemplified his understanding of republican as well as wifely—and, of course, religious—virtue. Martha's model was his trumpet call awakening *all* citizens to virtue through religion. "The tendency [of religion] to promote human happiness and its sovereign efficacy to tranquilize the mind and administer consolation under afflictions" was the only ideal powerful enough, both Ramsays believed, to elicit cooperative citizenship under the new constitution. They knew their friend Rush had pressured a very reluctant Mrs. John Witherspoon to leave her native Scotland by means of a biblical image; that is, that she must follow her husband "like another Sarah" to the Promised Land as Abraham's wife had followed him. In Mrs. Witherspoon's case, Princeton, New Jersey, was the Promised Land where her husband would assume presidency of the College of New Jersey and advance the cause of higher education in the new nation. Her consent-submission was essential to his leadership image. [32]

David and Martha's causal, instrumental view of religion's relation to citizenship made them "puritanical republicans," citizens who sought "a moral solution" to establishing and preserving the new republic. Agrarian republicans, on the other hand, believed that "better arrangements"—better socioeconomic structures, a better governmental environment—was necessary to ensure the new nation's health. A significant point of difference in their marriage was that David Ramsay, by temperament, was one of the nation's early environmentalists, although his writings employed a puritan-republican vocabulary. As a progressive medical leader in Charleston, he promoted higher urban sanitation standards (including clean drinking water) and civic improvements like a canal to speed the transportation of crops to the harbor, and even a new Fulton steamboat for use in the Charleston harbor. As part of his environmentalism, words themselves were a manipulable element. "The Press, the pulpit and all the powers of Eloquence should be exerted to counter-act that ruinous propensity we have for foreign superfluities." Words were perhaps his most congenial environment, since he managed them with more success than most other elements in his career. [33]

The Laurens standard of citizenship had been pronounced by Martha's father before she was born: citizens are responsible to and for the community. "Obedience to Law is the Duty of every Member of Community & it should be each ones study to cause as little trouble as possible to those who take upon them the burthen of seeing our Laws duly executed . . . *private Interest must not be set in competition with public good*."[34] Reared in that paternal ideal, Martha felt bound to uphold rather than challenge the gender and marriage systems of patriarchal culture, which meant supporting the implicit equation of dependence and womanhood despite its incongruity for a person of her accomplishments. In contrast with the forward-looking modernity she pursued in her standards of mothering and teaching, Martha's diary dialogues, filled with discontent over unspecified trials, begged God for the opposite: an all-but-stoic equilibrium.[35]

On the other hand, she had been raised as the apple of her father's eye—not prepared to be second in anything except to her older brother John. Martha's republicanism was cast in and through eighteenth-century Anglo-American gender prescriptions, even as she inhaled the same idealism of independence enjoyed by white property-owning males like her brother. At the same time, her self-image would not have been able to tolerate the thought of social chaos resulting from any abrogation of wifely, marital, or familial duty. Probably she wouldn't have had to write and pray so earnestly for the submission of her will to God's, nor would her principled wifely subservience to David have loomed so large for him, if in fact she really were unassertive and docile. Submission was her goal in religious and marital achievement.[36] Martha's religiously encoded selfhood, invisible within her ideal marriage, stands as an analogue for the impotence secretly lamented by many intelligent, ambitious women in a male-defined adult world.

David Ramsay's marital republicanism was visible first in the fact that he conceived a print memorial for a female, his wife, and second in the unequivocal way he credited her as his intellectual equal—the equal of any man. He called her his superior, not just his equal, in household skills and management, in her disciplined and productive use of time, in her "discharge of relative duties" (a phrase meaning the nurture and honoring of relatives), in her abilities and mental range as an educator, and in the depth of her religious authority as spiritual intercessor for their family.[37] But the most interesting example of her husband's republicanism was his uneasy discussion of Martha's domestic subservience to male authority. That he bothered to address it was significant in and of itself. Editor Ramsay portrayed this remarkable feature—subservience to the authority of the male head of household—as *her choice*, his wife's insistence on his primacy as a matter of principle. He argued via textual polemic, pitting the Bible against what was then avant-garde feminist philosophy (especially Mary Woll-stonecraft). Ephesians 5:22–24 made his point: "Wives, submit yourselves unto your own husbands as unto the Lord, For the husband is the head of the wife, even as Christ is the head of the church." Wives who embodied this ideal could halt the dissolution of virtue in the republic, he proposed; against the widespread diminishment of respect for traditional authority and custom in their times, David offered his wife's model as the ideal instrument to shore up the moral and social order.[38]

He began by describing Mrs. Ramsay's standard of domestic felicity: to love, honor, and obey her husband, in effect endowing him with all her worldly goods (the King James biblical language in the Episcopal Office of Matrimony in the *Book of Common Prayer*). This was the more impressive because she was a sophisticated woman, "well acquainted with modern theorists who contend for equality of the sexes; and few females could support claims to that equality on better grounds than she." The triumph of their marital republicanism, David Ramsay pronounced, was that a female paragon like Martha, who certainly merited independence from him, her husband, "yielded all pretension on this score"—out of choice, out of principle, and "in conformity to holy writ that outweighed whole volumes of human reasoning." He assured potential skeptics that such scriptural "reasonings" and rational principles were not "*imposed* on the subject of these memoirs," by him, by their clergy friends, or by anyone. Ramsay the idealist resisted admitting dependence (the essence of anti-republicanism) in one he admired vastly, to the point of implicitly questioning the male marital preeminence that was the cultural standard. Whether he intended his pro-woman thesis to embrace all women in the republic, however, especially those less superior than Martha, is questionable.[39]

To present-day readers, the editor-husband's long footnote elaborating his wife's high marital principle (and his calling to immortalize it) suggests a certain defensiveness. David Ramsay's peroration in this footnote might today be seen as overkill: "Such were the principles and conduct of a wife who had *read* [Mary] Woolstonecraft's *Rights of Women* but *studied* her *Bible* . . . as the standard of faith and practice." Portraying Martha as fulfillment of the canons of puritan republicanism—under scriptural rather than temporal or cultural authority—would, he believed, disarm doubters and skeptics. His hyperbole led him to overlook an essential nuance of Wollstonecraft's thesis about independence—that husband and wife enjoy a reciprocal independence primarily because they exercise interdependent functions within a family.[40]

David Ramsay idealized a competent woman whose principles "led her to make all her conduct subservient to her husband's happiness." Piling proof on proof, he recalled that Martha "gave up every separate scheme," possibly a reference to his use of her inheritance from father and uncle, although South Carolina law precluded her retaining legal control over those resources after marriage. She "identified her views and pursuits" with his: joining his church and leaving hers; supporting his political positions instead of harking back to her father's; perhaps most tellingly, beginning to express moral disapproval over the institution of slavery, although that would never appear in print. She "arranged all domestic concerns" to provide him with time for writing his books and delivering the great civic orations he so much enjoyed. She agreed with his enlivening history with celebratory biographies of "our Great characters," not just because he included her father and brother but also because "[such idealizing] is quite a republican custom and sanctioned by the example of the illustrious antients." Martha, having arranged for him "as complete exemption from the burden of domestic cares as was possible," even assisted in troublesome medical diagnoses. Here Dr. Ramsay was remarkably forthright in his era, crediting the medical competence she established during her French residence. "With the same virtuous habits and the same energy of character," she schooled herself in his medical texts, becoming an autodidact in the diseases of women and children. Since she, like her father, was a light sleeper, needing only "four hours in twenty-four," she was the one who intercepted the requests for his professional presence in the "hours allotted to repose" and "so arranged things that there was the least inconvenience to him."[41]

The capstone of Martha's canonization, in his eyes, was her avoidance of controversy, gracefully and on principle, in politics and religion—the two areas unfailingly contentious in marriage as well as in less intimate social exchange. In David Ramsay's pantheon of republican virtues, harmony was the true patriotism and the necessary counterweight to the new century's belligerent factionalism. He reflected the cultural expectation that the wife's role was harmony, bragging that Martha "*shunned all political controversy*" and idealizing prayers as the only patriotic service she would offer her country. She also wisely avoided theological "disputes on minor unessential points . . . injurious to peace, harmony and the best interests of religion." Clearly she exemplified a 1790 summary of "Rules and Maxims for Matrimonial Happiness." The eighth rule bluntly advised: "Dispute not with him be the occasion what it will; but . . . deny yourself the trivial satisfaction of . . . gaining the better of an argument . . . [and thereby] risqué a quarrel or create a heart-burning which it is impossible to know the end of."[42]

In the second edition of *Memoirs*, a belated encomium (added to the preface) by the Rev. Benjamin Palmer summarized that heroic characteristic more elegantly—Martha's "wonderful faculty" of masking her own "uncommon superiority" beneath a veil of "apparent unawareness."[43] To the Ramsays' circle of high-minded civic leaders and literati, public partisanship was a disturbing development. In 1786 Dr. Ramsay, then in the U.S. Congress in New York City, first expressed his disgust at the emerging disunity, noting that "there was more patriotism in a village (in 1775) than is now in the thirteen states."[44] An 1801 editorial in the *National Intelligencer and Washington Advertiser* trumpeted a unified nation, "undivided in political opinion," as one of the "accumulating triumphs of republicanism."[45]

The more ideological the observer in the early 1790s, the easier it was to trace threats to the new republic as emanating from unsound principles—historian Forest McDonald's puritan-republicans.[46] The Ramsays' federalism believed sound principles were the essential basis of national survival, "sound" meaning biblical Protestant unanimity of values and views held by educated, virtuous citizens. People must "obtain that knowledge indispensable to the support of Republicanism, and implant the principles of virtue and rational freedom in the minds of the rising generation," intoned one of the many pro-republican essays in the print public sphere. Dozens of such formulations, many written by their friend and fellow-historian Rev. Jeremy Belknap, provided a politico-religious creed that Dr. Ramsay endorsed with his portrayal of Martha.[47]

If the Ramsays were linguistically and emotionally united in their version of republicanism, however, a point of troubling disunity was money. First, David Ramsay's more humble origins led him to romanticize Martha's background. His own words about Martha's young adult experience exhibit bedazzlement: "from nurse's chamber in a remote country [southern France] . . . to head of the table for a minister plenipotentiary" in Paris. That she escaped moral and sexual ruination in such head-turning settings was due to the solid religious footing that "kept her from intoxication and follies," he pronounced. But promoters of meritocracy were vulnerable to confusing their own financial improvement with higher societal rank, and Dr. Ramsay was no exception. As a newly graduated physician, he confided to friend Benjamin Rush, "I am disposed to be thankful both to God & man for settling me in Charleston, where I hope I shall be able to be some good to the public, and especially to myself." He was the self-made man who "married up" through each of his three wives, a trajectory into political and historical significance as instinctive for him as Martha's Carolina aristocrat birthright.[48]

At the time of their marriage, 1787, Martha was still cocooned in her father's legendary prewar wealth and status. Readers might like to think that a woman born as an heiress enjoyed "a large proportion of temporal blessings," David's biographical introduction to *Memoirs* cautioned, but in Martha's case, "prosperity and adversity alternated. Good and Evil followed each other in succession." By the 1790s, any hopes of a monetary cushion from her Laurens inheritance was gone. David's historiographic instinct led him to list explanatory economic facts in a footnote to convince readers who were unaware of the Laurenses' devastating financial decline. First, Georgia lands that Martha inherited from her father "produced nothing but the annual taxes" for fifteen years; finally sold in 1793, the buyer was never able to raise the $30,000 sale price, so the properties constituted a total loss. Second, two houses Martha had inherited from her Uncle James Laurens burned in 1796; then in 1804 a hurricane ruined the sale of another portion of her inherited land, along with most of her husband's remaining properties. (He neglected to mention his own bankruptcy proceedings in 1798 and the lawsuits filed against him by Martha's only surviving brother, Henry Laurens Jr.)[49] His list concluded with the acknowledgment that his investment in the Santee Canal company in 1792—$25,000 of her patrimony— was a patriotic gesture that returned no income to him or anyone. From hindsight, patriot Ramsay could see that it had been "privately ruinous," but at that point he still maintained it would one day be "publicly beneficial."[50]

Martha's diary in 1795 revealed her nuptial loyalty but also her ambivalence about their financial troubles. She vowed "to make no unnecessary demands on my dear & affectionate husband, that [his] desire of largely supplying my wants or wishes may not be a snare to him, to make him engage in large schemes for riches." She did not want her past to goad him into unwise expenditures. Besides, wifely ethics required that she accept some of the burden. "To this I feel particularly bound, by my father's having been permitted to give us so small a portion of his fortune, compared to what he had declared to be his intention." Unsparing honesty made her add: "on the strength of which I lived less frugally in the first years of my marriage than I should have done." While her husband made idealistic investments and was constantly engaged in litigation—in marked contrast with her father's conservative approach to business and money—Martha

[margin annotation: financial troubles]

struggled to make her peace with their principled poverty in the year when her mental stability was already under siege (chapter 8).[51]

In actuality, her taste and manners as a child of the Charleston elite were fundamentally more egalitarian than husband David's: she had less need to make a big impression. In 1778, adolescent Martha had loftily disclaimed snobbish class distinction: "I should have no good idea of any [believer] who could not delight in a sermon, however excellent, that was not delivered with the embellishments of oratory, or could not like any book which was not dressed with the graces of fine language. A diamond though unpolished possesses intrinsic worth." Even more loftily, middle-aged Martha would write her son: "I feel more pride, more consciousness of being a lady, by having everything about my person and the persons of my children and household in the plainest style of decency than I could by endeavoring to cover our modest circumstances by a tinsel veil of finery." Martha's birthright identity as a Laurens sustained an unassailable corner of self-worth for her, except in her dark year of depression, 1795—when financial woes, inability to protect the family reputation, and anxiety over sin in general overwhelmed her.[52]

A difference of opinion about their eldest son's educational development and preparation for citizenship was one of their last recorded disagreements. Dr. Ramsay had been eager to boast that his son attended his own alma mater in Princeton, in company with other sons of the Carolina elite. Martha knew that a boy David Jr.'s age would be much "better off at a grammar-school than among juniors at college," and much less vulnerable to being misled by false companions.[53] The father prevailed, against Martha's better judgment.

Although David and Martha were Federalists, David revered egalitarianism almost as a sanction for his poor-boy-makes-good ambitions. Martha's egalitarianism was deeply principled, except, like mothers the world over, for her own children. Her English friend Miss Futurell, who helped Martha as a nanny and tutor when the children were little, assured Martha that her son David Jr. would indeed become a model citizen, one day. "He knows the truth; he has imbibed sound principles; from time to time in his life he has thought very seriously; he will do you no discredit; and he will become a valued member of society."[54] Unfortunately no such written prophecy was bestowed on the Ramsay daughters: educated, serious young women minus the all-important dowries to underwrite a suitable marriage connection were historically easy to dismiss, no matter how intelligent and useful they were.

Incidentally, those same daughters must have heard their mother tell a bizarre incident harking back to her years in France. An aggressive potential suitor had been outwitted through careful planning—the third anecdote they thought appropriate for insertion in the 1845 edition of their mother's *Memoirs* (published by the American Sunday School Union). While living with her uncle and aunt, "a gentlemen of latitudinarian sentiments paid his addresses to her, and a plan was laid to bring about a forced marriage." Martha resolved to escape the snare by concealing herself on his next visit, but told Aunt Mary her hiding place would be kept secret to prevent the aunt from having to lie. "Her aunt was interrogated and with a charged pistol pointed at her head, was told to reveal [Martha's whereabouts] but her character for truth was such that there was no doubt about her ignorance." The rejected lover then "swore vengeance upon the head of anyone who should marry Miss L. Some years after, the lover happened to be in the same house. Mrs. Ramsay as she then was, saw him and made some excuse to retire" without his awareness that she had become Mrs. Ramsay. "Her husband and former lover passed a very pleasant evening together, never suspecting each others' relation to Mrs. R." The Frenchman who courted her in Vigan must have traveled all the way to South Carolina, since David Ramsay was never able to afford Europe travel. The story's likely intended moral (and reason for insertion in that later edition) was to underscore Martha's commitment to truthfulness rather than to evoke a more adventurous and romantic image of her.[55]

Martha's primary cross to bear in her "joint pilgrimage" as Mrs. Ramsay was uncomplaining submission to financial hardships. She was the one who thanked God that they had not been reduced to selling their remaining household slaves in 1806. She was the one who reminded God in 1801 that both she and David relied on divine Providence for "the wisdom, prudence and discretion" so urgently needed in their money troubles. It was her religious sensibilities that were offended when her husband casually referred to the unexpected payment of a long-due medical fee as "luck." She abhorred luck or "chance" as a godless concept and recorded this morality tale in her diary to ward off such inappropriate or dangerously irreverent language. "June 2, 1808: My dear husband who is certainly a true believer and a great noter of Providence, having received two dollars from a casual patient said to me, 'here are two dollars which I have got just by chance.' I said thank ye but don't, at this time, when we are in such want of money, say that any comes *by chance*. He smiled with his usual kindness, and said, 'I only meant that I got it from a passing and not a stated patient.' About two hours after, he sent me up twenty dollars, just after I had been earnestly praying that the Lord . . . would send some supply to my necessities and those of my family which were very great. And covering the twenty dollars was the enclosed paper which I will keep with this note on it, to remind me of the great goodness of my God." Dr. Ramsay's note of capitulation—included in *Memoirs*—read: "Twenty dollars, not sent by chance, but by God. An unexpected volunteer payment of a doubtful old debt!"[56]

That vignette illustrated the psychic chasm between husband and wife that had to be bridged by Martha's language of submission. To a daughter of Henry Laurens, money was the economic bedrock of a mutual marriage—something to be counted on and counted up. Financial responsibility was too important to treat lightly, to be separated from religious duty, to merely "happen." Money was an unacknowledged component of Martha's sense of well-being and of God's favor, not just the basis of her family's physical survival. For her, spiritual signs were as visible in financial transactions as in sermons, fire, earthquakes, and sudden deaths. "On the evening of this day, Dec. 21, 1806, I . . . received a mercy, an answer of prayer, almost next to miraculous: a sum of money exactly suited to a particular engagement I had entered into for the first of January, with more of trust in the Lord than of outward certainty about it. This sum of money coming to me so unexpectedly, with regard to the quarter from where I received it, overcame me perhaps even more than some afflictive circumstances have done; for I felt . . . as if I should faint and die from the mingled emotions of surprise, gratitude and awe." David's view of money, by contrast, was cavalier, instrumental, and unrealistic.[57]

Both Ramsays saw themselves as serving the republic by guarding public virtue rhetorically. While David wrote books and gave speeches, Martha channeled her wifely principles into the design of an education to "give *a right bias* to the energies and sensibilities" of her young. The right bias she intended elevated virtue in the republic above the taint of commercialism.[58] Only when the "ruling passion" of "self love" was replaced with "perfect disinterestedness" would Patriotism, the "noblest of all social virtues," truly reign.[59] Here again she departed company from her husband, whose virtue had room for enlightened self-interest. Martha's innate approach to instructing virtue echoed her father's blend of Anglican Calvinist piety and duty, Lockean practical psychology, and Scottish common sense. Martha was no sentimentalist. Though she and her daughters read fiction celebrating the personal fulfillment to be found in domestic virtue, like *Pamela* she was too much her father's daughter to content herself with cultivating the "culture of the heart" only in her home school. Her larger societal responsibility embodied the Spartan view that women were to evoke virtue from men.[60]

Children in the new republic—in her case, her numerous offspring, Laurens nieces and cousins, children of household slaves, and young male boarders—all had to be convinced to merge their ambitions with the larger good. Public virtue depended on private virtue cultivated through that particular kind of "right bias." Educated parents like Martha welcomed that spiritual challenge as something they could actually *do*, in contrast with their Calvinist forebears' helplessness in the face of a doctrine like election to salvation, and infant damnation. Martha gladly became a pedagogue of virtue as well as of intellect, never fully repudiating the Calvinist view of human nature's original sinfulness but energetically investing herself in the mother's new role of citizen formation. She substituted the language of virtue for the terms "salvation" and "conversion," a sign of her modernity. "Using Burkitt's help and guide to christian families," she strove to enlist all her kin in the behavior-management system she honored, which alone would produce the principles guaranteeing virtue.[61] Martha focused on practicalities rather than belaboring theological doctrines: she aimed to establish the attitudes and habits of virtue before their opposite could take root in her children's goals and actions.

For example, in an impassioned letter to her son at Princeton in 1810, she worried that his "chief ambition [was] to wish at least to be *richer* than your father and mother, without caring whether you are as wise or as good." Martha equated intensity of effort with nobility of motive, one of her measurements for the right bias to energies and sensibilities. She saw herself engaged in a "cosmic struggle between the forces of industry and idleness" over the souls of her children. For her, effort itself was "the battleground for personal salvation," since it was under human and not merely divine control.[62]

Her specific calling, in her mothering and teaching, was to bind her children-pupils into the obligations of citizenship with strong emotional, not just intellectual, ties. Public Virtue was that "sacred precept of doing good to others as we would have others do unto us," but not just to ourselves—"to society in general." An essay in *The Columbian* by Honorius cataloged the traits of public virtue; they were communal, not individual. Private virtue's familial base linked citizens with each other, and in turn with the republic: "The virtuous man who beholds *the wife of his bosom* . . . and *his tender infants* . . . cannot surely indulge himself in . . . extravagance,

[or] indolence . . . [his virtue will inform his life] *As a son . . . as a husband . . . as a father . . .* ; and *as a man,* benevolent to men."[63] Honorius had no need to address female virtue because he and his readers knew that was subsumed under the male's.

Wifely republicanism, then, was domestically "political" for Martha, shaping her management of the relationships in the home. Her contribution to the establishment of public virtue led her to stud letters to children with maxims and apothegms of private virtue. Her talented daughters were shaped by her own feminine credo of gender compromise: they must actively manage their lives, not let life just "happen" to them. But they must also be "ever ready to reciprocate the tender charities of domestic endearment, ever cheerfully sacrificing something of their own convenience for the advancement of their brothers." Her male progeny, properly armed with private virtues, were directed to citizenly virtue in the public sphere but not "to vie with the sons of rich planters . . . whose lives are as useless as their expenses."[64] In her firm maternal oversight, each of Martha's children must be answerable for his or her own citizenship in this world and the next.

If the Ramsays' own economic slippage made Martha hypersensitive to the interrelatedness of financial irresponsibility and a shortage of virtue in the republic, she had public rhetorical support for seeing self-indulgent "happiness" as a symptom of her culture's moral decay. "Our citizens seem to be seized with a general emulation to surpass each other in every article of expense," Thomas Reese fumed in a 1788 Charleston publication; "they contract debts which they have no rational prospect of discharging." Abhorrence of debt-contracting without clear prospects of repayment was a Laurens taboo that raised an unspoken barrier between the Ramsays— between the pre-Revolutionary Laurens business principles, and the more adventurous investments of postwar entrepreneurs like her husband.[65]

In 1799 she recorded in her diary a moving meditation about David: "Bless my very dear husband; point out to him the path of duty; make all his way plain; bring him through these worldly perplexities; make me a comfort and blessing to him and to his children while my life is prolonged; and so help him in his difficulties and trials that he may say, this is the Lord's doing and it is marvelous in our eyes." Whatever the actual references behind that prayer, it ended with the following poignant plea: "In God is my trust; in his hands are the hearts of all men. I will not then fear what man can do. May [God] enable us to be just and upright to all, and not permit any to oppress and be hard to us."[66]

Probably Martha's ultimate gesture of republicanism had been her marriage to an "unpolished jewel" of a husband, known for his twisted stockings and disheveled jacket along with his optimism, political idealism, and "northward" disapproval of the labor system relying on slavery.[67] But the solid financial foundation she needed to undergird that idealism and the ambitions of their idealized joint hopes[68]—making them affordable, so to speak—demanded more religious forbearance and exterior social dignity in the long run than she had anticipated. In covenant and partnership with God and Dr. Ramsay, Martha juggled the modern, rational sensibility of the new American woman within a Calvinist-language armory of objectives and ideals—not an easy combination. The Ramsays defined themselves in civic responsibility as devoted to the mental and moral welfare of their community. Within their home on Broad St., religion and republicanism attempted to walk hand in hand although the burdens of each were not distributed equally between them. David Ramsay offered his histories—of the Revolutionary War, of medicine, of the Circular Church, and of the first president of the nation—and his marital idealization as political and spiritual contribution to the new nation's virtue. He made an American adage out of Martha's "maxim" that citizens were "not to complain of God but to complain to God."[69] In that regard, impecunious but high-minded citizens like the Ramsays, who calculated their worth in terms of principles rather than wealth, believed they bore the most crucial of all responsibilities in the era of nation-building.

Ironically, the *Memoirs* of David Ramsay's wife may indeed have turned out to be his lasting contribution to the new republic, not so much for its political influence or power to inspire reform but for its preservation of the marital and domestic tableau of its time. Her memorial volume provided an angle of vision into their joint efforts to craft a republican marriage, and actually embodied the ideal expressed in a self-congratulatory advertisement for an end-of-the-century compilation entitled *The American Spectator, or Matrimonial Preceptor.* This idealization proclaimed the new nation's grand belief that "the female mind is, probably, no where [else] so generally cultivated, and adorned with that knowledge and sentiment, which qualify for conjugal, and parental relations." In America, "THE RIGHTS OF WOMEN, as well as of MEN, are acknowledged and[,] a few instances excepted, in which the application of *American* or *Republican* to the title of *Husband* is a mere solecism [—] they [husbands and wives] are caressed as the first and dearest friends of their partners."[70] Martha's matrimonial politics, including all the mutual affection and proto-citizenship credits that gleam through her husband's adoring tribute, encompassed all the patriarchal assumptions and compromises that no woman in the new republic could avoid.

6 | "Relative Duties"

Women's Proto-Citizenship in the Constitutional Era

HAD SHE BEEN ASKED ABOUT her citizenship in 1788, the year in which South Carolina ratified the new national constitution, Martha Laurens Ramsay would likely have quoted an answer from the *Great Catechism of the New Protestant Episcopal Church in the USA* (1784). The church's teaching from her childhood on prescribed her (and all human beings') role in life on this earth as "laboring diligently in my family and station."[1] She had been married just a year (and had given birth to her first child) to a physician husband who had been active in state politics since 1776, and who, elected to the government of South Carolina, was enthusiastic about the new federal constitution. Martha herself was no novice in the role of laboring diligently in family maintenance. Previously, Martha's contributions to family and station had found her managing her invalid uncle's household in a foreign country and directing a village school to teach the local French children to read. She had survived a protracted battle of wills with her Papa about her first matrimonial life choice; she had served as hostess at her father's diplomatic dinners in Europe during the peace negotiations of 1783–1784; and recently she had hovered over her father's poor physical health and helped him petition Congress to recover war damages and unpaid expenses for his service to the government.[2] This religiously ingrained understanding of duty sustained her as she reestablished herself in her war-marked city after a decade abroad.

When an ill Henry Laurens gave his matrimonial blessing to her union with the twice-widowed physician and patriot Dr. Ramsay, her duties to family and station geometrically expanded: tutoring her stepson, John Witherspoon Ramsay, as well as her orphaned niece, Fanny. Obligations for the young in her care would shortly extend even further to creating her own curricula for the family "school," plus assisting her husband's literary and professional functions. In the new nation, highly competent women like Martha Laurens Ramsay were quietly assuming expanded authority within the family, taking responsibility for aspects of family management that expressed a new, practical equality with men in the everyday arena.[3] Some women were beginning to see their wifehood as a type of

family manage-ment

proto-citizenship for themselves, without thus naming it, within their religiously and culturally ascribed locations of family and station (or role).

If she had felt a need to explicate a theory about women's citizenship, Martha would have expressed it through the two major languages in her mental world: first, a personal religiosity beginning to expand its meanings and reach, thanks to the new currents of British evangelicalism, itinerant Quakers, and postwar openness to new ideas; and second, the classical-republican ideal powerfully appealing to the intellectual elite of the new nation, a balanced social order where no single group would exercise dominating power.[4] Her response to the idea of citizenship would not have mentioned invidious differences between the citizenship privileges and duties open to males and females, though that is a typical concern for twentieth-century scholars. Sophisticated, serious-minded American women did not think or speak of actions and roles external to family and station; diligent response to their in-house duties was accepted as their Christian and domestic "citizenship," important and fulfilling.

"To protect and improve social life is . . . the end of government and law," orated the Honorable James Wilson of Philadelphia at a celebration for the establishing of a law school in the new nation. "If . . . you [females] have no share in the formation of [the government and laws], you have a most intimate connection with the effects of your system of law and government. That the plan of education which you promote will produce and preserve such a system is an important object to you," he told ladies in the Philadelphia audience for his introductory lecture.[5] To them of course the word *citizen* itself meant "male," yet he included their contributions in the national challenge. As for a legal definition, however, women in the new United States were citizens only at one remove—through their male relatives, and then only if those husbands or fathers were white property owners, not slaves or indentured servants.

Martha Laurens Ramsay, however, could assure herself, as a large proportion of American women could not, that the "virtual representation" she enjoyed in her country's governmental structures through her famous father and her author-physician husband made *her* proto-citizenship valuable.[6] In contrast, the post-Revolutionary daughters' generation was already beginning to question limiting females' sphere of influence to family and station or, as Martha called it, to "relative duties."[7] Priscilla Mason, salutatorian of the Young Ladies' Academy in Philadelphia in 1793, pointed out in her graduation address that "citizens of either sex" had historically enjoyed the right to plead their own causes before the bar. She seconded the idea of females participating in the duties of governing through "a senate of women," a proposal first made as far back as Roman times.[8] Martha might have been amused at that youthful audacity in the same way she indulged evidence of her own daughters' precocity. Although Martha might allow herself hints of despair over her personal legal and financial impotence, in the secrecy of her diary, she never had serious doubts about her usefulness to family and station, and through them to the nation.

Though adolescent Priscilla Mason was one of the first American females—along with Boston author Judith Sargent Murray—to apply the word *citizen* to her own sex, neither she or other educated noncitizens of that era would have intended anything political (as we today understand it) by that term. Those for whom citizenship in the early nation was an only a dream were not thinking about the ballot box, necessarily, but more about being a participant in the popular meaning of liberty.[9] By *liberty* they intended something less tangible than the vote—more a kind of spiritual and social arrangement by which liberated, religiously enlightened human beings would help build the virtuous institutions that could preserve the new nation and make it live up to its highest ideals. Women born into the natural aristocracy of the founders of America, like Martha, were already confident of their influence, their ability to impact the moral, religious, and ethical context of political decisions, through their men. Martha and those of her contemporaries who were active, principled, and progressive kin-keepers and educators enjoyed the sense that they were already engaged in citizenship.[10]

Its essential building block in the new democracy was a new understanding of intention—an individual's conscious choice about ideology, identity, and resultant actions, an element of commitment women understood very well. The war over and the nation's independence from Britain established, the discourses about citizenship in newspapers, constitutions, and sermons emphasized intent as much as structures. Consciousness of the grand new national experiment in which they were all engaged, and its vulnerability, was addressed explicitly and implicitly in both organizational and emotional terms.[11] Women knew they were essential to the *implicit* creation of citizenship. For example, in their principled choice of educational philosophy and pedagogic techniques to shape virtuous future republicans, women were major contributors to the new institutional structures. For women who had the learning, the domestic support staff, and the intellectual capacity to undertake it, teaching within the family was indeed proto-citizenship. Women's calling to be responsible Christians in the new nation found an even more generic expression of proto-citizenship in the way they discharged the role of kinkeeper, along with educational and spiritual guardianship. Women's "relative duties" could be expanded to encompass the new society itself.

In eighteenth-century rhetoric, kinkeeping—Tamara Hareven's twentieth-century concept for the female family member who took upon herself the emotional and practical maintenance of family ties, bonds of affection, and rituals—meant duties toward one's kin relations.[12] Conscious of her birthright as female adjunct to men who were pillars of the republic, and "ever ready to reciprocate the tender charities of domestic endearment," Martha had exercised spiritual and relational oversight among her kin from the time she wrote her adolescent covenant; when she became a mother, "relative duties" defined and expressed "the exact bounds of maternal prudence." Martha's adult kinkeeping ineluctably reached beyond immediate family on "an overflowing tide of affection."[13] Kinkeeping was female virtue incarnate and one of the crowns awarded Martha in her husband's *Memoirs* biography. To make yet another mark in the public sphere of national print, he intended to present Martha's wifely excellence as a model for American women.[14]

Internal kinkeeping in the Ramsay family or any household—the actual physical and emotional managing of parent-child, aunt-niece, and husband-wife relationships—was culturally rooted in and interpreted through a Protestant Christian plan of management. "A good Mistress of a Family will make herself the mistress of the *should be,* the *why,* the *wherefore* and the *how,*" novelist Samuel Richardson preached to the many readers of *Pamela,* including Martha and her daughters.[15] His pithy mapping of the family's moral domain gave women authority equal to that of a clergyman in his pulpit. But a wider, extra-family or community dimension of kinkeeping was similarly authorized by religious precept. New Englander Benjamin Wadsworth's well-known sermon, *The Well Ordered Family,* had lent its subtitle—*Relative Duties*—to republican moral discourse as a generic label for advice givers. David Ramsay used that phrase to substantiate his claim for a public platform for Martha. "Never was there a daughter more devoted, attached, and obedient to her parent; and her conduct flowed not from instinct, accident or example, but from principle." Martha herself, if asked, might more modestly and realistically have subscribed to Richardson's kinkeeping aphorism for *Clarissa:* "A worthy daughter would rather wish to appear amiable in the eyes of her own Friends and Relations than in those of all the world besides."[16] In Martha's own scale of values, her relatives were indeed the measure of her public worth.

In the vivid letter Martha wrote her husband, David, who was away at the state capitol in Columbia about the end of Henry Laurens' life, she paid a final daughterly debt of devotion. At one level, Martha's letter, written after she had returned to Charleston from the plantation where her father had died, was an almost clinical recital of his body's succumbing to death. She knew her physician husband would appreciate such detail and also that rehearsing it in writing could help to soothe her deep mourning.

Her trip to Mepkin had been initiated by a sudden, urgent need to see her father—so that, at great inconvenience to her own schedules and plans, she launched herself into a carriage with her nursing infant and a slave nurse Tira. Henry was thankful she had come, she recalled, and gave her a kind of patriarchal blessing, carefully cloaked as "conversing on indifferent matters"—avoiding talk of death despite his obvious fragility. He retired shortly after 7:30. When she greeted him the next morning and learned of his uneasy, "wakeful night," however, he had already launched the day's routine, been up and "given out the barn door key, as usual"—a surprise considering his feebleness. Martha left for a hasty breakfast, but by the time she returned, his speech had already begun to thicken, his mind "to waver a little." No longer leaving decisions to him, Martha dispatched an urgent messenger for a nearby doctor, though her father declared himself content "in my skill." His breathing became "laborious"; he could not respond to her agitated questions. "Almost immediately [he] fell into his last agony," the coma that masked from him the last struggles for breath of his dying flesh. Twenty-four hours later he slipped away without regaining consciousness.[17]

The grief following this progression of physical symptoms was surprising in one who had armed herself with deep Christian faith, a measure of that death's "blow." She described herself as literally prostrate, at the nadir of loss and physical depletion. The funeral ceremony on which Henry Laurens insisted was the final straw to Martha after the strain of watching at his deathbed. The bizarre rite of cremation made her suffer profoundly and evoked a primal cry for her husband's presence at her side—"feeling more than ever my dependence on you [David] for countenance, support and kindness." Even this most dutiful child revolted at her father's choice of burial.[18]

Editor Ramsay made a special point of his wife's paternal devotion in his biographical sketch: it "flowed not from instinct, accident, or example, but from principle," thus making it an expression of religion, citizenship, and moral decision making in terms of will or intent. Daughterly devotion by itself was already expected, but in combination with highest religious principle it was exemplary.[19] Family legend held Martha responsible for her father's exotic (she thought execrable) funeral. Her narrow escape as an infant, nearly being buried after supposedly dying from smallpox, was seen as one explanation of Henry Laurens' instruction to "wrap his body in twelve yards of tow-cloth and burn it on a pyre until totally consumed."[20] Fear of being buried alive was an oft-recorded specter in eighteenth-century nightmares. Her sole surviving brother and numerous other witnesses watched in fascinated horror, but not Martha. One neighbor, Margaret Izard Manigault, reported: "a prodigious concourse of people are going out of [Charleston] tomorrow to see old Mr. Laurens on his funeral pile,"[21] the common understanding of his cause of death being gout in the stomach. Martha, having discharged her filial duty of seeing his body properly "laid out" for "the awful ceremony," timed the start of her departure specifically to avoid it.[22]

The adjective "fatherless" is a heavy choice for the death of an ailing (and at that time elderly) parent, yet that was her self-descriptive adjective. The most significant indicator of her outsize devotion to her father, in her husband's eyes, was her willingness to violate her own firm standards of Sabbath rest if or when her father needed something. Any other summons was unworthy of interrupting her cherished Sabbath break. Among the benchmarks of the fervent, rational piety to which Martha aspired, that kind of legalistic rule observance was seen to exemplify religious citizenship and membership in a divine social order. Her stance on the biblical commandment about suspending any "labor" on the seventh day was a point of principle to be kept inviolate *except* in conjunction with the other commandment "honor thy father." Undoubtedly, Martha intended more than earthly parents: it would include her sense of social structure, the religious roots and traditions that upheld it, and the entire societal understanding that told her who she was. Yet even in the extremes of mourning her last "duty" to her father, Martha-the-wife had been too well schooled as Martha-the-daughter to argue with God's dealings. Instead, she pledged not to rail against God in even a letter to her husband. Martha promised herself, her husband, and God that she would neither protest her "father's removal by death" or her husband's absence from her side by politics, even in her hour of deepest existential woe.[23] Martha's comfort would be found in assuming the role of family kinkeeper as caretaker of the Laurens name.

At a public level she had already signaled that commitment in the naming pattern—as long as her father was alive—of the first four children born to her and David Ramsay. Her first babies, all girls, were christened with both her father's names: Eleanor Henry Laurens Ramsay (1787), Martha Henry Laurens Ramsay (1789), Frances Henry Laurens Ramsay, who died in infancy (1791), and Catherine Henry Laurens Ramsay (1792). Honoring her patriarch in a public way was the most concrete reverence she could personally render to a superannuated Founding Father—a coded testament to her guardianship of the family name.[24] Interestingly, Martha ceased this singular practice when her fifth-born child and fourth living daughter was born in 1793, the year after her father died; that child was christened Sabina Elliott Ramsay, the name of David Ramsay's first wife. (Dr. Ramsay had brought the family name of his second wife to their marriage in a son named John Witherspoon Ramsay, who went off to Princeton while some of Martha's children were still young.) The daughter named Catherine honored Martha's English friend and mothers' helper, Miss Catherine Futurell, who lived in Charleston with the Ramsays during those years of child producing. Martha's choice of children's names expressed her principled intention to honor with her own living tributes all those lives were closely linked with theirs.

When Martha and David's own first male child arrived in 1795, she named him David Ramsay Jr. rather than for her father—a conscious shift. As long as she had only daughters, their names were a daughter's only means of saluting her lineage. But with the advent of a son, she embarked in a new direction, the task women were increasingly claiming as their contribution: preparing male heirs for citizenship and leadership.[25] After honoring Uncle James with her James (1798), the other two sons were named after her husband's brothers: Nathaniel (1801) and William (1802). Interestingly, none of them were called Henry Laurens Jr., possibly because a living brother carried that name and it was "his" to bestow—or because she had already set her own pattern of claiming his names for the females in the family.

Dr. Ramsay's emphasis on intention—averring that his wife's conduct "flowed from principle," not instinct or habit, or anything less substantive and rational than a conscious mental choice—was the principle element that transformed the dynamic of kinkeeping into proto-citizenship for women. Intention was the defining quality of any contribution by any citizen in a democracy. Editor Ramsay's own intention—to celebrate Martha's religious integrity and graceful management of kin relationships in the face of painful financial and social loss—carried political overtones. Rational, conscious intent made an act—one formerly taken for granted as instinctive, like family caretaking—"political" for women. The dialogue that emerged in the constitutional era about citizenship enjoyed elaborating just such invisible but psychologically significant themes. David, and Martha herself, intended to elevate intentional, principled kinkeeping as the standard for American women's religious, republican "citizenship."

The taproots of Martha's proto-citizenship reached back to the piety of seventeenth-century English women whose thoughts and writings had filled her youthful library hours: writers like Elizabeth Bury, Elizabeth Rowe, Elizabeth Carter, and Hannah More. They were the literary voices that first elevated the role and work of domesticity to the level of an intentional, religiously sanctioned choice and calling, enlarging the meanings of housekeeping and family care as considerably more than something one fell into through the event of marriage.[26] Then friendship was exalted, further expanding women's importance in her own domestic culture. Treated as a religious activity in sermons and essays, and in women's own correspondence with each other, females began to honor the ideal of friendship with intentionality—as a serious expression of their highest selves. Christian theology hallowed this new kind of leisure-time writing as an aspect of spiritual development, legitimating a moral and spiritual guardianship role beyond as well as inside the family circle. Christian friendship assumed additional possibilities in the lives of literate, religiously serious women like Martha. (Dr. Ramsay included a few examples of this expression of women's friendship in appendix 6 of *Memoirs*. They illustrate Martha's conscious imitation of the heavily prescriptive style and sermonic tone popular in that style of letter, transforming religious thoughts and concerns for the recipient into the noblest expression of affection and concern.)[27] Viewing domesticity as a social and religious calling exalted the formerly unexamined role of housewife or female household manager; an easy next step validated the role and activity of friendship theologically. From there women's mental and spiritual participation in "citizenship," heavenly and earthly, was a simple extension of spiritual friendship bonds, outward into civic activities and the church community. The mechanism enlarging all these "natural" female duties by accretion was principled intention.

Conscious, rational intention further impelled a mother's citizenly responsibility for virtue in the republic, which in turn influenced her selection of educational content, moral precept, and feminine symbolism.

Women like Martha considered extra-family "leadership"—being known for good works and charity in church and the surrounding neighborhood—as a way of putting their abilities to patriotic use. Martha assumed that her kinkeeping and proto-citizenship must diffuse her enlightened view of what was meant by "social affections" into the wider political family—a logical expectation for educated women with leadership inclinations in the 1790s.

Martha chose especially to be self-consciously modern as the family educator. Until John Locke's philosophical formulation about instructing children in 1692, the instructional ideal had been catechetical, authoritarian, and imitatively European; Martha intended to be Lockean—enlightened, progressive, and pragmatic.[28] She had been conditioned to weigh a course of action and decide on it inwardly, her own father's pattern. (Because he had needed to determine the truth of troublesome language in the historic Athanasian creed to his own "certainty" about words that to him were "a stumbling block in the cause of Religion in general," her father developed opposition to bigotry and hard-line zealotry in "Mother Church" as a young man, and maintained it throughout his life.)[29] Soon after Martha married David and began rearing their children, she undertook a thorough evaluation of materials over which she was to be the family authority, weighing all theories and approaches in up-to-date French and English treatises on education as grounding herself thoroughly in the "nature and extent of her new duties." "Mrs. Ramsay is among the number of those who are anxiously waiting for the publications of your lectures to young ladies," David wrote their author, his Philadelphia colleague Benjamin Rush, in 1788. A fresh copy of Dr. Rush's *Thoughts upon Female Education* became an instant part of Martha's self-education for shaping the next generation of American women, her first responsibility the orphaned niece, Fanny (brother John's only surviving heir).[30]

Martha's intellectual horizon perused Fordyce's *Sermons to Young Women,* Lady Pennington's *A Mother's Advice to Her Absent Daughters,* and George Ballard's *Memoirs of British Ladies of Achievement.* Undoubtedly, she had read Mrs. Chapone's *Letters on the Improvement of the Mind* (1772) while living in England and France during the war years. She enjoyed the palatable didacticism of Richardson, who, in his novels *Pamela, Clarissa,* and *Sir Charles Grandison,* "attempt[ed] to steal upon the world *reformation* under the notion of *amusement . . .* pursuing to their *closets* those who fly from the *pulpit,* and under the gay air and captivating semblance of a Novel, tempt[ing] them to the perusal of many a persuasive Sermon." Like

Richardson, she wanted to instill "a right bias to energies and sensibilities" in children almost without their knowing they were being instructed. She was the progressive parent who wanted to fascinate the young into learning, instead of relying on fear or force.[31]

Martha as teaching mother embodied the "emergence from nonage" wafting through the educational philosophy of her time—the refreshing belief one could confidently trust one's own senses, reason, and perception instead of merely submitting to an unreasoning, automatic rule. "Before you proceed much farther in history," she advised her oldest daughter, Eleanor, "read Priestley's Lectures on that subject . . . [but] Bear always in mind that he is a Socinian. Profit by his science, while you lament his errors in divinity." Despite her vow to shape children's expanding minds into "the right bias," she instinctively encouraged their individual capabilities rather than trying to fit their gifts and personalities into a fixed model. She endorsed the Lockean thesis of children's learning through experience; she expressed that theology in a letter: "We hear good sermons, we read good books, but whole years of hearing and reading do not teach us so much . . . as the running dry of one spring of earthly enjoyment." As a pedagogue she chose to persuade and demonstrate. Young children, she cautioned the eldest family siblings, learn a lot by osmosis—"whether you curb your temper, whether you begin wisely to observe those laws of self denial which will make you happy to yourself, and pleasant to those about you." She chose to cultivate the children's own capacity for self-governing. She instructed them to "Ask yourself what am I about?" when they became conscious of "the encroachments of vice." They must be their own monitors and ask, "Where is my conduct tending?"[32]

No instructional efforts were too demanding for Martha if they contributed to her children's advancement, her husband recalled. She tried to "keep them constantly in good humor; gave them every indulgence compatible with their best interests, partook with them in their sports, and amused their solitary hours so as often to drop the 'mother' in the 'companion' and 'friend.'" Instead of class sessions on a rigid schedule and dictated by fiat, she opted for fun and participation. "I delight to hear everything about you," she wrote her college-age son in 1810, "and you can have neither pleasure nor pain in which I do not sincerely and affectionately participate." Learning their first letters was indeed a kind of play, thanks to the Lockean multisided alphabet block; she believed children should experience languages other than English in the way children in France learn French, through using them.[33]

To encourage her future citizens' ability to speak in public in an authoritative style, "she placed her children around her and read alternately with them," teaching them pronunciation and articulation though "the art of reading with emphasis and propriety." The style of their declamation— of Scripture verses, Aesop's fables, improving religious stories by the child-centered British writer Mrs. Trimmer, and hymns by her favorite, Isaac Watts ("O God Our Help in Ages Past," "Joy to the World")—was as important as the content. A second instructional principle focused on comprehension instead of rote learning. Reading the materials she had selected "with care and attention, and repeatedly," was intended to let "the substance, not the words of what they read, [become] imprinted on their minds." She further adapted the standard question-answer method by devising her own questions—guiding what they read but encouraging them to respond in their own words. Children must "answer from their general knowledge of the subject without committing the answers to memory,"[34] she believed, a progressive modification of the catechetical style.

Martha's own education had been unusually broad. As a girl she had absorbed Latin from her brother's tutors, the new scientific interest in taxonomy and "drawing from nature," and the standard feminine requirements of music and needlework.[35] David Ramsay credited her as "apt" in philosophy (Watt's *Logic*), biography, astronomy, chronology, and travel literature; she could even commend Plutarch to her children. Her book consumption was "astonishingly great" and included the best fiction, but her editor trimmed specific listings in the *Memoirs* to titles that fit his program of religious excellence.[36] His verbal portrait of Martha implied that, had she spent the entire span of the war years in the company of English aristocrats and poets rather than in provincial France, she too would have qualified as a genuine bluestocking.

And Martha's own mental world continued to expand in the midst of intense "relative duties." For example, she was enthralled with the idea of incorporating democratic symbolism into the plan for a new church building—a circular design that would allow the entire congregation equal view of the pulpit in an antihierarchical space—"a layman's church," in contrast with the Anglican model in which she grew up. Putting thought into action, she completed a first drawing in 1803 of what then became the architectural design for Charleston's Circular Church (as it became known).[37] Interestingly, her husband was able to credit her initiative in *Memoirs;* but after her death, when he wrote an official history of the church, that was not mentioned. Claiming such public conceptualization for a female, even one as talented as his wife, may have been farther than even David Ramsay could go. Martha also continued her self-education through the process of writing out lengthy book abridgments in outline form, a typical method of mastering new material.[38] Her husband quoted one such example of her work, an abridgement of John Flavel's *On Providence, or On Keeping the Heart,* in a very long footnote that filled the better part of four and a half pages in *Memoirs* (32–36).

A prescription for the educational production of Americans appeared in 1787, the year of the Ramsay's wedding; it was one of many published in the *Columbian Magazine.* A pseudonymous *Pro Republica* built it around the kinkeeping metaphor: though Americans knew the term *citizen* meant male, using terms of "family" and "social affections" included female, an expansion of "relative duties" Martha could certify. In a state of civil society, the essayist argued, man is a member of a great political family, connected with fellow citizens by ties of interest and benevolent attachment. His social affections must be drawn beyond a narrow circle of immediate relatives and friends until they encompassed his entire nation and community, as in the illustration number 5 following page 104.[39] American citizens' *mentalite* must be transformed through this wider meaning of "social affections" to include and represent the wider political family—a bond that could be produced in the curriculum via education in virtue. Or, as Martha would say, by the conscious shaping of the right bias in children's energies and sensibilities. In circular reasoning, the essential component of citizenship in the new nation was conscious and principled intention; this required enlightened pedagogy, which in turn hallowed and exalted kinkeeping. The entire holistic philosophy was summarized as the "culture of the heart."

A mother's love for her children, if it was merely instinctive and lacking focused patriotic intent, was by no means sufficient any longer. Linking female nurture literally with the culture of the heart and citizenship, New England author Enos Hitchcock equated the practice of breast feeding with virtuous female citizenship—mother's milk a contribution to the nation's constitutional model as well as to a child's bodily constitution. "The quality of the food fixes the state of the constitution," was the Rhode Island preacher's avuncular pun.[40] Martha herself embodied this severe republican standard in her fifteen years of childbearing, her husband proudly recorded. "She suckled all her children without the aid of any wet nurse; watched over them by night and day; and clung to them in every moment of sickness or pain." Martha's principled parenting illustrated the new nation's metamorphosis of modern parenting: child rearing could no longer be left to or blamed on divine providence. Rather, the model was now anxious parental watchfulness over, and responsibility for, their children's welfare.[41] Again, intention—rational mental conviction—was the essential element.

Children must be taught to submit their passions to the rule of reason and religion, to practice self-denial for the greater good of the community, even to resist the importuning of present pleasure and pain for the sake of what *reason* pronounced appropriate and right. Martha's methods intermingled religion, knowledge, and behavioral psychology. Use the "excellent understanding God has given you," she advised her eldest son, to "regulate your conduct and harmonize your passions." She modernized the Calvinist language of her own upbringing with a note of persuasion. "Every act of self denial will bring its own reward with it, and make the next step in duty and in virtue easier." Her generational sweetener was that, since practice makes perfect, a growing competence in being good and pleasing one's parents would be its own reward.[42]

Her educational credo can be seen to link the "new" Enlightenment belief in reason's authority with the inculcation of moral standards. Subordination of self was the highest form of self-fulfillment, for Martha and women in general; it was also necessary for a balanced society in the larger kin network, the nation. A generation earlier her father cited "the benefits of Living in a large Community, in those Bonds of Love and Harmony which we admire in a well-regulated Family." Reared in such an atmosphere, his children could be engaged in "Acts of Benevolence & be pleased with [a] nearness of Equality," as children raised in "Poverty, Sin and Wretchedness" could not; Martha intended her children to be equally formed for virtue.[43] But in her generation of parents, a further urgency and intention was popularly discussed: their responsibility for shaping the new republic into a "dominion of reason and religion." The politico-religious motto of essayist and Ramsay friend Rev. Daniel M'Calla expressed this responsibility in patriotic terms: "Democracy is the only form of Government ever approved by God."[44]

The Reverend M'Calla, a Presbyterian fellow alumnus of David's from the College of New Jersey, published a series of essays in the Charleston newspapers under the pseudonym Onesimus (a word meaning helpful, profitable). His announced theme was that Americanized education must separate itself from the past standards, must innovate in both content and methodology. One urgent improvement had to be an updated "chronology"—the periodization of Western civilization that children were to memorize; it now must include revolutions, French and American. (He did not include the Haitian revolution of 1792, since it was not viewed with the same uplifting idealism, but indeed the opposite—more on that in the next chapter). A second improvement was the new study of geography, made possible by the invention of globes that constituted "one of the eyes of history, looking to place as the other looks to time": American children must be equipped for wider horizons, "know[ing] something of the world beyond their own country and residence."[45] He recommended elementary cartographic training that started at a child's own house and gradually extended her mapping skills in ever-wider concentric circles from home base. M'Calla's pedagogic goal, recognized and approved by Martha, was to establish the child's logical, experiential mastery of his and her own territory—the essential basis for progressive expansion in the new nation.

In spite of advocating the study of British literature rather than Greek classics, Onesimus revealed a hearty anti-British tone, perhaps gratifying the memory of David's experience as a captive during the American Revolution. In the 1790s, the amount of still-raw hostility toward England startled a young Briton arriving to teach at the newly founded College of Charleston (on which founding board of trustees Dr. Ramsay was serving). "The people of this State though wealthy and very luxurious, have not yet got over the baleful effects of the revolutionary war," he reported back to his parents in England. "Their independence cost the Carolinians much blood & treasure. Pillage, fire, and sword are said to have marked the footsteps of the British army in these States. Cornwallis . . . is seldom mentioned without a hearty curse."[46] Onesimus and the Ramsays shared a bifurcated cultural bias in this section of their political and educational ideals: they pushed for more American "productions" but also relied on British cultural standards along with imported goods.

As one who had "a long and intimate intercourse with many of the first characters in her native country and in Europe"—David Ramsay's summation of his wife's qualifications—Martha could discuss philosophies of education with the Reverend M'Calla or any other leading citizens. One opinion regarding gender, however, would surely have roused Mrs. Ramsay's genteel disagreement. Onesimus philosophized: "The laws and government and other political subjects which occur in learning this science [geography] may very well be omitted by young ladies. Their particular province in society by no means requiring [such] knowledge, and their native dignity and importance rather lessened than increased by them, [that topic] ought to be omitted." Martha Laurens Ramsay was one Charleston matron unusually well equipped to point out that women's "respectability and usefulness" was indeed augmented rather than diminished by that kind of knowledge.[47] Dr. Ramsay's entire conception of *Memoirs* was an implicit rebuttal to M'Calla's denigration of women's political intelligence—though both he and Martha were repulsed by the scornful journalistic epithet "female pedant."[48] Even so, the husband of Henry Laurens' daughter would have to dismiss the suggestion that female dignity was lessened by acquaintance with laws, distant geography, and politics—rather the opposite. In his view, this daughter and sister of Revolutionary heroes embodied a sense of responsibility for the nation equal to his own. At the same time, however, Martha was too well bred, too conscious of being a Laurens and kinkeeper to the nation, to adopt the controversial public stance of Mary Wollstonecraft; unlike her New England counterpart, Judith Sargent Murray, Martha never seriously considered earning a living by her writing or teaching. In Martha's mental world, laboring diligently in family and station would carry the day by example, and far more effectively than tendentious and divisive argument. Martha's life itself expressed the form of independence possible for a female like her, in Wollstonecraft's own aphorism: "The being that discharges the duties of her station is the autonomous woman."[49]

Martha was not a rebel, nor did her preserved record allow much humor or winsomeness to shine through. If she had been less high-minded or her editor less agenda-conscious, more informality would have appeared, since liveliness and wit animated her intimate correspondence. Being a Laurens daughter undoubtedly made relative duties a burden sometimes, but Martha was the staunchly loyal female, first to her patriarch and then her husband. In her middle years, the same passionate intensity once invested in preserving her father's reputation as statesman shifted toward the legacy being created by her husband's publications. Rather than steering David Jr. into grandfather Laurens' financial footsteps—though she commended that model of integrity to her son—Martha's vision for him was white collar (our twentieth-century anachronism): meriting and inheriting his father's literary status. Like all mothers who want only the best for their own, she saw him as belonging among men "of literary and public consequence."[50] Leadership in the new arenas of public rhetoric and political oratory, for this oldest son, would be a satisfactory replacement for the once-vaunted Laurens commercial stature.

In the uncertain postwar Charleston where her children's energies and sensibilities must be given the "right bias," Martha's favorite guidebook was Burkitt's *An Help and Guide to Christian Families*. She saw no irony in relying on British child-rearing precepts for her new Americans, since Burkitt's larger goal was, like hers, "relative duties." The major citizenship themes were harmony, frugality, and self-discipline; his model of domestic order was balanced, rational, and distinctly hierarchical—which she also saw as necessary along with her bent toward modernity. For example, under "Particular Advice for the Well-Managing of Every Day," children had to learn "that much of the life and power of religion consists in the conscientious Practice of Relative Duties"—the term *relative* here given both specific and societal connotation.[51] The proto-citizenship key for Martha was contained in his interpretation of the fifth commandment: "Whom understand you by father/mother?" was the question. The answer listed vertical levels of application: "My natural Parent or my Father that begat me; my political and civil Parent, or the Magistrate that rules over me; my ecclesiastical Parent, or the Minister that instructs me, and my domestical Parent, or the Master of the Family that provides for me."[52] Child-rearing advice by American authors, like that pronounced through Hitchcock's fictional Mrs. Bloomsgrove, was also newly emerging in popular magazines and epistolary novels.

"Politics at present divide the country, and the parties of Federalists and Anti-federalists are in the extreme," reported the British aspirant for teaching in the College of Charleston, and he affirmed the streets-paved-with-gold myth that lured immigrants then as now. "There are so many ways of turning money to a good account that a person who is saving and possesses but a moderate capital, may, if he pleases, rapidly increase his fortune . . . almost everyone here [who has] any capital speculates in landed property, the produce of the country, or merchandise."[53] Having described David Ramsay by type if not in person, young Mr. Cotton's irresistible-gain theory was one symbol of the greed corrupting the new state of South Carolina. Private, personal virtue untainted by commercial chicanery was still considered the seedbed of public, civil, unselfinterested patriotism. Thomas Reese had warned Charleston about financial competition in "An Essay on the Influence of Religion in Civil Society" (1788).[54] Martha's own husband was uniformly unsuccessful in these terms, his reputation correspondingly diminished in a new national mood associating "virtue" with business acumen.[55]

Everything in Martha's character resisted the possibility that her children might take privilege rather than the stern obligations of citizenship for granted as entitlement from their distinguished lineage; she could not have known that her enlightened educational approach cultivated that very assumption in them. Try as she might to direct their ambitions toward "social affections," they nevertheless imbibed pride in their genes as much as in their nation's ideals. Fiscal realities also contributed to forcing Martha's republican idealism to a high principle: she and her husband were sometimes barely able to sustain their middle-class mode of life in the three-story house on Broad Street. The expense of supporting their eight living offspring during the first decade of the 1800s left little for social gatherings except church. Their friends now were David's Princeton colleagues and the benevolent, civic-minded cognoscenti of Charleston like Thomas Coram, the painter and benefactor of the Orphan House, and his wife.[56] By the late 1790s, even if republican frugality had not been a point of pride, the Ramsays could no longer fraternize at the high-society level of her father's contemporaries—the Manigaults, the Izards, the Hugers, the Rutledges, the Pinckneys.

Martha had been raised to champion the ideal of egalitarianism for the nation, ignoring its contradiction in her own birthright among the Charleston elite. In her household she upheld the strict image of a nation that cared less about "dainties for the palate" than "wholesome food for the mind."[57] Their friend M'Calla, writing as Demophilos in 1798, went so far as to suggest that the president of the United States be titled "*head servant*, not through affectation of singularity but as according to the true sense of the constitution"[58]—pushing self-righteous meanings of equality to the edge. Of all the cultural negatives against which Martha cautioned her young—such as monetary irresponsibility and disregard for inherited standards of respectability—the characteristic she feared as most destructive to citizen virtue was irreverence—a want of seriousness. The religious poet she quoted a great deal in her adult life, Dr. Edward Young, in fact extolled "a serious mind [as] the native soil of virtue."[59]

Yet another moral factor undermining her parental serenity in the new republic, though it was unnamed in public and in her own writings, was the troubling issue of slavery. Martha included household slaves in her "relative duties" by instructing her "white and black" family in their Sunday catechism at the same time, according to her husband. Martha's life ended before widespread justifications of slaveholding were publicly and theologically elaborated in the 1820s.[60] Already in her lifetime, violence was understood as "justified when the public weal is at stake," and it was assumed to be essential for keeping "social order" and keeping the city's huge African population in subservience. Emotional and moral accusations about slave-owning were nevertheless stirring just under the surface of public avoidance of the topic, making their mark on Martha's religious awareness. British antislavery literature by a fellow bluestocking—the message in Hannah More's 1790 poem, "The Black Slave Trade," for example—was intended to elicit acute embarrassment and guilt among slaveowners: "the outraged Goddess, with abhorrent eyes, sees MAN the traffic, SOULS the Merchandise."[61]

Even if Martha verbally rejected Wollstonecraft's call to a female independence that included economic self-sufficiency, as her husband was delighted to report, intense internal conflict over both kin and finances are visible in many diary self-reflections.[62] Martha belonged to a generation and a religious mind-set that could never totally detach itself from the deep cultural blame of the biblical figure Eve for woman's lot in life.[63] What she seemed to do was accommodate and transpose it, making her ideal (claim?) of humility into a matter of principle, intentionality, and pride. Her husband fondly believed that her customary closing salutation, "your obliged and grateful wife," represented considerably more than mere convention. There were women in Martha's neighborhood who experimented, in the secrecy of a Commonplace Book, with less-than-joyous expectations of wifehood, as Martha herself may have, in writings she did not preserve. Ann Cleland, for example, transcribed two poems into her private journal that demonstrated the contrast involved in two different life stages, the first viewing youthful feminine dependence through pink clouds; the second uneffusive by comparison, and succinct:

> *O let me live on my own, and die so too*
> *To live and die is all I have to do*
> *Maintain a lady's dignity and ease*
> *And see what friends and read what books I please.*[64]

Ideally harmonious relations between husband and wife were the propagandist's most useful metaphor for relationships between "rulers" and "ruled" in early national discourse.[65] Educating students in virtue was the wives' school of influence for Martha Ramsay (and her fictional counterparts, *Pamela* and *Mrs. Bloomsgrove*), as well as the engine of social mobility for citizens born more humbly than she, like David Ramsay. But such a practice required increasingly well-educated females. While the ballot box was not at this point a symbol around which women in South Carolina were tempted to rally, better education for females was. In 1801 a southern journal entitled *The Toilet* announced itself as vowing to banish forever "the look of stupid indifference" from American women's faces. It proclaimed the thrilling thought that female education was finally being given "an attention due its importance."[66]

While opinions supporting women's *capacity* for equal status with men were occasionally supported in the print public sphere, most white American males viewed the call for general female equality as morally deformed or outrageous. Spokesmen like Dr. Ramsay, expatiating on his wife's proto-citizenship in every other sense, carefully dissociated Martha's marital republicanism from Mary Wollstonecraft's version of female equality.[67] Modern women who boasted a "firm, gymnastic nerve" instead of the standard "coy reserve" were laughable as "arrogant, political, philosophical courtezans . . . emulous of the fame of Mary Wollstonecraft . . . petticoat cheats."[68] These were literally unthinkable images to the doctor, and his wife either agreed with him or let him believe that she held the same opinion.

American women were major participants in the groundswell of public celebration and pageantry honoring their national father, the first American president, at the end of that momentous century; in some cities women even organized their own public demonstrations. The ladies of Trenton, New Jersey, in 1789 recalled Washington's military triumph over the British at the bridge to Princeton by erecting a "triumphal arch" that sported "13 pillars, 20 feet wide" entwined with evergreen, laurel, flowers, and a huge banner. Gilt letters proclaimed "TO YOU ALONE," General Washington—"THE DEFENDER OF THE MOTHERS WILL BE THE PROTECTOR OF THE DAUGHTERS"—invoking of the circle of affections that bound the father of the nation to his female proto-citizens. While Charleston women apparently did not mount such a personal welcome, Martha would have read about her New Jersey white clad and bonneted sisters—a "numerous train of women leading their daughters by the hands assembled at the arch," who "presented [President Washington] with a card printed with a Sonata," a three-stanza poem of welcome.[69]

Charleston produced its own gala for President Washington's 1791 visit. The big reception appropriated the Thomas Heyward house, most elegant in the city, for the occasion—described with local pride as "almost a museum" with its library of thousands of rare books, score of splendid paintings, and garden "of choicest flowers." Though Martha's preserved words made no comment on it, *all* important citizens were involved; perhaps editor Ramsay chose to omit any mention she may have recorded as irrelevant to his wife's "seriousness." The republican Mrs. Ramsay might inwardly have wanted to censure all the expense and fussiness of detail, but she would equally have wanted to bask in the president's remembrance of her brother John, one of his beloved young aides, and of her father. Martha's clergy wife-friend Mrs. Keith, in her written report of the grand event, managed a tone implying censure along with pride. The Charleston reception committee had at personal expense attired itself elegantly in "sky blue jackets," a colorful choice that Mrs. Keith approved; many of the women at the ball were "decked out in great glamour, perhaps too much for the simple country farmer from Virginia," which she disapproved. The president was met with two bands "discoursing music" and a procession to the Exchange, preceding the grand ball.[70] Martha was temperamentally likely to have shared a young Briton's disdain for the display of opulence. "Never were any Women fonder of dress than the Charleston ladies, the fashions are not out in London three months before they become the rage here." That observer considered such concern for style pretentious, since "apparell of all kinds is extremely dear" in Charleston.[71]

Upright citizens like Martha undoubtedly preferred to see women's impact on the body politic take a less ornamental, more morally signifi-cant form—like their emerging involvement in public benevolence. A rare newspaper editorial supporting women's education praised new vol-untary charitable associations for women as "political," meaning that they provided an approved way for females to contribute to and participate in the public order. *The Providence Phoenix,* 21 September 1802, praised both "the female world [which] has produced many who have shone on the political as well as the literary stage," and those men who were finally paying the attention to the education of daughters "which they fully merit."[72] Groups of women organizing, under a religious banner to accom-plish a societal task were adding another dimension of their proto-citizenship.

The first president of the Charleston women's benevolent organiza-tion was Martha's friend, Mrs. Rev. Hollinshead, wife of her senior pastor; the Mrs. Rev. M'Calla was yet another fellow member. Their stated purpose was to "distribute practical books of Piety and Religion among the Poor and sending Preachers of the Gospel to such parts of our country as are destitute of the means of Salvation."[73] A secondary, implicit benefit was their conversation and sharing of domestic concerns—sociability sanctioned by a religious intention. Since women's names were supposed to appear in public newspapers only when they married and were buried, announcements of the new women's associations were extremely discreet;

still the title they chose was its own signal that women of Martha's generation were taking public initiative to improve their own society.

Public virtue, to be nurtured in the domestic "culture of the heart," gradually emerged as "a large abstract ideal" for the new nation, even if anchored securely out of the public sphere, in the private realm of family, church and school, and legitimating a kind of proto-citizenship for women.[74] Male citizens could invoke and praise the ideal without responsibility for implementing or incorporating it. At the turn of the century, the *Baltimore Weekly* predicted: "Nothing short of a general reformation of manners would take place" if women fully discharged *their* religious, educational, marital, and system-maintenance proto-citizenship. Public decency would become "fashion," public virtue the only style.[75] Martha Ramsay was one who wholeheartedly subscribed to that type of fashion; public virtue was what she intended to incarnate, the very duty she intended to discharge to relatives.

Martha's principled kinkeeping was of course her explicit version of relative duties: "Christ said to his disciples in general ye are the lights of the world," she wrote in her diary; if that is so, how "defective [are those] who aren't *at least* the light of their own family."[76] The way she interpreted the educational, social, and civic dimensions of kinkeeping distinguished her, David proudly wrote, from any radical call for equality of the sexes. Martha knew perfectly well that proto-citizenship for women meant more than maintaining harmony, contributing to relatives' well-being, and guarding the virtue of the social order, but she maintained a stance of contentment while trying to exemplify all that—and avoiding more overt language. She was confident that her diligent contributions in the familial and marital station to which God had assigned her were essential to the new nation, they were her particular niche in the women's consciousness that would evolve in future generations.

7 | Slavery and Silence

MARTHA REFERRED TO SLAVERY in only a dozen places in her published *Memoirs,* requiring us to read around and between her words. The contexts and pressures surrounding those few words were varied and overlapping: her brother John Laurens' proposal to free and arm slaves during war against the British; her admiration of a British aristocrat whose ardent religiosity was untroubled by slaveowning; her much-respected senior pastor's example of caring for slaves religiously; and her own father's lifelong ambivalence about slaveowning and management, in contrast with her Uncle James' outright resistance to it. Further, Martha could not avoid the intellectual influence of burgeoning antislavery societies in the new nation, or the fear of slave uprisings that permeated white Charleston after the Haitian revolution, and the impact of some few outspoken American antislavery voices, one belonging to David Ramsay's best friend, Benjamin Rush.

Although in her preserved writings Martha herself was too intentionally discrete to provide us easy explanations, her silence around slavery is stark. Granted, this was a topic largely invisible in the polite conversation and literature of her times, but it was also an institution that impinged on every aspect of the Ramsays' social and material world.[1] Her silence about slavery was, it appears, the result of choice rather than unconscious omission; whose choice, hers or her editor's, remains the unresolved question. The editor's own selections and inclusions, as well as Martha's recorded vocabulary, are literally unhelpful in this puzzle, but they do provide a composite picture of the verbal customs they shared. The life she lived, and that part of it she had time to inscribe in a secret diary, were made possible by the labor of her household slaves, but the *Memoirs* do little to dispel the silence around that assistance, or hint at the way of living it presupposed. Reconstructing the various ideological and structural influences that shaped her thoughts helps ground the few fragmentary and elliptical references that, by themselves, leave us uninformed; we can only surmise her actual attitudes from those more clearly expressed by her nearest and dearest—most critically, her brother, father, and husband.

In 1793 an unsigned letter on the matter of slavery thrust David and Martha Ramsay into the public eye. It was published in the letters section of *The Ladies Magazine and Repository of Entertaining Knowledge,* a new venue of public print from Philadelphia.[2] An anonymous Providence, Rhode Island, correspondent was reporting on the recent South Carolina debate over suspending the slave trade for two years and whether or not to "cut . . . off further import of slaves from Africa and the West Indies." In that State House session, the debate had been contentious and wearying. According to Gabriel Manigault, it was tedious beyond belief when "two members spoke between them three hours." Martha's only surviving brother, Henry Laurens Jr., was among the legislators supporting the bill.[3] In the Senate the debate had moved further along but was stalemated in a tie vote: "The count was seventeen for, seventeen against." The letter writer then editorialized: "Happily for the oppressed of mankind, the chair [of the state senate] was filled by the illustrious Dr. Ramsay who, soaring above the prejudices of his country men, pronounced the following elegant, momentous and feeling decision."[4] The letter's adjectives conveyed awe. "I am now called on to discharge an official duty which renders the present moment the most important of my life," David Ramsay was quoted as saying. "I have violated my own feelings and the most tender attachment, that I might be here this day, to support the bill." Readers in 1793 would have known that his "tender attachment" was his third wife, Martha Laurens, eldest daughter of Henry Laurens, renowned as the American diplomat imprisoned in the Tower of London during the late war. Dr. Ramsay had artfully joined an important family name from the nation's founding with his own, dramatizing the "recent melancholy domestic event" of "the death of his Father-in-Law Mr. Lawrens during this very debate," as the letter writer explained.[5]

In the normal course of events, Dr. Ramsay continued, husbandly duty and patriotic obligation toward a distinguished founding father would "call . . . for my presence with an afflicted family, far distant from this place" (Columbia, South Carolina, to which the state capitol had relocated in 1790). Having invoked the solemnity of that family event, he continued: "But the subject of our present debate has absorbed all private considerations. As my vote is to be of such deciding consequence, I shall ever rejoice that I sacrificed private feeling to public duty." Ramsay set the stage for his stirring peroration by positioning himself rhetorically between duty to family and duty to principled governing and history. "Firmly believing as I do that the further importation of slaves is contrary to the true interests of Carolina, I will not only give my vote for the bill, but if necessary would seal it with my blood."[6]

By the time Dr. Ramsay unfurled this verbal banner he was already known nationally as a published historian and locally as the adopted

Charlestonian whose enthusiasm led him to establish, in 1778, the Fourth of July anniversary as an occasion for patriotic orations.[7] Much as he may have relished his decisive role in the 1792 debate, his previous public speeches had addressed broad, elevated themes of civic virtue and avoided the topic of slavery altogether. In the letter writer's view, however, here was a spokesman from the heart of slaveland making him an ideal champion of "the oppressed of mankind."[8] What David Ramsay may have intended by this putative gesture requires an understanding of racial attitudes in that specific social and cultural setting, and an awareness of his accommodations over the years to married life in a slaveowning society. Even with his imported (born in Pennsylvania and schooled at Princeton, New Jersey) negativity toward the institution of slavery, he had not hitherto condemned it publicly.

The scene described in the anonymous letter sounded authentic, since Ramsay was a man given to grand rhetoric and always passionate in patriotic expressions about the new nation. Nevertheless, the appearance of this vignette in the emerging sphere of print inserted it into the public arena, fact or legend.[9] *The Ladies' Repository* had been launched as a journalistic platform for female participation in public issues: to enable the "fair sex" to shrug off its "stifling female delicacy" and be a medium through which educated women of Martha Ramsay's status could, without public embarrassment, publish opinions about topics like slavery that were otherwise beyond the pale of polite discourse. Aimed at *rational* public discussion—to prove that women were capable of it—the entrepreneurial magazine promised an appropriate opening for females who chose to "seize the laurels of" this form of public debate. But no respectable woman of that era would use her own name in a public vehicle, let alone advance a partisan position about a highly charged topic like slavery—thus the anonymity of the letter writer.[10] Internal evidence, including its emphasis on the emotional background and the educational, social, and civic dimensions out of which the South Carolina senate president spoke, suggests that the letter was written by a female who was glad to use Ramsay's speech for making her own point.

The import of this "nodal event"[11] in Martha Laurens Ramsay's story resides in her husband's dramatic forthrightness about a topic that was usually invisible, all but unmentionable in public conversation and rarely discussed, even in the private papers of late-eighteenth-century white Christian citizens who owned slaves—with the all-important exception of business correspondence. That David Ramsay's inflammatory statement appeared at all, even in an obscure new journal, illustrates the point. Despite lives totally intertwined with slaves and slavery, white citizens in Martha's hometown preserved an all-but-total eclipse of the topic in both written record and public utterances during the postwar decades. If slavery appeared in personal letters, it was most often treated as an integral component of an elite society's gracious self-image—while northern criticism of it was dismissed as ill-informed and unaware. Joseph Alston, a Carolina contemporary of Martha's, used elaborate irony to detoxify the negative images of slavery that horrified his northern fiancé, Theodosia Burr, in the 1790s. He ironically juxtaposed Carolina's paradisial climate and fragrant beauty with "the scream, the yell of the miserable unresisting African, bleeding under the scourge of relentless power." Alston assured her that New Englander Jedediah Morse was responsible for such a lurid description of North, not South, Carolina, which was presented to her by friends wanting to dissuade her from marrying him. True, South Carolina society contained two elements: the very rich and the very poor. "The possession of slaves renders [gentlemen] proud and impatient of restraint ... [but that is accompanied by] a high sense of honour, a delicacy of sentiment." Slavery was intrinsic to the "polished state" of Carolina culture, a benign component of its sound morality, hospitality, and characteristic honesty.[12] Charleston as geography was every bit as healthy as Rhode Island, he claimed, and no more infatuated with "love of torture" and cruelty to its bondsmen than the North. In fact, Charleston, "the Montpelier of the South," produced "a liberality of mind" that one would seek in vain among "the more commercial citizens of the northern states."[13] Sophisticated regionalism could easily explain away the misinformation received by non-southerners.

David Ramsay's heroic declaration shocked readers because it was indeed unique. In Charleston the number of white spokesmen against the slave trade was miniscule, despite the frequent invocations of concepts like liberty and independence, left over from the recent war. Those terms had given new moral leverage to critics of slavery in the mid-1780s, so that early in the new century John Parrish of Philadelphia could write, "Slavery has become less excusable since the revolution."[14] Dr. Ramsay's spoken words thus constituted a thunderclap piercing the public silence about slavery. And his melodramatic vow to "seal it with my blood" placed him unequivocally in the antislavery camp, in marked contrast with the earlier public ambivalence of his civic activity in Charleston, as we shall see. If he intended, finally, to align himself publicly with his closest ideological friends in the North, Dr. Benjamin Rush and the Rev. Jeremy Belknap, known opponents of slavery, that senate speech would do it. It may also have raised a tension between David and Martha, with David's public role drowning out family considerations, as had been the case with Martha's father and brother. Indeed, for Mrs. Martha Ramsay, her husband's moment of glory was bound to have aroused a kaleidoscope of emotions— although there is no known record of her reactions.

At the end of 1792, Martha was psychically besieged on several fronts. Antislavery literature was challenging the assumptions of the intelligentsia to which she and her husband belonged. Its texts attacked the institution of slavery, slave traders and owners, and—through a few female activists like the anonymous letter writer—the social mores excluding women such as herself from serious public commentary. More deeply, her own religious practice rendered her exceptionally vulnerable to the new moral accusations about slavery; her wide reading exposed her to the emerging theological meanings beginning to be associated with benevolence and humanitarian empathy. Indeed, Martha's serious Christian study placed her in the company of enlightened citizens who would embrace as spiritual progress compassion for undeserved human suffering—the new literary convention undermining the rationalizations that had previously supported slavery (enslavement in order to Christianize the African).

Martha's fiercely self-evaluative persona trapped her in a family triangle on this issue, between a father for whom slavery had been *the* profitable commercial enterprise ("black gold"), and a husband whose origins allowed him to condemn it on principle, although living in and benefiting from a society where it was endemic. From her covenant at the age of sixteen, she had engaged in the anxious spiritual catechizing of the smallest decisions and actions, searching out anything within her consciousness that could be called sin. Raised to honor patriarchal authority in spirit and actuality, Martha was confronted by the newly circulating antislavery texts with both a soul dilemma and a real-life dilemma—for being her father's daughter and her husband's wife.

Behind the Laurens-Ramsay joint pilgrimage, differing class origins could well have increased her embarrassment at David Ramsay's rhetorical boldness. As "Daughter of her Father," her previous "importance in Society" could not smother all unfavorable comparison with her status as "Wife of her Husband."[15] Gossipy Charleston could enjoy Dr. Ramsay's eminence as an author while also jesting at his lack of social grace and wrinkled stockings.[16] Martha, too principled to record derogatory thoughts about her husband even in her secret diary, knew how to suppress unflattering thoughts. Her revered father might within the family lament the slave-labor system, but he had long ago made the moral adjustment necessary to preserve his sanity, and most of the time he placated his conscience by his self-image as a just master.[17] By contrast, her husband now apparently felt free to denounce slavery in an emblematic gesture. *His* self-image allowed his conscience to reject slavery but—until the 1792 legislative drama—had heretofore kept him silent in public.

Martha and David both employed the euphemism *servant* for their household slaves, along with others in their time, place, and class. Avoiding the word *slave* in face-to-face conversation with and about one's property was a well-established convention in eighteenth-century elite culture, and in Martha's family. Her father spoke of "my Negroes." The cultural fiction that servants preferred to think of themselves as "belonging to" rather than "slaves of the Massuh" was so ingrained that even those open to criticizing the institution, like the Ramsays, unthinkingly employed it.[18]

Inside her house on Broad Street, the domestic organization over which Martha presided was of course legally under the governance of her husband. For all her independence of mind and spirit, Martha's life as a wife was circumscribed by and defined within the household. In this era, white married women of her class, however competent as household managers, were in fact totally dependent on what the controlling males in their lives did or did not permit. An adoring husband like Dr. Ramsay was happy to proclaim it "her" territory, administratively and emotionally, and home was indeed woman's arena as nothing outside it could be. Martha probably had expected David to exhibit an updated version of her father's paterfamilias style—in which her Papa's views had prevailed on everything.[19] Indeed, Martha deferred to David as the patriarchal head of household both because it was proper and because she expected her marriage to be the highest example of domestic harmony and herself to be a model of wifely "meekness." However, she was fortunate to have a husband who credited her with greater superiority of judgment than did most of his colleagues of their wives. She may never have realized that a more defensive, misogynist spouse would have been far less indulgent toward a wife with her strong personality. Or she may have adapted herself and her ways to his with such skill that he did not fully realize her strength and independence of mind. All readers today have to puzzle over the fact that so little of Martha's struggle about the issue of slavery is visible in her preserved writings.

Martha first confronted the moral embarrassment of slaveowning through her childhood idol, older brother John Laurens. During the decade she lived abroad, John was also in London studying law at the Inner Temple. His circle of sophisticated British friends included the writer and antislavery poet Thomas Day.[20] When Martha met the young author in the 1780s, she confronted perhaps for the first time open efforts by British abolitionists to name and publicize the brutal realities of the slave labor system. Their cudgels were eyewitness reports from fellow Englishmen of the inhuman treatment slaves routinely received in the British West Indies. Day's much-reprinted poem, "The Dying Negro"[21] (about a recaptured slave whose only remaining power was that of suicide), had ignited the conscience of much of educated Britain, including the Church of England firebrand and reformer the Rev. John Wesley—author of imagery her brother John himself began to quote and employ.[22]

Wesley as crusader accused slaveowning Americans of self-delusion for trying to equate British taxation policies with enslavement. "But who is the slave? the Negro, fainting under the load." The audacity of supposedly mistreated British citizens? "One is screaming, murder! slavery!, the other silently bleeds and dies. You and I and the English in general go where we will and enjoy the fruits of our labor; this is liberty. The Negro does not: *this* is slavery."[23] During 1778, when John was establishing himself as aide to Gen. George Washington in the new nation's army, he had first broached the idea of freeing slaves and arming them as fellow fighters—but his idealism reached well beyond military victory: "I have long deplored the wretched State of these men," he wrote his father on 14 January 1778, "the bloody [African] wars to furnish America with Slaves, the groans of despairing multitudes toiling for the luxury of merciless tyrants."[24]

John Laurens cast his youthful radicalism in the emotive vocabulary characteristic of the new humanitarianism (*wretched* state, *bloody* wars, *despairing* multitudes, *merciless* tyrants),[25] rather than in John Wesley's simple declarative sentences—but his intent was the same. He was aflame with his generation's outrage at a rhetoric that twisted the noble ideal of liberty into white slaveowners' self-justification. In a letter to a fellow southern youth, John revealed his moral awakening: "How can we whose Jealousy has been alarm'd more at the name of Oppression than at the Reality, reconcile to our spirited Assertions of the Rights of Mankind, the galling abject Slavery of our negroes?"[26]

Ultimately, John's proposal died by inaction. In his homeland, South Carolina legislators—except for the support of Dr. David Ramsay, not yet his relative—were unwilling to disarrange their labor system and thus their economy. And Henry Laurens himself, no matter how critical of slavery within the family, responded to his son's potentially anarchic ideas without ambivalence. Henry Laurens' priorities were stated as clearly as his peer Pierce Butler, an important customer for highly skilled rice-cultivating slaves. The Laurens children's inheritance must not be jeopardized by John's "zeal for the public service [and] ardent desire to assert the rights of humanity."[27] Slaves were *property*, the economic "life's blood" of his family. John's early rallying for "the Coloured, the blacks, the subhumans because of skin," would shortly transform him into one of the antislavery legends of the South. His romantic war persona—where he was often referred to as "the Bayard of the American Army"—attracted additional layers of legend.[28]

There is no record of nineteen-year-old Martha's response to her brother's idealism. She might have felt a secret pride at his pushing far ahead of other Americans, or she might have been embarrassed by his challenge to their father's world. Unable to sway his father or enough of his fellow southern legislators to free and arm slaves, John achieved his public martyrdom in military rather than human-liberation terms. He met his death at age twenty-seven in one of the last battles of the war—"a paltry little skirmish"—on 28 August 1782.[29] His commanding officer wrote, "I wish his fall had been glorious, as his fate is much to be lamented . . . The love of military glory made him seek it upon occasions unworthy his rank. The state will feel his loss, his father will hardly survive it."[30] David Ramsay had eulogized Martha's brother in his book *The Revolutionary War in South Carolina* as "zealous for the rights of humanity, contending that personal liberty was the birthright of every human being, however diversified by country, colour or capacity." His fulsome language knighted John verbally: "the idol of his country, the glory of the Army, and an ornament of human nature."[31] Martha's sisterly tribute to John was her vow to educate his orphaned daughter, Fanny, in the highest standards of Laurens respectability and service, a determination all but destined to backfire. By the time of Dr. Ramsay's 1792 antislavery declaration, this Laurens' niece was already resistant. In a few years John's descendant, Fanny, would elope to a life well away from Laurens' control, with a man "all Charleston" considered unsuitable.[32]

After the war, in 1785, visitor Timothy Ford from Morristown, New Jersey, a contemporary of Martha's, was gratified by the beauty in Charleston buildings and streets, even by its police and firefighting system; but he also saw that something was very wrong. There, "in a land of

Liberty and Christianity that boasts and builds upon the irrefragable rights of human nature, [many are] torn from the enjoyment of them and devoted to perpetual slavery for no other cause than that God has formed them black. It begets a strange confusion of ideas and contradiction of principles. The general rule is Liberty but the Exceptions form a majority of five to one."[33] Obviously, other young postwar citizens were also incapable of ignoring the contradictions that John Laurens dramatized.

John's remarkable attempt to wrench the concept of liberty into a more enlightened stance vis-à-vis slavery proved to be in marked contrast with Martha's experience, two years later, with a titled Englishwoman. When Henry Laurens participated in the postwar peace negotiations in 1783, with Martha acting as his clerk and hostess, they came to know Lady Selina Hastings, the countess of Huntingdon (1709–1791), an aristocratic widow who had placed her personal fortune and large reputation in service of the new evangelical movement.

At the time of her widowhood, the countess found solace in evangelicalism's ardent challenge to the Church of England's staid hegemony. (In America that reform movement would spin off a new denomination called "Methodism," its name rising from the spiritual "methods" or disciplines of devotion and self-improvement viewed as essential by its intense Christian adherents. Once awakened, Lady Selina Hastings aligned herself with the branch of evangelicalism led by the Rev. George Whitefield, her mentor and friend. This touring originator of "field preaching" had earlier electrified black and white Christians in South Carolina, including Henry Laurens, who broke with his rector, the Rev. Alexander Garden, in order to welcome Whitefield.[34] The countess had built and paid for several of "her own" chapels and created "her own" college in England to train young clergy in the style of "high voltage preaching" that she approved. Eighteenth-century women were entirely invisible in Church of England except as pious worshippers before the imperious countess arrived on the scene. Miss Martha Laurens, invited to join the countess' personal entourage for a time in the summer of 1783, found her mental horizon vastly expanded by what this Christian female could accomplish—a woman whose wealth and rank enabled her to defy and ride high-handedly over church authority. By then twenty-five years old and experienced in the expatriate life of Paris and Bath, England, Martha could not fail to be impressed with this "monument of piety."[35]

The countess' male contemporaries—Church of England clergy and some evangelical dissenters themselves—were less charitable, declaring her guilty of an "excess of passion" and "choleric temper." Contrastingly, admirers praised her devotion as well as her zeal. In the words of a biographer, "wherever she was called by the providence of God she was acknowledged as 'a burning and a shining light,' [for her] spiritual leadership."[36] The Lady was clearly able to have her own way in an established eighteenth-century hierarchical and patriarchal church.

Crucially for Martha's developing conscience about slavery, Lady Hastings saw no dissonance between slaveowning and missionary outreach. Determined to spread the Gospel, the countess purchased slaves for field labor at "her" missionary outpost at Bethesda, in the colony of Georgia, which Whitefield had established and she funded. While enlisting Henry Laurens' reputation for honesty to straighten out the mismanagement at Bethesda, the countess entertained Martha and her younger brother Harry. Early in her philanthropy, the countess had financed young Church of England clergy (and first British evangelist/missionaries to the colony of Georgia), the Wesley brothers, John (1703–1791) and Charles (1707–1788). But disagreements between the brothers and the Georgia colonial government soon created complications, followed by a similar tangle with the countess.

John Wesley gained his firsthand experience of slavery on that missionary tour, although he did not publish his *Thoughts on Slavery* for another half century. But his direct experience of slavery, with its dehumanization of black slaves that kept them ignorant of Wesley's God and salvation, offended him. That, and his own problems with the colonial authorities as well as the countess, fostered a split among evangelical reformers. "Arminian" or Wesleyan, and Calvinist or Whitefieldian "methodists" became opposed and competitive, the countess remaining in the authoritarian Calvinist wing.

The Wesleys and their supporters developed the more generous "Arminian" theology of free will, individual grace, and salvation for everyone, including slaves and not just the predestined "elect." Martha's inclinations aligned her with the more democratic Arminian view that would be visible in her later diary writings, but the countess' model of religious initiative was bracing. Both groups of reformers continued to be members of the Church of England, since they saw evangelicalism as revitalizing a dormant institution rather than initiating a religious revolution. If the Laurens visitors to the countess had expressed ecclesiastical partisanship, their loyalties might well have been divided. Budding Americans had to be critical of aristocratic privilege, but as committed Christians they had to applaud good works, even by aristocrats.

John Wesley's concern that all converts be able to exercise their own free will constituted a threat to the social order, in the countess' view.[37] In the spiritual autobiographies and diaries he encouraged his followers to keep, he encouraged individual decisions that could undermine English rank and custom. Wesley treated hierarchy as antithetical to personal salvation; further, he allowed women to exhort (preach informally at public gatherings), an undoctrinaire privilege that the countess could scarcely consider Christian. Martha, having been reared in the American rhetoric of Anglican deference and her father's Calvinist view of authority, had no trouble understanding the countess in this regard, if perhaps ultimately differing with her about slavery.

Critics accused Lady Huntingdon of believing that God had called her as directly as men were called into the ordained clergy. Despite the disadvantages of being unordained and female, she never doubted her own divine mandate. The male clergy she selected to do "her" evangelical work were willing to please a wealthy patron. Martha, aware that her own ambitions for spiritual achievement were externally circumscribed, had to be impressed by that. Expecting deference from inferiors, the countess remained unaligned with either Arminian or Calvinist reforms, and also had no doubts that a biblical curse destined some human beings—with African features and skin color—to be slaves, "Sons of Ham,"[38] though of course deserving Christianization.

Henry Laurens' admired the countess' investment in charitable works and agreed to straighten out the finances of her Georgia project. Martha admired her Gospel spreading, her fervent piety, and her ability to override the male clergy system. The countess' lack of concern over the morality of slaveowning provided Martha with an interesting contrast to the antislavery literature she was reading. After Martha became his wife, David Ramsay was proud of the special regard in which the countess of Huntingdon held Martha. Even that quintessential American patriot was not immune to the lure of a titled British admirer. His wife's ease of comportment among the elite of Europe was something grand, in his view, and his loving word-portrait of Martha's deathbed scene (in chapter 10) carefully noted the hymn she wanted read to her—a favorite from the gift book presented to her by the countess in 1784.

Notably absent from the *Memoir's* wide ranging list of human beings associated with Martha Ramsay was any person of African heritage. In the published version of her writings, there is no mention of the originally African hands who cooked the meals and polished the marble steps at her house on Broad Street in Charleston. There is never a mention of who stitched diapers for and rocked her eleven infants, after attending their births and boiling the bed linens. Or who kept anxious vigil with a distressed mother during the heartrending deaths of three of them. No mention also of who it was that actually boiled, scrubbed, starched, and ironed the ruffles for four little daughters and hovered near them protectively in the streets; no mention of those human beings who freed Martha from household duties to pore over textbooks and write her own curriculum for her family "school"; no mention of those whose physical labors allowed her to search her husband's medical books for diagnostic clues that assisted his work and helped him with the correspondence necessary to assemble the multitude of facts he needed for writing his histories. Disappointingly, there is no acknowledgment that other humans' labor gave her the additional time to train her growing daughters to be skilled copyists for their father's publications.

When her father's death coincided with her husband's antislavery gesture in 1792, Martha had been married five years to her "diamond tho unpolished," the Charleston champion of "the oppressed of mankind." She would have understood perfectly her neighbor's summarizing dictum about the Good Wife in their social world: "The rank of a good woman in society leaves her little to complain of. She frequently guides where she does not govern, & acts like a guardian angel by preventing the effects of evil desires." Needless to say such women's names are "not brought forward [made public] . . . they enjoy the internal sense of their own abilities."[39] Left unstated was the undergirding of goodwife Mrs. Ramsay's way of life at every turn by slavery. Apart from an occasional name in a diary entry or family letter, slavery and her slave helpers might not have existed. That total institutional invisibility suggests that Martha took slaves for granted, as a kind of furniture and also as a type of extended family. All the actual household duties of cleaning, cooking, bathing, and polishing within her household—even preparing her father's body for cremation—were performed by this slave labor force. The scope of silence about slavery in the *Memoirs* and in most public print in her times was its own testimony to the existential ambiguity in which she and her society had to exist.[40]

The *Memoirs* contain two mentions of the institution of slavery, both from the pen of her editor, Dr. Ramsay, and a half dozen mentions of individual slaves made by Martha herself in intimate letters to family. David Ramsay first used the conventional phrase "young white and black family," signifying the interdependence of human beings of differing skin color and power relationships within the same house, about his and Martha's household in the biographical introduction to *Memoirs.*[41] He then elaborated, in a footnote, the theme of Martha's commitment to slave discipline as a way of directing readers' interpretations of Martha's diary self-criticisms.

First, writing about his wife's high-minded, covenantal religious direction of household routines, Dr. Ramsay singled out her methodical plan for keeping the Sabbath. Her "young white and black family . . . both [received] catechetical instruction at the same time," he wrote. David's description of her habit of daily Scripture reading and prayer with her "domestic circle," was his way of celebrating her household harmony. His use of the label *family* revealed his agenda for her *Memoirs:* prescribing the ideal that the white Christian wife and mother should model in a slaveholding society. Within a system he opposed on principle, he thought Martha the best available example.[42]

"Black and white family" became an oft-employed euphemism by the mid-nineteenth century, because white Christians found it comforting.[43] It implied they were indeed discharging the religious duty owed their slaves, whether or not that image actually influenced the physical treatment their slaves received. Dr. Ramsay intended to present himself and his idealized Martha as devout human beings, "walking in the way of the Lord." Though today his language seems effusive and hagiographic, David Ramsay intended *Memoirs* to promote a living image of virtue that combined religious concern with respect for the enslaved—the kind of stance some historians later dismissed as "moonlight and magnolia apologetics."[44] Ramsay however was expressing the accepted Christian ideals in his place and class, not attempting to address the more unsettling moral questions of antislavery crusaders like Wesley.

David Ramsay's second editorial insertion used the topic of slavery tangentially, as background for his tempering the many self-accusations of unworthiness in Martha's diary entries. By the second decade of the 1800s, when he was editing her *Memoirs,* the language of Calvinist self-abasement may well have lost some of its ability to certify the ideal of humility, so he may have felt that Martha's fervent self-condemnation needed a mitigating context. He selected Martha's words about her failure to keep slaves from "vice" and "intemperance" to make his point.[45]

Dr. Ramsay had good reason to use this topic to contradict his wife, since drunkenness was a well-known problem afflicting all classes in America, and was one of his own major concerns (with no overt awareness that drink was one of the means of subverting owners' authority actually available to slaves). He and his northern allies, Dr. Rush and the Rev. Belk-nap, had committed themselves to a campaign of letters to newspapers and medical associations promoting abstinence from alcohol. *Memoirs* thus provided him with a covert platform for additional lobbying.[46] Among the various infractions of which young slaves might be guilty, a principled matron like Martha would view drunkenness as particularly heinous, shaped by her father's Calvinist attitude toward self-indulgence. Even the reasonable Henry Laurens, when Martha was a girl of six, had severely punished an intoxicated slave who also made a sideline of dealing in alco-hol. Amos, who had a tendency to "turn Rum Merchant," had been ordered to receive "39 sound stripes" and be forced out of his owner's protection—"turn[ed] out of the gate."[47] Martha's responsibility for keeping the instru-ments of vice away from servants epitomized the direction in which personal religion was moving in the eighteenth century. Instead of the for-mer emphasizing the quest for personal (and familial) salvation as primary, some organized religious bodies had begun to turn their focus outward, their efforts expended to "cleanse the world" from sin.[48] If the world had any chance of becoming more orderly, more pleasing to God, Christians were the essential agents of change: it was they, like Martha, who must wall off, protect, and direct in the right way those most vulnerable to sin.

David Ramsay also saw the topic of slave discipline as a means of high-lighting Martha's efficiency in domestic oversight, the new American model of female competence. Many white Americans believed that, since the slave system existed and they were helpless to abolish it, their path of duty required them to impart Anglo-cultural expectations, morals, and mores to their slaves. As a child, Martha watched her mother instruct ser-vants for their "improvement." Slaves must learn their owners' meanings of right and wrong, understand marriage as Christian whites did, and replace African practices with Americanized English customs.

According to David's annotation, Martha often vowed to be more consistent in discipline overall, and she "particularly" resolved "that every young negro, in addition to moral means [lectures, instructions], should be severely chastised for each and every single act of intoxication." He coun-tered her self-chastisement ("my easily besetting sin") by listing her virtues ("meekness, never angry or bitter").[49] This was to prevent readers from associating Martha with the distasteful feminist assertiveness of the noto-rious Mary Wollstonecraft, a point he was proud to make in another long footnote.[50] In fact, today the tone of her written prayers sounds anything but meek.

David Ramsay's praise for Martha, however, allowed him to comment indirectly on the theological and spiritual problems of slaveowning. As property, slaves' condition of servitude—less than fully human—made them highly vulnerable to alcohol's narcotizing qualities. An owner who ignored slaves' access to liquor was actively preventing one of God's creatures from healthful rather than destructive habits, to say nothing of physically damaging his or her own investment. Society's vulnerable members must be protected from the dangers of alcohol by the owner's vigilance. But Dr. Ramsay's comments added further to *Memoirs'* ambiguity. Did the Ramsay household have a hidden problem with drunkenness? How much moral instruction did this family offer its slaves? Did Martha "severely chastise" the young slaves? Martha's preference for persuasion over punishment for her own children makes such a reading unlikely. When she resolved to be more diligent about discipline, was that specific toward slave management or simply one more step in her pursuit of religious excellence?

Martha herself made five mentions of individual slaves in *Memoirs:* "Nanny our servant," who "died suddenly of an apoplexy"; the baby nurse Tira, who accompanied Martha and the breastfeeding infant, Kitty, to her father's plantation in November 1792 for his last hours on earth; the servant Coony, a driver or coachman whom she commissioned to deliver an anti-smoking pamphlet to David Jr., who was already on board a ship bound "northward" for college at Princeton; and two references in letters that mention an aging butler or dining-room waiter Jack.[51]

One note about Jack gave Martha the excuse to remind her son David Jr. in Princeton of the well-bred slaveholder's household etiquette: no revelatory conversation when a servant was present. Family dinner tables were expected to suspend any substantive discussion "until a servant is disengaged," she reminded him—an implicit acknowledgment of slave intelligence. Her motherly nudge undoubtedly recalled many impatient pauses endured by the Ramsay young. David Jr.'s mother wanted to touch his heart with the image of their smaller assemblage—"our lessened board"—since he was away at the College of New Jersey and his younger brothers were attending the Rev. Dr. Waddel's local boarding school, from which he himself had just graduated. Such a reduced number of diners made even "slow paced Jack more than we want [need]," she confided.[52]

Martha's second reference to Jack, in a note to her niece, accompanied information about the death and funeral of Thomas Coram, the family friend and professional colleague.[53] This in turn raised the topic of another funeral: "This afternoon or evening our poor Jack will [also] be carried to his earthly home."[54] Perhaps she implied that she and some of her children would attend poor Jack's burial service, or even that the pastor from their church would conduct Jack's funeral for the white and black family.

To date, historical records of slaves' adaptation to Anglo-Christian worship services before the 1820s consist only of mentions in the rare sermon or letter of a pioneer black preacher, or the testimony of slave women "filtered" through the record maintained by white preachers— proof that slave women had converted to Methodism.[55] Owners like Martha and David were among the local white Christians who would expect family slaves to attend church with them, though again such weekly routines were rarely mentioned in letters or diary. Their minister Hollinshead provided an exemplary model in their own backyard, so to speak—though here other silences in the record also leave room for ambiguous interpretation.

The Rev. William Hollinshead (1772–1817), senior pastor at the Circular Church, was an important mentor to Martha, although his unusual devotion to the Christianization of slaves appeared only at the margins of his posthumous record, almost an afterthought. His official biography noted his high esteem in Charleston, including board memberships in "every institution either literary or benevolent . . . which a minister of the Gospel could fill." Only years later did an addendum to the record cite his unusual "interest in the coloured population, his anxiety for their religious instruction, and his zeal for the welfare of their souls."[56] Though that tardy information was meager and perhaps amplified by mythology like David Ramsay's 1792 gesture, his influence on a devoted parishioner like Martha had to have been important.

"On every Sabbath morning, a considerable number of the coloured members of his church met at an early hour in his yard, and conducted their religious exercises alone in one of his outbuildings," began the letter appended to his biography. Pastor Hollinshead included his slaves in family worship, like Martha, and was known to explain the Scripture "in a language adapted to their comprehension." After a hymn and prayer, the slaves would "retire to their respective homes, to join afterwards in the public services of the sanctuary,"[57] seated in a segregated gallery. Clearly some slaves attended Anglo-religious services in addition to their own because of this white pastor.

Martha and David's slaves attending the same Circular Church on Sunday mornings provides evidence that some white Charlestonians admired educational and spiritual ministry to the souls of bondsmen and women; perhaps Martha's cryptic reference to laying "poor Jack" to rest conveyed meanings to her contemporaries that are unapparent today. The Rev. Hollinshead's historical reputation and his deep influence on Martha support the view that slavery as a topic was consciously suppressed in *Memoirs:* either Martha eliminated any thoughts admitting controversy about it or her husband omitted reference to racial issues because he feared such might depress its sales.

Of course the Ramsays and their contemporaries never employed the word *race,* except in hymns and poetry, any more than they did the word *slave.* High-minded Christians used *race* in religious terms rather than as linguistic fact.[58] The only time it appeared in Martha's diary was in a quoted hymn, where it meant the entire sinful race of human beings, not dark-skinned servants in bondage. British hymn writer Charles Wesley was a rare poet who employed "race" to address both salvation and skin color. His "For the Heathens" in 1780s England asked if God's grace could have been intended "for Adam's race" (white) alone, and was answered in resounding negatives. Using the Hebrew scriptural trope of slaves as descendants of Noah's son Ham, Wesley's third stanza read:

> *The servile progeny of Ham*
> *Seize as the purchase of thy blood;*
> *Let all the heavens know thy name;*
> *From idols to the living God*
> *The dark Americans convert,*
> *And shine in every pagan heart.*[59]

The few other references to slaves on Martha's list are also personal, rather than institutional. Two prosaic uses of the word *household* suggest she wanted to idealize the inclusiveness of her daily human context. A diary prayer in May 1806 asked that "all of my household" be impressed by her ardent efforts "to walk uprightly" in "faith, hope, sincerity, desire, and endeavor," instead of being disillusioned by her "imperfections." Since her Doddridge covenant, her explicit goal was to offer a witness powerful enough to convert everyone around her—not just blood kin but servants and people in the community. And in an undated letter excerpt, she invoked a poetic image of household—her "morning bible-readers, my noonday catechumens, my evening hymnists," obviously embracing all members of her black and white family.[60]

Martha's most complete diary entry about slaves was dated 4 May 1806, when family finances were extremely precarious. "The providential mercy of God did again interpose for us," Martha rejoiced, "that the servants whom we feared to lose and who feared to lose us are still in our possession." Modeling the owners' concern for slave dependents despite dire financial hardship, the Ramsays would have considered it unforgivable—too calculating, mercenary—to sell the black members of their family. Martha's prayerful thanks epitomized the forbearance required of Christian slaveowners, and was intended as a virtuous affirmation of masters' responsibility.[61]

The Ramsay household had apparently experienced something Martha called a miracle of deliverance. Obviously their enormous debt, or their creditors, might have forced them to exchange their slaves for cash. After confronting what would have been a tortuous rupture of relationships (and a blow to that aspect of her self-image), her daily world righted itself toward what she knew as normal. Somehow that fearsome possibility—a genuine sin of irresponsibility in Martha's eyes—had been resolved in "circumstances that give us reason to hope they [the slaves] will still continue in our service and in their comfortable situations." Though human beings' commercial value was the unavoidable subtext of this entry, her words focused on the personal and emotional ties rather than the institutional issue of owner and owned.[62]

One more direct reference to slavery, in Martha's words, cited a gesture that typified master-slave relations in the slave labor system: "giving out the key" was code for daily order and authority, on any plantation. In Martha's December 1792 letter reporting her father's final hours to David, she cited the reassurance (false, it turned out) she had read into her father's ability to execute that routine function, mere hours before he had slipped into his final coma. Propelled to his Mepkin plantation by providential leading and intuition—"so inexpressible a desire to see him"—she had hurried from Charleston to his side at the Mepkin plantation, accompanied by nursing infant Kitty and "faithful Tira," the slave who was the Ramsay baby nurse. The morning after arrival, she had awaked to find that her father had "already been up and given out the barn door key as usual."[63] For an instant, according to her letter, everything had seemed normal; knowledge that the master was monitoring the day's supplies and assignments had deluded her into assuming that the domestic world was still intact.[64] But despite that plantation routine, her father had slipped into unconsciousness later that morning and died within two days.

During the father-and-son confrontation over freed-slave soldiers for the Revolutionary War—John's translation of his father's ambivalence about slavery into new emotional and legislative territory—Martha's loyalties had been stretched. Now, in 1792, she faced another pull on family loyalties: the convergence of a husband's public anti–slave trade declaration and a father's end, his name and reputation unalterably linked in the public mind with the slave trade. On one hand, Martha knew only too well how much personal fortune and health Henry Laurens had "sacrificed" to his country. Indeed, her own period of exile from Carolina, patriarchally arranged and justified, had made her a participant in that sacrifice. And on the other hand, there was her husband. She idolized her father and believed he deserved his country's thanks and tribute (which was as yet unrepaid financially) for serving the new nation during its birth. And with her eldest brother, John, dead, Martha had assumed care, figuratively and literally, of the Laurens name: as family kinkeeper she would have been forced to face her own position on slaveholding. Martha and John had, each in their own way, absorbed the inherent contradictions of owning human property long before they could reason them out. Henry Laurens' ambivalence about slaving had long been visible in the tension between his genuine humanitarian concern for the realities experienced by his human labor force and his hard business sense. The tension was exhibited in his variable treatment of slaves. At one time he would instruct the overseer to give slave Castillo his "full deserts" of harsh whipping for circumventing plantation authority; at another he ordered that old May, weak and infirm, be given "very little work" because "he is a human Creature whether you like him or not."[65] Writing about a cruel overseer Gambrell, whom he later fired, Henry demonstrated more interest in character than skin color and rank as he thanked his brother James: "Your handling of Old Cuffy was kind and wise. Do write that old Man . . . a line of comfort. O that wretched Gambrell. He is not the tythe in virtue of that Black Man, Poor old Cuffy." Henry knew his employee, however: "If Gambrell was to hear [me say] this he would fly into madness."[66]

But along with his determination to be a reasonable master, Henry Laurens was first and foremost a businessman, a product of the previous century's Huguenot diaspora that created a transoceanic "Protestant International" of skilled, practical, and successful merchants. Having been "regularly bred to merchandise," and naming trade, family, and religion as the rhetorical lodestars in all his correspondence,[67] he was ultimately more concerned with the integrity of the merchant economy that undergirded his business dealings than the humanitarian treatment of his laborers.[68] Confronted by hard choices, Laurens usually chose "good business." This became more obvious during the war. In 1765 Henry had refused a business offer that required "the unnecessary division of Fathers, Mothers, Husbands, Wives & Children who tho Slaves are still human creatures & I cannot be deaf to their cries." But during the 1770s, economics gained precedence. Affronted by what seemed to him disloyalty, he commanded overseer William Smith to sell a particular slave. "I will not keep a runaway, the first and only one I ever had. The rest are in general very orderly and give me but little trouble. Sell him as best you can."[69]

Laurens' attitudes toward the idea of emancipation conveyed the same ambivalence. In 1771, sorrow over the "pitiable and deprived" condition of his slaves elicited compassion and real identification with them as human beings: "How much do I pity those poor unhappy Men, Women and Children to whose Distresses and Starving Conditions the Rice Planter is indebted for the vast Advance of Price for his Produce. Have I any cause to complain? when I reflect one moment upon their miserable Circumstances and compare my own."[70] Then in 1776, the year family letters bristled with anger at the British Parliament, he enjoyed the luxury of blaming England for the entire evil system. "I abhor Slavery," he wrote John. "I was born in a country where Slavery had been established by British Kings and Parliaments as well as by the Laws of that country, ages before my existence." He admitted confusion over the issue that would trouble Martha's conscience in 1795: "I found the Christian Religion & Slavery growing under the same authority and cultivation—I nevertheless disliked it." Still, he insisted, disingenuously, "I am not the man who enslaved them, they are indebted to English Men for that favour." At that early point in the war (August 1776), he told his son that he was "devising means for manumitting many of them," despite the opposition that would rise against him, of "great powers . . . the Laws & Customs of my Country, my own and the avarice of my Country Men."[71] But thereafter, anxiety about his diminishing estate pushed aside that plan. Philadelphia Quaker abolitionist Anthony Benezet, a fellow Huguenot descendant, named Henry Laurens (among others) under his blanket indictment of greed—the only real motive for slaveowning.[72] While Laurens would have smarted at that accusation because he saw himself as a devoted Christian, he also had to preserve his wealth, which consisted of slaves and the land they made productive: "What will my Children say if I deprive them of so much Estate?"[73]

On one hand, Henry Laurens' defense of slavery was objectively economic. On the other, deep emotions tapped by individual slaves gave rise to contradictions, making him uncomfortable with it. By the time of the war, his ambivalence about slavery had created a rumor that he was a "promoter" of "strange . . . dangerous doctrines," attributed to his "inborn [Huguenot Protestant] instinct of fairness and liberty."[74] Still, worries fueled by the war's uncertainties and slaves lured by British promises of freedom were vexing. In 1773 he had exclaimed about an overseer's cruelty, "For what signifies his knowledge of Planting if through those faults he drives away the People without whose aid he can neither plant nor beat out his Crop? I would rather be without Crops of Rice than gain the largest by one single Instance of Cruelty or Inhumanity."[75] Yet in 1775 that same Henry Laurens gave his support to the physical mutilation of Thomas Jeremiah, a free black convicted of trying to mount a slave insurrection. However reluctantly, he viewed such a public bloodletting as necessary to allay white slaveowners' fears in the approach of war.[76]

During the same period, Henry spelled out a different set of ambivalences over the "Scene of my foolish Rascally Robert," a personal slave who was with him in England. In a letter to his English partner George Appleby, Robert's owner recited the slave's "comical Narrative of Bigamy & Burglary" as proof that English law was itself at fault. Shouldn't a slave receive the same punishment as a white man for the same crime? Henry's rascally Robert would likely get off "the present Indictment" with "the Light penalty of Transportation." Of course if he were returned to America, Robert would still be a slave, in which case "no man in the World has So just a Claim upon him as I. He is *my property according to the Laws of this Land, as well as of that Country*," Henry fumed.[77] At Robert's own earnest petition, owner Laurens had saved him from being sent to the West Indies in return for Robert's repeated promises of improvement. "I have treated him with all that humanity . . . one . . . ought to extend to every Creature in Subjection to him," Henry believed. Against his own better judgment that slave had been vaccinated against smallpox, and Henry really did not want him severely chastised. "Bad as he has been, I would not wish him Hanged for Stealing Bacon."[78]

Disillusionment with rascally Robert likely compounded Henry Laurens' disgruntlement over his niece Molsy's fall from grace and proper society at the same time, and prompted his rare epistolary outburst about race and sex. British women, particularly working-class females, were unabashedly responsive to Negro sexuality, noted the upright Mr. Laurens; they actually praised it as "mending the breed of English Men." Against such flagrant sexual disorder the "supineness" of British lawmakers was too much for him. No legislation against it meant that responsible citizens in

Britain were simply caving in to "the Merit of the female Gust." If the "man-ufactory" of "unfettered sexual congress" were not halted by some legal restraint, there would be twenty thousand "mulatties" in London alone in another five years.[79] Here he was echoing the cries of British journalists who sold newspapers with their warning that natural British looks and coloring would be hopelessly stained with "the morisco tint" unless Englishmen took steps to cut off the source of such contamination, which was granting citizenship rights to imported Africans. Henry Laurens had no problem with the "pitiless racism" thus printed, and perhaps viewed it as a necessary counterbalance to the incendiary revelations then being published by Eng-lish abolitionists.[80]

In the year of the war's beginning, 1776, Henry reported with pardon-able pride that "My Negroes in Georgia and South Carolina are attached to me, not one has attempted to desert."[81] But within a year his letters carried a less sanguine incident about a male slave named Scaramouche. "If he should elope and you can recover him, after due Correction cause Irons to be put upon him and keep him confined at work," Henry wrote the over-seer. Regretting this "first Instance of any Negroe of mine put in Irons," he justified its severity because of the slave's "Ingratitude."[82] What he did not need to make explicit was that "due Correction" meant a resort to flogging— the whip. The casual order for "discipline" often meant something as rela-tively mild as a change in work conditions, but the word *punishment* meant the lash.[83] Insubordination affronted the slaveowner's sense of control and required the most cruel tool of management they had: physical pain. Its message was a contradictory admission that he or she was human.

Whipping as the accepted mechanism of control was a cultural given for Martha Laurens Ramsay, an unquestioned detail on the canvass of slave society.[84] Yet it was no more mentioned in Martha's writings than slavery itself.[85] In 1777 Henry Laurens stated his alternatives for slave control: "Severity or Separation . . . the former may reduce and reform but I prefer the latter." Mary, the mother of Cuffee and "long the bane of" a group of his Negro families, was to be sold far out of proximity to any of his three plantations. "The removal of such leaven may stop a contagion," he hoped, discarding his own previous dictum about preserving slave families.[86] Every master who wanted to be viewed as kind believed that loyal slaves were a testimonial to his humane management, but an outsider during the Revo-lutionary War saw the prevailing South Carolina plantation system in its rawest conditions: "Negroes must be kept very severely . . . naked, living in miserable huts, a poor diet of crushed corn or rice boiled . . . not only in terms of their subsistence, but also to the punishments executed against them," revealing the way whites' demonized slave disobedience. The hard view was that slaves were "revengeful" and "as obstinate as undomesticated cattle," their use of "Guinea language among themselves" merely compounding owner anxieties.[87] The contradictions of slave intelligence and cleverness simply proved their humanness rather than their bestiality.

In late summer 1777, Henry Laurens' humanity made him order blankets for his slaves against the coming winter, despite a short money supply: "I would rather strip my pocket naked than suffer my Negroes to be so on a winter's night," he assured John Gervais.[88] And when a formerly obedient, valued slave named March maimed himself by cutting off his left hand above the thumb Henry was deeply affected—even forced to question his own talent for judging slave character. March had always been a "man of placid and obliging disposition," and "a good and faithful Servant." Henry's dismay at such self-mutilation made him glad to focus on a scapegoat— the corrupting female Mary, on whose account March had already been "cruelly whipped by Morgan."[89] A subversive influence on March, Mary would have to be sent to Georgia and sold, clever and valuable though she was. In a written sigh, Henry added that he felt obligated to punish March as well. Ordering him to be whipped was "a necessity due to the public," since March had dared alter the conditions of his own servitude. "Otherwise, from the reluctance I feel I believe he would escape [it.]" Yet another slave fracas brought the order for instant sale of three culprits. Applying his own theory of reciprocity, he believed those slaves would confront terrible dangers away from his beneficent ownership. "If they knew . . . my intentions toward them . . . my Negroes would esteem a change of Masters to be the heaviest Punishment that could be inflicted on them."[90] Martha echoed that mind-set in the 1790s about the possibility of having to sell her household slaves.

In his own eyes, Henry, and slaveowners like him, with a preference for management by "Separation" rather than "Severity," saw themselves as responsible masters employing the modern theory of sentiments.[91] He believed his slaves benefited from the civility with which he treated them, that slaves and masters were sharing "social bonds." But when necessary he could resort to the whip—the unfortunate management tool embedded in "deep custom and prejudice," within their complex labor system and the sacred law of private property.[92]

Although ambivalent about slavery, Henry Laurens was nevertheless galvanized by his son's uncompromising plan to dismantle or rearrange slavery in 1778. John had sounded wildly visionary when he talked about freeing slaves to fight against England. His idea was presented in sequential steps, tentatively: "First I would advance those who are unjustly deprived of the Rights of Mankind to a State which would be a proper Gradation between abject Slavery and perfect Liberty—and I would reinforce the Defenders of Liberty with a number of gallant Soldiers."[93] But the anarchy potential in his son's proposal unleashed Henry Laurens' primal paternal instincts. Employing a broad verbal arsenal—irony, sarcasm, and public disdain—he spelled out its reputational and financial disaster: "Not a man in America is [of] your opinion." John should tread warily, lest "without effecting any good," his plan would do worse than make him a laughingstock—"a bye word." He might instead be "transmitted to your Children's Children" as a fool rather than a patriot idealist.[94] The father-son debate by letter continued into 1779, and at one point Henry Laurens actually borrowed his son's image as an attempt to bolster General Washington's mood: "Had we arms for three thousand such black men as I could select in South Carolina I should have no doubt of success in driving the British out of Georgia." The 1782 South Carolina legislature, where John proposed his idea, found his fellow slaveowners (with the exception of a few like Dr. Ramsay, not yet his brother-in-law) more concerned to preserve their slave property than defeat the enemy.[95]

Toward the end of his life, Henry Laurens expressed his frustration over the society he had helped construct: "Though I may cry out that I am constrained to dwell, etc., yet I must dwell [in a slave society] and probably all the remainder of my life, which can last at most but few years longer."[96] On 7 July 1790, aware of his increasing fragility, he made a gesture that gave concreteness to his longing. He dictated a letter of manumission for his personal slave. Son-in-law Dr. Ramsay was appointed "guardian of George—to be called George Laurens, son of Mr. Beekman's Neptune and Mr. Laurens' own slave Old Lucy"—who should be free after his master's death. (The letter noted that George had been offered full freedom earlier and refused it.) At his manumission, George Laurens was to receive $120 in silver for tools, clothes, or whatever he needed for self-maintaining work.[97] Finally, at the end of his life, Papa Henry's compassion took concrete (and symbolic) expression in that single act.

Yet another factor in Laurens ambivalence was the position of Henry's brother, James, whose negative view of slave trading Martha often heard during her residence in his household. His sighs of concern over business were often implicit disapproval of making money through slave imports, and in a 1773 letter to Henry he gave a rare explicit rejection. A business friend angling for entry into "the Affrican & Commission business" worried Uncle James into stating his commercial (and by implication, moral) distaste: "I disapprove and will have no concern in the Guinea trade. You may remember I refused it in the year 1767 when you were so kind as to make me an offer of your interest in that business, & thank God, neither my circumstances or inclinations make it more necessary [now] to engage in new concerns." He cloaked his objections in a desire for "more and more …retirement and freedom from all perplexing cares,"[98] itself a polite bridge over the moral gulf between brothers on this topic, although his reservation was likewise unmentioned in Martha's preserved thoughts.

What had Martha gleaned from her father about slavery? Gender constraints would likely have made her frame any criticisms in an externally dutiful support of all her father's views. Elite daughters learned very early to subordinate their own inner convictions, at least verbally; they knew well how to mask inner disagreement and resistance—to themselves as well as their fathers. Intersecting messages about race and gender in an upper-class family of property nourished a healthy sense of caution about female independence, even the intellectual variety. Underneath all the ambivalent questions in her world was the deeper awareness that unchanneled, uncircumscribed female sexuality was viewed as danger on a par with free blacks: both were fearsome portents of disorder in a patriarchal system that depended on unquestioned authority. Further, from her father's ambivalence she would have focused her own fears of possible anarchy and unthinkable chaos that would be the result if slaves were not controlled. Clearly, the earliest and most tenacious roots of Martha's ambivalence must be traced back to Henry Laurens' yearning to be rid of that tyrannical system, the mixed message she too embodied.

Henry's heirs, coming to maturity during the Revolution—Martha, David, sons John and Henry Jr., and youngest daughter Mary Eleanor (Polly)—were affected by the emerging literary idealization of compassion far more than their father could have been. They were constantly exposed to the new literary view that a person without compassion, "unmoved by the pains and joys of another," was unnatural, even inhuman—an internal moral evaluation that began to meld seamlessly into existing religious definitions. Worldly authors like Adam Smith named pity—"the emotion which we feel for the misery of others"—a new moral imperative, and this attitude was diffused by print opinion-shapers such as the British import *Gentleman's Magazine*. The Ramsays read and quoted British writers like

Richardson and the great Dr. Samuel Johnson, who, along with the few American antislavery voices, were leading their readers along newly mapped channels of empathy toward innocent suffering and thus to a different self-assessment. Under these expanded standards of emotional and religious nobility, individual Christians were beginning to acknowledge the experience of guilt when they confronted the extent of slaves' unmerited suffering.[99]

Fellow Huguenot-American Anthony Benezet (1713–1784) was a seminal figure in creating this negative response to slavery.[100] Known to readers of the *Columbian Magazine* for having established his own Philadelphia school for free blacks, and more for his powerful abolitionist writings, he was the colonial American who challenged the countess of Huntingdon to face her complicity in slaveowning (by sending her John Wesley's 1774 *Thoughts on Slavery*), and one of the first to name greed as the chief motive behind slavery. In one of his pamphlets, after citing such craven depths of inhumanity as flogging pregnant slave women (staked face down over a hole in the ground to receive their enlarged abdomens), he wrote this warning: "It cannot be that war or contract can give any man such a property in another as he has in his sheep or oxen. No human law can deprive any human being of the liberty which he derives from the law of nature. Let none serve you but by his own voluntary choice."[101]

Antislavery arguments specifically addressed to the consciences of good, churchgoing citizens in the new United States were expressed entirely in religious language and were couched as pleas for religious and personal internal (rather than institutional or constitutional) reform. For example, Martha's New England contemporary Sarah Osborne, widely known for sympathizing with and educating slaves in her Newport, Rhode Island, home school, described her efforts to bring slaves salvation in terms of religious rather than bodily "freedom."[102] The unarticulated logic of making spiritual reform a prime antislavery mechanism was based on the assumption that when Christians revived their own inner and behavioral commitment to true religion, all social ills would automatically wither and disappear, including slavery. Thus antislavery pronouncements of John Wesley, John Newton, and Anthony Benezet scolded Christians for their spiritual lethargy, the weakness of their lukewarm "philanthropic energy." Even though the language was indirect in terms of civic, earthly application, the meanings of "reasonableness" and "right" were gradually being changed and redefined.

From the earliest English antislavery voices of Lord Shaftesbury and Granville Sharpe, through Dr. Samuel Stanhope Smith (a Scottish friend of the Ramsays who would be president of the College of New Jersey when David Jr. attended as a student from 1809 to 1811), print arguments were expanding the purview of religious duty in regard to slavery.[103] David and Martha were among those who enjoyed critical engagement with all modern ideas and religious thought. Writers Martha used and recommended for her own children—Bible storywriter Mrs. Mary Martha Sherwood, the British Christian mystic and poet William Cowper (who wrote a famous poem "The Negro's Complaint" in 1793), and their own friend Dr. Rush— were tenacious and outspoken voices against slaveowning; Rush's "The Paradise of Negro Slaves, a Dream" appeared in the *Columbian Magazine* the same year Martha and David were married.[104] In England, the publishing of first-person narratives by former Africans—Ignatius Sancho's *Letters* (1782), Ottobah Cugoano's *Thoughts and Sentiments on the Evil of Slavery* (1787), and Olaudah Equiano's *Interesting Narrative* (1789) were creating a print sensation (John Wesley particularly named this last as having a profound impact on his thinking). To educated, conscientious white Christians, books written by former slaves in literate English—books using the same logic, concepts, and vocabulary as white authors—were incontrovertible proof that slaves must be recognized as fully and equally human, not as a species for whom theology was irrelevant.[105]

A layered portrayal of mid-eighteenth-century unease about slavery was captured in a book, *The New Pilgrim's Progress* (1748), something Martha's Uncle James might well have imported to sell. Its title signaled an updating of the challenges faced by John Bunyan's famous "Pilgrim" a century earlier: those were personal and dramatic moral battles against evil and soul-destroying sins, for example, sloth and vanity. In the modernized version, the tests challenging the soldier of faith (an ordained Church of England missionary to the New World) were sociological rather than internal: he confronted issues of race and rank, societal inequality. A fictionalized travelogue made up of tales within a tale, the book dramatized the moral dilemmas presented by the new transatlantic world and unflinchingly mirrored the rationalizations of white Christian slaveholders in the West Indies and the Carolinas. The modern Pilgrim recognized sin in his New World adventures by the inner religious disquiet it created, the very message a Christian woman of Martha Ramsay's mind-set would recognize. *The New Pilgrim's Progress* displayed both the unquestioned Anglo ethnocentrism of its times and the foundering of Christian antislavery preaching on the rocks of white commercial and cultural resistance.[106]

Poetry, a less prosaic avenue into Martha's consciousness, may have penetrated more deeply than imported British prose by or about enslaved Africans. The Rev. George Whitefield and the countess of Huntingdon had praised an American poetess, the freed New England slave Phillis Wheatley, and rewarded her with a trip to England some years before Martha herself was "very much noticed" by the same titled lady. Phillis Wheatley had been thrust onto the American national literary horizon because she, too, like the former African slave authors in England, wrote like "a [white] woman of refinement." She too was entertained in the very household and honored by the same eminently pious female as Martha.[107] And Martha, her husband recalled, "highly prized the company of such persons": pious and "literarily talented" women.[108]

Wheatley's achievement, lionized in London as "genius in bondage," was seen to establish once and for all the intellectual and esthetical equality of slaves with white, educated human beings. A white American contemporary of Martha's under the pseudonym "Matilda" celebrated that new "fact" in a 1796 poetic tribute, "On Reading Poems of Phillis Wheatly, African Poetess." Matilda rejoiced that dark skin, the former excuse for enslavement, had lost its *rational* (or rationalizable) authority. Reason was now tilted firmly in the opposite direction: enslaving fellow humans because of color was *ir*-rational. Her final triumphant lines read:

> *Tis done! at length the long withheld decree*
> *Goes forth, that Afric shall be blest and free;*
> *A Phillis rises, and the world no more*
> *Denies the sacred right to mental power.*
> *Heav'n inspir'd she proves her Country's right*
> *To freedom, and her own to deathless Fame.*[109]

If Martha had written anything poetic about this same literary milestone, she too would have employed the language of "rights" and idealized her country's "righteousness" for its tribute to the "right to freedom." She and husband, David, cherished their own "right to mental power." As determinedly reasonable, rational Christian citizens, they welcomed that quality in others and cultivated it in their young—even if the poet's assertion that *Africans* had a "right" to freedom raised conscience-searing questions.

Martha Ramsay's silence about slavery was naturally affected most by the ambivalence of husband David Ramsay, her closest companion in adult life. He had moved to the South in 1773, eager to participate in the political and organizational life of Charles Town, to make his mark in literary, scientific, and governmental arenas in the emerging nation. His being held as a British prisoner-of-war during the struggle for independence from Britain was the defining event in his life.[110] He believed his skills and service validated his aspirations to civic eminence in his adopted city, despite his being a "northward man."[111] Happy as he was in his new setting, his negativity toward slavery constituted an ideological gulf between him and the family of his third wife. The year after he married Martha, David confided in a letter to Benjamin Rush a hearty wish that "it had been my lot to have spent my days where slavery was unknown!" Existential experience of its moral burden made him add, "To speak as a Christian, I really fear some heavy judgment awaits on that very score."[112] Some of his Carolina compatriots knew his critical view of what they called their way of life, and he was considered an outsider even after his marriages to Charleston women. Still, he enjoyed enough recognition and support in Charleston to be elected to the state senate eight years, spending six as its presiding officer. David Ramsay's ambivalence made him a highly complex character.

Though his private epistolary words about slavery may have been less guarded before he married into the Laurens family in 1787, they remained mild and relatively unchallenging, for a time, compared with his incendiary statement in 1792. From the time of his arrival in 1770, this intelligent, impulsive physician from Philadelphia Medical School *knew* that Charleston society was committed to economic and cultural justifications for slavery. He found himself—like the traveling clergyman in the *New Pilgrim's Progress*—a captive of its defensiveness. Businessmen like his esteemed father-in-law were convinced that Carolina could not make agriculture economically productive without slave labor. If Martha's father had known that brash newcomer Ramsay credited the 1779 British invasion of Carolina with the "great service to the state . . . by diminishing the number of slaves," Henry Laurens might have given his new physician a cooler welcome—or summoned a different local doctor.[113] After the war, in 1783, Dr. Ramsay regretted, but at that time did not publicly oppose, the resumption of the slave trade. By then he was already too aware that the "Don Quixot who would attempt" to abolish it, who even dared address it, would receive "public odium" for daring to breach the public silence.[114]

Given David Ramsay's less than complete adaptation to the Carolina ethos, it should hardly have surprised him or Martha when, during his 1788 campaign for a seat in the newly formed United States Senate, that damaging topic was made public in a newspaper debate. How could a Pennsylvania-born northerner suitably represent South Carolina's "interests" (read:

solidly proslavery) in the new national forum, his opponent William Loughton Smith asked. "Though Ramsay denies it, it is very well known that he is principled against slavery, it is idle for him to contradict what is so universally known," Smith's letter stated, boring in on the issue of character. "Either the Doctor must act according to his principles and injure the country [South Carolina]" or deny his convictions and "serve the country thwart"—reveal himself to be a hypocrite who "opposes his own sentiments and principles." Dr. Ramsay's dilemma was daunting, especially to the principled, pillar-of-the-church citizens whose votes he wanted, where one's word or conviction was assumed to be sacred. Second, and more significant for his elective future, his ambivalence about the rightness of slavery had already aroused the commercial interests in the community. Could Carolinians really be expected to believe that Dr. Ramsay had *"never* declared that he thought slavery ought to be abolished," his opponent queried? The rhetorical question carried its own arrow into the viscera of voters. They could hardly be asked to trust the interests of Carolina to one whose "necessary inclination" would be "to injure me [and all of you]" financially.[115] Lifelong Charlestonian Martha knew well that maneuver and justification.

In fact, a smaller, more homely crime related to mistrusting his antislavery inclinations was what actually brought down the Ramsay electoral ambitions: his role as a known conduit for antislavery literature. The Ramsay house on Broad Street held not only his medical office and family home but was also a central depository for a vareity of imported print materials—and two major antislavery pamphlets printed in Philadelphia had been seen there. The print contamination of which he was accused happened to be two tracts, "Clarkson's essays": *An Essay on the Slavery and Commerce of the Human Species* (Philadelphia, 1786) and *An Essay on the Impolity of the African Slave Trade* (Philadelphia, 1788), reprinted from young Thomas Clarkson's prizewinning Cambridge University thesis. Viewed as a scholarly antislavery urtext in its time, it documented the history of slavery in the Western world to the present, including recently published materials about slaveowners' barbarity in the British West Indies' sugar and rum trade. The new abolition societies in America were quick to republish and distribute the Clarkson pamphlets through their network.[116]

The Clarkson name, then, was recognized as the leading edge of antislavery assault on the South, an ideal trigger for the outrage of white Charlestonians who wanted to think of themselves as "good." One of the inflammatory, eyewitness accounts of white inhumanity cited by Clarkson

had been written by the Rev. James Ramsay, a Church of England missionary "in the British Sugar Colonies" (no blood kin of David as far as is
known), that supported and reiterated the accusations of Wesley and
Benezet.[117] A British clergyman and outspoken humanitarian, the Reverend
Ramsay's vivid metaphors portrayed white owners treating slaves as "mere
machines or instruments of profit," with total disregard for their suffering.
His riveting "I was there" tone pierced the self-protective Carolinian
cocoon even more effectively than Clarkson's own academic prose, forcing
the horrors inherent in a slave system right through the insulated fabric of
daily life for Martha and her contemporaries. To admit that such human
depravity was true meant that she, for one, must question every rationalization for its existence that she had absorbed since childhood. And what
then? To even contemplate the idea of abolishing slavery meant the end of
all certainties: her family and heritage, her culture and education, her
assumptions about normality, the very ground of her morality, and her
understandings of what was good and what was evil.

The Ramsays were among the local literati who enjoyed the elite status of owning and circulating cosmopolitan reading materials. For Martha,
it began with her Uncle James' book business. David himself had become
known for collecting subscriptions to support the publishing of their New
England author compatriots, and for acting as the agent of distribution,
since new books needed a point of entry into a given locale. Both Ramsays
had reputations of being related to and associated with books—Martha
bestowing them as gifts, David not only writing them but also promoting
their readership and sales.[118] His attempt to explain away the dangers of the
Clarkson accusation started with this defense: Charleston newspaper readers knew that all kinds of books and pamphlets were often "left at my
house, in my absence, by . . . unknown person[s], without any letter to
me."[119]

The full electoral uproar over David Ramsay's possession of antislavery materials (no doubt along with other incriminating books, his enemies
suspected) continued to focus on whether or not Dr. Ramsay had actually
passed them along, actively crusading against slavery. At this point, however, ambivalence led him to overplay his hand. David Ramsay reiterated
his self-image as innocent literary middleman, coming up with a legalistic
denial that ignored the substance of the charge. He had often passed along
unopened packets to the "particular gentlemen" on the address, he
explained, "forward[ing] them as letters without knowing their contents
till after they were opened." Totally unwitting on his part, books like the

Clarkson pamphlets might easily have been part of such a transaction. Then overexplaining, he condemned himself: "My own copy I never read nor circulated." Voters were expected to take his word that he too disapproved of the Clarkson pamphlets and that those alone, out of the many books he passed around, had never left his house.[120]

The volume of print flowing across the Ramsay threshold could in fact legitimate his claim that any single publication was an easily ignored bubble in that rushing stream. However, critics already knew that the Ramsays had long subscribed to the racially and politically liberal *Columbian Magazine* from Philadelphia and were close to Dr. Benjamin Rush, its widely read author of federalist and antislavery essays. A case of condemnation by literary association was easy to make.[121] But David Ramsay helped them; his public wavering was embarrassing. His disingenuous explanation revealed only too clearly his discomfort at "standing against the cherished beliefs of friends and neighbors."[122] In 1788 he would confess to John Eliot in Massachusetts that he had lost that election "because I was a northward man and represented as favoring the abolition of slavery. Such is the timber of our people here that it is unpopular to be unfriendly to the further importation of slaves."[123] David Ramsay's experience in this debacle foreshadowed what became a Charleston truism: that in terms of public reputation, it was safer to be "slightly Tory" than to be "slightly abolitionist."[124] It also made his no-turning-back declaration in 1792 the more remarkable.

Martha must have suffered with and over her husband's political ambitions in that first year of their marriage, 1788, perhaps rationalizing his defeat as the result of campaign trickery. She would have sympathized with his disappointment, whether or not she was embarrassed by his misjudgment of political strategy and poor explanation in a crisis. In 1792, for once he stepped out from behind his ambivalence—the complicated mix of admirable ideals, failure of will, and impulsive words comprising his electoral Achilles heel. By 1835, a generation later, being found with antislavery materials would produce far weightier consequences; that year the possession of antislavery print was an excuse for a public conflagration.[125]

Perhaps the most significant element in Martha's silences, for interpreting her "being of two minds" about slavery, was her husband's editorial eye and pen. As he compiled her "literary remains" in the immediate weeks after her death in 1811, his own embarrassment during the 1788 election was revived and he had to weigh the cost of antislavery sentiments in their world. If or when David Ramsay made a reluctant decision to omit from the published *Memoirs* any writings about slavery that Martha had committed to the secrecy of her diary, community ethos triumphed. His biographer, Arthur Shaffer, suggests that, in the end, David adapted himself to the Carolina environment, becoming more a part of his wife's familial and cultural orbit than her of his. Martha's "northward" husband accepted acculturation into her world as the price of survival. All he loved and worked for was there, along with the abhorrent institution of slavery.

Shaffer also suspects that Martha's husband may have confronted his double-bind about slavery in 1790, when he began compiling the statistics for his comprehensive two-volume *History of South Carolina.* That research involved vast correspondence for which he credited (unusual in an author of his time) his wife's extensive assistance.[126] His published analysis of the state's inhabitants simply omitted information detailing the African population. He acknowledged slave labor, domestic and plantation, in his "Miscellaneous History" section, under "Manners and Character," but directed his severest criticism at the "lowest grade of [white] people, called squatters," who were denigrated as mere nuisances.[127] That particular silence—ambivalence incarnate—was surely David Ramsay's "no comment" about slavery—eloquent testimony that he had learned the public price of deeply held "principle" on that topic. Not wanting to jeopardize potential sales of his *History,* he chose to ignore much about the majority of the state's labor force. Such an omission could scarcely have been accidental, given his national reputation for vast, inclusive compilation of facts; he was widely known as an early American statistician, by which he meant documenting interesting information—for example, a list of white citizens over one hundred years of age.[128] Possibly after collecting black numbers that were disproportionate, but unable without betraying his true sentiments to credit slaves (rather than their owners) for South Carolina's economic progress, David opted for authorial excision. Thanks to the many personal and political challenges he endured between the conception and publication of that study, Ramsay had plenty of opportunity to edit out a section, an editorial technique he may well have used again with Martha's *Memoirs.*[129]

Martha knew and loved her husband's enthusiastic idealism, and they both exhibited confidence in their Enlightenment-era education: a commitment to the importance of reason and reasonableness, a certainty that principled rhetoric by good men, good people, had the power to bring about a good society. Martha also knew how profoundly her husband's self-esteem had been enhanced by election to public office, and the depth of his disappointment at being denied that possibility because, at least in part, of his antislavery sympathies. Though she admired his eloquence on nearly all occasions, she could still internally deplore his public reference to the house-divided position on slavery that characterized their Laurens-Ramsay union. His legislative apotheosis at disrupting "slave imports" very likely seared the heart of his own "tender attachment," though she would never have criticized him for it.

Martha Laurens Ramsay actually had to negotiate degrees of loyalty to her husband's and her father's differing worldviews over everything, not just slavery and finances. The Ramsays' marriage coincided with the brief period at the end of the eighteenth century when slavery could be a relatively open topic. This required a juggling on her part that might have upset their marital equilibrium if Dr. Ramsay's admiration for his father-in-law had been less vast and respectful. The new organizations actively promoting the abolition of slavery were one more phenomenon about which she had to examine her conscience and ponder a response.

Because Martha's innate Laurens drive had chosen religion for the arena in which she could strive for distinction, the new, religiously authenticated truths about conditions on slave ships and the Middle Passage, and about the unthinkable cruelties so-called Christian owners visited on their human property, had to be especially wounding. Because she had covenanted herself as a co-worker with God and she was a serious Christian, she would have found it impossible to block out awareness that slaves were fellow human beings in the eyes of God, that they possessed "a sense of human sameness in feeling."[130] Since adolescence her religious application had been more personally intense than was usual among her contemporaries; by all accounts she was in no way like them spiritually—typically "easy and tolerable, polite without cultivating the principle, religious without feeling."[131] The new theological condemnation of slavery would have led her in the direction of her husband's position and altered her emotions around her Laurens legacy in profound ways.

Martha's and David's expanding realization of slavery's moral and ethical burden had to have been counterbalanced by their cultural Anglo-British view of dark skin color, hair, and facial features as esthetically inferior—an impersonal evaluation only a Benjamin Rush could at that time call racist.[132] Second and more ironic, the domestic management skills required for a household encompassing a black and white family had to complicate her "two minds" about slavery. By class and race, she had to be counted among the highly privileged women of her time who "revelled in their privilege"; she was at one level a predecessor of the antebellum white slave mistresses who "saw themselves . . . as warm, God-fearing, decent, even exemplary in white society."[133] David Ramsay was fulsomely proud of the dispatch and dignity with which Martha managed their often penurious establishment and the backdrop of slave labor that maintained it. Martha's ambivalence interlayered the common domestic space of husband, children, boarders, guests, relatives, and household servants. On the surface she continued to honor the arrangements of a system she knew from birth as normal and orderly. But a mature, ethical mind like Martha's couldn't help but recoil at realizing that "her" system, slaveowning, treated human beings as commodities. While she found ways to live within the cognitive dissonance thus created, maintaining the social charade must have increasingly affronted her spiritual intelligence.

David's friend Benjamin Rush, actively promoting antislavery societies in the 1780s, could have become an irritant in Martha Ramsay's conscience, however much she may also have admired him. Knowing that Rush had urged English abolitionists, early on, to "tease your Parliament every year with petitions . . . and anecdotes on the injustice and cruelty of the African trade,"[134] might well have made her defensive. Rush was not modest about proclaiming the successful establishment of antislavery societies in Connecticut, New York, New Jersey, Pennsylvania, and Delaware. It was "the glory of our nation to have originated a system of opposition"—the antislavery network—to commerce "in that part of our fellow creatures, who compose the nations of Africa." He actually went so far as to equate patriotism itself with the total abolition of slavery—his version of cleansing America religiously.[135] In 1794 Rush addressed the Convention of Abolition Societies in Philadelphia, and the copy of that collection of speeches that was printed specially for circulation in South Carolina contained a final added paragraph that directly encouraged his friend Ramsay—urging that the existing two-year ban on slave imports, for which Dr. Ramsay had cast the deciding vote, be expanded to total abolition. Another antislavery address, this by Dr. George Buchanan (*Oration on Slavery,* delivered to the Maryland Anti-Slavery Society at its 4 July 1791 meeting in Baltimore), proved that yet another piece of Martha's family history had been mythologized.

The Ramsays enjoyed reading that other cities were imitating the practice David had originated, of celebrating Independence Day oratorically, and that in the case of Buchanan, a physician in Baltimore and member of the esteemed American Philosophical Society in Philadelphia, antislavery rhetoric had become part of the occasion. This orator, probably unknown to the Ramsays, employed the historically honored name of Laurens to make the argument that antislavery sentiments were universal, that they could be born and flourish even in a "slave state."[136] In the same rhetorical style as the anonymous homage to Dr. Ramsay in the *Ladies' Magazine,* Martha's brother was cited as adulatory "proof" that a southerner could be an antislavery hero. As Buchanan retold it, John Laurens (already a full generation earlier) had dared assert that slaves were wrongly derogated as subhuman and that they were in fact as capable of valuing liberty as their white masters. However, Buchanan transposed John's reputational legacy into military history. "Witness also the valour of a few Blacks in South Carolina [during the late war]," he wrote, "who under the promise of freedom joined the great and good Colonel John Laurens, and in a sudden surprised the British and distinguished themselves as heroes." Did Martha wince at this revisionist use of her family name? Dr. Buchanan, himself a child during the war, was mythmaking—transforming the martyred John Laurens into a southern hero who not only valiantly opposed slavery but also enabled slaves to enact military heroics. John's reworked youthful fame returned to his middle-aged sister as a "vibrant semantic link," in Winthrop Jordan's contemporary phrase. Buchanan's historical error must have reconnected Martha with her European years and the troubled family correspondence at that time, including John's antislavery arguments.[137]

The specter of slave uprisings was an ever-present, underlying threat in the atmosphere white Charlestonians inhaled. For example, Martha's colleague Mrs. Manigault addressed it in code in a letter to a friend the day before Christmas in 1790. "Our great holidays [are equivalent to] the Saturnals of the Romans," she wrote with irony. "All our domestics have their heads turned . . . [and] dream only of drinking, eating, dancing and amusing themselves well during the three days they are given." Of course "those who serve us well during the rest of the year" merit this "little vacation," but this particular year that acknowledgment also evoked a foreboding image from another state. "But in these times (you understand me) we are not perfectly in a state of security and repose. You have doubtless heard talk of the Virginia affair," implying but not naming the Gabriel conspiracy in Henrico County, "happily failed." In its aftermath, rumor had it that "innumerable troops of those wicked faces" had been allowed to enter upper Carolina, intensifying slaveowners' fears. Thus when "the cry 'fire' [was] heard at 2 a.m. last night," Margaret Manigault had experienced "a terrible start," imagining it the signal that slaves were rebelling on home territory. "I am sick from it today. But my fright was baseless." Only one house burned, and "order & tranquillity were immediately re-established."[138] Her discreetly worded summary could rely on a set of shared assumptions—acknowledging the state's huge African population; implicit recognition of its intelligence (or craftiness); and the uncertainty basic to a system maintained by brute force. Naturally the news of a successful slave insurrection in the Caribbean—the actual founding of a "black republic" named Hayti—could turn white Charleston frantic. David and Martha would not anticipate how such an outside event would totally cut off the flow of abolitionist ideas that was beginning to appear in public print dialogue.[139]

The January 1792 *Columbian Magazine* arriving at Martha Ramsay's house gave print legitimacy to her city's self-devouring racial nightmare. One story reported that Port au Prince, the capital of the new republic of Hayti, was "being destroyed by mulattos" and that even the seven thousand troops promised by France would not be sufficient to quell the black barbarism ravaging the island of Santo Domingo.[140] The writer, of course, did not report that extreme black atrocities were the pent-up response to the white torture and butchery routine in slave punishment there (documented by Rev. James Ramsay, among others). Martha and David Ramsay were among Charleston residents likely to credit missionary accounts of the mutilation and sadism wreaked on slaves in the sugar colonies, but they were also among those attempting to remain rational in the rising hysteria. A few years into the new century, Dr. David Ramsay became president of a Charitable Society in Charleston, founded to aid the white refugees fortunate enough to flee the black revolution.[141]

At the beginning of 1792 (the year that would bring her father's death and her husband's legislative drama), Martha, despite prayerful attempts to remain reasonable, read monthly reports inflaming fears of about the Haitian uprising. "The . . . free black population in Charleston" was recently doubled, she read, by "many light-skinned *gens de coleur* from St. Domingue."[142] February brought a rumor that the Negroes in Jamaica intended to follow the frightening example of Haiti.[143] Month by month the "terrible news" arrived: whites had been most barbarically murdered. Accounts of the insurrectionaries' "treatment of matrons, virgins, and infants" were enough to "make a Negroe blush"—a thoughtless journalistic cliché under the circumstances.[144]

A separate news article appeared in the March 1792 *Columbian* that clearly expressed the Anglo-European perspective on both race and class in a menacing description of "mulattos," the term the British used for mixed-race people.[145] Mulattos, "a yellow tribe," were neither African nor European in color, therefore dangerously void of "attachment to either land."

Their loyalties, practices, and political propensities were fearsome because unpredictable.[146] *They,* the creation of racial mixing, were the new enemy to be feared. The writer's anti-French bias allowed him to blame French entrepreneurs for begetting this kind of threat, while ignoring the British barbarities of punishment that had actually ignited the uprising.[147]

Scholars today are reexamining the agency of slaves in mounting the 1790s rebellion in Santo Domingo and in causing a disproportionately fearful reaction in white Charleston. The nearby establishment of Haiti as an example of black power created an all but total intellectual blockade against the liberationist ideals that had begun emerging in the late 1780s. David Ramsay's civic leadership in a refugee organization and Martha Ramsay's diary record of emotional turmoil during these years provide a kind of evidence that their individual double binds about slavery were colliding. At the beginning of 1795, a Charleston gathering of Methodist ministers—in themselves alarming because they were successfully converting slaves—added to the local paranoia by passing an official resolution for "the immediate emancipation of slaves."[148] That same year Martha's spiritual condition reached its nadir of despair. If converging worries about slave uprisings, fire, and hellfire for slaveowners were contributing factors, her written record as preserved names none of these dramatic portents. The factor she could name was her self-imposed regimen of fervent, rational piety—a personal discipline that in ordinary times helped subdue her inner turmoil but this time was unavailing.

Since Martha's lifelong goal of self-improvement required her to distinguish herself in mastering the highest religious reasoning, she might well have begun to admit to herself that a life enmeshed in the institution of slavery fell drastically short of her own severe Gospel standards. Still, in order to continue functioning, she had to believe that she was discharging the duties of her station, including the management of slaves, in a righteous, Christian manner. Whether or not she could quiet her conscience on that score as effectively as had the countess of Huntingdon, Martha remained bound, by her own habits of mind, to the authority system embodied in the men who defined her existence. On balance, the symbolic metaphor used by Martha and her husband, "black-and-white family," enacted by her as "mother-instructor" of such a household, brings the actual treatment of her slaves as close to modern scrutiny as is possible. Dr. Ramsay's summary of Martha's household administration, philosophical and abstract rather than concrete and practical, was: "These and several other rules of conduct in the discharge of relative duties were not taken up at random but derived from reason and reflection, and especially from an attentive consideration of the preceptive part of the word of God." A monitory conclusion made his agenda explicit: "Happy would it be for society if all its members used their Bibles for similar purposes."[149]

During the war for independence some slaveowners, including Henry Laurens and Pierce Butler, had already begun to admit to each other that slavery was increasingly uneconomical, unchristian, cruel, and physically dangerous. Charleston-born Henry Clay, who would become the mid-nineteenth-century's great statesman of compromise over slavery, wrote in 1798, "All Americans acknowledge the existence of slavery to be an evil."[150] But only the rare few could act upon it. The Laurens-Ramsay record literally displays ambivalence and silence instead of action.

In the Charleston of their time, a united front of custom and government silenced all local or federal political efforts to regulate or abolish slavery or the slave trade. In spite of the antislavery challenges in which the Ramsays played small, ambivalent parts, David Ramsey was, finally, out of his depth: not proslavery enough to suit the people among whom he must live and write, not antislavery enough to live an openly oppositional life in Charleston. Martha, in her silence, was also out of her depth on this issue: unable to criticize her cultural heritage, but also unable to fend off her soul's awakening to the sinfulness of slavery and the burdens of its evil.

After the turn of the century, David Ramsay directed some of his energies into safer channels. The topic he could unproblematically champion—religion—allowed him to apply his editorial skill to Martha's posthumous modeling of religious life and consciousness, as his service to the public. Whether or not he protected her by omitting any of her writings that he deemed controversial, the long shadow of slavery and regionalism clearly shadowed all his efforts. Martha's spiritual agonies—"I am in straits, trials and perplexities of soul and of body"—may well have concealed unarticulated dismay at the "monstrous system" of slavery all around her even as her published record remained opaque.

Meanwhile, their friend Benjamin Rush was also experiencing a reality check in Philadelphia: facing the hitherto ignored (by whites) gulf between the races in religious observance. Earlier he enthused to his and David's mutual friend Belknap, in Boston, that he "love[d] everything about the poor negroes, even the name of Africa." His affections, similar to many of his white antislavery colleagues, addressed the converting of dark-skinned people to Anglo-Christian salvation rather than their political and physical freedom. "When shall the mystery of Providence be explained, which has permitted so much misery to be afflicted on these unfortunate people?" Perhaps slavery in this life was their part in an equation intended to offset "misery *hereafter*"—hell—in the next life. But since Negroes partook in original sin along with whites, they should also enjoy "the benefits of the atonement. For they are our brethren not only by creation but by redemption." The Ramsays of course would agree that Christ's death redeemed all humankind, not just whites.[151]

By 1792 Dr. Rush was writing to that same colleague that white Christians in Philadelphia had opposed the mingling of races in church via seating arrangements. As a result, "the Africans have lately formed themselves into a religious society in our city" with governing principles of their own, having walked out of churches where they were treated as second-class and segregated. The established churches (Episcopal, Presbyterian) had responded with shock, "look[ing] shy at them." Apparently "each [church] have lost some of its members by the new [racially separate] association." Worse, free blacks holding their own worship services represented the possibility of whites' further loss of control, making owners more edgy. What if free blacks' demand for autonomy of action extended beyond church services? "The gospel now a days seems to require total separation from all sects," lamented Doctor Rush—people, he felt, were "more devoted to their own forms or opinions than to the doctrines and precepts of Jesus Christ."[152]

Of course, "in spite of neglect" (or active opposition), the Negroes would succeed in establishing their "independent church," Rush believed, and would erect their own building with which he personally assisted them. At present they were meeting in a schoolhouse that "accommodates about 500 persons" and worshipping in services that were simple "but uncommonly solemn." Despite Rush's disappointment over the race separation within churches and denominations, he too honored the unwritten code of not censuring white fellow Christians for *their* racial intransigence. The letter's final, prophetic sentence cautioned that these musings about black religious independence were not intended for public discussion: "all this is between friends." Antislavery sentiments, even from Benjamin Rush, were being returned to the closet.[153] For the next half century, earnest Christians musing over ideas like emancipation and justification for blacks would share them primarily among the like-minded. At the beginning of the nineteenth century, the residue from the upsurge of antislavery activism in the 1790s was bruising, existential ambivalence—as witnessed so pervasively by Martha Laurens Ramsay's silence.

8 | 1795

"Dark Night of the Soul"

THREE DAYS BEFORE HER DEATH on 10 June 1811, Martha Laurens Ramsay finally told her husband about the diary she had kept for at least fourteen years of their married life. She also told him where to find it—in which drawer it and a few other precious private papers were concealed at their Broad Street home in Charleston. In the *Memoirs* posthumously compiled from those writings by Dr. Ramsay during the immediate weeks after her death, the largest portion he printed from her diary was dated 1795, the year Martha had suffered a major depression. His editorial instincts had led him to preserve a remarkably explicit account—an interior description of a psyche disintegrating for a time, then gradually restored—of a mental illness recorded in the terms of analysis available to an eighteenth-century victim.[1]

Religion—Martha's framework—was both the language and the organizing principle for expressing her inner state of turmoil, context as well as subtext of what she called her "dark dismal night of trial" in 1795. Because her times had no other conceptual language for emotions "in the depths of despair" or the "dark night of the soul,"[2] religious phraseology became the tool for explaining her misery and despair to herself. "I am in straits, trials, and perplexities of soul and of body," the first entry of 1795 reads. "My outward affairs can only be helped by thy providence; my spiritual troubles by thy grace."[3] That passionate written cry illuminates the anguish of a mind constrained by the circumstances of her time and place. Martha's "agony of spirit" in 1795, creating an eighteenth-century psychological intersecting of history and autobiography, elevated to public visibility the convictions, shocks, and converging influences of her era and worldview—thanks to her husband's editorial labor.

David and Martha had both been reared to believe that the printed word itself had the power to convert and reform; they thought that reading about good people would somehow help produce good people. The British Pietist Philip Doddridge, whose devotional instructions Martha deeply assimilated in her adolescence, urged all Christians to keep spiritual journals in the hope they might well exercise posthumous witness later through being published in print, so her last-minute revelation was appropriate.[4] As her husband began to compile Martha's *Memoirs*, his first instinct was to honor the "lively sentiments of fervent rational piety" he found in her diary by letting them speak for themselves. On second thought, he changed his mind: without some "account of the author . . . many of the reflections of the writer would be comparatively uninteresting, if not unintelligible." Readers ignorant of Martha's "losses and crosses" would puzzle at such self-accusatory exclamations as "Oh! sins against vows; sins against light."[5] In addition, a biographical sketch would allow him to paint an exalted word portrait of her life that could help allay his bereavement. The result, his forty-seven-page biography-introduction portrayed the "dark night" of Martha's soul in vivid (if not very explanatory) strokes. David's hagiography simply heightened the meanings Martha herself brought to that darkest year of her life, the phrase she oft invoked—"darkness"—then being the reigning metaphor for everything regressive and terrifying.[6] Significantly, when she again could write about "light," that was a signal that her despair and darkness were beginning to lift.

The background to Martha's musings, not spelled out by her husband since it could be assumed by her contemporaries, included the shattering effects of post–Revolutionary War inflation and the doctor's perilous professional income. The cost of fabrics, books, and spices, was an everyday component included in "the present intricacy of several of my worldly concerns" contributing to the larger trauma. Her life consisted of woman's highest calling—to labor "diligently in my family and station"—but she, born and raised a Laurens, had not foreseen having to scrape and juggle to maintain respectability or having "to watch against extravagance and self indulgence," let alone confront the specter of bankruptcy.[7] Her husband's unpopular disapproval of slavery added yet another layer of tension to all daily neighborly interactions. On top of everything, including giving birth to her first son that year, Martha had experienced painful defeat in her attempts to control and rear her niece, brother John's orphaned daughter, Fanny. Early that year, Fanny had eloped on what Martha knew would be a disastrous marriage. To Martha, this was the last straw, an indication that she was failing in her religion—and that it was failing her. Apparently her prayers were impotent in the face of "those afflictive Providences which force our consciences to a stand."[8] She could neither protect foolish Fanny from herself nor the Laurens name from Fanny's disgrace. The combined blows of economic distress, anxieties over social standing and family reputation, and the perception of failure in the religious domain of her own household, where she had thought herself preeminent, opened an abyss in her soul that plunged her into a profound depression lasting into the first months of 1796.

Martha met the crisis in her usual forthright way, attempting to mobilize the full range of resources her husband aptly called her "fervent rational piety." To her diary, but apparently to no person—neither husband, pastor, nor friend—she confided her petitions and confessions, her moral vows, trying both to express and interpret the loss of confidence in herself that she could neither suffer passively nor, for a long time, succeed in exorcising. Those intimate pages record a travail of "drooping spirits, and . . . dying faith."⁹ They show her struggling to get a mental grip on irrational feelings, to reassert intellectual competence, to impose a sense of control upon all the uncontrollable factors in her world. The mind-set and personality that led her to berate herself for her inability (or unwillingness) to accept the surcease of spiritual surrender, in the face of depression, was shaped by a rational stance toward responsibility that could only reject passivity. Martha's enlightened Calvinist childhood had created a problematic, if not paradoxical, persona for her: when her rationality and piety converged and contested with each other, and since she felt equally committed to both, that strong, managerial sense of her own self had to crumble.

I

In her teens, making a covenant with God had been young Martha's self-dramatizing way of raising a moral defense against the kinds of trials she might have to confront as her life unfolded; it was her first major attempt to translate human problems into spiritual routines. She had inwardly determined to become as expert in religion as her older brother John was in political and civic affairs. These being their father's two primary concerns, each of the two oldest Laurens children grew up to be a distinct yet complementary chip off the paternal block. While displaying the same drive for leadership as brother John, Martha's ambitions were directed into the religious sphere, which took her out of direct competition with him. But she was a Laurens as well as a Christian; her youthful heart could no more fail to strive for distinction than could her brother's. In the dark night of 1795, that religious dedication served not to relieve but to exacerbate her mental and spiritual torment.

Martha and David agreed on many things, including grand ambitions about the number of children their union should produce for the new republic. She was so happy in being pregnant that it scandalized some of their friends. "Mrs. R at present is in a thriving way," wrote one of them to another, and "says it is her highest ambition to have twins, I think she had better wish for a litter at once. The act of getting them from the sweet Dr. must be very delightful for when you hear people talk of such things, you can't help bringing to your mind that situation."[10] The first dashing of her parental hopes, the death of her third child, Frances Henry Laurens Ramsay, in 1791 impelled her to begin a secret diary—perhaps as a confidential repository for her anguish, or (at the subconscious level) to establish an autobiographical record of her pain for future reflection. If there was ever an event for which one wanted, and needed, to blame the entire universe, it was the death of a child. But her diary writings reveal a careful attempt to contain and redirect that despair, away from blaming God. Catherine Henry Laurens Ramsay was born in 1792, the year of her father's death. In 1793 another daughter, Sabina Elliott Ramsay, arrived, but at the same time Martha's only sister, Mary Eleanor Laurens Pinckney, died. As caretaker of the Laurens dynasty, Martha had endured three profound bereavements in as many years.[11] Early in 1795 her first son, David Ramsay Jr., was born, although according to her diary, rejoicing over the long-awaited male child was subdued; her husband's frequent absences, as an elected representative in the South Carolina House of Assembly, meant he was often away in Columbia.[12]

David was an unusual husband in that he enabled Martha to speak for herself in print (through the *Memoirs,* for the most part in her own words and voice); in this he contrasted favorably with other contemporary male editors of female papers for whom the wives were "mere extensions of their husbands, and [the males] themselves . . . the real subjects of their wives' memoirs." Martha's "reasonings . . . on the condition and duties of wives were not imposed or even suggested" by her husband, he asserted with pride; "they were entirely her own."[13] For him her intellectual and spiritual superiority translated agreeably into a wifely stance of principled defer-ence. In his eyes Martha made an ideal analogue for civic cooperation and selflessness, since her dutifulness was practical and culturally appropriate as well as symbolic.

In 1795, to all outward appearances, Martha had everything conducive to contentment: the heritage of a respected name, a growing bevy of prom-ising children, a fond husband who was a leader in civic affairs, and a secure place in world of elite Charleston society.[14] She enjoyed the Independent Church which she had joined upon marrying David, a congregation pastored by a succession of friends from David's college who also became her friends.[15] She had, as well, the advantages of an exceptional education for a woman of her time and place, creating a reputation comparable with a contemporary Englishwoman reputed to be "a living library."[16]

In her life's upheavals to that point, Martha had always been able to rely on the deep foundations of her faith; yet in 1795, for the first time in her privileged existence, she found herself completely powerless. "Out of the depths have I cried unto thee, O Lord," she wrote. "Out of the depths now I cry unto thee again O My God." This time her calls for help remained unanswered, and she was forced to record: "My mind has been more exercised both from outward pressure and inward conflict than I can ever recollect it to have been, since I gave myself to be the Lord's"—that is, since her adolescent covenant signed in 1773. Worse, because there seemed to be no response from God, she was guilty of "add[ing] sin to sin" by despairing. "Oh no!" she recoiled, "let me not add to my other guilt the guilt of unbelief."[17] The ultimate humiliation of seeing herself as an insult to religion rather than its handmaid loomed before her.

Nature and its order, reason and its gratifications, both remained unavailing in 1795, that "worst year of [her] life." Martha besieged the intermediary of Providence: for God's self-disclosure and rescue from her anguish: "by thy Providence clear up my darkened skies," 1 March 1795; for helping her recall "the divine providential dealings with me over these troubled three years," 3 July 1795; please send "a special interference of Providence in the life of one for whom I pray so earnestly," 7 September 1795; and thanksgiving that providence was beginning to meliorate her cloud of darkness, 3 January 1796. The sense of depression seemingly would not lift, however, leaving her "exercised with inward conflicts and sorrow of heart under which I have groaned for near eleven months past." The agony of this trial was unique in her life thus far, due to "some peculiar circumstance [that] have [made it] *exceed* in kind and continuance *all the other sorrows of my life.*"[18] Could suffering over a niece be that profound?

An additional subterranean strain, of course, widely known and dubiously viewed, was the Laurens-Ramsay relationship with slavery. Though her father's fortune derived from it, one of Henry's contemporaries, corresponding in 1785 with Thomas Jefferson about the abolition of slavery "in all the States except the *Carolinas* and *Georgia*," had heard Mr. Laurens say "that in his own State he [now] has the whole country against him."[19] That family burden surely constituted a fault line of moral responsibility and social anomaly for a woman of her high conscience and self-esteem.[20]

The troubles overwhelming Martha in 1795 brought to a head many interior strains: tension between pride in her rationality and her powerful call to piety; the circumscription and narrow channeling of her own exceptional intellect and capacities; the changed community identity for a wartime hero's daughter now wedded to a man who was decidedly different from her father. All these fostered dissonance between her public and private selves. Her chosen field of achievement was religion, so in her domestic circle she had a mandate to be religion's successful representative. Such achievement, symbolized by triumphant rearing of the young in her care, would in her own secret calculus confirm her familial, spiritual, and social worth; it would compensate for some other chafing disappointments. To fail in the special responsibility that she had willingly undertaken, for Laurens' posterity—the niece who rejected her and her counsel—had to be triply disheartening.

II

In her diary entries, Martha pursued a logic of spiritual and psychological debits and credits, the literary strategy shaping her written conversation with God. "How lately hath thine afflictive Providence been wringing my heart with a two-fold anguish, the loss of my sweet baby [Frances H. L. Ramsay], and the consideration of those sins which required this chastisement."[21] Concerns of this life had to be balanced with concerns for the next. Pain could only be relieved by locating the wound in one's own soul; attributing loss to personal deserving brought the struggle with heaven into manageable human terms. The lament, "O how does the remembrance of my sweet [infant] Fanny press upon my memory," had to be succeeded by self-reproval: "How good is God that though cast down, yet my heart is kept from murmuring, and aches more for my sorrow causing sins, than for the sorrow itself." Hymns that were the coinage of much devotional literature focused on a mothers' struggle to accept grim death for a beloved infant, the stanzas bathed in their tears as they argued God's greater need for their babe (in heaven) as reason to cease their earthly mourning. One hymn, subtitled "Supposed Conversation between the Mother and the Child after Death, concludes with the infant's reassurance to the grieving mother: "Then cease t'indulge th' falling tear, / I now with Jesus ever dwell; / If you my praises did but hear, / You'd surely say that all is well."[22]

Another hymn, intended as a comforting litany to the mother, had a repeated final theological doctrine to end each stanza: "He [God] doth what seems him good." The first stanza read: "God hath bereav'd me of my child; / His hand in this I've view'd; / It is the Lord, shall I complain? / He doth what seems him good." The fourth stanza acknowledged human frailty: "Yet nature feels—but ah, *he's* gone— / For *him* my tears have flow'd; / It is the Lord, his hand I own, / He doth what seems him good."[23] By late 1791, when Martha was again pregnant, she had wrestled her emotions into the proper balance of blessing and obligation. "I thank thee who art a God that givest as well as takest. I praise thee, that I have one child in heaven. Lord have mercy on those which remain on earth." Loving a dead infant too much, mourning too deeply, meant pitting one's will against God's; Providence in this case was both comforting and terrifying.[24]

Through 1794 she groped for an explanation of "the tumult of my thoughts." (Today, physical contributors to her gloom might be understood as rising out of bodily depletion from her repeated pregnancies, lack of calcium, or postpartum depression.) A devastating yellow fever epidemic was raging in Charleston but was "said to be confined to strangers or people who live irregularly," so she could dismiss that as a cause. Worries about the dangerous nursing-to-weaning transition for infant Sabina were past because the child was now eating well. Once external causes were ruled out, Martha's unease had to turn inward, to something she obsessively called her "easily besetting sin." In mortifying vulnerability, she bared her spiritual Achilles' heel: "*I cannot perceive an increase in sanctification, according to my desire.*" Spiritual ambition was the unseen worm in the bud. From adolescence on, she knew Doddridge's strictures about any "secret misgiving of the heart," and that she must painfully scrape away the "artful coverings for what you cannot forbear secretly condemning," rather than "endeavor to palliate the matter before God."[25] Profound self-examination, at a level well beneath her normally confident piety, must inexorably search out an unwelcome dark corner in her heart.

In a footnote explaining that he himself was mystified about the nature of Martha's "easily besetting sin," David assured readers he had no clue to what she "so pathetically deplored throughout this diary." To him, "easily besetting sin" denoted a character flaw, such as anger—something toward which one has a "strong propensity, either from the constitution, or the temperament of the body, or some peculiar circumstances of the times, of situation, profession, or mind, body, or outward estate." He was confident that her flaw, if indeed she had one, could not have been anger or rebelliousness. He recalled her as an ideal mother who had an "excess of . . . love, tenderness and anxiety, for the comfort and happiness of her husband

and children, . . . [if anything] mak[ing] too large sacrifices of her own enjoyments for their accommodation."[26] His reading of her diary glossed over the emotional ferocity visible to a twentieth-century reader.

Martha may have intended the metaphor, "easily besetting sin" (Hebrews 12:1), to imply something in simple behavioral terms, such as being too busy to keep regular times for praying in the midst of daily routines—although that defies other references to her efficient management. Or it could have meant a general inability to forgive herself, a psychological imperative that set impossibly perfectionist standards in order to magnify religious self-chastisement. Such morbid Protestant martyrdom exalts suffering to exaggerate an ultimate surrender to the divine, a scenario likely somewhat melodramatic for one as forthright as Martha. A more subtle reading suggests that she was forced to recognize (and abhor) a component of spiritual pride in her disappointments. Any dutiful reader of Richardson's novels, especially one of Martha's well-grounded religious sensibilities, knew that "Spiritual Pride is the most dangerous and the most arrogant of all sorts of Pride." She who had avouched, in Doddridge's verb, to use her efforts for God rather than her *own* ends, was vulnerable in that regard; with all internal barriers down, she must accuse herself of daring to presume that her goals and ideals would automatically be granted since she had become God's coworker.[27]

And her view of partnership with David has to be added to potentially damning religious self-aggrandizement. Martha had not been schooled to accept limits gladly; she idealized her parents' marriage as a "matrimonial partnership."[28] She married David in high anticipation of their "joint pilgrimage here on earth"[29] because of their shared views on religion, politics, and education—even if, by Laurens' standards of practicality, he was something of a disheveled intellectual. It was common lore in Charleston that Martha jested affectionately about her "unpolished Jewel." Yet even if David had not "studied the graces" as thoroughly as he knew medicine and history, there was no doubt of his being an appropriate spouse for her.[30] Expressing the slightest disloyalty to God or David was unthinkable in Martha's self-image. Because neither anger nor a sense of betrayal of her own deepest wishes could be admitted consciously, despair about these two anchors—husband and God—had to be subsumed under her "most easily besetting sin."[31] Even in the diary that phrase was never given specificity.

By itself, a husband's social fallibility would not have threatened Martha's self-esteem or fine-grained sense of spiritual well-being; after all, she was a Laurens. But in combination with financial and familial fallibility, it became another matter. Being unsure of spotless credit for daily necessities, for the first time in her life, was a new and unwelcome reality (even if no Laurens exhibited the fondness of opulence that characterized other South Carolina aristocrats); being unsure of future necessities was basic and terrifying. Regrettably, by 1795 their finances were out of control.[32] Twenty-five thousand dollars of her inheritance had been invested in the "publicly beneficial but hitherto privately ruinous" canal-building project of which David was president in 1795.[33] "It will be a better property than any bank stock," he promised an investor in 1794, "but in the meantime, money going out and none coming in suits very few Carolinians."[34] Sales of the books David published did not cover their printing costs, let alone show a profit.[35] Payment for his medical services remained unpredictable; competition among the physicians of Charleston was brisk. The Ramsays were forced in this dreadful year to mortgage their home—legal rituals of dower renunciation (27 March and 7 November 1795), when Martha, as legatee, voluntarily relinquished at the lawyer's office all claim to the properties she had brought to the marriage. That, a jolt to her psychic bedrock, might have helped foster a heart "bursting with grief."[36] At age thirty-six, Martha instead needed a "good report."[37]

Added to money that was owed everywhere was family disgrace, the impetuous niece who ran away. Fanny had come into the world in London in 1777 while Martha's brother, John, marked time until he came of age and could enlist in the glorious American struggle. After a perfunctory marriage to the infant's mother, Martha Manning (youngest daughter of Henry's British business partner), Fanny was born. Meanwhile, Fanny's dashing young father sailed off to fight against her mother's homeland and was killed in 1782.[38] A true orphan (the young mother died when the child was only one year old), Fanny was brought back to America as Martha's protégé. She was to have been Martha's first achievement in the rising generation.[39] But at the age of independence, Fanny fled to London with a husband of whom the family could not approve. Martha failed to preserve the Laurens name and the wayward creature herself—impotence that symbolized her spiritual Waterloo.[40]

If, however, spiritual pride was the sin that so easily beset Martha, it was also her primary defense. If she sometimes suffered from a secret tendency to think rather better of herself and her heritage than of many other people (perhaps including on occasion her own husband) this innate sense of self was her final remaining resource. Martha did not possess David's protean personality; his ability to adapt and rationalize was very different from the rock-solid presence of her father. Although her husband found the fluid atmosphere of the 1790s heady and exciting, it dismayed her.[41] David could call his opportunism "virtue" because he intended the large purpose of serving the public good; Martha's ambitions could not be considered virtuous for a woman; they had to be concealed and spiritualized, loyally disguised even from herself in her one secret companion—the diary. The year 1795 meant "coming into relationship with reality" and discovering that life was not at all what she had imagined it would be when she penned her covenant—not even the special part of it that she supposedly orchestrated.[42]

In late May 1795, Martha listed her catalog of miseries retrospectively, with specific calendar dates (but without further detail: they alone sufficed to evoke vivid, painful recollection): "the 27th of January . . . the 7th of February . . . the 1st and 11th of March."[43] April 14 was a day so bleak that "heart and flesh . . . were both going to fail," even without "bodily indisposition." That may have been the day niece Fanny dramatized her ingratitude by announcing her determination to leave. Reliving these horrors, Martha wrote: "Oh! who but the Maker of my frame, and the former of my spirit, could ever know what I underwent on this awful day. Had I turned to any creature, none could have understood my case, much less could they have helped it." That epic distress thrust her "in a plunge again, and my skies, which seemed to be clearing away, are now obscured by clouds and darkness," unrelieved and abysmal. Earthly terrors compounded spiritual ones. "Wo is me, for fear I have sinned away God's mercy."[44]

June was a dreary and afflicted time. "I can no longer say the skies are darkening, for they are so darkened that I see no light." In the diary, listlessness alternated with feverish claims on God. Raw, obsessive phrases inscribed and reinscribed her feeling of entrapment. "If it be not thy will, to grant me the prayer, which I believed thou wouldst have done, having had my heart so drawn out to pray [for it]," she lamented, "at least" prevent my being "so entirely depressed, as to be useless and worthless in that state of life to which thou hast called me." Were her aspirations to establish her niece's future, to arm her children with virtue and a proper station in life, not from God but from the evil Enemy himself? That a pragmatic Laurens would countenance such self-doubt indicated her psychic fragility. "If I may not record that the Lord hath heard and granted my request, at least enable me to know and feel, that he hath given [me] brokenness of heart" and "the frowns of his providence," she chided herself bitterly. Shifting to direct address, she reminded God that even "the *remembrance* of the especial times" of his favor would be "a cordial to support my drooping spirits, and revive my dying faith." If an approaching Sabbath could make God "draw nigh," and if he would only give the "death stroke" to "my most easily besetting sin," then she might "be able to add [the word] *hitherto* to my past experiences"; then the sufferings of today could be recorded in the past tense. But a few days later it was again worse: "I am so vile and wretched, that I am now afraid almost even to pray . . . I am so vile, that I am a terror to myself."[45]

"How long, O Lord . . . hast thou appointed, that I shall labor under this perplexity?" In her desperation, Martha tried renewing her "often broken covenant." To each of its planks she added a new dimension intended to strengthen her bargaining position with God. More than just warding off the easily besetting sin, she would burrow beneath it by asking, often, each day, "what I am about in this respect?"; instead of just reading the Bible in a mechanical way, she would do it *"with meditation"*; instead of trying merely to control her thoughts, she would trace them to their very origins, asking "'whence comest thou and whither goest thou?'"; instead of just dragging through her daily tasks, she would be "vigilant" against any trace of "indolence" (an unlikely possibility given her temperament). And concretely she would "watch against extravagance and self-indulgence and . . . walk more usefully than . . . hitherto." She tried to assure herself, "God is leading me by a way that I know not," but she felt impelled to add, as if the words themselves could summon conviction, "I am persuaded it will be the right way."[46]

Martha's negotiations with God exhibit the variety of ways she addressed the question that motivates all autobiographical writing: "where do I fit in all this?"[47] The diary was a literary tranquilizer when she had nothing to relieve her angst except herbal teas or tepid baths, both too passive to soothe her frantic mind. Determination, ingrained Laurens determination, was stubbornly blanketing her darkened spirit. "I am waiting upon God for a mercy which I have sought so long and so earnestly, that I cannot but think God has drawn me to pray for it." In fact her prayers were unceasing: "Many a thought [has been] sent thither in the course of every hour, while at the necessary avocations of my situation." Wearily, she had to acknowledge, "Thou *hast* answered prayer; but Oh, in how different a manner from what I expected."[48]

In July, Martha's despair shifted from unanswered prayers and events gone awry in her life to her own lack of spiritual prowess. At all crucial points her grief and disappointment was turned back on herself, made into her own failure. "I have been many years a professor," she lacerated herself; "instead of having just life enough to be grieved at [my] sin, . . . *I ought to have made great advances in sanctification, and to have been eminently pious,* instead of being saved as it were by fire." Neither visionary nor mystic, Martha was the prisoner of her rationalist mind-set. She treated herself as alone responsible for bringing all the disappointments that were subverting her sanity under the control of her reason. She noted the topics of sermons dutifully but the bindings of her own mental straitjacket kept her in the depths. In a world where family name or inherited standing were affording only diminishing comfort, spiritual pride and despair were her nemeses. Yet she could not free herself from them. "I am a wretch . . . afraid to make any more resolutions; afraid to hope that ever I should be better."[49]

Profound depression kept her away from the first gathering of "a prayer society" at the pastor's house on 23 August 1795. In her normal state she would have been a leading advocate of any new activity promoting "the good of souls" and religious awakening within the congregation. But in her dark night, she wrote, apathetically, "my own mind is not yet made up about attending them." In despair she was unable to enjoy David's triumphant archaeological display at their home of fossils uncovered in digging the Santee Canal; even that remarkable scientific find was unable to penetrate her psychological fog.[50]

In late August, Martha undertook the abridgment of a treatise by the British Pietist John Flavel, titled *On Keeping the Heart*. It may have seemed just one more among many such exercises in a lifetime of self-education; more likely she hoped the act of note-taking would distract her from her soul's agony. Flavel's first stern note—against antinomianism, enthusiasm, and other "Spirit marks"—reinforced her instinct to get a grip on herself. No true Christian would toy with those dangerous shortcuts and such escapism. "Since both Scripture and Experience do confute this Dotage, I hope you will never look for comfort in that unscriptural Way," the introduction warned. Flavel recommended, instead, examining one's heart *rationally* as the only legitimate means to comfort a ravaged soul—"not by any extraordinary Revelation but by subjecting [one's] Understanding to the Scriptures, and comparing [one's] own heart with them."[51]

Even in Martha's disturbed state, Flavel—a pedagogue of piety who carefully numbered his theses and subpoints—was easy to outline. She wrote down his six "Exhortations for keeping the heart" and used the phrase "heart work" to summarize his introduction: "To keep the heart is hard work, constant work and the most important work." In Martha's

Protestant mind-set, religiousness was associated more with effort than with quiet, mystical communion; heart *work* may have struck her as hopeful, as something she could actually *do*. Her abridgment included the topic sentences from paragraphs titled "Motives for keeping the heart" (ten), "Special means for keeping the heart" (six), and, touchingly that August, "Words of consolation to those who are plying heart work, groaning and weeping in secret, over the hardness, pride, earthliness, and vanity of their hearts" (three). Connecting the maxims in the abridgment with her preoccupations that crucial week suggests that helplessness, so grotesquely painful for a Laurens, was the pivot. Flavel's prescriptions focused on agency, on the person taking charge of her own heart by reinstituting a right relation with God. The sixth in his list of "Rules to keep the heart from distractions," the final section on which she took notes, pointedly directed her back into this world: "Endeavor to engage . . . in *duty,* if thou wouldst have thy [distractedness] *cured.*" His didactic admonition was the old prescription: work is the best medicine.[52]

For pietists like Flavel, "Heart" was the central metaphor, "the noble faculty of the Soul," that helpless human beings were as unable to "keep [in the right path] . . . as . . . to stop the Sun in its Course, or make the Rivers run backward; . . . we may as well be our own Saviours, as our own Keepers," the author scoffed. In the impossible psychic dilemma of the Calvinist, Martha must strenuously strive, even if striving by itself was like trying to make "the Rivers run backward." His remedy for human helplessness, however, was one she already knew, one that enlisted God in the soul's initiative: Flavel suggested "well composed, advised, and deliberate vows." They alone could "overawe" her soul and "preserve [it] from Defilement by [those] special Heart-corruptions" that had indeed been her preoccupation and grief.[53]

Martha concluded her abridgment with a dedicatory prayer of contrition, a solemn dating (28 August 1795), and a self-reminder that memorizing Flavel's rules was "evidence to my own mind, that I am in earnest about religion." The prayer consisted of six agonized petitions, each beginning with "Oh God" or "Oh Jesus," followed by lengthy pleas filled with demanding imperative verbs: hold me up, keep me, help me, save me. The entire exercise may have crystallized her perspective on those "sins, over which I hoped I had gained some power." Or perhaps by embracing a model that combined agency *and* submission, she was enabled to begin encompassing her disappointments, her spiritual pride, and a new energy—instead of drowning in their torment.[54]

On 7 September 1795, Martha wrote down startling testimony to some kind of turning point. On that Monday morning she was able for the first time to list the themes in her depression, systematically named and numbered in the Flavel pattern. Three things had been "particularly on my mind" all this miserable year, she wrote. First and foremost was the "easily besetting sin," still unidentified but now destined for its "death's wound."[55] Second was her intense longing to be the one who effected "the thorough conversion of a very near and dear friend." Informed conjecture locates that "near and dear" cause of Martha's anguish in niece Fanny. Her flight with Francis Henderson, "the ugliest man in Abbeville or elsewhere," would last less than a year, and local society watchers called it a "freak of Venus"— utterly déclassé for a Laurens.[56]

A kinkeeping defeat was of course spiritual failure. Martha's ambition to shape and educate Fanny could be compared to Pamela's for the wicked Mrs. Jewkes: "To pluck such a brand as this out of the fire, and to . . . quench its flaming susceptibility for mischief."[57] The young aunt Martha had set herself to woo and shape her brother's child into an honorable Laurens, but physical desertion put Fanny totally outside her reach. Martha had to confront the powerlessness of her early vow—"that all others, so far as I can rationally and properly influence them, shall serve the Lord"—though in her diary she does not reveal more than the longing to prevail over, be the agent of salvation for, someone "near and dear," unnamed.[58]

The third theme releasing her paralysis of spirit concerned her husband; for the first time she wrote prayers expressly about him and their monetary straits. David's financial slippage was called "worldly entanglements" that she bemoaned as endangering his soul. He must be "enabled so to manage his earthly affairs, that they . . . never interfere with his heavenly business." Allusion to his economic ineptitude, however, roused her wifely loyalties; the diary's next sentence was a vow "that we may rather be satisfied with a smaller portion of this world's goods, than to run the risk of being greatly involved" in bonds and debts.[59]

Loss of reputation, dearest relations, "some threatened stroke upon their property"—all were converging in that hellish year.[60] Once having named her demons, Martha could face them with Flavel's recommended heart work: she formed yet another version of her vows. She would, in the case of the first, prevent the easily besetting sin from even coming to the surface of her conscious mind: "avoid the occasions of sin, more especially of the sin over which I have so much mourned." Second, turning the defeat with Fanny into resolve, she would "walk" so "holily and uprightly" that her

Kinkeeping

conduct could not possibly "hinder [those who love me] from entering on a religious life." And third, she would accept personal responsibility for the times when "I lived less frugally in the first years after my marriage than I should have done."[61] Legends of Laurens' prewar elegance must not give her husband any excuse for rash profit-making ventures. In the long darkness of 1795, these renewed vows were the first to carry anything like her former sense of self-command and were a portent of the darkness beginning to recede. A letter from her husband, away at Columbia during the last month of 1795, alluded to his awareness of her emerging from depression: greeting her as his "greatest earthly comfort & Joy," he enveloped her in gratitude for being "a partner whose good sense delights me—whose judgment assists me in every difficulty—whose many virtues command my esteem while her love & attachment deserve and & command such an ardent affection." He concluded with fervent hopes for her recovered equanimity and health, "the source of all my earthly comforts."[62]

At the beginning of 1796, though still not totally free of the depression "under which I have groaned for near eleven months," Martha attended church as usual with the family. That Sabbath meal, the Holy Communion, became an epiphany, the moment of spiritual illumination for which she had been longing: "there Jesus made himself indeed known unto me in the breaking of bread." The possibility of holy food and drink becoming "manifestations of his presence" was not unknown to eighteenth-century Pietists, although for a rational Calvinist it had to seem a miraculous intervention in nature. "With inexpressible sweetness of acquiescence," Martha suddenly found herself able to give up "all to God, though in that *all* was comprehended that for which I had been praying for many months." Her weary spirit was able to make its peace with defeat.[63]

Moments of transfiguration invariably elude verbal description, but Martha wanted to try: "I cannot describe them in any suitable manner; nevertheless I will record them to the glory of God's grace, and as memorials against my heart, should it ever be so treacherous as to forget them." She wanted to mark with suitable words the moment when her fierce determination had been lifted from her will, her volition itself suddenly "annihilated." And she cast that release in terms of the surrender she had so bitterly fought; her description was "such a swallowing up of my will in the will of God, that my soul lay, as it were, prostrate at the foot of the Cross."[64]

Martha had experienced a flash of psychic integration, a transcendent force flooding her inner being. Her soul "lay meekly and sweetly at the foot of Jesus, saying, Lord! not my will but thine be done; Lord, let thy will be done in me, and by me, and upon me." Suddenly she felt at one with the whole of creation and the author of her salvation. Her youthful vow "to believe that every particular circumstance is ordered for some wise and good end" was given new and shining illumination. Martha had come to that most difficult existential awareness: admitting that she, Martha, was not in charge, was not God—but also that she was no longer alone and need never be. "Whether he gives or takes, he is still my God."[65]

The rest of that day she basked in serenity, and all the next; by Tuesday she had received "assurance about the affair which has so long perplexed and bowed me down." Whatever that indicated—her niece's defection, momentary relief from financial distress—she knew she was no longer estranged from God. A new peace and certainty, and some of her former optimism, appeared in the diary. "And now God, who has done so much for me, will not leave his work unfinished."[66] Martha's dark night of the soul had lifted.

After such a New Year's beginning, Martha's troubles ought to have disappeared. But her remaining years continued to be shadowed by financial stringencies, endless debt litigation, declining health, and anxieties for her children in a new, less gracious era. The crowded Ramsay house on busy Broad Street in the bustling center of Charleston was undoubtedly a confining contrast, when she dared admit it, with the broad gardens and spacious rooms of her childhood home on East Bay Street. Though her diary writing tone did not become visibly lighter, she never again descended to the nadir of 1795. Nor was her spiritual equilibrium ever again in such jeopardy. The stormy passage into middle age had been negotiated, and Martha Laurens Ramsay now directed her religious anxieties into educating her young and carrying on her own heart work.

The kind of spirituality tested during Martha's dark night was often overlooked in eighteenth-century literary documents because of its private religious application. Yet it constitutes one example of the stepping stones expanding nineteenth-century women's religious sensibilities and actions. She was less visionary and more theologically rational than seventeenth-century Puritan and Quaker prophetesses, and more domestically circumscribed or constrained than her nineteenth-century successors would be. Those women, empowered by the revivalist energies of the second Great Awakening, would carve out experimental forms of religious activism—mothers' clubs, prayer meetings, missionary work, Sunday schools—as Martha did not. But many of them would consider themselves her heirs when they read the memoir of her dark night of the soul and were inspired by the profound if homely story of her survival.[67]

9 | Filiopietism As Citizenship, 1810

AFTER MARTHA LAURENS RAMSAY KISSED her oldest son God-speed on his departure northward to college on 7 May 1810, she went to his room in her Charleston, South Carolina, home and burst into tears. "The first thing I did when you left me, dear David," she wrote him, "was to retire for a few moments to your chamber and relieve my laboring heart, by commending you solemnly and affectionately to the good Providence of our heavenly Father." Her streaming eyes gazed unseeing at his childhood mementos as she tried to compose herself. Suddenly they focused on a pamphlet that his father, Dr. David Ramsay, had given his departing name-sake just a few days earlier. It was a polemic against the snares of "smoking tobacco," written by a distinguished Briton and addressed to Cambridge University students. In her mind's eye, that little brochure was to have been an angel in her son's pocket—symbolic assurance that family moral guardianship surrounded him far away from the parental nest. Yet here it was, left behind.

Her tears dried, banishing the moment of emotional indulgence. She quickly sent her trusted household slave Coony to the sloop *Pennsylvania,* still at anchor in the harbor, where he pressed the abandoned leaflet into the very hand of passenger David Ramsay Jr.[1] Martha herself thought this pamphlet salutary enough to have presented it to "half a dozen . . . persons in whom I am much less interested than in you," she reminded him in the accompanying note. Her central admonition was both prayer and charge: "I hope its contents will not be lost upon you, nor the book itself lost by you."[2]

Though only Martha's side of this mother-son correspondence has survived, the Enlightenment article of faith animating it is evident: knowledge itself should produce good behavior. If Davey read about the dangers of smoking, he would not smoke. This incident suggests that some part of her highly rational mind-set nourished the irrational hope that if he even carried the antismoking text on his person it would somehow protect him from giving in to smoking. Her rationale, however, was specific to the era in which these nine missives of parental aphorism and endearment were written: a sense of personal obligation to rear a citizen worthy of the new nation and of his distinguished Laurens and Ramsay bloodlines.

Two concerns dominate her letters in the final section of *Memoirs*. Those concerns were, in her own formal yet passionate diction, an "overflowing tide of affection," and, second, sometimes overwhelming the first, "anxiety that you should behave well and make the very best use of your collegiate opportunities." This literary legacy was addressed to her first and only offspring to go away to college, the oldest of their four sons after four daughters.[3] Written during the final eighteen months of Martha's life, the letters exhibit a patriot-mother's strategies for shaping a son in and for the new republic and demonstrate a parental anxiety that is unchanged across the centuries: mothers still implore their collegians to write home more often (today, telephone) and study harder.[4] In addition, the letters track a republican-instructional trajectory—from parental goals and the son's resistance, to a crisis in the relationship, to a final ending in generational accommodation. Between the lines as well as in them, the letters demonstrate a mother's attempt to persuade, inspire, and manipulate a fifteen-year-old-boy into the mold of citizenship she regarded as essential.

Martha Laurens Ramsay styled herself a woman of reason, a female who gloried in the use of her own mental powers and enjoyed epistolary oversight of a citizen under construction—the duty that her father had assumed in her childhood. As well as being a family standard, reason was valued for its own sake. Unlike mothers with less education and less confidence in their own authority, Martha Ramsay took it for granted that she was the one to maintain the letter connection between the parental nest and the distant son and heir. During her adolescent years, physically separated from her father because of the Revolutionary War, Papa's letters had been her solid anchor. Within her frame of reference, filiopietism was the weapon of choice for her son Davey.

Further, when Martha was the same age as Davey, she herself had taken a significant step into adulthood. Unknown to anyone at the time, even during the years she was writing these letters to her son, she had a secret "solemn spiritual covenant," the documented vow that remained her lifelong moral and emotional beacon. That action, independent of any parent or mentor, had been her coming-of-age ritual, the true Lockean moment of independence, her "pinch of destiny."[5] But that was long ago in 1773, when cultural currents still flowed primarily toward America from across the Atlantic. By 1810 the new generation of young Americans saw the English devotional models that had been significant in her youth as outmoded. And, of course, her citizenship instruction had been gendered. Hers was the all-encompassing mandate of "relative duties" that aligned women with family concerns and emotions, something with which males were almost never attuned. Caring for and serving one's kin or relations was the way in which Martha was expected to serve community and nation. A male, by contrast, would be expected to "regulate [his] conduct" and "harmonize [his] passions" for public and national, rather than purely domestic, reasons. Martha had two generations of model for Davey, making filiopietism both logical and practical for him.[6]

The descriptive noun *filiopietism,* the metaphor underlying Martha's adjurations though never her actual word, was eighteenth-century code for a dynastic perspective on citizenship. In a new nation, barely thirty years old, honoring Revolutionary fathers was the pertinent generational ideal. The Founding Fathers' heroism had plowed the soil of optimism and opportunity and planted the seeds of epistemological exhilaration.[7] Young David's own father had written, in *History of the American Revolution* (1789), that as long as Americans were constrained by "the leading-strings of the mother country," they could have no sense of "scope or encouragement for exertion"; but once that dependency on Great Britain was thrown off, the "War not only required but created talents." David Sr., son of an ordinary Pennsylvania farmer, was the typical self-elevated citizen who now "spoke, wrote, and acted with an energy far surpassing . . . expectations" for a child of his humble origins before the war.[8] An ambitious idealist who had established himself in part through marrying into influential families, David Sr. recognized no limits to the possibilities for the sons and grandsons of the white, educated elite citizenry. Perhaps because his historical writings promoted many "great characters" (including his father-in-law, Henry Laurens) for his fellow Americans to revere, he was glad to delegate the actual formative instruction of David Jr. to his capable wife. After all, more exalted levels of leadership descended from her side than his.[9]

Quite apart from her husband's enthusiastic patriotism, Martha, as oldest daughter of the patriot Henry Laurens, was intent on passing along to future generations the shield of family honor. The Ramsays and their contemporaries, friends like Benjamin Rush of Philadelphia or John Adams of New England, naturally envisioned a dynastic lineage. But close to her father as Martha had been, a Laurens female could achieve significance only through the men to whom she belonged. The Laurens name had been as notable in Carolina mercantile circles as that of the Brown family in Providence, Rhode Island, for the same commercial achieve-ments;[10] and David Ramsay Sr.'s name was respected in Europe as well as in literary circles up and down the eastern seaboard. If his mother's dream came true, Princeton-bound David Jr. would achieve at least the level of his father's "public consequence," if not the more towering recognition accorded grandfather Laurens.[11] A dynastic imperative undoubtedly helps account for the moralizing tone (in twentieth-century ears) of Martha's fil-iopietism. Her maternal goal for this eldest Laurens grandson had explicit ancestral parameters. David Jr., however, was part of the generation for whom the war was already myth rather than experience, and he was some-what less in awe of those bloodlines than his mother.

This archetypal drama of cross-generational communication (and miscommunication) was preserved in the *Memoirs* of David Sr.'s deceased wife. Since editor Ramsay could not have foreseen the perennial dimen-sions of her parental emotions and ambitions, his decision to include her "college letters" was a shrewd calculation of their timeliness for a nation-building era. Here was a veritable curriculum for citizenship, based on the key ideals of usefulness and honor—a literary package of expert advice for youth far away from their parents, at "seminaries of learning."

Reading Martha's motherly sermonettes about family honor and indi-vidual character required a late-eighteenth-century, post–Revolutionary War lens, while son Davey already wore the brash "new American" lenses. To her, honor meant an ingrained discipline and grace arising from self-respect and the respect of one's peers, not false European presumptions of rank and status.[12] The Laurens' view of honor, which she assumed David Jr. had imbibed with his mother's milk, was intended as psychic and patriotic replacement for formerly British cultural practices of deference based on rank and status. Martha's ideal of honor invoked a sturdy self-reliance that linked it with usefulness in community as well as family. But the central concern of her "overflowing tide of affection" and general "maternal anxi-ety" was character, the goal firmly fixed in the cross-hairs of her north-ward-yearning gaze. Her distant son must implant an internal governor on his youthful passions, and she must direct that implantation through long-distance "cultivation" of his interior life—his character. Fortunately, she believed that a son's inner life provided the best possible location for such maternal groundwork.[13]

Women like Martha viewed as their foremost mother's task the estab-lishment of "the reins of government" in sons. Replacing the need for the "leading-strings" that had once tied America to British cultural patterns with "habits of the heart" essential for the new earthly (and heavenly) citizenship required a firm foundation in a son's mind and body.[14] Martha's belief system encompassed the sense of "providence extend[ing] to every event and every circumstance of the life of every human being." She expected to see the hand of Providence not only in prayer but also in events, conversation, observations, actions, and dreams. Martha gladly accepted responsibility for guardianship of public order. She knew that what made a citizen "useful" was grounded first in familial honor and virtue, to be realized later in the social institutions created by people who embodied that honor and virtue.[15] This was the mechanism of filiopietism she intended to transmit to David Jr. under the rubrics of honor and usefulness.

The style of her written discourse also added psychic weight to her letters: religious rhetoric signaled emotional seriousness. In the cosmopolitan Laurens-Ramsay world where letter writing was both art and skill, religious language was the highest, most profound vocabulary available. Correspondence was an index of one's ability to articulate as well as a means of coping with events, small and momentous. Grandfather Henry Laurens' letters to *his* children had intermixed spiritual admonitions with observations about windmills and fruit trees; they had linked the family across oceans, assuaged his griefs, debated the outrages of English soldiers in Carolina, and worried endlessly about finances.[16] After Martha's mother's death, when Martha was eleven, letters were her means of connecting with an absent father. Throughout the years of exile from her father—which encompassed the terrible traumas of her youngest and oldest brothers dying—letters were her lifeline. Because letter writing had always been crucial to her, Martha took it for granted that an adolescent son steeped in filiopietism would emulate that practice.

David Jr., however, was a product of the invigorating postwar climate. He elicited special motherly vigilance, perhaps because his optimism seemed a clear genetic inheritance from his father. Though Martha Ramsay and other progressive parents educated their daughters as seriously as sons of that era, she especially welcomed the challenge of preparing sons for college, an intellectual achievement rare enough in her era and location that it would later be noted in her public obituaries. From time to time, she revealed some maternal ambivalence over the potentially conflicting demands of usefulness—earned esteem from others for self-giving—and honor—fulfillment of family expectations. In typical motherly complexity, her son must become useful, a valued member of society, not one to lord it over his peers; at the same time, however, he must also be outstanding, an honor to his inherited family names.

The generation of parents contemporary with Martha and David Sr. were no longer content to leave their children's spiritual well-being to God's inscrutable design, as their Calvinist forebears had believed they must; the modern parent considered herself answerable for it. And since Martha's scrutiny of young David's "habitual practices" must be conducted via letter, abstruse theological points were superfluous. She addressed habit rather than doctrine, echoing her father's epistolary pragmatism. She believed insight would eventually follow behavior. In her view, a collegiate citizen needed a map to follow—an undeviating pathway to adult usefulness and honor.

Martha hoped that the family's sacrifice (sending a son to Princeton was costly) would loom large in Davey's consciousness, since it was a guarantee of and "the foundation of his future usefulness." A college degree was already considered essential for young men who expected to "furnish [their] states with Legislators and Judges"—to be future leaders who would "infuse [an Enlightened] spirit into the politics and councils of our country." Unlike the self-made commercial eminence achieved by Grandfather Laurens, Davey's father received professional education after graduating in 1765 from the very same College of New Jersey. David Ramsay Sr. had then studied at the Medical School in Philadelphia and also had become a published author, important in national associations of physicians and literary publications as well as in hometown Charleston. This gave young David's destiny an imaginable shape in the parental eye. Although distinguished heritage was no help with tuition, the Ramsays had been able to scrape together the money for his all-important "sojourn" at "a temple of learning." Once there, young David must "lay in a sufficient stock of knowledge, and . . . attain such literary honors" so that he could both serve the nation and earn a livelihood—his parents' definition of "future usefulness." Such a heavy dynastic yoke on youthful shoulders might have dampened Davey's excitement at embarking on a ship northward to Princeton, but his mother's letters suggest otherwise.[17]

In point of fact, a bachelor's degree from his father's alma mater would be the only fortune David Jr. would ever "inherit." As one "of a large not rich family," the oldest of four sons and four older, unwed sisters, he would have "no patrimony" to "lean upon." Martha reminded him several times that he would be solely dependent on whatever "cultivated talents" he acquired at college. After the two years so carefully budgeted into the family's scant income, these talents must be "ready to be brought into action." He was expected to emerge from college "capable of building up a fortune"—livelihood and reputation—on his own.[18]

Finances had always been a particularly tender topic for the Ramsays, and nothing had improved in that regard. The Charleston citizenry were unconscionably slow to pay for the doctor's services. On the literary side, his histories sold barely enough copies to meet their printing expenses, let alone produce income. Before the Revolution, Martha's father had been one of the richest men in Charleston. After the war, chaotic inflation devoured her dowry, the land she inherited proved worthless, and her husband's high-minded but disastrous investment in patriotic projects demolished the rest. Consciousness of the decline from prewar Laurens status was a gnawing subtext for Martha, in spite of her loyal efforts to ignore it. Financial setbacks and a blow at Laurens family honor had combined to plunge her into a deep depression in 1795, the very year David Jr. was born. Three years later, in 1798, David Sr. had been forced to declare bankruptcy, and in 1803 her only living brother, Henry Laurens Jr., sued him for vast overdue loans.[19]

So in spite of the fact that the Ramsays were prestigious members of the new nation's literati, their daily circumstances were hard-pressed. Concerns about money and the future hopes of his seven siblings all devolved squarely on young Davey: whatever he could recoup would be their only recompense. "Give me thine heart," his mother wrote in July 1810, using biblical diction to hallow the emblem of familial bonds. "Any heart worth giving," or for that matter "worth having," would "seldom [be] refused" one's parents, "the authors of our being, the protectors of our infancy." In his case, that meant a father "whose fond ambition it is to see his son distinguished in life," a mother who is "continually addressing the throne of heaven for the welfare of [this same] son," and four sisters, aged twenty-three, twenty-one, eighteen, and seventeen, all exceptionally well educated and eminently marriageable except for the fatal lack of dowry. Even in that hopeless circumstance, these sisters were the kind who "ever cheerfully sacrifice some of their own convenience for the advancement of their brothers," Martha reminded him. His younger brothers were then twelve, nine, and eight years old.[20]

Martha's letters to the family scion always ended in a list of combined maxims and prayers. A contemporary novel helps depict the moral primacy attributed to the role of mother in that era. The female sex has the immediate province of implanting "the first lessons of instruction in the infant mind," the anonymous female author had written. Ideal mothers "detest" whatever subverts "principles of morality"; patriot females know that "right sentiments" will always be a "faithful Monitor" internally and "adorn the name of Americans." Martha coined her own version of that sentiment in practical terms: Davey must form "a right bias to energies and sensibilities," and know how those aspects of character can be cultivated, lest they "make you foolish and miserable [when] wrongly directed." To that end, Martha's "overflowing tide" of maternal affection assumed the form of directives.[21]

The first letter contained seven. They provided, in slogan form, a methodology of usefulness and honor: be respectful to your superiors, live affectionately with your equals, make yourself a party to no broils by minding your own business; give dignity to the Carolinian name; write home accurately about every subject that concerns you; and be not ashamed of religion—read your Bible diligently. Her benediction was a daughterly tribute to her father's preachments. "Your grandfather Laurens used to say if men would make a good use of" only one part of the Bible, "the book of Proverbs, there would be no bankruptcies, no failures in trade, no family dissentions"—none of the "widespreading evils which desolate human society." His enemy, like hers, had been "the careless conduct of men" who would mismanage "the common concerns" of a city like Charleston or a nation like the new United States. Grandfather's practical Huguenot ways would make young David "wise unto salvation," his mother assured him, and be "excellent direction for your conduct in the affairs of this life."[22]

Her warning to mind his own business undoubtedly reflected her fear of negative influences as well as her desire to protect the long friendship between the adult Ramsays and the president of the College of New Jersey, Samuel Stanhope Smith. Three years earlier, the parent generation had been scandalized by the Collegiate Disorders of 1807. At the apex of College of New Jersey's most successful era since its founding in 1746—two hundred students enrolled and a full faculty of president, four professors, three tutors, and a French instructor—the students had staged a rebellion against excessive rules and regulations. Adults viewed the upheaval darkly. It was "irreligion against religion," boys of "jacobinic . . . principles who made hostility to religion and moral order" their major tenet. One hundred and twenty-five students were sent home that year, "a blow . . . of which the College did not recover for many years."[23]

The unrest had beginnings back in 1800, escalating from relatively minor infractions like drinking at the tavern, "tying a calf in the pulpit of the Prayer Hall," or blasting the dinner trumpet in the hall during hours rigidly reserved for room study, to creating distractions during the tutors' lengthy morning prayers. The suspension of three seniors in February 1800 incited a mini-riot of pistol shooting and crashing bats against the walls— a general uproar but still harmless—until President Smith's appeal for order took hold. Then one of the expelled culprits who remained "loitering in the town" persuaded some of his colleagues in the dormitories to "roll a three-pound cannonball down the hallway" during quiet hours. The tutor blamed for the three initial suspensions became so enraged that he ran into the hall, unsuspecting, and was roundly beaten. Tutors, only a few years older than the students but expected to wield the institution's punitive powers, were *the* accessible target.[24]

In the next few years student anger began to coalesce around the enemy behind the tutors: arbitrary, rigid college rules. In March 1807 the new colonials, as the students saw themselves, united to "draw up a remonstrance" against the unnecessarily harsh punishment that had suspended the three students. Systematically canvassing each room, they collected signatures from the entire student body. This insubordination, however audaciously modeled on their fathers' dealings with Great Britain in the Revolutionary era, all but demanded punishment from the authorities. The damning evidence was in writing—a document accusing the faculty of "act[ing] precipitately and contrary to the 'principles of justice.'" Further, the students had defied the college rule that forbade the "forming [of] combinations to resist the authority of the faculty and trustees." Such a petition could not be ignored or acknowledged (except in reaction to it). College faculty gave students the option of "removing their names from it or themselves from the college." The trustees concurred. "We must either govern our own college or resign it to the government of inconsiderate boys [and] passionate young men," the board of trustees' declared.[25] A genuine riot then ensued, and the entire college was closed down till after spring vacation.

College student unrest in that first decade of the nineteenth century— similar outbreaks occurred at Harvard and Yale—was viewed by the parent generation as little more than youth in need of tougher discipline, although later interpreters would call it a tributary to the stream of increasing secularization that undermined clergy control of higher education. But later, in 1821, the Episcopal clergyman who was President Smith's biographer would connect the Princeton rebellion with a much larger current of change and challenge to governing authority. "The French Revolution which [then] had just taken place . . . did not confine its effect to the limits of that kingdom," he wrote. "In no country was [it] felt more sensibly than in our own . . . on account of the severe struggle from which we had just released ourselves in the establishment of our independence."[26]

As early as 1790, the popular New England novel *Memoirs of the Bloomsgrove Family* sounded the same note of alarm: junior Americans were exhibiting too much independence within the social order and thereby unwittingly jeopardizing it.[27] "Enthusiasm in favour of the civil rights of mankind," with its "tendency to extravagance and excess," an undoubted residue of revolution, was nothing less than an "infection spread . . . among our youth, who strange to tell, carried these false notions of liberty . . . into our seminaries of learning," its author intoned. President Smith's biographer also believed that the "spirit of insubordination," traceable to a foreign revolution, was responsible for "storm after storm" at Princeton during Smith's presidency, constantly testing his "readiness of resource, his firmness and decision of character."[28]

Long before the 1807 debacle, generational conflict at Princeton was a topic in the national literary journal, the *Columbian Magazine.* CAELO, pseudonym for a graduating senior from the College of New Jersey, submitted a poem titled "Valedictory to Scholastic Education" that extolled freedom from "tyrannic tutors." One of its biting couplets was a calculated anticlerical insult: "Adieu ye reverend hypocrites! / Ye holy despots, little wits!" Martha Laurens Ramsay deplored such public disrespect.[29] And the specter of a Laurens-Ramsay scion being suspended was unthinkable. Since David Jr. was not enrolled at Princeton until 1810, this upheaval was already history, though fairly recent. A mother could easily worry in any case about residual rebelliousness lurking in the walls themselves.

Besides warding off potential anarchy, then, Martha the mother must advise son Davey about fiscal prudence, regional identity, and seriousness—some of the characteristics defining "usefulness" in a collegian. When he had been away only a few months, her son must have written something resistive about the academic routine.[30] In July 1810, his mother responded, using the rhetorical apothegm for a person who tries to get something for nothing. "Can you go through any virtuous course without economy, industry, self-denial," she demanded. "Can you fit yourself for usefulness on earth or happiness in heaven," in any way other than "doing your duty in the station in which God has placed you?" As he should know, this was his mother's own republican and Anglican credo. Davey had not been born into just any family but to the "station" of a Laurens-Ramsay.

"And if your chief ambition is without caring whether you are as wise or as good, to wish to be richer than your father and mother," she waxed eloquent, "the readiest method to fit you for eminence in whatever profession you choose," the way to "attain this golden treasure," is "diligent attention to collegiate studies and duties." Her intention was to penetrate his youthful imperviousness by reminders of his relatively privileged location in life. "I assure you, many young men with less means than you . . . have felt it a great privilege to go through a collegiate course, and afterwards come to be eminent, respectable and wealthy." Particularly because of the Ramsays' monetary constrictions, Davey must include honest financial gain in *his* definition of usefulness. His generation had not only ample permission but even obligation to blend filiopietism with commercialism, for its own and the nation's sake.

Indulged sons of southern planters had been blamed for instigating the 1807 Princeton rebellion. "Carolinian triflers . . . have brought the colleges such as Princeton into disrepute" was Martha's epithet. She detested Charlestonians who "carry their idleness, their impatience of control, their extravagance, their self consequence" everywhere, including northward to college. It was a pity. Even "the best of them are, in general, far inferior" to their potential. Why? Because they lacked the desire to be useful, to "make the virtuous endeavor" that would employ their "quick capacities, and lively imaginations."[31] It grieved Martha that youth from her state were the ones credited with flouting the new nation's standards of appropriate public behavior.

Ironically, that very constituency—rich sons from southern families—had been deliberately cultivated by the College of New Jersey in 1796. Early in Smith's presidency, a committee charged with reinvigorating the college finances set out to attract students beyond the local Jerseyan context. They drafted a kind of marketing statement to justify petitioning the state legislature for financial aid. In it they pointed out that Princeton was already known as "the principle resort of American youth from the Hudson to Georgia." If the "south of this country" had not yet fulfilled its potential, it was undoubtedly due to "something in the state of society and in the habits of the people in the southern states, which has hitherto prevented that success . . . [that might be] expected to attend their literary establishments." The "something" alluded to was the institution of slavery, which the College made no secret of opposing. One could also read in that indictment implicit reproof for southern tardiness in developing its own educational institutions. However, Princeton stood ready to help. Since citizens in the

Carolinas and Georgia already had to send their young men somewhere else for schooling, the trustees felt it would be "no inconsiderable glory to New Jersey to be the fountain of education to so large a portion of America." And it would certainly be good for college business.[32]

David Ramsay Sr. himself was a product of the successful link between the College of New Jersey and the South. After medical school he had selected Charleston as the place to seek his fortune. The Independent Church of Charleston, of which he and Martha were prominent members, consistently elected Princeton-trained preachers as their bulwark of orthodoxy against trends toward free thinking in religion. Even the new science taught at the College in Princeton was presented, in the words of its first professor of natural philosophy, as the friend of traditional religion rather than its enemy. Studying science was "a continued act of devotion," according to the 1788 lecture inaugurating the college study of science; "the immense, beautiful, and varied universe is [itself] a book written by the finger of Omnipotence."[33]

Young David was expected, then, to rise above the negative, self-indulgent regional image. Also, he should exhibit "a laudable pride" in his "father's literary reputation, [at] the college where he was educated and of which he has made so excellent a use," Martha advised in another letter. He would benefit from the "great improvement made in every branch of science" since his father's college days. Actually, his father's literary reputation embraced science as well as history—that is, his publication tracing the eighteenth century's improvements in medical practice. In 1805 Dr. Ramsay wrote President Dr. Smith to interest him in the purchase of a "cabinet of natural history" for the college as a rival for Mr. Peale's Museum in Philadelphia. He himself had collected "Specimens in the history of nature" from the southern part of the country.[34] Filial duty could measurably strengthen Davey's "improvement" in the area of science since both his parents appreciated the new factual approach to botany and medicine. Then Martha rang a generational peal on the age-old theme: wait till you have children of your own. The more you love your father and mother, "the more you [will] endeavor to oblige them," she wrote, "and the wiser, the better, the happier you will be." The child's reward for this duty would be the "consciousness of having been a good son." If at his stage of life, praise for being a good son was not entirely persuasive, it would surely become so "when, at some future period, you stand in the relation of a parent yourself." However, her letter sighed, no mere collegian could be expected to understand this; parents have "sensations unknown to all but parents."[35]

In August 1810, Martha urgently addressed the topics of wasting time and bad companions. She could no longer repress her worst fears. Usefulness in a collegiate life meant productive use of one's time; bad companions were the enemy of honor *and* usefulness. "I hope you are not trifling away this prime of your days," she worried. If her son turned out to be "content" with "such attainments as will excuse you from censure"—that is, merely passing grades—his mother would be terribly disappointed. Why could Davey not be "emulous of ranking with the most studious, most prudent, most virtuous of your companions?" To her it was impossible to overemphasize the importance of right companions. "The society of the virtuous is to youth, what a good climate is to the [physical constitution] and the waters of the heavens to the fruits of the earth," ran an aphorism in the *Columbian Magazine.* His mother made the point her own way: "I wish I could inspire you with a *laudable* ambition." This she defined as "feelings that would make you avoid any unnecessary intercourse with the bucks, the fops, the idlers of college" who were anathema in her eyes. The usefulness for which he had been sent to a seminary of learning was entirely opposite: it was "to attain science, and fit you hereafter to rank among men of literary and public consequence."[36]

She could scarcely have cast "laudable ambition" in more explicit dynastic terms. Her earliest ideal for men of public consequence was her father. As for literary consequence, Dr. Ramsay qualified. Further, he had written a hagiographic biography of George Washington, the first national exemplar of public consequence. His friends Jedediah Morse, Jeremy Belknap, and Benjamin Rush were contributors to the nation's intellectual fabric—all from cosmopolitan locations. Local friends of mental and civic eminence included the artist and engraver Thomas Coram, head of the board of the Orphan House in Charleston and designer of a medal for the state. Davey's father had observed, in his *History of the American Revolution,* that in "the *establishing* of American independence, the pen and the press had equal merit to that of the sword."[37] These were the men of consequence Martha wanted young David to emulate, examples she hoped were brilliant enough to penetrate his collegiate fog.

Even his "upcoming college vacation" would have its dynastic educational purpose. He was to spend it with Nathaniel Ramsay, his father's lawyer brother in Baltimore, "the third city in the United States." One day when there was more money, Davey would visit Boston and New York and travel to England to "survey that world of wonders, London." But for the present, family connections were logical, safe, and affordable. Even his travel from Princeton to Baltimore required strict frugality. This supported Martha's argument that "the sons of rich planters" were a bad influence: they "only go to college for the sake of fashion," their lives "as useless as their expenses," and they have plenty of money for vacations.[38] As the College at Princeton symbolized an anchor against modernism for traditional religion, kin represented a safe haven for an unfinished collegiate lad, to a mother who was increasingly anxious and ill.

The September 1810 letter reached a zenith of concern about character. "Your judgment ought to be well informed," Martha began. A Laurens-Ramsay heir would have lived "within the sound of good advice" from infancy, not in a wilderness like the one Rousseau had popularized. Up to that point Davey had not seemed "restive" about his mother's advice. She hoped he still possessed "[an] ingenuous disposition," one that welcomed "effort on the part of your parents and friends to make you wiser and better." Having already lived fifty years, Martha knew many young folk in their echelon of Charleston society who were given "every possible advantage" in terms of "cultivating their talents, improving their minds, and becoming estimable members of society." Yet even some of these had become lost "to self, a disgrace to their friends," and "plagues to society, or mere cyphers in it, through indolence." A larger meaning than physical laziness irradiated these phrases; his mother was zeroing in on "a *slight* manner of pursuing their studies" (emphasis added). The visible signals of "slightness" were a flippant approach to life, plus smoking, drinking, "drap[ing] themselves in finery," and associating with "trifling" company. Surely Davey knew his mother's reputation for skillful management of time, and that she, a Laurens like her father, was "uncommonly economical" of it. A Spartan rhetorical charge from the *Columbian Magazine* would have been appropriate: "Does the blood of heroes fill thy veins? . . . consider how thou mayst assert this honor . . . by brilliancy of thy virtues, not by ostentation." Literary quotes—Scripture and other reinforcing mottoes—were standard ammunition for Martha.[39]

All possible motherly wiles were brought to bear on the terrifying mental picture of youths who were nothing but plagues and cyphers; Martha even included a rare allusion to her own physical debility. If you only knew how much I love you, she began, "a spirit of compassion for *an afflicted friend* would make you conduct your self wisely." Even if he totally lacked "nobler motives," that unusual plea might jolt his thinking. In Martha's cosmic struggle against uselessness, the mere idea of failure— "thoughts of how I stand among the persons [who have] sons exposed to such a calamity"—was enough to reduce her to "death-like faintness." In order to "ward off such a stroke," her own fervent prayers were offered "with streaming eyes, and bended knees."[40]

Then his mother suggested a more positive image as counterweight. Look at "those who with very scanty means," like Davey himself, but with "every possible *dis*advantage" which was not his case, who have still "risen as lights in the world." Such poor-boys-made-good were their "own best friends," their "own fortunes"; they merited "the smiles of heaven." She discerned an achievable middle ground between the plague-cypher types and the light-of-the-world types: those "situated . . . under happier circumstances," as he was, who did not have to "struggle . . . constantly against wind and tide, supported only by their own efforts." Those sons were not alone, as he was not, and they did exactly what was wanted of him. They "repaid the labors of a father and the tender exertions of a mother by doing their part well and returning home from their different seminaries of education, such as their parents could wish." God grant our story may end thus, Martha concluded. Though his financial future was up to him, a solid family network was ever surrounding and cheering his efforts. Her benediction addressed Davey in third person: "Let him not waste the morning of his days in any trifling pursuit, or disgrace it by anything vicious or ignoble."[41]

The previous day, a Sunday sermon by another Princetonian, the Rev. Dr. Isaac Stockton Keith, had furnished Martha with the term "errors." In her 11 September 1810 letter she employed it to cover the topic her generation would have known as the doctrine of original sin—the scriptural image for human perversity that obeyed self rather than divine wisdom and guidance. The "error" she wanted to address was "slightness"— youthful insouciance, lack of seriousness once again. "By nature," she quoted from the sermon, everyone has "some secret error, some constitutional defect or vice." Davey ought to watch carefully for his "error" and "break [its] bias" or power over him, lest it "become too strong for us . . . our curse and our master as long as we live." Over her lifetime, his mother had entrusted many examinations of her own "secret error" to her diary— her "easily besetting sin," in the devotional terminology learned in her youth. At his stage in life, she knew that young men were "apt to think themselves very wise, and to pay very slender attention to the advice of their superiors." That itself indicated a tendency to slightness and was his error—in fact his "very *great* error." Resistance to learning from the experience of "those who are older and wiser" made youth "very unlovely in their tempers," especially "to those who reprove or advise them," that is, to parents or teachers. (She had earlier included a comparative remark about how highly his older sisters had profited from the advice and example they received from their mother's friend and helper, Miss Futurell, now departed back to England.) Ingratitude for one's advice is very galling to the giver. There was still time for him to triumph over this particular error, while it was yet a "pygmie" habit rather than "a giant cruel and severe." The remedies she recommended for it, as usual, were diligence in the pursuits of "useful science," and "mak[ing] friends to yourself among the wise and the good." If youthful obtuseness still rendered him impervious to parental wisdom, Martha comforted herself that Dr. Smith, president of the college, was at hand, "the very dear friend of your mother." He was a figure "so accustomed to youth as to know every twisting and turning of their hearts, [and therefore] capable of giving . . . the best advice."[42] Advice was the summum bonum of her generosity, the measure of usefulness in mothers (and other wise adults) that was equivalent to the standard of diligence and honor in sons.

By November 1810 Martha had rallied from another spell of "severe affliction" that left her much "occupied and agitated." She was in despair over receiving no letters from him: "It is very mortifying to a parent so tenderly attached to a child as I am to you, to think that in the leisure of a whole vacation, you have written but once." Though his father had tried to defend him against her worries about dangers or foolhardiness, calling him their devoted son who would "never act materially wrong," she reported to the errant Davey Jr. that her motherly rejoinder to his father's meliorating words had remained cool. "I pray God you [David Sr.] may be right. [If so] I shall rejoice in having judged erroneously," she wrote. She returned to her worries: if "a boy does not write fully, freely and frequently to his father and mother," how shall she, the fondest, tenderest of mothers, avoid the foreboding sense that "all is not right with our son?"[43]

To arm him against peer pressure, Martha next set up and demolished a straw man—"the character of [a] young man of good family and slender fortunes" who does *not* "take an early turn to learning and science." The application of that phantom? Davey's "time for improvement" would be "quickly past," and if he had not "improved it," he would find himself "grown up with the pride of what you call a gentleman" and little else. Its moral? Ultimately, the "meanest object in creation is a lazy, poor, proud gentleman, especially if he is a dressy fellow." Martha, ill, worried about money, and single-minded in regard to this precious emblem of their future, had no energy to report the usual tidbits of local gossip, "domestic matters of news and amusements." Rather, "terrified as I am by hearing nothing of you, *nothing from you,* and interpreting this *no news* from a cherished son as *bad news,* my mind is quite out of tune for anything of the lighter kind." The very different context of generation and gender that had shaped her mind-set when she was his age lends perspective to what today would be called her psychological manipulation. "I was so much attached to my father, and to the uncle and aunt who brought me up, that I lived in the habit of greatest intimacy with them." What she meant was a trust that depended on verbalized affinity of interests and goals, rather than geographic proximity. Then as if crossing her literary fingers, she added, "This is so generally the case, with virtuous and affectionate children, that wherever there is silence I dread lest there should also be mystery." Yet Davey's self-absorption was apparently equal to fending off even that guilt-inducing appeal.[44]

The following March, three months before she died, Martha penned the most withering letter of all. She applied scorching rhetoric to her usual concerns, exposing them in a more damning light. Armed with quotations from letters Davey had written home three years earlier (from Mr. Waddel's boarding school in Willington, near Abbeville), she confronted him with the evidence of slippage from his own former ideals. At age twelve, Martha reminded him, he had exulted in being "a very reputable member of society . . . made very much of by Dr. Waddel [the headmaster] and . . . respected by all the good boys in the school." Now he dared pontificate to his parents about "the necessity of spending much money in order to maintain [a] genteel standing in college"—something "necessary [in order] to be respected." Worse, three years ago he had sworn he would never "omit going to college, for any consideration," because it was impossible to have "an extensive practice of any profession" without a college degree. Now he had unwarily suggested that perhaps "a collegiate course is not very necessary to eminence in a profession." Poor Davey, trying to mimic the high rollers at college, had foolishly quoted the dreaded "fashionists."

Martha's wrath was especially fueled by his request for money to buy extra clothing rather than books or travel. She recalled a parental warning from President Smith in 1804: "Every parent may be absolutely assured that, if his son is solicitous to procure . . . much larger sums, under the idea that the stile of living at the College requires them, or under ANY PRETENCE whatever, he has formed some imprudent connexions." She was armed with facts. First, the mother of one of his friends reported that $400 covered "every expense" for her son, an amount Davey had already received, and more. Second, the idea of $100 spent on clothing was shocking evidence that he had used poor judgment in his purchases; they were either "unnecessarily costly, or miserably laid in." He knew better than to pretend that such a request "will not be felt by your parents; you are well aware that it is with much exertion we provide what is comfortable, and have no money to throw away." In desperation Martha added an atypical derogation. "What a weak mind you must have, how I have been deceived in its texture, if you suppose that foppish clothes . . . or what you call a genteel appearance, will make you respectable." One hundred dollars would go a *very* long way "with prudence." Without it, ten times that much would be like pouring water into a sieve. Third, a lad of "perhaps the richest parents in Carolina," who had "only one brother to divide the inheritance" instead of Davey's many siblings, had requested that *his* mother never send *him* more than $500, "let him solicit ever so earnestly." His prim words pointed to parental indulgence as the culprit in any such "shameful dissipation." Fourth, an already distinguished Charlestonian, Thomas Smith Grimké, only a few years older than young David, had assured Mrs. Ramsay that *he* lived very comfortably at Yale in Connecticut on $400 a year and was still able to buy all the necessary virtuous "impedimenta." At this point, Martha acknowledged wearily, "But why multiply examples?"[45]

In Martha's view, David Jr.'s real blasphemy was unwillingness to face the major reason he was at college: the dynastic necessity of "lay[ing] in a sufficient stock of knowledge and . . . attain[ing] such literary honors as may be the foundation of future usefulness." His parents already knew the actual monetary charges as well as he, which had been spelled out in a printed statement. *They* could "calculate what . . . is necessary for clothing, pocket money, and conveniences" —*if* a young man did not use his college days for the wrong reasons: "to be a fashionist, to sport various changes of apparel, to drink, to smoke, to game."[46]

Had his mother suspected attraction to the opposite sex was giving rise to these "fashionist" impulses, she might have cited an aphorism from a recent novel the family had recently enjoyed about male "triflers." "Vanity is the companion of an empty mind, [and there are] as . . . many vacant heads in the one sex as in the other, nor is beauty less destructive to the understanding of the gentlemen, than the ladies."[47] And finally, in case he was serious about returning to Charleston immediately after college, forget it. Wasted though her physical strength might be, his mother would "oppose all my influence to so mad a scheme. You should rather spend

them in the Indian country, and learn the rugged virtues of savages than
… the desultory, dissipated habits of Charleston."[48] Martha was echoing her
father's despair over the way slavery in a society ruined its white youth
through demeaning menial labor. In a society where only slaves did it, children were not taught to develop serious work habits. Her idealization of
the virtue to be found in a life among the Indians was perhaps inspired by
a book the illustrious cleric Jonathan Edwards had fashioned from the
journal of an early New England missionary to the Indians, consumptive
youth David Brainerd—or even in the wooded and Spartan rural setting of
Dr. Waddel's school, which Davey had attended before going north. Davey,
not even born until 1795, may not have known the theological referent of
his mother's scathing remark but he could not mistake the intent behind
her use of "Carolinian" in her letters. Sometimes it was purely negative,
other times an exhortation to regional pride. Her idealization of stern character, in the mold of his grandfather Laurens, pictured Davey as both
descendant and future American leader, but also implicitly it addressed the
peculiar institution that lay behind her misgivings about Carolina indolence. This harsh dismissal of her son's proposed plans was the closest
Martha Laurens Ramsay came to expressing open disdain for the burden
of slavery in their culture. Interestingly, it came out in terms about which
she did not have to be ambivalent: she could openly regret the way slavery
damaged Carolina's own young white citizens.[49]

Impotent in the face of Davey's noncommunication and further dis-
comfited by "the silence of [Princeton president] Dr. Smith, after having
been my correspondent for so many years," poor Martha ended this letter
somewhat helplessly, commending both her fears and her son to God.

A week later, a note from young David—"more judicious, better rea-
soned, [and] in every respect more worthy of yourself"—mollified his ailing mother. Davey's letter had been mailed before her excoriations could
have reached him, which made its conciliatory tone all the more genuine
and welcome. In what turned out to be her farewell note to him, she
acknowledged how ill she had been when she wrote the previous letter—
"confined for upwards of a month by indisposition." Her explanation
verged on apology. As if to prove that she now exonerated him from the
dangerous pro-fashionist tendencies she had deplored the week before, this
letter conveyed a monetary blessing to her darling, "a $50 bill as will pass in
the northern states" that his father had "procured … with great difficulty."
For the present, that symbolism must suffice. "I avoid all remark, advice or
other matter." Perhaps she was weakened by her deepening illness, perhaps

she recognized the futility of further railing at him on paper. Her written benediction beseeched God "to bless you, my dear son, and make you a son of comfort and honor, to your dear father and your most affectionate mother and friend."[50]

Martha's letter-closing flourish invoked not only the biological bond, "your affectionate mother," but also its larger, modern, and voluntary frame, "and friend." Among parents in the new nation, a current of idealism was gradually replacing force with reason and suasion—the appeal to a child's basic good nature. "The voice of undoubted friendship has a great influence over the human heart," New Englander Hitchcock explained through his fictional mother, Mrs. Bloomsgrove. When children know that their "good" is their parents' dearest concern, that is a "greater inducement to fidelity" than anything else. This up-to-date attitude toward child rearing eschewed heavy-handedness in the belief that "lay[ing] hold of the best affections of human nature" gained a kind of "ascendancy over the [child's] mind which an exertion of authority could not effect."[51] Martha's softened tone in the money-bearing benediction suggested that she had recovered enough to recall that principle. Perhaps she also sensed her days approaching their earthly conclusion.

Though her husband was the wordmaster crafting many admired speeches and books, the domain of internal family relationships was one he had gladly surrendered to his wife. He would soon use her model in *Memoirs* to preach the ideal of beneficent domestic management, the effectiveness of her "culture of the heart" over threats or punishment. Martha was his exemplar of modernity as a mother in the way she would "drop the [label and role of] mother in [that of] companion and friend" in their home. She was the children's confidante as well as instructor, a parent who ruled out "the use of severity, sarcasms and all taunting, harsh, unkind language, overbearing conduct, high toned claims of superiority, capricious or whimsical exertions of authority, and . . . other particulars" as a matter of principle. Parents in the new, egalitarian America were reciprocally obligated to "curb their own tempers," he would explain in her *Memoirs*, "to make proper allowances for the indiscretions and follies of youth, and to behave toward their offsprings in the most conciliatory manner so as to secure their love and affections, on the score of gratitude."[52] Her epistolary hectoring was intended only to accomplish that which in David Sr.'s eyes she had achieved, and more.

Martha's exacting standards for herself explain some of her late-life advisory tone. She had consciously selected the most enlightened child-rearing theories available and combined them with the best, most enlightened family governance known to her generation of parents.[53] Yet she could not be fully confident of the outcome. The only shepherding pattern she had to imitate was the style her father had employed in advising her—a blend of cautions, concerns, dreams of aspiration, and goals. Long-distance participation in her son's college life, and the success for which it was intended to prepare him, expressed her "filiapietism."

If, in her letters to the Laurens-Ramsay standard-bearer in the brash new nation, this dying mother sometimes exceeded her ideal of "conciliatory manners," the fifty-dollar gift was her rainbow. After the storms, overarching love bridged the miles and the generations. Martha Ramsay had done her utmost, within the prevailing cultural understandings of motherhood, for the citizenry of the new republic.[54] Sadly, death came before Martha could reap the tangible reward of the college degree—the very foundation of her son's future usefulness, she believed—bestowed on David Jr. at Princeton in 1812. If she had survived, she would have proudly accepted that sheepskin as her own well-earned "laurel wreath."

Epilogue

The recipient of these "college letters" returned to Charleston after his mother's death and his graduation, prevented from further schooling by the continuing shortage of money. He apprenticed in medicine and became a physician, later marrying his first cousin (daughter of his mother's only sister) Eleanor Pinckney and fathering three children. After David Sr.'s death in 1815, the surviving Ramsay offspring faded into relative obscurity—the usual accompaniment of poverty. David Ramsay Jr. died of unrecorded causes in 1826, when he was only thirty-one, well before his progenitors' dynastic hopes could be realized.[55] Since none of the Ramsay daughters—Eleanor, Martha, Catherine, and Sabina—had any prospect of a dowry, they supported themselves by keeping school in their family home on Broad Street.[56] After their father's death in 1815 (shot on the street by a mentally deranged patient), the entire family of eight children were left with nothing, "dependent on . . . reputation alone."[57]

10 | "Discontented with Nothing but Her Heart"

FROM AS FAR BACK AS HER mid-teen years, while her brother dreamed of becoming a hero in the war for independence from Britain, Martha Laurens Ramsay had also dreamed of heroism—in a necessarily feminine and religious version: "the heroism becoming a woman of an honest and a pious heart."[1] Her way of writing about that ideal in her adult years employed the concept of "providence" in the same way that idealizing reason and her capacity for rational thinking had formed an intellectual banner in her youth. The mediating concept of Providence became her lifelong means of coping with many negative and a few happy experiences, in fact it became the only acceptable way she could express the otherwise unthinkable stance of differing from or opposing God.

Martha's religious mentality, like that of her less serious peers, had been nurtured through sermons, deep conversations, and soul-sharing correspondence with women friends; she had read, marked, and inwardly digested shelves of books portraying a divine being who spoke through humans embodying as much frailty as triumph and strength. Economic buffetings and concerns for the new American experiment in civil government—the idea that "the people" both represented ultimate authority in the new nation and were responsible for preserving it—were exhilarating and exhausting during her adult married years. Amid the vast changes in the nation, and despite her modern views on the educating of her children, Martha's spiritual and mental roots were anchored in an eighteenth-century framework. However reasonable and progressive-minded she tried to be, however open to new ideas in her emotional solar plexus, the "Providence" she had absorbed as a child remained a useful part of everyday thinking, and her operative literary tool.

Readers like Martha Ramsay understood exactly what a contemporary English fictional heroine meant when she said, "It is the office of Religion to reconcile us to the seemingly hard dispensations of Providence." Early novelists such as Mary Wollstonecraft in *Mary, a Fiction* (1788), enveloped the metaphor of Providence with contemporary associations.[2]

Providence had become an important means of religious rationalization in seventeenth- and eighteen-century devotional literature,[3] an helpful conceptual link between doctrine, theology, and the exigencies of daily life. It became second nature to expressive, high-minded women like Martha who continually struggled "to discern what end [their] various faculties were destined to pursue."[4] In the uncertainties and hopes of late-eighteenth and early-nineteenth-century Americans, a woman's religious cosmos needed the idea of Providence for active assurance and explanation, as well as for seemingly fatalistic resignation on occasion.

When her life ended in 1811, Martha had been married nearly twenty-five years to a husband whose rhetorical exuberance about the new nation and its constitution was infectious: in his 1804 oration celebrating the accession of the Louisiana Territory, David Ramsay had trumpeted: "Our present form of government is the very best on earth for a great country; . . . an improvement on all the governments that have gone before it."[5] He was a great articulator of the Revolutionary generation's belief in American exceptionalism or "chosen nation" symbolism (the phrase used to describe experience in the nation's first two centuries). Increase Mather had traced the strange, remarkable evidence of God's hand in transplanted Anglo-Christian culture in the wilderness as "providences."[6]

Some historians have described the era of Martha Ramsay's life span—revolution, constitution, and early nationhood—as a time of religious decline, a period when membership and commitment to religious life and institutions had sunk to a low ebb. The Episcopal Church of Martha's childhood was stereotyped as dwindling to near extinction. Bonomi's *Under the Cope of Heaven* disproved that assumption with a concrete picture of church membership and religious practice during the prewar period.[7] American religious historian Edwin Gaustad located that postwar history, the period when Martha and David were rearing a family, within a wider context of religious reorientation and restructuring rather than decline. Among the currents of religious change occurring during Martha's adult life (1780–1810) were the disestablishment of the dominant church in a given locale—abrupt for Anglicans in the South, gradual for Congregationalists in New England; increasing anticlericalism or religious resistance to the authority of clergy in nonparish affairs, the religious organizational counterpart of Americans' rebellion against governmental hierarchy and domination; challenges to both inherited and traditional (the Bible and revealed religion) sources of religious authority, under the impact of European Enlightenment thought; and the rise of competition among organized religious bodies—between denominations—along with numbers of voluntary associations, within and across denominational lines.[8]

Some of the harshest Calvinist doctrines, such as infant damnation, were losing influence as parents embraced child-rearing goals over which they themselves had control—for example, the ideal of republican virtue that they were responsible for inculcating.[9] New forms of charity carried out specifically by women had emerged a decade earlier: in Martha's locale, there was one of the first church-sponsored women's prayer groups, followed shortly by a Charleston Woman's Society for Distributing Books and Starting Schools (1804). In New England, among many comparable organizations, the Female Charitable Society of Providence, Rhode Island, had come into being four years earlier, in 1800. Such cross-denominational organizations allowed women to write and administer their own "constitutions" (not unlike their husbands crafting new structures of civil government) and to develop a new form of religious activism. Women continued to do the basic hands-on work of benevolence with neighbors, slaves, and sick relatives while also engaging in these newer, more corporate activities. The ways in which Martha Ramsay employed Providence in her thinking and spiritual life supplies the evolutionary process under these innovations and illuminates the female religious cosmos at the turn of the nineteenth century.[10]

In the diary entries preserved in *Memoirs* from 1791 to 1808, Martha invoked Providence on more than twenty-five occasions, a number that reflects only those times she actually sat down to record it. Readers must estimate, as she herself writes regretfully, the countless times it was silently, fleetingly invoked—in the multitude of crises inescapably accompanying wifehood, childbearing, child mourning, the death of relatives and friends, psychic depression, money worries, declining health, and the competitive new society that was replacing her ordered childhood world.

Although Martha was the intellectual peer of her elite fellow citizens and shared the public assumption that Providence had given Americans politico-religious support for independence from Great Britain, gender led her to apply it differently—domesticate it, so to speak. However capable she was of phrasing her religious thoughts in sophisticated, literary discourse, Providence was more often a basic psychic tool for her, an all-but-instinctive cry from the heart; for example, on June 20, 1808, "the many gracious providences I have experienced." Her diary meditations usually ignored the specifics of an event that precipitated a particular reflection, but this one, among the last entries published in *Memoirs,* documented a profound feeling of divine deliverance: their house had not burned to the ground during a terrifying neighborhood conflagration.

Fire was a consuming anxiety in early American cities because of the way the buildings were constructed, and in Charleston because of the unexpressed but ever-present belief that arson would be the weapon of choice in a slave uprising.[11] The "dry situation of these wooden buildings, with their appurtenances, so nearly connected," she wrote, might easily have resulted in the three Broad Street townhouses (the Ramsays' being the middle one) going up in flames "in less than fifteen minutes" due to tumultuous winds. Fortunately, the storm had struck before ten in the evening, while the neighborhood was "yet up and awake." Human intervention— the "timely discovery" of the blaze "before the fire had arisen to a great height"—was the agent of Providence. Martha and her family were all right, she recorded in a timeless affirmation: "God, who is rich in mercy, is better to us than our fears." Characteristically, that entry also carried a subsequent application: "May the recollection of this goodness keep my heart quiet and submissive under the various cares that, at present, torment it. Whatever anxieties assail me, may this and the many other gracious providences I have experienced, silence my fears, encourage my hopes, and enable me to go on."[12]

Providence first entered the preserved diary along with motherhood, as had the diary itself, perhaps. After falling into the fireplace, another potential trauma haunting any mother of a two-year-old, dear little Patty (Martha Junior) was saved. Fortunately, Martha had been close by and "by God's good providence" pulled Patty to safety, able to smother the flames before she was seriously burned. That occurred in November 1791, the same day her husband left for Columbia, South Carolina, and a meeting of the state legislature. The underlying motif of that particular entry was larger than that the fireplace accident, however: it was grief for her sweet infant Fanny (Frances Henry Laurens Ramsay) who had died. A harried, burdened mother of thirty-two, however helpful her household slaves, needed a place outside herself to record God's providence and preservation of her pious, honest heart. Her diary became a symbolic closet in which she could unburden her soul.[13]

Yet the next two years brought two more baby girls, with a mix of emotions she never recorded. Catherine Henry Laurens Ramsay was born the year her Grandfather Laurens died and her father, David, made his public antislavery declaration at the state capitol. Sabina Elliott Ramsay arrived in 1793, the same year Martha's only sister, Eleanor (Mrs. Charles

Pinckney), died—an "exceeding heavy stroke of thy Providence," she confessed in the diary. It made her "heart . . . too full to write on this subject." A year later, in 1794, Martha used the diary and Providence to argue herself out of what her rational mind assured her was unwarranted melancholia—a rebellious spirit that could not be quelled or rationalized and that she could not prevent from interfering with her ability to submit to dark Providence. Conversely, "Providences" were high on the list of changes in habit she hoped could dispel her cloud of depression: "I would wish to be more diligent in self-examination, more watchful to prayer, more steady in resisting temptation, more careful in the instructions which I give my dear children and in the example I set before them, and *more attentive to providences.*"[14]

Late in 1794, Martha was already pregnant again (with Davey, her first son) when a young friend—a bride of only twelve days—died suddenly. Martha's shock at this unexpected death produced her awed pledge to ponder deeply such inscrutable happenings, no matter how painful. "God grant that no such awful and awakening providence as the removal of a young person, so lately full of life and health . . . should pass, without some earnest desire to have my loins girt, and my lamp burning." Her invoking the biblical images of preparedness was a verbal totem, a means of fending off fear and gloom. A well-filled, brightly glowing lamp and being properly clothed for any eventuality were homely images of concrete action she could take as a hedge against arbitrary fate, inspired by a watchful Providence. Of all her fears, unexpected death was the most constant. "Our Taper of life is not always consumed by its own Flame," warned a seventeenth-century French pietist Martha relished especially in her final illness; "many unkind Blasts and showers often [prematurely] extinguish it."[15] Even though all women of her class were schooled in handling physical death—supervising the bathing and laying out of the corpse, dressing and sprinkling it with petals—the confrontation of a bridal bier, early in her own marriage, impelled Martha to want to placate Providence.

The central portion of her diary (the year of her soul's dark night, 1795), cast Providence as religious intermediary between Martha at the point of nervous collapse, and a God who seemed suddenly remote, unheeding of her prayers. Providence was somehow the comforting entity in the daunting abyss between the all-knowing if unresponsive Creator of the universe and galling human helplessness. While she, a Charleston "first family" heiress, struggled to make sense of the cumulative blows to her sense of self-worth, Providence became the thread sustaining her sanity, a fateful mediator through and to whom she could plead and rage. Though Providence was acknowledged to deliver both good and bad "mercies" and "judgments," Martha had believed that her own powers of reason were sufficient to discern which were positive and which were chastening, even in the midst of a spiritual and physical depression. During that dark night of soul, the most painful negative she assigned to Providence was the desertion of friends who had been glad to admire the Ramsays in their more affluent times. "The grave covers the most of those with whom I kept up much intimacy," she had to record, "and various providences have changed the hearts of some who yet remain."[16]

Once, Martha cited the popular Providence of the Enlightenment mind, the heavenly engineer who set the world in motion, the clockmaker in the sky who inscribed the miraculous laws of nature in the minute perfection of a leaf—quoting the psalmist, "O God whose providence is over all thy works." A widely reprinted sermon, typical of many she read and heard, celebrated the optimism of educated Christian citizens in her time based on "the development of the Arts and Sciences." The preacher warned: "As a Clock will shew the Hour of the Day without any further interposition of the Artificer that made it," thoughtless humans may delude themselves that "Nature may and does produce every Effect which we see about us without any further Interposition of God." Such unthinking assumptions led humans to ignore, at their peril, the maintenance required by a clock: it could be kept in motion only by gravity operating on its "weight of lead" (the pendulum). The awesome cautionary moral was: "In the great [clock] Machine of the World, who . . . shall hang on its weights?"[17] Who is actually in charge and keeping it running? One of the burdens in Martha's religious worldview, and contributing to her depression, was the belief of her era that *she personally* must be the one "to hang the weights" in her moral and physical domain to keep it running, and she must also be responsible for guarding the new nation's virtue to keep it running. For enlightened folks like Martha and her husband, the new understandings of nature and reason were awesomely expressed in such mechanical imagery.[18]

At the beginning of 1796, Martha had found a providential interpretation of her debilitation. She had experienced a visitation of healing (she called it "surrender") during the semiannual communion service at the Circular Church, which providentially revived her inner spirit even if her life was not as she wished or had imagined it could be. Still, spiritual lessons were never a once-and-for-all learning, something that once endured and conquered was finished forever after. Life's circumstances were never so neat: within a half year, by November 1797, an agonized entry again begged for "a gracious revival, a merciful, providential lifting up." This followed a period of fierce bargaining with God. Another infant had hovered near death, a daughter named Jane Montgomery, and Martha recorded spending every available hour "prostrate before [God]." She had pitted her own value in God's eyes against her infant's recovery. "I thought that if the life of the child should be granted me, it would be an evidence that the Lord, for Christ's sake had forgiven me those things I had bewailed before him . . . [But] My child was taken, and I was plunged into . . . a double sorrow."[19] Since she was the one who had enlarged the stakes, her loss had to include God's favor as well as the infant, a combination that made her physically ill. "Since the death of this baby . . . [there have been] other trials of a temporal nature I have also undergone at this time; even now many things seem to be going against me." The only mitigation she could think of was to reinvoke the powers guaranteed in her youthful covenant: "enable me O my God to walk as under the bonds of [my] covenant, and in all sorrow, to take hold of covenant consolations."[20]

Several years later, Martha described herself as "hanging on Providence for the events of the next two days" (3 February 1799). Those events included the death of yet a third newborn daughter and all but unbearable anxieties about her husband's "worldly perplexities"—lawsuits, money shortages, general litigiousness, and public humiliation. "Bless my very dear husband; point out to him the path of duty; make all his way plain; bring him through . . . his difficulties and trials, that he may say, this is the Lord's doing, and it is marvelous." God knew the "groanings" of her heart. In fact she could intellectually affirm that God already held the hearts of all men, all humanity, in His hands. But she had to remind herself: "In God is my trust; . . . I will not then fear what man can do. May He enable us to be just and upright to all, and not permit any to oppress and be hard to us." This veiled reference alluded to the news that her brother, Henry Laurens Jr., had filed bankruptcy proceedings against her husband.[21]

Although Dr. Ramsay continued to hold positions of leadership in the civic affairs of Charleston, the Ramsay financial condition remained unimproved.[22] Martha's next recorded conversation with Providence, in March 1802, was a thanksgiving and lecture (to herself) about a momentary financial deliverance which turned into a positive link between answered prayer and the Bible, which she happened to be holding in her hand when it arrived. While intending to search the Scriptures for guidance, her mind had drifted toward the perilous state of their finances. She upbraided herself for such faithlessness: "What do you read your Bible for, but to fetch from it instruction and consolation, suited to all your circumstances!" Within a miraculously short time her husband unexpectedly brought her "a sum of money more than adequate" to meet their most pressing debts, an action she recognized and had to name. "This is but one instance of the manifold interventions of Providence which I have experienced and which, although not written down in books, are deeply engraven on my heart, and treasured up in my memory." In fact, she apologized to God and berated herself for all those examples she had *not* recorded. How could she, who recognized that God was the provider of "necessary food for my family," not also record the gift of "the bread of life to feed our souls?" Holding up her family in prayer—her dear husband "on this sweet and solemn occasion" (unexplained), Miss Futurell (the now-departed English tutor and mother's helper who had lived with them during the children's early years), and all the younger generation themselves—she especially begged for a "restraining providence" who could bring about "an early conversion" for her dear children and thus direct their potential for youthful folly into safer paths.[23]

One of the books Martha read in 1811, during her final illness, reinforced her consciousness of the providential hand in human lives and the way lives of believers were intertwined via a web of associations and blessings. *The Power of Religion on the Mind, in Retirement, Affliction and at the Approach of Death* was compiled by one of her favorite editor-authors, the Rev. Lindley Murray.[24] This last of his books consisted of relatively brief orations of deathbed wisdom by religiously famous and sometimes titled Europeans as well as a very few Americans. One such was Anthony Benezet, the antislavery activist in Philadelphia, for whom their friend Benjamin Rush had written a posthumous panegyric in the kind of terms Martha most admired. He was "a truly pious man," Rush had eulogized, "and one who loved virtue wherever he found it," including among deprived slaves and free blacks—one of their rare contemporaries who saw and admitted that.[25]

Like Martha's own father, Anthony Benezet had been a successful Huguenot merchant (in his case, later become a Philadelphia Quaker spokesman and leader) who also accumulated great wealth. In Rush's obituary praise, however, his major life accomplishment had nothing to do with riches but rather with devoting "himself to ameliorate the condition of the negroes," and efforts toward "entire abolition of the [slave] trade." Dr. Rush praised Benezet as the American who had single-handedly generated "the spirit of inquiry into [the blacks'] situation, and sympathy with their distresses, [which] have spread over the world, and will, ere long we trust, destroy this system of inhumanity and in-justice," quite an encomium in the Ramsay view. His concluding paragraph traced Benezet's funeral procession through the streets of Philadelphia—a grieving cortege attracting "so many Negroes" that Benezet was in a figurative sense "embalmed with tears." A former officer in the Revolutionary Army, probably a contemporary of Rush and the Ramsays, witnessed that emotional procession and "pronounced this striking eulogium" that Rush was pleased to quote from a newspaper account: "'I would rather be Anthony Benezet in that coffin, than the great George Washington with all his honors.'"[26]

Dr. Rush's Charleston friends had to be moved by a tribute that linked the deep concerns they also shared: religion, virtue, and racial injustice. Perhaps they were inwardly embarrassed for the constraints on their own actions imposed by their geographical location. Despite internally opposing the slavery in which they felt embedded, and despite their community status as upstanding religious voices, Martha and David Ramsay were likely to have privately admitted their impotence in that moral dilemma. They could applaud visionary, providential activism in Benezet and in their friend Benjamin Rush. But if the Ramsays rejoiced, in their own home, over Benezet's antislavery influence, Providence may also have helped them rationalize their own inaction.

Dr. Ramsay's biographical introduction to Martha's *Memoirs* contained several pages of philosophy that set the stage for his description of her deathbed drama, the essential capstone of print memorials in that era. Since his subject had been so exemplary in every respect, in his view, readers would likely expect a life "crowned with a large portion of temporal blessings." As it happened, in her case "unpropitious events" had instead produced "perplexing embarrassments," a euphemism for financial limitations and reputational reversals. Martha herself was responsible for none of these, he cautioned, and her self-reproaches were in no way "accessory to them."[27]

In the financial arena, all Providences had been afflictive and adverse for the Ramsays, even as Martha herself had remained steadfast, "discontented with nothing but her heart." She was the "same self-possessed, unrepining, submissive, satisfied Christian" in those "unpropitious events" as she was in health and prosperity. "The burden of sin [always] lay heavier on her mind than the burden of outward troubles," was her husband's summary. Whether his philosophizing captured Martha's true feelings or remained solely in the eye of the beholder allows for an interpretative question: did she really welcome death more for "closing the scene of her sinning" in this earthly life than for ending her physical suffering?[28] In that regard she undoubtedly modeled her soul's triumph over debility and diminished energy after the medieval female saints "of pious and honest hearts" she had long studied and tried to imitate; she clearly intended her life's valedictory scene to follow the pattern established in many religious memoirs. Hers should also be recorded, and similarly preserved.

David Ramsay established the proper tone for her final tableau by discussing a speech she had brought to his attention shortly before her final illness—one delivered at the grave of a pious Englishman more than a century earlier. (He recorded that she found it on page 352 in Isaac Watts' *World to Come*. Such careful detail, one of rare such instances in the *Memoirs*, creates a sense of immediacy for the reader even two centuries later). Martha had handed it to him underlined and notated, as "expressive of her feelings," which he explained as her willingness to face the "truth" of the grave and its portents of physical dissolution. This was a theological indication measuring her courage, in his eyes. The speech was addressed to the grave that would receive the body of "our dearly beloved in the Lord"; that body, weakened and weary from long affliction and anguish, would only welcome "a quiet rest from all its labors."[29]

Determined not to flinch from graphic depiction, Martha wanted the grave to be called "a devourer" that would "swallow up forever" the "dishonor" of humanly corruptible flesh "as [its] proper prey." This was not an image of dread, however, since that same flesh housed a soul, "a divine relation[ship] to the Lord of life" that the grave could by no means retain; at some unforeseen season that "being" would return from God's hand in "incorruption, honor and power." The body, like so much seed, must be sowed [in the grave] in the dishonor of physical death, in order to be resurrected in glory—sowed in weakness and returned from the upper realms in power, sowed as a "natural body" but "returned a spiritual body."[30]

Her husband credited Providence for the graceful and dignified manner she exhibited in all physical and financial hardships. These had created "a secret connexion with our future and most important destinies"; they had helped her forge the "necessary links in the chain conducting [Martha] from earth to heaven." The intimate recital of her last twenty-four hours followed a script she planned "with the same calmness . . . she would have done in the days of her best health, preparing for a journey or voyage."[31]

First, her pain-wracked body was tenderly lifted into a warm bath. Having studied Drelincourt thoroughly in those final weeks, Martha could view her diseased body as "this rotten Lodge," anticipate the "Palace of Immortality" she would inhabit after death, and willingly pray, in his words, "Let my Bed remember me that I must shortly lie in a Bed of Dust." She wanted soothing water to mark the moment "when Death comes to break the strings of this wretched Body" and "the Soul enters into the River of Living Water, into an Ocean of Celestial Felicity."[32] That last symbolic bath was Martha's end-of-life sacrament, comparable in her eyes with baptism at the beginning of her life and her secret covenant on the brink of adulthood; she needed a religious initiation into each succeeding stage of spiritual life, including this final one into heavenly life hereafter.

While resting in the bath, she called for a treasured artifact from her youth, the hymnal given her by the countess of Huntingdon in those long-ago days in England after the war. The hymn she chose to sanctify her watery suspension was filled with ineffable images of light overcoming pain and decay. Each stanza repeated "sweet" providential transformation as a foreshadowing of her immanent release: "sweet to look inward and attend / The whispers of his love; / Sweet to look upward to the place / Where Jesus dwells above."[33]

She was able to whisper the word *sweet* as each verse was read, assuring her watchers that she was still conscious and able to join them in the hymn's vision. Drelincourt had promised that the only death-soothing narcotic needed by believers was to "already feel Heaven in the Soul."[34] In fact, the hymn ended: "If such the sweetness of the streams, / What must the fountain be, /Where saints and angels draw their bliss / Immediately from Thee."[35] Martha was departing from a world on images that themselves could lift her soul into transcendent reality. In the curiously contentious logic of early pietists, Drelincourt's theme argued its own proofs: "If Life and Death were not in God's hands, there would be nothing settled or constant . . . prophets would be found in grievous errors" [no one could trust holy Scriptures], and The Eternal Election would be totally abolished" [heaven and its promises could not be counted on].[36] Circular as this sounds today, it reified the certainty undergirding Martha's final moments.

She had planned the sequence of her dying rituals—the coffin, the laying out of her body in the clothing she was to be buried in, the funeral itself—as religiously (and administratively) as any of the other tasks she skillfully accomplished in her life. She had chosen the Scripture readings, the hymns to be sung, and the particular clergyman to officiate—the friend she regarded as her chief pastor, the Rev. Mr. Hollinshead. She had ordered her own coffin, proudly specifying plain Carolina cedar. She had arranged for the family's continued management by preparing her daughters to care for the household, their father, and their brothers. And she had ensured her own memorial, three days before her death, by telling her husband where to find her diary and the other secret documents unknown to him or anyone else, now to be preserved as her major legacy.

The last act in her drama, "about four o'clock in the afternoon of June 10th, 1811," required her to ask the ultimate question that closed the death scene in a pious memoir—whether the grieving mourners around her deathbed were "willing to give her up." This ritual was intended to affirm the dying person's faith one last time: she must say she was now ready to meet God face to face. Further, the mourners must consent to her leaving their circle, to surrender their claims on her in favor of God's. Martha, three weeks before, had read yet another pious memoir, this one of British scholar and pietist Elizabeth Carter, which had made her eager to meet its author in heaven.[37] And Martha had armed herself for the final farewell to her family with Drelincourt's motto: "Death my entrance to the presence of my God."[38]

The grieving husband recorded that their children, ranging in age from twenty to nine, were made distraught by her asking that final question. Knowing its significance, they resisted, weeping and begging her not to leave them. In the end, Martha herself was the one to make the necessary gesture: she "assured them that God had now made her entirely willing to give them all up, and in about an hour after, expired." In the eyes of her witnesses, she had fulfilled the vow of her youth, "to do honor to religion in that last finishing scene, and to glorify thee, dear Lord, with my expiring breath."[39]

Nearing the end of his biographical introduction, her husband summarized his editorial commission: "The subject of these memoirs was neither the first nor the last of the favorites of Christ whom he has led to heaven otherwise than by a path strewn with flowers." Undoubtedly, the "storms of adversity" she faced were "highly favorable to her improvement in the Christian virtues of patience and resignation." He then pronounced an avuncular benediction: "The workings of her mind . . . as recorded in her manuscripts, prove her high attainments in the Christian life, and were probably one cause of them."[40] In his view, *Memoirs* was a conclusive demonstration of female virtue as the essential armor of exalted womanhood, of reason as elevating motherhood and piety, and of Providence itself as the sustaining hand. If a new nation would only heed her cautionary model, all civic ills would disappear and the republic would indeed flourish.

Martha's dying suggestion that her diary become "a common book of the family" transformed Dr. Ramsay's grief into entrepreneurial energy. Since there was already a well-established tradition of treating family papers as a special legacy, sometimes even having them privately printed, he required only one further nudge. That was an ethical one: "How far it would be proper to withhold them from that more enlarged sphere of usefulness which would result from their publication?"[41]

Scarcely two and a half weeks after Martha's death on 10 June 1811, David had in hand the sanction he needed. He had consulted his friends at the Circular Church, one of whom was his fellow alumnus from the College of New Jersey. The Rev. Dr. Keith's letter encouraged Dr. Ramsay to "yield to *the call of duty,* consider yourself as *rendering an important service to the public,* and a due *tribute of praise* to the God of all grace, by consenting to publish these valuable papers." Rev. Dr. William Hollinshead, head pastor, agreed. The volume David Ramsay was creating would promote much-needed public virtue in a troubled time and would immeasurably gratify "a numerous circle to whom every memorial of their beloved departed friend will be precious." It would also "embalm the virtues" of and preserve "a lady of a very superior mind, of accomplishments derived . . . from the best education, and from a long and intimate intercourse with many of the first characters in her native country and in Europe." Martha's posthumous print emblem, measuring three and one-half by six and one-half inches, would comfort and inspire her fellow Americans, "who walk in fear and darkness" because they lack the spiritual knowledge she had mastered, of coping with daily trials and earthly disillusion. By all three men's standards, transforming Martha into a religious icon for the new nation's women was also perfect republicanism. Her voice and example, preserved in a print memorial, would become "a weapon to combat corruption" in the new republic.[42]

At the personal level, Martha's diary was her soul's confidant and battlefield. At a political level, it was a sectarian treatise in an era that still sanctioned lay patriot preaching by citizens like David Ramsay.[43] Two years after Martha's death (1813), David recognized the deep solace he had received from the task of compiling her *Memoirs:* "I know from experience that in a late severe family affliction I found my mind wonderfully composed by thinking and writing on a dear deceased friend."[44] Martha would have been thankful that editing her papers banished his grief. She would undoubtedly have viewed being the subject of his print monument as an honor. Although a reviewer of *Memoirs* in the new literary magazine *Portfolio* expressed an opinion that the editor had been carried away by "the fallacious standard of his own feelings,"[45] we today can be grateful that providence led him to alchemize his grief editorially.

Martha's religious cosmos epitomized mainstream knowledge and religious belief in her time. The theology she lived and recorded in her diary and letters was indeed "a solvent of the intellectual and social climate of its period,"[46] an interpretive system that helped her translate disasters into vehicles of grace. It gave her a sense of having fulfilled the words of her father's commission in her youth—"the heroism of a woman of a pious and an honest heart."[47] Reconstructing the life and times of a woman like Martha Laurens Ramsay, in the era of the new republic, requires modern scholars to somehow reappreciate the religion that was her vital cultural medium—a spiritual ground enhanced by women's new confidence in the ability to use their reason, and confidence in Providence as their special instrument.

Notes

Preface

1. Walter J. Fraser Jr., *Charleston! Charleston! The History of a Southern City* (Columbia: University of South Carolina Press, 1989), 30, 41.

2. Ibid., 47, 62, 98.

3. A recent English literature study traces twenty-six seventeenth-century English women's "journals," diary-eulogies, and "memoirs" in religious language. Avra Kouffman, "The Cultural Work of Stuart Women's Diaries" (Ph.D. diss., University of Arizona, 2000).

4. Sarah Josepha Hale, *Woman's Record; or Sketches of All Distinguished Women from "The Beginning" till A.D.* 1850 (New York: Harper & Brothers, 1853).

5. Samuel C. Smith, "'Through the Eye of a Needle': The Role of Pietistic and Mystical Thought among the Anglican Elite in the Eighteenth Century Lowcountry South" (Ph.D. diss., University of South Carolina, 2000).

6. Amanda Porterfield, review of Ann Taves' *Fits, Trances, and Visions: Experiencing Religion and Explaining Experience, from Wesley to James* (Princeton N.J.: Princeton University Press, 1999), in *WMQ* 57 (Apr. 2000): 432–34.

7. Henry Laurens to Martha Laurens, 17 Aug. 1776, in "Review: 'Memoirs of Martha Laurens Ramsay,'" *Portfolio*, 3d ser., no. 2 (1813): 53.

Chapter 1

1. Her diary comprises appendix 5, the largest single section (99–166), in David Ramsay, *Life of Martha Laurens Ramsay* (Charleston, S. Car., 1811). Page numbers throughout are from 1814 edition published in Boston by Armstrong.

2. David Duncan Wallace, *The Life of Henry Laurens* (New York: G. P. Putnam's Sons, 1915), 130, listed some 20,000 acres as his vast plantation holdings, along with their cadres of slave labor cultivating rice and indigo: Mepkin, Mt. Tacitus, Wambaw, and Wright's Savannah; in upper South Carolina, Ninety-Six; and in Georgia, Turtle River, Broughton Island and New Hope.

3. Josiah Smith diary, 1780–1781, *SCHM* 34 (Apr. 1933): 67. "Last Tuesday night [May 24, 1770] died, universally regretted, Mrs. Helena Laurens, wife of Henry Laurens Esq., as valuable a woman in all respects as any she has left behind."

4. Emily A. Smith, *Life and Letters of Nathan Smith* (New Haven: Yale University Press, 1914), 32. Dr. Smith, a correspondent of David Ramsay, founded Dartmouth Medical School in 1798.

5. The primary documentary sources about Martha are Philip M. Hamer, George C. Rogers Jr., David R. Chesnutt, C. James Taylor, Peggy Clarke, eds., *The Papers of Henry Laurens*, 15 vols. to date (Columbia: University of South Carolina Press, 1968–), and her husband's letters, Robert L. Brunhouse, ed., *David Ramsay, 1749–1815: Selections from His Writings* (Philadelphia: American Philosophical Society, 1965). Biographies are by Arthur H. Shaffer, *To Be an American: David Ramsay and the Making of the American Consciousness* (Columbia: University of South Carolina Press, 1991), and Wallace, *The Life of Henry Laurens.* See Donald J. Winslow, *Life Writing* (Honolulu: University of Hawaii Press, 1980) for evolution of the genre "memoirs."

6. HL to Elias Ball, 6 Nov. 1764, sending "583 yards of Negro Cloth" to Wambaugh Plantation; Hamer, *Papers of Henry Laurens*, 4, 493.

7. George N. Edwards, *A History of the Independent or Congregational Church of Charleston* (Boston: Pilgrim Press, 1947), 35.

8. David Ramsay, *History of the American Revolution* (Philadelphia, 1789), 2:316.

9. Sarah Jane Hennen, ed., *Sentiments and Experience and Other Remains of Lucy Cobham Hennen* (London, 1846), x, characterization of a compiled memoir; Ramsay, *Memoirs*, 47–54.

10. Ramsay, *History of the Revolution of South Carolina* (Charleston, 1785), concluded with an appendix of "great characters," including Henry and John Laurens. Shaffer's characterization, "cultural nationalism" in *To Be an American*, 87; William J. Free, *The Columbian Magazine and American Literary Nationalism* (The Hague: Mouton, 1968), 102–3.

11. Subsequent editions of Ramsay, *Memoirs*, were unchanged except for letters of commendation added to the preface of the second and succeeding editions. The exception is the 1845 American Sunday School Union edition in which three anecdotes were inserted, probably by her school-keeping daughters, in the biographical introduction (this edition cited where applicable).

12. Avra Kouffman, "The Cultural Work of Stuart Women's Diaries" (Ph.D. diss., University of Arizona, 2000), is one of the latest in-depth explorations of previously ignored women's diary and devotional writings from seventeenth-century England.

13. See Laurel Thatcher Ulrich, *A Midwife's Tale: The Life of Martha Ballard, Based on Her Diary, 1785–1812* (New York: A. A. Knopf, 1990), 8, for previous historians' dismissal of Martha Ballard's diary.

14. Felicity A. Nussbaum, *The Autobiographical Subject: Gender and Ideology in Eighteenth Century England* (Baltimore: Johns Hopkins University Press, 1989), 137.

15. Ramsay, *Memoirs*, v, iv.

16. Ibid. Real-life events include the following: 100, the death of baby Fanny (1791); death of baby Jane (1797); sister's death (1793); 104, death of servant (1791); 110, death of Mrs. Petrie; 138, death of Mrs. Keith; 164, Mrs. Howell funeral, death of

two Ramsay nieces (1806); 106, baby fell into fireplace. Illnesses: (her own) sick with grief after sister's death, 110; darkness of 1795, 111; heart and flesh failing, 114; daughter Eleanor and self ill with fever, 138; after death of infant Jane, weakness, 140; constitution enfeebled, 153; pained body, drooping mind, 158; thoughts of death, 160; weakness of body, 163. "Easily besetting sin," 99, 101, 102, 108, 119, 133.

17. Janet Varner Gunn, *Autobiography: Toward a Poetics of Experience* (Philadelphia: University of Pennsylvania Press, 1982).

18. Births of daughters in 1787, 1789, 1790, 1791, 1792, 1793; a son in 1795; another daughter in 1799; and three more sons in 1798, 1801, and 1802. David Ramsay gave "An Address to the Freemen of South Carolina on . . . the Federal Constitution" in 1788, for example; a "July 4th Oration" in 1794; and an "Oration on the Death of Washington" in 1800. Brunhouse, *Writings of David Ramsay.*

19. Ramsay, *Memoirs,* 198.

20. Ibid., 43. *Heart religion* became code for self-focus in late-seventeenth and early-eighteenth-century English and American popular religious literature.

21. Ramsay, *Memoirs,* 102. Her usage employs the word *profess* to indicate proclaiming one's Christian faith and identity, not an academic occupational role.

22. He cited Gen. 6:5, Jer. 17:9, and 2 Tim. 1:15.

23. Ramsay, *Memoirs,* 102–3 n. 81. "Why should such persons [joyful in their communion with God] be censured by their brethren as enthusiasts? [and called] religious over much; . . . let such cool religionists be rather animated by these instances of holy fervor."

24. Ramsay, *Memoirs,* 14, 19, 29, 199–219.

25. Ibid., 103.

26. Henry F. May, *The Enlightenment in America* (New York: Oxford University Press, 1976), 75.

27. HL to Augustus Johnston, 19 Aug. 1769, Hamer, *Papers of Henry Laurens,* 7:118 n. 34; Geoffrey Adams, *The Huguenots and French Opinion, 1685–1787* (Waterloo, Ontario: Wilfred Laurier University Press, 1991), chaps. 18 and 19.

28. William James, *The Varieties of Religious Experience* (New York: Simon & Schuster, 1997), 387.

29. Albert H. Keller, *A Brief History of the Circular Church, Charleston, South Carolina* (undated pamphlet, circa 1988).

30. Jay Fliegelman, *Prodigals and Pilgrims: The American Revolution against Patriarchal Authority, 1750–1800* (New York: Cambridge University Press, 1982), 3.

31. Carla Mulford, ed., *Annis Boudinot Stockton: "Only for the Eyes of a Friend"* (Charlottesville: University Press of Virginia, 1997); *Columbian Magazine and Universal Repository,* 1786–92.

32. Ramsay, *Memoirs,* 72, 73.

33. Ibid., 170, 184, 191.

34. Judith Sargent Murray, *The Gleaner,* 3 vols. (Boston, 1798), 1:vi, vii, viii.

35. Ibid. Martha's design for the Circular Church, Ramsay, *Memoirs,* 10; scientific assistance, Ramsay, *Memoirs,* 30.

36. Nussbaum, *The Autobiographical Subject,* 175: "Autobiographical texts encouraged organization, and self-regulation . . . [and were almost] a technology of the spiritual self" in the newly accepted experiential codes.

37. Ramsay, *Memoirs,* 47.

38. HL to ML, 17 Aug. 1776, Hamer, *Papers of Henry Laurens,* 11:255. When David Ramsay edited that letter for her *Memoirs* (1811), he substituted "Spirit" for "Heroism" in the original (52).

39. Ramsay, *Memoirs,* 73, emphasis added.

40. E.g., two of many Providence-tracing sermons in the Metcalf Collection, John Hay Library, Brown University, Providence, Rhode Island, are by Henry Stebbing, "Discourse Concerning the Governing Providence of God," 6 Feb. 1756, London; and Joseph Lathrop, "The Constancy and Uniformity of the Divine Government," 7 Apr. 1803, Springfield, Mass.; also David D. Hall, *Worlds of Wonder, Days of Judgment: Popular Religious Belief in Early New England* (Cambridge, Mass.: Harvard University Press, 1990), and "On Common Ground: The Coherence of American Puritan Studies," *WMQ* 54 (Apr. 1987): 193–229.

41. Joan W. Scott, "Deconstructing Equality-Versus-Difference," *Feminist Studies* 14 (spring 1988): 33–50; Ramsay, *Memoirs,* 107, 110.

42. Ramsay, *Memoirs,* 87, 111.

43. Hall, "On Common Ground," 214. Ramsay's *Memoirs* epitomize what was formerly undealt with as "minor literature" in the academic study of religion, more recently appreciated as "almost as valuable as the classics," though "without [the same] authority" as formal scholarly writings. Ernest Campbell Mossner, *Bishop Butler and the Age of Reason* (New York: Macmillan, 1936), xiii.

44. Ramsay, *Memoirs,* 171; Mossner, *Bishop Butler,* 14; Hall, "On Common Ground," 219; Ann Janine Morey, "In Memory of Cassie: Child Death and Religious Vision in American Women's Novels," *Religion and American Culture* 6 (winter 1996): 87–104.

45. Scholars today are mining such collections of personal writings by women for their perspective on their times; e.g., *Milcah Martha Moore's Book: A Commonplace Book of Early American Literature,* ed. Catherine L. Blecki and Karin A. Wulf (University Park: Penn State University Press, 1997) and Wulf's forthcoming edition of the diary of Hannah Callender, an educated Quaker woman for whom slavery was troubling. Stockton's manuscript of poetry, circulated among friends, was her comment on public and private events (Mulford, *Only for the Eye of a Friend,* introduction).

46. Ramsay, *Memoirs,* vii, David Ramsay's oxymoron, also used by Judith Sargent Murray and others to emphasize women's view of reason as an integral component of spiritual excellence.

47. Philip D. Morgan, *Slave Counterpoint* (Chapel Hill: University of North Carolina Press, 1998) is the most comprehensive study of South Carolina slave structures and relationships to date.

48. Elise Pinckney, ed., *The Letterbook of Eliza Lucas Pinckney, 1739–1762* (Columbia: University of South Carolina Press, 1997).

49. DR to BR, 11 Feb. 1786, Brunhouse, *Ramsay,* 98; also Jerome Huyler, *Locke in America: The Moral Philosophy of the Founding Era* (Lawrence: University of Kansas, 1995) for the effects of self-interested "interest groups" on Lockean idealism.

50. Jonathan Edwards Jr., "The Injustice and Impolicy of the Slave Trade and the Slavery of Africans," sermon preached at the Annual Meeting of the Connecticut Society for Promotion of Freedom and Relief of Persons Unlawfully Holden in Bondage, Sept. 17, 1791. Antislavery Pamphlets Collection, John Carter Brown Library, Providence, R.I. (New Haven, Conn: privately printed), 14. He was affiliated with the same short-lived denomination as the Ramsay's Circular Church in Charleston. Jedidiah Morse was David Ramsay's least antislavery correspondent: Larry E. Tise, *Proslavery: A History of the Defense of Slavery in America, 1791–1840* (Athens: University of Georgia Press, 1987), 214.

51. "Equal privilege for all, special privilege for none" was overwhelmed by defenders of slavery, the most vociferous political interest group. Huyler, *Locke in America,* 794.

52. Edwards, "The Injustice," 29–30.

53. Gregory D. Massey, *John Laurens and the American Revolution* (Columbia: University of South Carolina Press, 2000), chaps. 3–11, are by contrast filled with detail and revelatory comments—testament to the relative valuing of male versus female letters.

54. HL to William Manning, 27 Feb. 1776, Hamer, *Papers of Henry Laurens,* 11:124.

55. HL to John Laurens, 17 Aug. 1776, Hamer, *Papers of Henry Laurens,* 11:249.

56. HL to James Laurens, 23 Aug. 1776, Hamer, *Papers of Henry Laurens,* 11:261.

57. HL to ML, 17 Aug. 1776, Hamer, *Papers of Henry Laurens,* 11:253. His "War Letter" to John about slavery, 14 Aug. 1776, also employed the new vocabulary: "in the pay of the Colony or as I should now say, State" (223).

58. *The Papers of Benjamin Franklin I,* 1 July–31 Oct. 1779 (New Haven: Yale University Press, 1993); lxv, 30.

59. Carroll Smith-Rosenberg, "Subject Female: Authorizing American Identity," in *American Literary History* 5 (fall 1993): 481–511, naming the characteristics of "young Columbia" in Susanna Rowson's *Reuben and Rachel: A Tale of Old Times* (New York, 1798).

60. Thomas Mallon, *A Book of One's Own* (New York: Ticknor and Fields, 1984), 114.

61. Edith Gelles, *Portia: A Life of Abigail Adams* (Bloomington: Indiana University Press, 1992).

62. Frank Shuffleton, "Endangered History: Character and Narrative in Early American Historical Writing," in *Eighteenth Century: Theory and Interpretation* 34 (1993): 221–41, labels "biographic discourse" concerned with character, "historical discourse" focused on events.

63. Elizabeth Fox-Genovese, *Within the Plantation Household* (Chapel Hill: University of North Carolina Press, 1988), 251.

Chapter 2

1. The phrase used in the chapter title is quoted in HL to Lachlan McIntosh, 14 Jan. 1769, Hamer, *Papers of Henry Laurens,* 6:284.

2. Jack P. Greene, *Pursuits of Happiness: The Social Development of Early Modern British Colony Formation of American Culture* (Chapel Hill: University of North Carolina Press, 1988) 5, 147.

3. Charles Baird, *The Huguenot Migration to America* (Toulouse: Societé de Livre Religeux, 1886), 1:282–83; Richard Golden, ed., *The Huguenot Connection: The Edict of Nantes, Its Revocation, and the French Migration to South Carolina* (Dordrecht: Kluver Academic Press, 1988); Bertrand Van Ruymbeke, personal communication, 1998. For more on the Huguenot diaspora, see his forthcoming volume *From New Babylon to Eden: The Huguenot Migration to Proprietary South Carolina* (Columbia: University of South Carolina Press).

4. Sidney Charles Bolton, *Southern Anglicanism: The Church of England in Colonial South Carolina* (Westport, Conn.: Greenwood Press, 1982), 8–9, 63–64, 75.

5. Inventory, Hamer, *Papers of Henry Laurens,* 1:369–81.

6. Ibid.

7. See David Hancock, *Citizens of the World* (New York: Cambridge University Press, 1998), for London traders who initiated Henry Laurens' involvement in transoceanic commerce. See Hamer, *Papers of Henry Laurens,* 9:629, 5 Nov. 1774, for HL's shopping list sent to Capt. Robert Deans: artichoke seed, Battersea Asparagus, and "Colly flower, Sugar Loaf Cabbage, hemp seed, 5 bushels of best Seed Oats, Broccoli (purple, white, Green); Coss Lettuce, Golden Purslain, Garden Cress, Pease, Marrow, Windsor Beans, White Kidney Beans, ¹/₂ gal. Rape, sev. doz cuttings or sticks of Irish Willo for Hoop Poles, and 2 or 3 young Mountain Ash trees." Hamer, *Papers of Henry Laurens,* 4:31, 19 Oct. 1763, comment on business success.

8. Carl Bridenbaugh, *Myths and Realities: Societies of the Colonial South* (New York: Athenaeum, 1985), 65, quoting Rev. Charles Woodmason.

9. Ibid., 59.

10. Edward Ball, *Slaves in the Family* (New York: Farrar, Straus and Giroux, 1998), 190.

11. T. H Breen, "The Meaning of Things: Interpreting the Consumer Economy in the Eighteenth Century," in *Consumption and the World of Goods,* ed. John Brewer and Roy Porter, 249–60 (London: Routledge, 1993).

12. Thomas Savage and Robert A. Leath, "Buying British," in *In Pursuit of Refinement: Charlestonians Abroad, 1740–1860* (Columbia: University of South Carolina Press for Gibbes Museum of Art, 1999), 55–64; Marco Sioli, "Huguenot Traditions in the Mountains of Kentucky: Daniel Trabue's Memories," *JAH* 84 (Mar. 1998): 1313–33; Wallace, *Henry Laurens,* 27, 42.

13. Ball, *Slaves in the Family,* 153.

14. Breen, "Meaning of Things," 252, 257, quoting John Wayles; Thomas Savage, personal communication, 1997. See his "Material Culture in the Low Country," in

Southern Furniture, 1680–1830, ed. Ronald Hurst and Jonathan Prown (New York: Abrams for Colonial Williamsburg Foundation, 1997).

15. For naming practices see Cheryl Ann Cody, "There Was No 'Absalom' on the Ball Plantations: Slave Naming Practices in the South Carolina Low Country, 1720–1865," *AHR* 92 (June 1997): 563–96, multiple repetitions of the name Eleanor in Ball (and later in Henry Laurens) family.

16. Hamer, *Papers of Henry Laurens,* 6:140, little people; 7:335, affection; 7:298, true picture; 7:300, little flock; 8:15–16, mutual affection; 7:350, apple of eye, Deut. 32:10, Ps. 17:8, Prov. 7:2.

17. HL to Monkhouse Davison, 15 Oct. 1762, Hamer, *Papers of Henry Laurens,* 3:139.

18. Ramsay, *Memoirs,* 9.

19. HL to Lachlan McIntosh, 7 Mar. 1763, Hamer, *Papers of Henry Laurens,* 3:362.

20. Ibid., 5:570; see Ball, *Slaves in the Family,* 180, for Mepkin; HL to Joseph Brown, 1 Oct. 1762, Hamer, *Papers of Henry Laurens,* 3:128.

21. "Extracts from the Journal of Mrs. Ann Manigault (1754–1781)," footnote quoting *South Carolina Gazette* description of waterspout or hurricane hitting Charleston on Saturday, 9 May 1761, *SCHM* 20, 1 (Apr. 1919): 128–31, 137–38.

22. Richard J. Hooker, ed., *Carolina Backcountry on the Eve of Revolution, 1720–72: Journal and Writings of the Rev. Charles Woodmason, Anglican Itinerant* (Chapel Hill, North Carolina: University of North Carolina Press, 1953), 61; George Fenwick Jones, "The Siege of Charleston" (diary of Hessian soldier), *SCHM* 88 (Apr. 1987): 63–75, constant laundering; George C. Rogers Jr., *Charleston in the Age of the Pinckneys* (Norman: University of Oklahoma Press, 1969), 83.

23. HL to Thomas Mears, 22 Dec. 1763, Hamer, *Papers of Henry Laurens,* 4:99.

24. Recollection of Dr. Alexander Garden: "A large vacant lot on the NE part of town, adjoining Col. Laurens garden, which occupied an entire Square . . . was what we called Federal Green" (Charles Fraser, *Reminiscences of Charleston* [Charleston: South Carolina Historical Society, 1969]), 24. Wallace, *Henry Laurens,* 62, negotiations for property.

25. HL to John Coming Ball, 21 Mar. 1764, Hamer, *Papers of Henry Laurens,* 4:223; 4:224, boundaries of purchase of Ansonborough land. S.v. "Laurens Lands," in *Streets of Charleston* (Charleston: compiled for the Charleston Museum, South Carolina Historical Society, c. 1930). See HL to John Ettwein, 13 Mar. 1764, Hamer, *Papers of Henry Laurens,* 4:314, for delayed moving date.

26. HL to John Knight, 24 Aug. 1764, Hamer, *Papers of Henry Laurens,* 4:379.

27. Wallace, *Henry Laurens,* 63, "jerkin-head" roof, house plan; 11 Apr. 1764, bill of sale for slave bricklayer, Hamer, *Papers of Henry Laurens,* 4:241.

28. See Wallace, *Henry Laurens,* 63, for room dimensions, and Robert M. Weir, *Colonial South Carolina: A History* (Millwood, N.Y.: Kraus-Thomson Organization, 1983), 244–46, for fireplace mantles.

29. See HL to Issac King, 6 Sept. 1764, Hamer, *Papers of Henry Laurens,* 4:399, for careless packing; and Hamer, *Papers of Henry Laurens,* 8:61–62, for furnishings

listed from report (28 Nov. 1771) in *South Carolina Gazette* on lightning damage to HL house.

30. See Harriott Horry Ravenel, *Eliza Pinckney* (New York: C. Scribner's & Sons, 1896), 228, for neighbor comment; David Ramsay, *History of South Carolina,* 1:128; Rogers, *Charleston in the Age of the Pinckneys,* flower names, 83; fruits, 84.

31. Quote from Bartram, *Diary of a Journey,* 13 July 1765, p. 15; Hamer, *Papers of Henry Laurens,* 4:651; Jones, "Siege of Charleston," for streets.

32. See Fraser, *"Charleston!,* 135, for streets, clock in St. Michael's tower; HL to John Laurens, 1 July 1772, Hamer, *Papers of Henry Laurens,* 8:388, morality of time; Mark M. Smith, "Old South Time in Comparative Perspective," *AHR* 101 (Dec. 1996): 1432–69.

33. See Fraser, *Charleston!,* 40, 94, for churches.

34. HL to Augustus Johnston, 19 Aug. 1769, Hamer, *Papers of Henry Laurens,* 7:118. Also Thomas J. Little, "A Quantitative Analysis of Churches and Ministers in Colonial South Carolina, 1681–1780, OIEAHC seminar paper presented September 1997 contradicting South Carolina stereotype of indifferent church attendance; Fraser, *Charleston!,* 134, few gentry among serious church members.

35. Greene, *Pursuits of Happiness,* 196–98.

36. Hamer, *Papers of Henry Laurens,* 1:377, appendix, inventory of "sundry toys" in 1747 Laurens estate. See Charles Geoffrey Holme, *Children's Toys of Yesterday* (London: Studio Ltd., 1932).

37. HL to John Laurens, 17 May 1775, Hamer, *Papers of Henry Laurens,* 10:122.

38. See Ravenel, *Eliza Pinckney,* 113, for painless method of learning to read.

39. Ramsay, *Memoirs,* 10, family legend; see Kevin Hayes, *Colonial Woman's Bookshelf* (Knoxville: University of Tennessee Press, 1996), for early print availability.

40. Fraser, *Charleston!,* 130, dismissive view of female education; Patricia Cline Cohen, "Reckoning with Commerce: Eighteenth Century Numeracy," quoting George W. Fisher (1748), in *Consumption and the World of Goods,* ed. John Brewer and Ray Porter (New York: Routledge, 1993), 329.

41. Hennig Cohen, *The South Carolina Gazette, 1732–75* (Columbia: University of South Carolina Press, 1953), range of book imports, special books for children, 128, 138; parish letter to Alexander Garden, 10 Apr. 1754, Hamer, *Papers of Henry Laurens,* 1:243, signed by HL as one of the two churchwardens, plus seven vestrymen, about the memorial sermon; John F. Woolverton, *Colonial Anglicanism in North America* (Detroit: Wayne State University Press, 1984), 95–193, on the Church of England in South Carolina; see D'Alte A. Welch, *American Children's Books Printed Prior to 1820* (New Haven: American Antiquarian Society, 1972), xxi–xxxiii, for proportion of publications specifically for children.

42. Samuel J. Rogal, "Watts' *Divine and Moral Songs for Children* and the Rhetoric of Religious Instruction," *Historical Magazine of the Episcopal Church* 40 (1971): 95–100; Hamer, *Papers of Henry Laurens,* 7:20 n. 7.

43. HL to James Laurens, 5 Dec. 1771, Hamer, *Papers of Henry Laurens,* 8:68.

44. Cynthia Adams Hoover, "Music and Theater in the Lives of Eighteenth Century Americans," in *Of Consuming Interests,* ed. Cary Carson, Ronald Hoffman,

and Peter J. Albert (Charlottesville: University Press of Virginia, 1994), 338 n. 49; Hamer, *Papers of Henry Laurens,* 7:150 n. 5, tutors; HL to George Appleby, 26 Sept. 1769.

45. Betty Ring, "For Persons of Fortune Who Have Taste"—An Elegant School Girl Embroidery," *Journal of Early Southern Decorative Arts* 3 (Nov. 1977): 1–23; Thomas Woody, *A History of Women's Education in the U.S.,* 2 vols. (Octagon Books Reprint, 1974), 1:42–85, 28; limited schooling for most girls; see Hamer, *Papers of Henry Laurens,* 7:583, for art instruction.

46. HL to John Laurens, 8 July 1774, Hamer, *Papers of Henry Laurens,* 9:493, travel notes and instruction to children; HL to William Howells, 16 Jan. 1773, 8:527, emphasis on writing even for youngest; HL to John Laurens, 1 July 1772, 8:389, requiring memorization of catechism.

47. See HL to John Laurens, 19 Apr. 1774, Hamer, *Papers of Henry Laurens,* 9:418, for legible handwriting; L. H. Butterfield, ed., *Letters of Benjamin Rush,* 2 vols. (Philadelphia: American Philosophical Society, 1951), 1:865 (24 May 1803).

48. Edwin T. Arnold III, "Women Diarists and Letter Writers of Eighteenth Century South Carolina," in *South Carolina Women Writers,* ed. James B. Meriwether (Spartanburg, S.C.: Reprint Co., 1987), 127–40: "The Charleston society was in many ways a writing society . . . Young ladies were encouraged as part of their education to keep thought books, religious devotionals, and diaries as a form of private stocktaking" (128).

49. Michael Zuckerman, "Penmanship Exercises for Saucy Sons: Some Thoughts on the Colonial Southern Family," *SCHM* 84 (July 1983): 152–66; HL to Jemmy, 23 May 1775, Hamer, *Papers of Henry Laurens,* 10:138, Papa's preaching "brief rules"; Ramsay, *Memoirs,* 28 n, citing HL's opinion of Martha's handwriting.

50. HL to Jemmy, 24 May 1775, Hamer, *Papers of Henry Laurens,* 10:139.

51. Ramsay, *Memoirs,* 10, her studies; HL to John Laurens, 10 May 1774, Hamer, *Papers of Henry Laurens,* 9:440; HL to ML, 18 May 1774, Hamer, *Papers of Henry Laurens,* 9:457–58, reminding Martha of women's tasks.

52. HL to John Laurens, 1 July 1772, Hamer, *Papers of Henry Laurens,* 8:388–89, religious injunction; 30 May 1775, Hamer, *Papers of Henry Laurens,* 10:158, to John, children's inheritance; HL to Jemmy, 24 May 1775, Hamer, *Papers of Henry Laurens,* 10:141.

53. HL to John Rose, 28 Dec. 1771, Hamer, *Papers of Henry Laurens,* 8:141, education credo paraphrased; HL to James Habrsham, 4 June 1768, Hamer, *Papers of Henry Laurens,* 5:717, criterion of usefulness.

54. Wallace, *Henry Laurens,* 13 n. 3; Sioli, "Huguenot Traditions."

55. A. D'Auborn [John McGowan], *The French Convert, or A True Relation of the Happy Conversion of a Noble French Woman from the Errors and Superstitions of Popery to the REFORMED RELIGION by Means of a Protestant Gardener, Her Servant* (Haverill, Mass., 1794); see Fraser, *Charleston!,* 11, for French Protestant church.

56. Ramsay, *Memoirs* (1845 ed.), 14, probably added without attribution by one of her adult school-keeping daughters. It carried the following moral: "As very trivial circumstances in . . . childhood serve to show the disposition and habits

which afterwards appear . . . in the mature character, we cannot refrain from [inserting this] anecdote."

57. Ibid. 13, 14, 15.

58. Ramsay, *Memoirs* (1814), 10.

59. HL to Smith and Baillies, 30 Apr. 1764, Hamer, *Papers of Henry Laurens*, 4:257–58.

60. HL to Mathew Robinson, 30 May 1764, Hamer, *Papers of Henry Laurens*, 4:295–96.

61. HL to Mathias Holme, 24 Aug. 1764, Hamer, *Papers of Henry Laurens*, 4:375–76, "Nelly is no more"; HL to Lachlan McIntosh, 14–15 Aug. 1764, Hamer, *Papers of Henry Laurens*, 4:368; HL to George Appleby, 9 Nov. 1764, Hamer, *Papers of Henry Laurens*, 4:499–500.

62. Fraser, *Charleston!*, 134.

63. HL to Monkhouse Davison, 22 Apr. 1763, Hamer, *Papers of Henry Laurens*, 3:416.

64. Ibid., Dame School of Mrs. Stokes.

65. Ramsay, *Memoirs* (1845 ed.), 13–15.

66. Civic roles in Gazette notices 27 Nov. 1753, Hamer, *Papers of Henry Laurens*, 1:243; Bridenbaugh, *Myths and Realities*, quoting Rev. Alexander Hewatt (1745–1829), 113; Hamer, *Papers of Henry Laurens*, 5:278 for lawsuit; HL to Issac King, 6 Sept. 1764, Hamer, *Papers of Henry Laurens*, 4:401.

67. Kenneth S. Greenberg, "The Nose, the Lie and the Duel in the Antebellum South," *AHR* 95 (Feb. 1990): 57–74. Bertram Wyatt-Brown, "God and Honor in the Old South," *Southern Review* 25 (spring 1989): 283–96.

68. HL to James Habersham, 5 Sept. 1767, Hamer, *Papers of Henry Laurens*, 5:292–99.

69. Fraser, *Charleston!*, 51–52, 135.

70. HL to John Knight, 10 Aug. 1756, Hamer, *Papers of Henry Laurens*, 2:278, volatile prices for slaves; 2:317, H L to Richard Oswald & Co., 15 Sept. 1756; also in Elizabeth Donnan, *Documents Illustrative of the History of the Slave Trade to America*, 4 vols. (Washington, D.C.: Carnegie Institute, 1935), 4; HL to Peter Furnell, 9 Sept. 1755, Hamer, *Papers of Henry Laurens*, 1:33.

71. HL to George Dick, ca. 1 June 1764, Hamer, *Papers of Henry Laurens*, 4:299, evaluation of Abram.

72. HL to John Jackson, 19 Mar. 1766, Hamer, *Papers of Henry Laurens*, 5:91, high value of skills of American-born slaves; 5:370, HL to Richard Oswald, 16 Oct. 1767, female slave's value as breeder.

73. HL to William Fisher, 11 Feb. 1769, Hamer, *Papers of Henry Laurens*, 6:275, admiration for Quakers; 4:42, 10 Nov. 1763, identifying religiously with Moravians; 3:373–75, HL to Pastor Ettwein, 19 Mar. 1763, slavery detrimental to white citizens.

74. HL to Richard Oswald, 27 Apr. 1768, Hamer, *Papers of Henry Laurens*, 5:668, slaves as happy as circumstances permit; 6:149, HL to William Fisher, 9 Nov. 1768, indentured white servants.

75. Barnwell, Joseph W., "Diary of Timothy Ford, 1785–86," in *SCHM* 13 (July 1912): 130–47, 181–204.

76. HL to Joseph Brown, 28 Oct. 1765, Hamer, *Papers of Henry Laurens*, 5:29. He even offered to duel any one of them—a mode of problem solving he so detested that on the rare occasion in which he was a participant, he refused to carry a weapon.

77. Ibid., 5:28–29, n. 6.

78. Ibid., 5:30.

79. Ibid., 5:31.

80. HL to James Grant, 18 Aug. 1766, Hamer, *Papers of Henry Laurens*, 5:167, governor ill in Laurens house.

81. See HL to John Gervais, 1 Sept. 1766, Hamer, *Papers of Henry Laurens*, 5:184, for baby Jemmy and death of another unnamed infant.

82. See HL to James Habersham, 10 Apr. 1770, Hamer, *Papers of Henry Laurens*, 7:275, 27 Apr. 1770; 7:286, for last child's birth.

83. HL to Matthew Robinson, 4 May 1770, Hamer, *Papers of Henry Laurens*, 7:287.

84. HL to Henry Humphreys, 19 May 1770, Hamer, *Papers of Henry Laurens*, 7:298, phrases reordered.

85. HL to Matthew Robinson, 1 June 1770, Hamer, *Papers of Henry Laurens*, 7:300.

86. HL to Richard Grubb, 1 June 1770, Hamer, *Papers of Henry Laurens*, 7:302.

87. HL to Judith Ball, 5 Sept. 1770, Hamer, *Papers of Henry Laurens*, 7:333; 7:335, HL to William Fisher, 6 Sept. 1770, "children won't let me leave."

88. HL to Henry Bright, 10 Sept. 1777, Hamer, *Papers of Henry Laurens*, 7:350, cloud beginning to lift; 7:358, HL to Richard Oswald, 10 Sept. 1770.

89. HL to James Habersham, 1 Oct. 1770, Hamer, *Papers of Henry Laurens*, 7:374, 375.

90. Ibid.

91. Ibid.

92. HL to William Fisher, 2 Nov. 1770, Hamer, *Papers of Henry Laurens*, 7:396.

93. HL to John Polson, 13 Nov. 1770, Hamer, *Papers of Henry Laurens*, 7:400–401.

94. HL to John Hopton, 29 Jan. 1771, Hamer, *Papers of Henry Laurens*, 7:429, household ill, Jemmy choking.

95. HL to James Habersham, 3 June 1771, Hamer, *Papers of Henry Laurens*, 7:514.

96. HL to Thomas Corbett, 4 Apr. 1771, Hamer, *Papers of Henry Laurens*, 7:473–75.

97. HL to Ann Foster, 24 Oct. 1771, Hamer, *Papers of Henry Laurens*, 8:15–16.

98. HL to William Cowles & Co., 18 Apr. 1771, Hamer, *Papers of Henry Laurens*, 7:494, separating children, one gone ahead to England.

99. HL to John Moultrie, 17 June 1771, Hamer, *Papers of Henry Laurens*, 7:544, "your dear aunt's death."

100. Newspaper account of storm hitting Henry's house, 28 Nov. 1771, Hamer, *Papers of Henry Laurens*, 8:61–62.

101. Ramsay, *Memoirs*, 14–15.

102. HL to James Laurens, 26 Dec. 1771, Hamer, *Papers of Henry Laurens*, 8:123, emotional identification with slaves' lives; 8:178, HL to James Laurens, 6 Feb. 1772, out of slave trade, little ewe lambs; 8:290–91, John Gervais to HL, 5 May 1772, bad treatment by overseers, recommending kind treatment; 8:617, HL to Lachlan McIntosh, 13 Mar. 1773, financial loss better than cruelty.

103. HL to John Lewis Gervais, 10 Dec. 1773, Hamer, *Papers of Henry Laurens*, 9:191; 10:72, HL to John Laurens, 18 Feb. 1775, on "droll coupling" of Patsy's schoolmate to much older Mr. John Drayton.

Chapter 3

1. HL to Issac King, Hamer, *Papers of Henry Laurens*, 4:234 n. 6.

2. HL to James Laurens, 6 Feb. 1772, Hamer, *Papers of Henry Laurens*, 8:172–73. Henry recalled that shortly after sister Mary Bremar "Lay a Corps" on 9 May 1769, Leigh had "carried away M. Bremar to his Country Seat," Henry Middleton's former Cooper River plantation known as "The Retreat."

3. HL to James Laurens, 15 Apr. 1772, Hamer, *Papers of Henry Laurens*, 8:269.

4. James L to HL, 19 Dec. 1772, Hamer, *Papers of Henry Laurens*, 8:506.

5. Ibid., 8:507–8.

6. Ibid., 8:508.

7. Ibid., 8:509.

8. Ibid.

9. HL to Egerton Leigh, 30 Jan. 1773, Hamer, *Papers of Henry Laurens*, 8:556–63.

10. Ibid., 560.

11. Ibid., 562–63.

12. HL to James Laurens, 5 Mar. 1773, Hamer, *Papers of Henry Laurens*, 8:594, 595.

13. HL to John Laurens, 1 Feb. 1773, Hamer, *Papers of Henry Laurens*, 8:567.

14. HL to James Laurens, 1 Feb. 1773, Hamer, *Papers of Henry Laurens*, 8:571, worst fears for Molsy.

15. HL to John Laurens, 1 Feb. 1773, Hamer, *Papers of Henry Laurens*, 8:572, Uncle James' distress of mind.

16. HL to William Freeman, 9 Feb. 1773, Hamer, *Papers of Henry Laurens*, 8:577, gout.

17. HL to John Laurens, 25 June 1772, Hamer, *Papers of Henry Laurens*, 8:378–79. Henry Laurens idealized Geneva. "Be sure to study minutely in the constitution and form of the Government of that wonderful Republic so you can tell your English friends."

18. HL to ML, 19 Apr. 1773, Hamer, *Papers of Henry Laurens*, 8:670, convent; 8:688, HL to Uncle James, 19 Apr. 1773, Molsy's appearance of penitence.

19. In the style of travel journal he expected Martha to emulate, Henry noted great buildings, the poor quality of worship in the cathedral of St. Dennis (St. Denys), and the uncleanness of his hotel: a grand street floor but upstairs "a floor worse than my Barn or any Negro kitchen." HL Travel Journal, 25 Apr. 1773, Hamer, *Papers of Henry Laurens,* 9:18. Leigh had agreed to support Molsy financially but without acknowledging the perfidy of which she had formally accused him in her deposition. HL to James Laurens, 11 May 1773, Hamer, *Papers of Henry Laurens,* 9:40.

20. Henry Laurens Letterbook, 17 Mar. 1773, Hamer, *Papers of Henry Laurens,* 8:62; 8 Apr. 1773, 8:67.

21. HL to John Laurens, 8 Oct. 1773, Hamer, *Papers of Henry Laurens,* 9:120–21.

22. For Laurens-Ramsay relationship to that terminology, see note 3 in Gary B. Nash, "The Hidden History of Mestizo America," *JAH* 82 (Dec. 95): 941–964.

23. HL to John Wearat, 30 Aug. 1777, Hamer, *Papers of Henry Laurens,* 11:475.

24. HL to James Laurens, 7 June 1773, Hamer, *Papers of Henry Laurens,* 9:71–76.

25. Hayes, *A Colonial Woman's Bookshelf,* 39.

26. Lydia Dittler Schulman, *"Paradise Lost" and the Rise of the American Republic* (Boston: Northeastern University Press, 1992), 100; Donald S. Lutz and Jack D. Warren, *A Covenanted People* (Providence: John Carter Brown Library), 1987.

27. Rev. William Hutson, *Living Christianity Delineated* (London, 1760, pt. 1; Boston, 1809, pt. 2), *Diary of Mary Hutson, 1756,* 138. Many descriptions, books, and family scenes in this published memorial were echoed in Martha's adult diary phrases and vocabulary.

28. David Lyle Jeffrey, *A Burning and a Shining Light: English Spirituality in the Age of Wesley* (Grand Rapids: William B. Eerdmans, 1986), 97, 101–2.

29. Ibid., 28, spiritual logic.

30. Ibid., 31, prescribed by English reformer John Wesley in 1771.

31. Janet Payne Whitney, *Elizabeth Fry: Quaker Heroine* (Boston: Little, Brown & Co., 1937), 66.

32. Ibid., 69–72.

33. Massey Shepherd, *The Oxford Prayer Book Commentary* (New York: Oxford University Press, 1950), 292, Second Office of Instruction.

34. HL to James Laurens, 26 Dec. 1771, Hamer, *Papers of Henry Laurens,* 8:130; 8:546, 25 Jan. 1773, "[Tell] Patsy that writing this letter to you [James] will deprive me of the pleasure of finishing one I have begun to my Dear little Woman [Martha]."

35. Hayes, *Colonial Women's Bookshelf,* 31, quoting English divine Richard Baxter: Sermons are easily forgotten, "but a Book we may read over and over till we remember it . . . So that Good Books are a very great mercy to the world."

36. Rhys Issac, *The Transformation of Virginia* (Chapel Hill: University of North Carolina Press, 1982), 295. Also Mary Kelly, "Reading Women/Women Reading: The Making of Learned Women in Antebellum America," *JAH* 83 (Sept. 1996): 401–24.

37. Hayes, *Colonial Women's Bookshelf,* 32.

38. Ibid., 42.

39. Ibid., 51, 56. As an adult she gave the Doddridge book as a gift to young friends.

40. Ramsay, *Memoirs,* 12; Shepherd, *Prayer Book Commentary,* opposite p. 578, attributed the Great Catechism (1662 *Book of Common Prayer)* to unknown authorship, though Thomas Cranmer, then archbishop of Canterbury, "certainly had a hand in it." Anglican church history has not addressed congregational practices of devout families. The Episcopal establishment in Charleston was known for orthodox worship services and broadmindedness toward other forms of religion— a laity not interested in severe Calvinist preaching. Woolverton, *Colonial Anglicanism,* 154–72.

41. D. E. Huger Smith and A. S. Salley Jr., eds., *Register of St. Philip's Parish, 1754–1810, Charles Town or Charleston, South Carolina* (Columbia: University of South Carolina Press, 1971), 42.

42. Ramsay, *Memoirs,* 12. Shepherd, *Prayer Book Commentary,* 283–85, 579.

43. *Oxford English Dictionary,* 2d ed., 1069–70.

44. Shepherd, *Prayer Book Commentary,* 580, summary of child's version of the Ten Commandments.

45. James Boswell, *Journal of a Tour to the Hebrides with Samuel Johnson* (London, 1791), Sept. 14, 1746, 194.

46. Clifford Geertz, "The Pinch of Destiny—Religion As Experience, Meaning, Identity, Power," *Harvard Divinity School Bulletin* 27 (1998): 7–12.

47. "The Christian urged to, and assisted in, an express act of self-dedication to the service of God" (Phillip Doddridge, *The Rise and Progress of Religion in the Soul* [Philadelphia, 1810], chap. 17, 222–56, microfiche 3, no. 19978).

48. Ramsay, *Memoirs,* 56; covenant, appendix 2, 54–62.

49. Christopher M. Jedry, *The World of John Cleaveland, Family and Community in Eighteenth Century New England* (New York: W. W. Norton & Co., 1979).

50. HL to James Laurens, 15 Sept. 1774, Hamer, *Papers of Henry Laurens,* 9:559, Leigh's capitulation; 9:562, HL to James Laurens, 17 Sept. 1774, letter. Earlier in April 1774 Henry had expostulated: "[Leigh] is a Composition of Fox, Spaniel, Goat, some other bad Ingredients & a large portion of Monkey . . . what will be the end of his misconduct? . . . How can he shew his Head in that Country which he has Strove to Ruin. I lament for the prospect of his family's distress." HL to James Lauren, 13 Apr. 1774, Hamer, *Papers of Henry Laurens,* 9:405.

51. HL to Martha Parsons, 15 May 1775, Hamer, *Papers of Henry Laurens,* 10:121, Molsy's attempt at extortion.

52. James Laurens to HL, 20 June 1778, Hamer, *Papers of Henry Laurens,* 13:500 n. 8, Molsy's death.

53. See Elaine Forman Crane, *Ebb Tide in New England* (Boston: Northeastern University Press, 1998), chap. 2, for Martha's Rhode Island contemporary, Sarah Osborn (1728–1796), who employed "covenant" in organizational terms; Darcy R.

Fryer, "The Mind of Eliza Pinckney," *SCHM* 99 (July 1998): 215–37, cited Pinckney's vows about relationship duties as an informal covenant.

54. Edward D. Young, *The Complaint; or Night Thoughts on Life, Death, and Immortality* (Philadelphia: Prichard & Hall, 1787), 69, lines 557–60.

Chapter 4

1. HL to Harry, 6 Feb. 1775, Hamer, *Papers of Henry Laurens*, 10:55.

2. Ball, *Slaves in the Family*, 220; Council of Safety to William Moultrie, 7 Dec. 1775, signed by Henry Laurens, president, Hamer, *Papers of Henry Laurens*, 10:546, order to sieze "a number of negroes . . . said to have deserted [to Sullivan's Island]." Council of Safety to William Moultrie, 7 Dec. 1775, signed "HL, President."

3. Adrienne Rich, *Of Woman Born: Motherhood As Experience and Institution* (New York: W. W. Norton, 1976), 57.

4. Gregory D. Massey, *John Laurens and the American Revolution* (Columbia: University of South Carolina Press, 2000), re-creates this particular member of Henry's family, heightening the contrast in expectations for a son as compared with an eldest daughter.

5. HL to John Laurens, 4 Jan. 1775, Hamer, *Papers of Henry Laurens*, 10:72.

6. HL to John Laurens, 6 Feb. 1774, Hamer, *Papers of Henry Laurens*, 10:60, Martha's language skill; 10:17, HL to John Laurens, 4 Jan. 1775, needing a housekeeper "to save . . . Your Miss Patsy . . . from the trouble of improper branches of Housewifery in her present stage."

7. Ramsay, *Memoirs*, appendix 2, self-dedication and solemn covenant, 54–62.

8. Lydia Ginzburg, *On Psychological Prose* (Princeton: Princeton University Press, 1991), 18, suggests that in a pivotal era like the American Revolution, strong personalities seem to organize the inner self into an image aligned with the culture's meaning—giving that larger interpretation to one's life, fortune, and experiences.

9. Ramsay, *Memoirs*, 13–14; Barbara De Wolfe, "Discoveries of America: Letters of British Emigrants to America, on the Eve of the Revolution," *Perspectives in American History*, n.s., 1 (1984): 1–80, includes a 1774 letter to Scotland detailing the geographical challenge to which John subjected Martha: "I know of no hills within less than Eighty miles of the Sea, so high as to give prospect over trees that grow on the Lowest Swamps . . . the Sea Coast (and Charles Town) . . . It is one Continued dead Plain (69)."

10. John Laurens to HL, 4 Oct. 1775, Hamer, *Papers of Henry Laurens*, 10:451–53.

11. HL to John Laurens, 4 Jan. 1776, Hamer, *Papers of Henry Laurens*, 10:616–18.

12. Ibid.; John Laurens to HL, 26 Apr. 1776, Hamer, *Papers of Henry Laurens*, 11:204, Martha's confined life nursing uncle; 10:154, 27 May 1775, recommending Martha's tutelage in improvements and explaining Uncle James' troubles.

13. John Laurens to HL, 20 Apr. 1775, Hamer, *Papers of Henry Laurens*, 10:100, John's view of Uncle James' poor health habits.

14. Ramsay, *Memoirs*, 36.

15. John Laurens to James Laurens, undated letter (between 19 Dec. 1776 and 11 Jan. 1777), privately owned collection. Copies made available through Laurens Papers editorial office, University of South Carolina, Columbia. Hereafter cited as Private Collection (copy).

16. HL to John Laurens, 3 Feb. 1777, Hamer, *Papers of Henry Laurens,* 11:289; 11:324, HL to James Laurens, 28 Mar. 1777.

17. James Laurens to HL, 14 Sept. 1778, Hamer, *Papers of Henry Laurens,* 14:310 n. 2 promoting Nimes' climate.

18. James Laurens to HL, 16 Dec. 1777, Hamer, *Papers of Henry Laurens,* 12:160.

19. *Letters of Eliza Wilkinson Written 1776–1782,* ed. Caroline Gilman (New York: Samuel Colman, 1839), 88.

20. Ramsay, *Memoirs,* appendix 4, 66–98.

21. Young, *The Complaint,* Introduction to Night VII, 155.

22. Ibid., 72, 76, 79, 83, 71.

23. James Laurens to HL, 18 Sept. 1777, Hamer, *Papers of Henry Laurens,* 11:530, Martha's usefulness.

24. Ramsay, *Memoirs,* 89; Archbishop Fenelon, *Spiritual Letters to Women* (London: Longmans, Green & Co., 1921), 62, 63, 261, 262.

25. Ramsay, *Memoirs,* 69.

26. Ibid., 72, emphasis in original.

27. Ibid., 90, 71, 90.

28. Ibid., 94, 89, 90, 84.

29. Massey, *John Laurens,* chaps. 8–10. The amount of preserved detail about his adventures is evidence of the significance accorded male over female activities, even within the family.

30. HL to William Brisbane, 14 Aug. 1777, Hamer, *Papers of Henry Laurens,* 11:453–59.

31. HL to ML, 17 Aug. 1776, Hamer, *Papers of Henry Laurens,* 11:252–56.

32. Ibid.; see Robert A. Olwell, "'Domestick Enemies': Slavery and Political Independence in South Carolina, May 1775–Mar. 1776," *JSH* 55 (Feb. 1989): 21–48, for the case of Sampson.

33. "Rules and Maxims for Matrimonial Happiness," *Columbian Magazine* 4 (24 Jan. 1790): 24.

34. HL to ML, 17 Aug. 1776, Hamer, *Papers of Henry Laurens,* 11:253.

35. Ibid., 254; Nancy Ruttenberg, "George Whitefield, Spectacular Conversion and the Rise of Democratic Personality," *American Literary History* 5 (fall 1963): 429–58, analyzing religion's contribution to the forming of the democratic personality.

36. HL to ML, 17 Aug. 1776, Hamer, *Papers of Henry Laurens,* 11:254, his underlining.

37. Ibid.

38. Ibid.

39. Ibid., 256.

40. HL to ML, 16 Aug. 1776, Hamer, *Papers of Henry Laurens*, 11:256, quoting John's 20 March 1776 advice. HL to John Laurens, 14 Aug. 1776, Hamer, *Papers of Henry Laurens*, 11:222–35, Henry Laurens' "war letter" to John plus enclosures about the war, 235–346.

41. Ramsay, *Memoirs*, 17.

42. Ibid., 79.

43. HL to John Laurens, 3 Feb. 1777, Hamer, *Papers of Henry Laurens*, 11:296.

44. John Laurens to HL, 26 Oct. 1776, Hamer, *Paper of Henry Laurens*, 11:277; see also note 6.

45. Ibid., 11:277 n. Though Martha herself never put it into words, many of the women she read wrote of their wish to "metamorphosis from a sister into a brother": Sylvia H. Myers, *The Bluestocking Circle: Women, Friendship and the Life of the Mind in Eighteenth Century England* (London: Clarendon Press, 1990), 25, quoting Elizabeth Montague (1739). Within the Laurens family, little sister Polly innocently requested to be rechristened with a boy's name in order to wear pants and be like brother Harry (John Laurens to HL, 26 Apr. 1776, Hamer, *Papers of Henry Laurens*, 11:204).

46. Ramsay, *Memoirs*, 175–88, self-imagery in undated letters to friend Elizabeth Brailsford. Internal evidence locates the James Ramsay household en route to Teignmouth, in August 1776, the time of John's impatience for HL's permission to enlist; 14, final images.

47. Vivien Jones, ed., *Women in the Eighteenth Century* (London: Routledge & Kegan Paul, 1990), 2–4, quoting Edmund Burke's *Philosophical Enquiry into the Origin of Our Ideas of the Sublime and the Beautiful* (1757).

48. Ramsay, *Memoirs*, 18.

49. Ibid., 12, 21, 23, 29, 43, 44, among others.

50. Twenty-three published authors, nearly all English, are mentioned in Ramsay's *Memoirs*. Martha's biographer could not read French as she had.

51. Sheryl Kujawa, "Religion, Education, and Gender in Eighteenth-Century Rhode Island: Sarah Haggar Wheaten Osborn, 1714–1796," *Rhode Island History* 52 (May 1994): 35–47.

52. Whitney, *Elizabeth Fry*, 166–67.

53. Myers, *The Bluestocking Circle*, 8, emphasis added. Dr. Ramsay specifically cited Martha's admiration for Elizabeth Carter and the countess of Huntingdon to illustrate her likeness to similarly well-read women in her time.

54. Ramsay, *Memoirs*, 20; Whitney, *Elizabeth Fry*, 169. Martha's competence in French was documented in James Laurens' will: "Because of the difficulty I have explaining myself in France, . . . I have translated [my will] in English, . . . and Mr. Louis Gendre, Notary Public of . . . Vigan, 6 Sept. 1782, wrote it . . . dictated [in French] by my niece Martha Laurens" (Caroline T. Moore, ed., *Abstract of Wills of Charleston County*, Will Book A (Columbia, S.C.: R. L. Bryan, 1974), 88.

55. Ramsay, *Memoirs*, 87.

56. Cynthia A. Kierner, *Southern Women in Revolution, 1776–1800: Personal and Political Narratives* (Columbia, South Carolina: University of South Carolina Press, 1998).

57. Cynthia A. Kierner, *Beyond the Household: Women of the Early South, 1770–1835* (Ithaca: Cornell University Press), 70: "After 1776 . . . women in the southern states petitioned their legislatures in unprecedented numbers."

58. Henry Laurens wrote the American government from the tower (20 Dec. 1781), "Gentlemen: Almost fifteen mo. have I been closely confined and inhumanly treated, and even now I have not a prospect of release. There has been languor and otherwise neglect. If I merit your attention you will no longer delay the only speedy and efficacious means for my deliverance. Enter this, if you please, and what it may produce on the ____ Journal & pardon the omission of ceremony. I am full of love and respect for you" (Hamer, *Papers of Henry Laurens,* 15:393–94).

59. May 29, 1781, John Laurens to Martha Laurens, private collection (copy); Wallace, *Henry Laurens,* 481. John had been appointed to solicit aid in France for the Americans in December 1780. At that time, he inquired into his father's release and deposited money to his credit.

60. Martha Laurens to John Adams, 14 Nov. 1781 and 16 Jan. 1782, Adams Papers, microfilms 355, Letters and Other Loose Papers, June–Dec. 1781, Massachusetts Historical Society, Boston; Martha Laurens to Benjamin Franklin, 28 Apr. 1781 and 14 Nov. 1781, Barbara Oberg, et al., eds., *Papers of Benjamin Franklin,* 35 vols. to date (New Haven: Yale University Press, 1993–). Franklin requested assistance of the court to obtain Henry's release, but England resisted any exchange of prisoners. Benjamin Franklin to Samuel Huntington, 14 May 1781, Oberg, *Franklin Papers,* 35:61–64.

61. Stanley J. Izerda, ed., *Lafayette in the Age of Revolution: Selected Letters and Papers, 1776–1790* (Ithaca: Cornell University Press, 1977), 4:47, 19 April 1781: "Mr. [John] Laurens shows zeal . . . but not . . . in a manner suited to the nature of his mission [which must be] attributed to his inexperience in public affairs."

62. Ibid., 5:28–29, 14 Apr. 1782.

63. Carla Mulford, ed., *Annis Boudinot Stockton: "Only for the Eyes of a Friend"* (Charlottesville: University of Virginia Press, 1997), 120, poem honoring Henry Laurens' endurance in the tower and celebrating his release on 1 January 1782.

64. Wallace, *Henry Laurens,* 367.

65. Richard B. Morris, ed., *John Jay: Winning the Peace. Unpublished Papers, 1780–84* (New York: Harper & Row, 1980), 141.

66. Lafayette to HL, 3 Jan. 1778, Hamer, *Papers of Henry Laurens,* 12:258.

67. HL to ML, 18 May 1782, Hamer, *Papers of Henry Laurens,* 15:507–11.

68. Ibid.; HL to ML, 25 July 1782, Hamer, *Papers of Henry Laurens,* 15:541–43.

69. HL to ML, 13 Aug. 1782, Hamer, *Papers of Henry Laurens,* 15:565–68.

70. Ibid.; HL to James Laurens, 7 Aug. 1782, Hamer, *Papers of Henry Laurens,* 15:552–54.

71. Ibid.

72. HL to ML, 13 Aug. 1782, Hamer, *Papers of Henry Laurens,* 15:565–68.

73. HL to ML from Nantes, 18 Aug. 1782, Hamer, *Papers of Henry Laurens,* 15:574–79.

74. Myers, *The Bluestocking Circle,* 85, quoting both Jeremy Taylor's *Discourse on the Nature, Offices, and Measure of Friendship* (London, 1657), and Anne Donnellan (?1700–1762).

75. HL to Henry Laurens Jr., 20 Aug. 1782, Hamer, *Papers of Henry Laurens,* 15:580–81.

76. Wylma Wates, "Precursor to the Victorian Age: The Concept of Marriage and Family in the Correspondence of the Izard Family of South Carolina," in *In Joy and In Sorrow,* ed. Carol Bleser (New York: Oxford University Press, 1991), 3–14, a father warning his daughter not to "form an attachment in Europe," 6.

77. HL to Henry Laurens Jr. from Nantes, 22 Aug. 1782, Hamer, *Papers of Henry Laurens,* 15:583–85.

78. HL to Martha Laurens, 18 Aug. 1782, ibid., 15:574–79.

79. HL to Martha Laurens, 24 Aug. 1782, ibid., 15:589–91.

80. Ibid.

81. H. L. to M. deVerne, 13 Nov. 1782, Private Collection (copy).

82. HL to James Laurens, 17 Nov. 1782, HL to Mary Laurens, 30 Dec. 1782, Private Collection (copy).

83. HL to Martha Laurens, 7 Jan. 1783, Private Collection (copy).

84. Mr. L. Grand to HL, 13 May? 1783, South Carolina Historical Society, Microfilm Roll 15, Item 45b.

85. Henry Laurens to William Drayton, 13 Feb. 1783, emphasis added, Henry Laurens Collection, South Carolina Historical Society, Charleston; reference to "the American ladies," HL to Martha Laurens, 5 Feb. 1783.

86. Martha's much younger sister, Mary Eleanor, was the truly European Laurens, having attended school in France from age seven to fourteen. W. W. Abbott and Dorothy Twohig, eds., *Papers of George Washington,* Presidential Series, 7 vols. (Charlottesville: University Press of Virginia, 1993), 4:484, 14 Dec. 1789, Charles Pinckney to George Washington.

87. HL to John Jay, 5 Sept. 1783, Morris, *John Jay,* 582, conveying Martha's respects to Mrs. Jay and two daughters. On 6 Nov. 1783, she and her father stopped to rest with the Jays en route back to Paris after visiting Uncle James (634). Martha visited the Thomas Day family the next year (30 Apr. 1784), E. Day to HL, private collection (copy). Stanley J. Idzerda and Robert R. Crout, eds., *Lafayette in the Age of the American Revolution* (Ithaca: Cornell University Press, 1977), 142, HL's closing salutation to Lafayette (6 July 1783).

88. Alfred Barbeau, *Life and Letters at Bath in the Eighteenth Century* (London: William Heinemann, 1904), 161, cited Lady Huntingdon as a startling personage in English religious consciousness, "a star of the first magnitude in the firmament of the Church" for those who agreed with her. "There was a publicity in her religion that no one else, Dissenter, Puritan, or Anglican, had admitted at least since the Reformation" (161 n. 3).

89. Louis P. Masur, "Age of the First Person Singular": The Vocabulary of the Self in New England, 1780–1850," *Journal of American Studies* 25 (Aug. 1991): 189–211.

90. Tamara K. Hareven, *Family Time and Industrial Time: The Relationship between the Family and Work in a New England Industrial Community* (New York: Cambridge University Press, 1982), concept of "kinkeeper."

Chapter 5

1. David Ramsay, after the death of his first wife, served in Congress in Philadelphia and was the object of social polishing—"attention to his hair and the seam of his stockings"—from Benjamin Rush's sister-in-law Miss Boudinot. If her efforts succeeded, Rush speculated that Ramsay might be taking "a Jersey or Pennsylvania beauty back to Carolina with him" (Benjamin Rush to Jacob Read, 23 Apr. 1782, L. H. Butterfield et al., eds., *Letters of Benjamin Rush,* 2 vols. [Philadelphia: American Philosophical Society, 1951], 1:269). Ramsay's second wife was indeed the daughter of President John Witherspoon, College of New Jersey, in Princeton.

2. Ramsay, *Memoirs,* 146, 165; see Joseph J. Ellis, *After the Revolution* (New York: W. W. Norton & Co., 1979), for concept of the "new American"; Hareven, *Family Time and Industrial Time,* 101–9; see Margaret Miles, "Introduction," in *Immaculate and Powerful: The Female in Sacred Image and Social Reality,* ed. Clarissa W. Atkinson., Constance H. Buchanan, and Margaret R. Miles (Boston: Beacon Press, 1985), 3, for women's religious identity being stitched together like quilt pieces.

3. Ramsay's medical correspondence cited information she learned from "French Physicians" during her eight years in France. James A. Spalding, *Dr. Lyman Spalding* (Boston, 1916), 87.

4. Ramsay, *Memoirs,* 27–28 n.

5. DR to B Rush, 21 Apr. 1788, Brunhouse, *Ramsay,* 120.

6. Dominick La Capra, *Rethinking Intellectual History: Texts, Contexts, Language* (Ithaca: Cornell University Press, 1983) ; John E. Toews, "Intellectual History After the Linguistic Turn: The Autonomy of Meaning and the Irreducibility of Experience," *AHR* 92 (Oct. 1987): 879–907; Phyllis Rose, *Parallel Lives* (New York: A. A. Knopf, 1983), 7.

7. Ibid., 8.

8. Ramsay, *Memoirs,* 107.

9. Shaffer, *To Be an American,* 77.

10. Susanna Read to Betsy Ludlow, 8 Dec. 1787, Jacob Read Correspondence, South Caroliniana Library, University of South Carolina, Columbia.

11. Ramsay, *Memoirs,* vii, v, iv, v, vi.

12. David Ramsay, *History of the Revolution in South Carolina,* 2:230; Julia Spruill, *Women's Life and Work in the Southern Colonies* (Chapel Hill: University of North Carolina Press, 1938); Mary Sumner Benson, *Women in Eighteenth Century*

America (Port Washington, N.Y.: AMS Press, 1975); Ruth Bloch, "The Gendered Meanings of Virtue in Revolutionary America," *SIGNS* 13 (autumn 1987): 37–58; see Jan Lewis, "The Republican Wife: Virtue and Seduction in the Early Republic," *WMQ* 44 (Oct. 1987): 689–721, for the salience of marriage as image for the relationship between citizen/nation; Jean Matthews, "Race, Sex and the Dimensions of Liberty in Antebellum America," *JEAR* 6 (fall 1986): 275–92, for perception of the rhetorical issue of liberty; Joan Gunderson, "Independence, Citizenship and the American Revolution," *SIGNS* 13 (autumn 1987): 59–77, for the concept of women's virtual representation politically.

13. Ramsay, *Memoirs,* vi.

14. Ramsay, *Memoirs,* iii; Lewis, "Republican Wife," 689–721; "Thoughts on Matrimony," *Royal American Magazine,* Jan. 1774, 9.

15. Scott, "Deconstructing Equality vs. Difference," 33–50.

16. Ramsay, *Memoirs,* 28 n.

17. Anne Norton, *Alternative Americas* (Chicago: University of Chicago Press, 1986); Arthur H. Shaffer, "Between Two Worlds: David Ramsay and the Politics of Slavery," *JSH* 50 (May 1984): 175–96. Hamer, *Papers of Henry Laurens,* 3:373–75, 26 Dec. 1771, regretting the institution; 8:123, opposing the breakup of slave families by sale.

18. Henry F. May, *The Enlightenment in America* (New York: Oxford University Press, 1976), xvi.

19. Richard D. Brown, "Modernization and Modern Personality in Early America, 1600–1865: A Sketch of a Synthesis," *JInterH* 2 (1971–72): 201–28; Fliegelman, *Prodigals and Pilgrims.*

20. Sheila Skemp, *Judith Sargent Murray: A Brief Biography with Documents* (New York: Bedford Books, 1998), 68; Bloch, "The Gendered Meanings of Virtue," 47, 56.

21. Brunhouse, *Ramsay,* 141, letter 116 (10 Nov. 1787).

22. Gunderson, "Independence, Citizenship, and the American Revolution," 13; Carroll Smith-Rosenberg, "Misprisoning Pamela: Representations of Gender and Class in Nineteenth Century America," *MQR* 36 (winter 1987): 9–28, 11.

23. Michael Gilmore, "Eulogy As Symbolic Biography," in *Harvard English Studies 8,* ed. Daniel Aaron (Cambridge, Mass.: Harvard University Press, 1978), 131.

24. Ramsay, *Memoirs,* 207, urging son to avoid superficial peers and aim for distinction.

25. Ibid., 149–50.

26. Ibid., 99.

27. Ibid.

28. Ibid., 157.

29. Ibid., 119.

30. Ramsay, *Memoirs,* 69. Joanna B. Gillespie, "The Clear Leadings of Providence: Pious Memoirs and the Problems of Self-Realization for Women in the

Early Nineteenth Century" *JEAR* 5 (summer 1985): 197–221; Patricia Bonomi, *Under the Cope of Heaven: Religion, Society and Politics in Colonial America* (New York: Oxford University Press, 1986); Ramsay, *Memoirs,* 139.

31. See Hennen, *Sentiments and Experience,* x, for "literary remains." Ramsay, *Memoirs,* 118.

32. L. H. Butterfield, ed., *John Witherspoon Comes to America* (Princeton: Princeton Library, 1953), 73.

33. Ramsay, *Memoirs,* preface, iii; Gordon Wood, *The Creation of the American Republic, 1776–1778* (New York: W. W. Norton & Co., 1972); Forrest McDonald, *Novus Ordo Seclorum: The Intellectual Origins of the Constitution* (Lawrence: University Press of Kansas, 1985), 71; Brunhouse, *Ramsay,* letter 151, David Ramsay to Robert Fulton, cites "Hamilton Steamboat Company"; 6 Aug. 1785, Ramsay to the Rev. John Eliot, Boston, p. 90.

34. HL to James Cordes Jr., 31 Aug. 1765, Hamer, *Papers of Henry Laurens,* 4:67, emphasis added, property owners' responsibility to provide slave labor for road-work days.

35. Jean Matthews, "Race, Sex, and the Dimensions of Liberty in Antebellum America," *JEAR* 6 (fall 1986): 275–92. During Martha's final illness she read *The Memoir of Mrs Elizabeth Carter,* ed. Montague Pennington (Boston: Oliver C. Greenleaf, 1809), a British bluestocking renowned for having translated Epictetus, and idealizing the stance of stoicism for educated Englishwomen.

36. HL to Martha Laurens, 18 May 1774, Hamer, *Papers of Henry Laurens,* 9:457, her childhood request for globes; Matthews, "The Dimensions of Liberty."

37. Ramsay, *Memoirs,* 37; Benjamin Wadsworth, *The Well-Ordered Family; or Relative Duties* (Boston: B. Green, 1712), in *The Colonial American Family Collected Essays,* ed. David Rothman and Sheila Rothman (New York: Arno Press, 1972).

38. Ramsay, *Memoirs,* 37; David D. Hall, "Uses of Literacy," 43.

39. Ramsay, *Memoirs,* 37.

40. Ramsay, *Memoirs,* 39; Susan Groag Bell and Karen Offen, *Women, the Family and Freedom,* 2 vols. (Palo Alto, Calif.: Stanford University Press, 1983), 1:51. Mary Wollstonecraft defined "the being who discharges the duties of its station" as "independent" (61).

41. Ramsay, *Memoirs,* 38.

42. *Columbian Magazine or Monthly Miscellany* 4 (Jan. 1790): 24; Ramsay, *Memoirs,* 17, 31.

43. Ramsay, *Memoirs,* viii, "unconscious of her own uncommon superiority."

44. DR to Dr. Benjamin Rush, 11 Feb. 1786, Brunhouse, *Ramsay,* 98.

45. Issac Kramnick, "The Great National Discussion: The Discourse of Politics," 1788, *WMQ* 45 (Jan. 1988): 3–32. Editorial, *National Intelligencer and Washington Advertiser* 2 (20 Nov. 1801), emphasis added.

46. McDonald, *Novus Ordo Seclorum,* 163; David Ramsay expressed "hurt at the association [Paine's Age of Reason] occasions . . . that the great patrons of liberty are enemies to religion," DR to Rev. John Eliot, 11 Mar. 1795, Brunhouse, *Ramsay,* 139.

47. Ibid., 193. Anonymous, "Inducements for a Judicious Improvement of Our National Privileges," *Columbian Magazine* 12 (July–Aug. 1806): 148–51.

48. Ramsay, *Memoirs,* 19–20; Brunhouse, *Ramsay,* DR to Benjamin Rush, 29 July 1774. His father, James Ramsay, was a poor sharecropper on land owned by Leander Shoemaker near Philadelphia; his other professional brother, Nathaniel, became a lawyer and married Jane Peale, sister of Charles Willson Peale. Margaret Simons Middleton, *David and Martha Laurens Ramsay* (New York: Carlton Press, 1971), 53; Pauline Maier, *The Old Revolutionaries* (New York: Vintage Press, 1980).

49. Bankruptcy was a financial hazard experienced by many prominent citizens of his era. Richard Barry, *Mr. Rutledge of South Carolina* (New York: Duell, Sloan & Pearce, 1942), 359.

50. Ramsay, *Memoirs,* 41. Petition for Benefit of Insolvent Debtors, filed May 11,1798, Charleston District Judgement Rolls 1802, 413A, South Carolina State Archives, Columbia. In the *Charleston City Gazette* (1 Feb. 1804), the Santee Canal was saluted as the "dawn of a new era, in the true interests of [South Carolina] inhabitants bringing their commodities to Charleston by water" (Ramsay, *Memoirs,* 41). A month later (5 Mar. 1804) an anonymous note observed that a $3,000 cargo loss could have been prevented via the Santee Canal, saving both time and money. Their tone suggests David Ramsay's hand may well have written them.

51. Ramsay, *Memoirs,* 134; 111–37.

52. Ibid., 79, 180, 216.

53. Ibid., 213–14.

54. Ibid., 26, 31, 206.

55. This anecdote appears only in *Memoirs* (1845), 84–85.

56. Ibid., 163, 146, 164.

57. Ibid.

58. Robert Shalhope, "Republicanism and Early American Historiography," *WMQ* 39 (Apr. 1982): 334–56; Ramsay, *Memoirs,* 205.

59. Wood, *Creation of the American Republic,* 68; *Baltimore Weekly,* 20 Dec. 1800, 154, in *Documentary History of the Ratification of the Constitution,* microfiche supplement for Pennsylvania volume.

60. Bloch, "Gendered Virtue," 48–51, 53. David Ramsay named as Martha's favorite books only those portraying "rational piety." Others she owned, perhaps inappropriate to his editorial agenda, were left unmentioned; e.g., a picaresque thousand-and-one-nights French novella with virtue triumphant, *The Memoirs of Madame de Barneveldt* (Jean duCastre d'Auvigny, 1796); MLR's distinctive signature appears on the flyleaf.

61. Fliegelman, *Prodigals and Pilgrims,* 185; William Burkitt, *An Help and Guide to Christian Families,* 33d ed. (London: J. Rivington et al., 1767).

62. Kramnick, "The Great National Discussion," 17.

63. Honorius (pseud.), *Columbian Magazine* 1 (July–Aug. 1787): 177–79, emphasis added.

64. Ibid. *Columbian Magazine* 1 (July–Aug. 1787): 180. Hannah More, *The Complete Works of Hannah More,* 2 vols. (New York: Harper & Brothers, 1839), 1: 311–416, quoting the section "Strictures on the Modern System of Female Education"; Ramsay, *Memoirs,* 205, 208, 217, 211.

65. Wood, *Creation of the American Republic,* 416; Joseph Johnson, *Traditions and Reminiscences of the American Revolution in the South* (Charleston, S.C.: Walker and James, 1851), 326.

66. Ramsay, *Memoirs,* 145.

67. Ibid.

68. Joyce Appleby, "Republicanism," *WMQ* 43 (Jan. 1986): 20–34. "What was exhilarating [in the 1790s] was not the experience of organizing a society of new principles . . . but the *hopes* such a prospect inspired" (italics added).

69. Wood, *Creation of the American Republic,* 118; Ramsay, *Memoirs,* 43.

70. Anonymous, Boston, 1797, quoted in Benson, *Women in Eighteenth Century America,* 187.

Chapter 6

1. Ramsay, *Memoirs,* 166; Bridenbaugh, *Myths and Realities;* Rogers, *Charleston in the Age of the Pinckneys.*

2. Miscellaneous Family Records #2182 (Laurens Family), Southern Historical Collection, Manuscripts Department, Wilson Library of the University of North Carolina, Chapel Hill, has an extensive correspondence to and from Henry Laurens, before his death in 1792, about debt and financial records lost in the war. The records continue into the early 1800s to Henry Laurens Jr.

3. Elizabeth Fox-Genovese, "Placing Women's History in History," *New Left Review* (May/June 1982): 130–34.

4. Suspicion of domination—power imbalance—was an identifying characteristic of early national republican ideology (Wood, *The Creation of the American Republic;* McDonald, *Novus Ordo Seclorum*); James T. Kloppenberg, "The Virtues of Liberalism: Christianity, Republicanism and Ethics in Early American Political Discourse," *JAH* 74 (June 1987): 9–33.

5. James Wilson, Course of Law Lectures (Introductory Lecture, Philadelphia), quoted in *Universal Asylum and Columbian Magazine* 6 (Jan. 1791): 45.

6. Gunderson, "Independence, Citizenship, and the American Revolution," 63.

7. Ramsay, *Memoirs,* 37; Wadsworth, *The Well-Ordered Family,* 169.

8. Priscilla Mason, quoted in *Women and Religion in Colonial America,* ed. Rosemary Ruether and Rosemary Keller (San Francisco: Harper & Row, 1983), 2:406–8.

9. Jean Matthews, "Race, Sex, and the Dimensions of Liberty."

10. Quilt-piecing as the metaphor for women's assembled spiritual identity is cited here as an analogue for women's construction of a citizenship identity. Atkinson, *Immaculate and Powerful,* 3.

11. Ruth Bloch, *Visionary Republic: Millenial Themes in American Thought, 1756–1800* (New York: Cambridge University Press, 1985), 95. "The belief that America was destined to become . . . powerful . . . addressed both the fears and the wishes of ardent American nationalists."

12. Hareven, *Family Time and Industrial Time,* 101–9; Wadsworth, *The Well-Ordered Family.*

13. Ramsay, *Memoirs,* 204–5. Barbara Bellows, "My Children, Gentleman, Are My Own": Poor Women, the Urban Elite, and the Bonds of Obligation in Antebellum Charleston," in *The Web of Southern Social Relations,* ed. Walter J. Fraser Jr., R. Frank Saunders Jr., and Jon L. Wakelyn, 52–71 (Athens: University of Georgia Press, 1985).

14. Warren I. Susman, *Culture As History* (New York: Pantheon Books, 1984), 8–9, historian as myth creator. Linda K. Kerber, *Women of the Republic* (Chapel Hill: University of North Carolina Press, 1980). Brunhouse, *Ramsay,* 146, had already included biographies of her father and brother in other writings.

15. Samuel Richardson, *A Collection of Moral and Instructive Sentiments,* 1775 (Delmar, N.Y.: Scholars Facsimiles & Reprints, 1980), 53.

16. Ramsay, *Memoirs,* 36, 37 (emphasis added); Richardson, *Sentiments,* 169.

17. Ramsay, *Memoirs,* 173.

18. Ibid., 37, 174. Years later, Henry Laurens' exotic burial was mythologized; one writer (attributing it to Mercy Otis Warren's Revolutionary War history) implied that Henry had threatened disinheritance if his only surviving son, Henry Jr., refused will-mandated cremation; it implied that Henry thought his own body was "too good for worms" *(The Panoplist* 2, 9, 429–30).

19. Ramsay, *Memoirs,* 37.

20. Ibid., 9. The actual burial place at Mepkin plantation was a spot "worthy the illustrious man who cultivated and adorned it." The house itself, occupied by Henry Jr. and his family, was on a bluff of some thirty-five feet, surrounded by oaks "of a magnificent size" and a mill and granary, very large and featuring the protection of lightning rods. This visitor recalled Henry Laurens' name as "in the charge of history," and "the eyes in his portrait [hanging in the mansion] gazing with prophetic intuition into futurity." John Hammond Moore, ed. "The Abiel Abbott Journals," *SCHM* 8 (Oct. 1967): 245, quoting his 2 Feb. 1828 letter to his wife.

21. C. James Taylor, "Another Bicentennial! The Anniversary of the Death and Cremation of Henry Laurens," *Carologue* (winter 1992): 19; Wallace, *Henry Laurens,* 12–13.

22. Ramsay, *Memoirs,* 173.

23. Ibid., 173.

24. Joel Barlow's "Vision of Columbus," excerpted in *Columbian Magazine* 2 (Jan. 1788): 47, included Henry Laurens as a Founding Father who "ope'd the halls of fate" along with Adams, Washington, Franklin, and others.

25. Linda Kerber's coinage *republican motherhood,* refined and contextualized in Jan Lewis' "Motherhood and the Construction of the Male Citizen," in

Constructions of the Self, ed. George Levine (New Brunswick: Rutgers University Press, 1992), 143–63. For a nuanced reading of women excluding themselves from political citizenship, I am grateful to Edith Gelles, "Reexamining the Mother of the Republic" (unpublished paper, 1997), and Rosemarie Zagarri, "Morals, Manners, and the Republican Mother," *AQ* 44 (June 1992): 192–215.

26. Pennington, *Memoirs of the Life of Mrs. Elizabeth Carter;* also, Samuel Burder, ed., *Memoirs of Eminently Pious Women* (Philadelphia, 1835).

27. Irene Quenzler Brown, "Domesticity, Feminism, and Friendship: Women, Aristocratic Culture, and Marriage in England, 1660–1760," *JFH* (1982): 406–24; Brown, "Death, Friendship, and Female Identity during New England's Second Great Awakening," *JFH* (1987): 368–72; and Brown, "Leisure, Prayer, and Inclusive Friendship from Bunyan and Law to the Lowell Girls," unpublished paper presented at American Academy of Religion, Boston, 1987; Ramsay, *Memoirs,* 175–89, letters from Martha Laurens Ramsay to Miss Elisabeth Brailsford in 1770s England, and to Miss Sproat and Mrs. Keith, fellow church members in Charleston and Philadelphia, in the 1790s.

28. John Locke, "Some Thoughts on Education," [1692] in James Axtell, ed., *The Educational Writings of John Locke* (New York: Cambridge University Press, 1968); Margaret J. M. Ezell, "John Locke's Images of Childhood," *Eighteenth-Century Studies* 17 (winter 1983–84): 139–55.

29. HL to John Laurens, Hamer, *Papers of Henry Laurens,* 10:176–77, a copy of HL's speech to Congress.

30. Ramsay, *Memoirs,* 21. Brunhouse, *Ramsay,* 122–23.

31. Richardson, *Sentiments,* vi; Ramsay, *Memoirs,* 205.

32. Fliegelman, *Prodigals and Pilgrims,* 40–50; Ramsay, *Memoirs,* 171, advice on Priestly; 194, learning from deprivation; 169, older children's influence on younger; 168, students' own self-direction.

33. Ramsay, *Memoirs,* 39, persuasive theories of instructing; 203, involvement in all experiences of children.

34. Ramsay, *Memoirs,* 26, reading aloud as training for public speaking; 28, teaching comprehension; 23, anti-rote learning. Mrs. Sarah Kirby Trimmer (1741–1810), widely known as a Christian education writer, published *Easy Introduction to the Knowledge of Nature* (1782); *Bible Stories for Children* (6 vols., 1782–84); *The Oeconomy of Charity* (1788–89); and essays, *The Guardian of Education* (1802–6). One of these included detailed directions for explaining each item in the Church of England's Great Catechism (in question-and-answer form), plus her moral, for children's benefit. Beloved by Martha as a child, Issac Watts (1647–1748), *Divine Songs for Children,* 2 vols. (London, 1715), was another important source.

35. Spruill, *Women's Life and Work in the Southern Colonies,* 230–31.

36. Ramsay, *Memoirs,* 20, 189, 199. David D. Hall, "The Mental World of Samuel Sewall," in *Saints and Revolutionaries: Essays on Early American History,* ed. David D. Hall, John Murrin, and Thad Tate (New York: W. W. Norton and Co., 1984),

75–89; William L. Joyce, David D. Hall, Richard D. Brown, and John B. Hench, eds., "Introduction: The Uses of Literacy in New England, 1600–1850," *Printing and Society in Early America* (Worcester, Mass.: American Antiquarian Society, 1983), 1–47.

37. Ramsay, *Memoirs*, 28–30.

38. Circular Church Register, vol. 2, 1796–1806 (quoted with permission from the Independent [Congregational] Church, South Carolina Historical Society, Charleston), noted, "the Old Church having been voted for removal Oct. 19, 1803," David Ramsay presented the suggestion of a round design, and a special December 1803 meeting was convened to discuss it. On 13 February 1804, he presented a drawing of a plan (his wife was not named in that record); Richard Yeadon, *History of the Circular Church, Its Origin, Building and Rebuilding* (Charleston, S.C.: J. B. Nixon, 1853), and Edwards, *A History of the Independent or Congregational Church*, 35, provide David's description of the denomination symbolized in the building: "a free ecclesiastical democracy" that had women in its choir as early as the 1780s, when the Ramsays regularly attended.

39. *Columbian Magazine* 2 (Jan. 1787): 2.

40. Enos Hitchcock, *Memoirs of the Bloomsgrove Family* (Boston, 1790), 47, 79.

41. Ramsay, *Memoirs*, 22; Nancy Schrom Dye and Daniel Blake Smith, "Mother Love and Infant Death, 1750–1920," *JAH* 73 (Sept. 1986): 329–53.

42. Ramsay, *Memoirs*, 203.

43. Smith-Rosenberg, "Misprisioning Pamela." Hamer, *Papers of Henry Laurens*, 8:353.

44. Daniel M'Calla, *Works of The Rev. Daniel M'Calla*, 2 vols. (Charleston, S.C.: John Hoff, 1810), 2:183. Two of his "Hints on Education" appeared in the *Charleston City Gazette and Daily Advertiser*, 4 and 7 Feb. 1795.

45. M'Calla, *Works*, 2:179.

46. Caleb Cotton, "Letters of Charles Caleb Cotton, 1798–1802," *SCHM* 51 (July 1950): 75–81; 51 (Oct. 1950): 132–44; 51 (Jan. 1951): 217–28; and 51 (Apr. 1951): 17–25.

47. M'Calla, *Works*, 2:181–82.

48. Anon., "Prolonging the Happiness of the Marriage Union," *Columbian Magazine* vol. 1, no. 10 (Oct. 1787), 473, pronounced that "women of wit and fine reading, your Lesbias and Cleomiras," were as destructive to a husband's peace as their opposite, the illiterate housewife.

49. Bell and Offen, *Women, the Family, and Freedom*, 1:61.

50. Ramsay, *Memoirs*, 202, 207.

51. Burkitt, *An Help and Guide to Christian Families*, 22.

52. Ibid., 136.

53. Cotton, "Letters of Charles Caleb Cotton," *SCHM* 51, no. 2 (Jan. 1957), 222.

54. Quoted in Wood, *Creation of the American Republic*, 69.

55. Kramnick, "Great National Discussion," 22–23. Ramsay, *Memoirs*, 153.

56. Whaley Batson, "Thomas Coram, Charleston Artist," *Journal of Early Southern Decorative Arts* 1 (Nov. 1975): 38. Two Ramsay children served as executors of Mrs. Coram's estate.

57. Hitchcock, *Bloomsgrove Memoirs,* 33.

58. M'Calla, *Works,* 2:308.

59. Young, *The Complaint,* 155, Introduction to Night VII.

60. Eugene Genovese and Betsy Fox-Genovese, "Divine Sanction: Religious Foundations of the Southern Slaveholder's World-View," *JAAR* 55 (summer 1987): 211–34; Alan Gallay, "The Origin of Slaveholders' Paternalism: George Whitefield, the Bryan Family, and the Great Awakening in the South," *JSH* 53 (Aug. 1987): 369–94.

61. Fraser, *Charleston!,* 187. "Fourth in population among urban centers [in the new nation] Charleston had by far a denser concentration of Afro-Americans than the other three combined—New York, Philadelphia, and Boston." Hannah More, *Complete Works,* 2:115.

62. Ramsay, *Memoirs,* 38–39 n.

63. Beth Kowaleski-Wallace, "Milton's Daughters: The Education of Eighteenth Century Women Writers," *Feminist Studies* 12 (summer 1986): 273–93.

64. Ann Cleland, Commonplace Book (1785), South Carolina Historical Society, Charleston.

65. Jan Lewis, "The Republican Wife."

66. *American Periodical Guide,* Microfilm Reel no. 1.

67. Ibid., quoting *Massachusetts Centinel Extraordinary,* 1789; Ramsay, *Memoirs,* 39 n.

68. Richard Polewheale, "The Unsex'd Female," quoted under New Publications, *Baltimore Weekly,* 5 July 1800, 82–83.

69. *Columbian Magazine* 3 (May 1789): 288–90. The promptness with which this occasion was reported indicates the level of national interest: George Washington's visit was 21 April 1789.

70. Theodore D. Jervey, *Robert Y. Hayne and His Times* (New York: Macmillan, 1909), 10, quoting Mrs. Keith.

71. Cotton, "Letters of Charles Caleb Cotton," *SCHM* 51, no. 4 (Jan. 1951), 217.

72. *Providence Phoenix* 1, no. 20 (21 September 1802), 3.

73. *Charleston City Gazette,* 7 May 1804, 3. The Charleston Womens Benevolent Society's anniversary meeting at the Independent Church, Archdale, with Martha's friend the Rev. Mrs. Hollinshead presiding, featured a sermon and sacred music.

74. Bloch, "The Gendered Meanings of Virtue."

75. *American Periodical Guide* 1 (1 Apr. 1801): 241–42.

76. Ramsay, *Memoirs,* 159, emphasis added.

Chapter 7

1. The concept of silence in a specific culture's records or conversation about a topic so intense and fraught with significance as to be unmentionable is discussed by Jody Shapiro Davie in *Women in the Presence: Constructing Community and Seeking Spirituality in Mainline Protestantism* (Philadelphia: University of

Pennsylvania Press, 1995), 95. It indicates a culture's fears or desires and is itself evidence of the prevailing conditions in its time or setting. Victoria Lee Erickson's *Where Silence Speaks: Feminism, Social Theory, and Religion* (Minneapolis: Fortress Press, 1993), discusses its spiritual function: "the everyday is where silence speaks" (192). For silence in a national-cultural context, see Ernestine Schlant, *The Language of Silence: West German Literature and the Holocaust* (New York: Routledge, 1999).

2. Jan. 1793, 106–7; the table of contents for a December 1792 issue listed ten articles with content addressed to women; noted in Benson, *Women in Eighteenth Century America*, 212.

3. Michael E. Stevens, ed., *Journal of the House of Representatives, 1792–1794* (Columbia: University of South Carolina Press, 1988), xv. Gabriel Manigault to Mrs. Gabriel Manigault, 7 Dec. 1792, Manigault Family Papers, South Caroliniana Library, University of South Carolina, Columbia; Clerk's notes, filed with Stevens, *Journals of House of Representatives*, rough copy, South Carolina Archives; *Ladies Magazine* 1, no. 1 (Jan. 1793), 106–7.

4. Ball cousins of Martha's who vacationed in Rhode Island were possible correspondents (Joseph K. Ott, "Rhode Islanders in Charleston," *SCHM* 75 (July 1974): 180–83), or a Rhode Island female Quaker abolitionist. No one else thus far discovered cited David Ramsay's antislavery declaration, but others knew of it: a New Englander recalled that momentous event in David Ramsay's career in almost the same words. John Hammond Moore, ed., "The Abiel Abbot Journals: A Yankee Preacher in Charleston Society, 1818–1828," *SCHM* 68 (Apr. 1967), 66.

5. *Ladies Magazine* 1, no. 1 (Jan. 1793), 106–7.

6. Ibid.

7. Samuel Lorenzo Knapp, *American Cultural History, 1607–1829* (Delmar, N.Y.: Scholars Facsimiles & Reprints, 1997), iii, 104. Yale awarded David Ramsay an honorary degree in 1804 (Shaffer, *To Be an American*, 93). Ramsay's national reputation was reiterated in a posthumous tribute accompanying the presentation of his portrait and the portrait of father-in-law Henry Laurens by John S. Cogdell to Joseph Johnson, president of the Apprentices Library Society in Charleston (established circa 1815). Cogdell's letter of gift called Ramsay "the venerated, the distinguished Historian Dr. David Ramsay, personally so well known to you and Many Members of our Society." Johnson's acceptance of the portraits said: "The bright example of these distinguished Men will excite Emulation in the bosoms of our Youth, for whose beneficence our Society is established." Cogdell to Johnson, Johnson to Cogdell, 25 Aug. 1840, John Stevens, Diary and Letterbooks, 1808–41, 6 vols., Manuscripts Division, Henry Francis DuPont Winterthur Museum, Winterthur, Del.

8. See William Frederick Poole, *Anti-Slavery Opinion before 1800* (Westport, Conn.: Negro University Press, 1970), for antislavery optimism in that era.

9. See Warner, *Republic of Letters,* for the role of public print in legitimating political topics and a sense of national identity.

10. An exception in this decade was Judith Sargent Murray, who craved public recognition as a writer and confessed a "ruling passion to stand well in the opinion of the world"—in short, "to be an AMERICAN AUTHOR" (capitalization in original). Murray, *The Gleaner,* 1:vi, vii, viii.

11. See Rhys Issac, *The Transformation of Virginia* (Chapel Hill: University of North Carolina Press, 1982), 332, for "knots of dramatic encounter" in the evolution of social life.

12. Joseph Alston to Theodosia Burr, 28 Dec. 1800, Matthew L. Davis, *Memoirs of Aaron Burr,* 2 vols. (New York: Da Capo Press, 1971), 1:424–33.

13. Ibid.

14. Mary Stoughton Locke, *Anti-Slavery in America, 1619–1808* (New York: Johnson Reprint, 1968), 40, quoting John Parrish, Remarks on the Slavery of the Black People, pamphlet, Philadelphia, 1806; see George M. Fredrickson, *The Black Image in the White Mind* (Middletown, Conn., 1987), for the emergence of full-blown racism.

15. Wates, "Precursor to the Victorian Age," 9.

16. Johnson, *Tradition and Reminiscences,* 326.

17. See Philip Morgan, "Three Planters and Their Slaves: Perspectives on Slavery in Virginia, South Carolina, and Jamaica, 1750–1790," in *Race and Family in the Colonial South,* ed. Winthrop D. Jordan and Sheila L. Skemp, (Jackson: University Press of Mississippi, 1987), 37–80, for archetypal master-slave relationships, patriarchal to paternalistic (Henry Laurens in the latter). Hamer, *Papers of Henry Laurens,* 4:28–99; Malcolm Bell, *Major Butler's Legacy: Five Generations of a Slaveholding Family* (Athens: University of Georgia Press, 1987), 100, characterized Henry Laurens' slave management "with a light hand."

18. Tise, *Proslavery,* 126–27; Duncan Clinch Heyward, *Seed from Madagascar* (Columbia: University of South Carolina Press, 1993), 209–10.

19. Eighteenth-century Anglo-European fathers were expected to be autodidacts within their families. Thomas P. Slaughter, *The Natures of John and William Bartram* (New York: A. A. Knopf, 1996), 18; John Demos, "The Changing Faces of Fatherhood: A New Exploration in Family History," in *Father and Child: Developmental and Clinical Perspectives,* ed. Stanley H. Cath, Alan R. Gurwitt, and John M. Ross (Boston: Little, Brown & Co., 1982), 425–45.

20. E. Day to HL, 30 Apr. 1784, Private Collection (copy), Martha's visit to Thomas Day's mother; Thomas Day honored John poetically after his death in 1782. Hamer, *Papers of Henry Laurens,* 9:588 n. 4.

21. Gregory D. Massey, *John Laurens and the American Revolution* (Columbia: University of South Carolina Press, 2000), quoting Thomas Day, "The Dying Negro" (England, 1773); George Warren Gignilliat Jr., *The Author of Sandford and Merton: A Life of Thomas Day, Esq.* (New York: Columbia University Press, 1932), 102–10; Gretchen Holbrook Gerzina, *Black London* (New Brunswick: Rutgers University Press, 1995), 121.

22. John Wesley, *A Calm Address to Our American Colonies* (Philadelphia, 1775).

23. Warren Thomas Smith, *John Wesley and Slavery* (Nashville: Abingdon Press, 1986), 101. John Wesley preached at St. Philip's in Charles Town on 31 July 1736 to a congregation of three hundred with "some negroes in attendance"; some fifty received communion (45). Henry Laurens, not departing to England for business training until the following year, may well have attended. Olaudah Equiano's autobiography was read to Wesley on his deathbed, 22 Feb. 1791, its impact inspiring him to write parliament and the antislavery network.

24. John Laurens to HL, 28 Jan. 1778, Hamer, *Papers of Henry Laurens*, 12:392; see Peter M. Voelz, *Slave and Soldier: The Military Impact of Blacks on the Colonial Americas* (New York: Garland Publishing Co., 1993), 381–82, for view that winning the Revolutionary War depended on "which side can arm the Negroes the faster."

25. Norman Fiering, "Irresistible Compassion: An Aspect of Eighteenth Century Sympathy and Humanitarianism," *Journal of the History of Ideas* 37 (Apr.–June 1976): 195–218; Joyce E. Chaplin, "Slavery and the Principle of Humanity: A Modern Idea in the Early Lower South," *JSocHist* 24 (winter 1990): 299–315, slaveowners mixing "kindness and coercion" (311); Elizabeth B. Clark, "The Sacred Rights of the Weak: Pain, Sympathy, and the Culture of Individual Rights in Antebellum America," *JAH* 82 (Sept. 1995): 463–93, translating this sensibility into law.

26. Massey, *John Laurens and the American Revolution,* quoting John Laurens to Francis Kinloch, 12 Apr. 1776; Elizabeth Langhorne, K. Edward Lay, and William D. Rieley, eds., *A Virginia Family and Its Plantation Houses* (Charlottesville: University of Virginia Press, 1987), 132–41, citing another second-generation idealist, Edward Coles, 1806 graduate of the College of William and Mary who traveled west with his slaves for their freedom. The president of his college, Episcopal Bishop James Madison, admitted that slavery "could not be justified in principle . . . [and was] only tolerated because of the difficulties of getting rid of it" (133).

27. John Laurens to HL, 2 Feb. 1778, Hamer, *Papers of Henry Laurens*, 9:390; Bell, *Major Butler's Legacy,* 100.

28. Francis S. Drake, *Memorials of the Society of the Cincinnati of Massachusetts* (Boston, 1873), 226, quoting Odijah Baylies of Massachusetts, army colleague.

29. Joseph Lee Boyle, ed., "The Revolutionary War Diaries of Capt Walter Finney," *SCHM* 98 (Apr. 1997): 143. John Laurens' "eagerness" prevented him from waiting for backup, and he "precipitately engaged and in a few minutes fell a victim to his own inadvertance by the well directed fire of the enemy" (spelling modernized). His "untimely death," the phrase universally applied, deprived the state of "a worthy citizen" (173).

30. Nathanael Greene to Otho H. Williams, 17 Sept. 1782, Richard Showman, ed., *Nathanael Greene Papers*, vol. 11 (Providence, R.I.: Rhode Island Historical Society, 1976).

31. David Ramsay, *History of the Revolution in South Carolina*, 374.

32. "Reminiscences of Abbeville (S.C.) by Ex-Abbevillian of Over Forty Years: Notable Persons—Marriage and Divorce in High Life/ The Last Man Who Lost

His Life in the Revolution," in *Abbeville (S.C.) Press and Banner,* 19 Apr. 1876, centennial tribute to John Laurens and his only child.

33. "Diary of Timothy Ford," 1785–86, *SCHM* 13 (July 1912): 130–47.

34. Sylvia Frey and Betty Wood, *Come Shouting to Zion: African American Protestantism in the American South and British Caribbean to 1830* (Chapel Hill: University Press of North Carolina, 1998), 91–92, slaves' response to Whitefield's evangelizing seen as "implicit recognition" of their "intellectual equality."

35. Boyd Stanley Schlenther, "'To Convert the Poor People in America': The Bethesda Orphanage and the Thwarted Zeal of the Countess of Huntingdon," *Georgia Historical Quarterly* 72 (summer 1994): 225–56; Lady Hastings (about Martha's visit) to HL, 22 July 1783, Private Collection (copy).

36. David Lyle Jeffrey, Introduction, *A Burning and a Shining Light: English Spirituality in the Age of Wesley* (Grand Rapids: William B. Eerdmans Publishing Co., 1987), 15, quoting A. C. H. Seymour, *The Life and Times of Selina, Countess of Huntingdon,* 2 vols. (London: Painter, 1844), 1:86–87.

37. Another titled woman reproved the countess for her "methodist impertinence." "It is monstrous to be told that you have a heart as sinful as the common wretches that crawl the earth. This is highly offensive . . . that your Ladyship should relish . . . sentiments so much at variance with high rank and good breeding." A. Barbeau, *Life and Letters at Bath in the Eighteenth Century* (London: William Heineman, 1904), 164.

38. Schlenther, "To Convert the Poor," 226–30; Albert Brown-Lawson, *John Wesley and the Anglican Evangelicals of the Eighteenth Century* (Durham, England: Pentland Press, 1994), 335–53; Benjamin Braude, "The Sons of Noah and Construction of Ethnic and Geographic Identities in Medieval and Early Modern Periods," *WMQ* 54 (Jan. 1997): 103–42, background of biblical curse; James H. Sweet, "The Iberian Roots of American Racist Thought," *WMQ* 54 (Jan. 1997): 143–66, skin color in views of race; and David Brion Davis, "Constructing Race: A Reflection," *WMQ* 54 (Jan. 1997): 7–18.

39. Ramsay, *Memoirs,* 180, phrase in text not applied specifically to husband; phrase from letter, *Ladies Magazine* (Jan. 1793): 1; Wylma Wates, "Correspondence of the Izard Family," 9.

40. Davie, *Women in the Presence,* 94–95.

41. Eugene Genovese, "Our Family, White and Black: Family and Household in Southern Slaveholders' World View," in Bleser, *In Joy and in Sorrow,* 69–87.

42. Ramsay, *Memoirs,* 75.

43. Genovese, "Our Family White and Black."

44. Ibid.,106.

45. Ramsay, *Memoirs,* 106 n.

46. Dr. Benjamin Rush. Letter to Rev. Jeremy Belknap, 19 Aug. 1788, 161.A.170, Belknap Papers, Massachusetts Historical Society; also printed in the *Collections of the Massachusetts Historical Society,* 6th ser., vol. 4, 416–18. "Let us try the force of the press upon spiritous liquors in every part of the U.S. *Dr. Ramsay will be our*

coadjutor in S. Carolina (emphasis added). By the year 1815 a drunkard I hope will be as infamous as a lyar or thief, the use of spirits as uncommon in families as drink made of arsenic or hemlock" (417).

47. HL to Abraham Schad, 30 Apr. 1765, Hamer, *Papers of Henry Laurens*, 4:616.

48. See Davis, "At the Heart of Slavery," *New York Review of Books* 43 (17 Oct. 1996): 51–53, for this stage in the abolitionism movement.

49. Ramsay, *Memoirs*, 39, 105–6.

50. Karen A. Offen, "Was Mary Wollstonecraft a Feminist? A Contextual Re-Reading of a Vindication of the Rights of Woman, 1792–1992," in *Quilting a New Canon: Stitching Women's Words*, ed. Uma Parameswaran, 3–24 (Toronto: Sister Vision Press, 1993); see Annis Boudinot Stockton to her daughter, Mrs. Benjamin Rush, 23 Mar. 1793, for an evaluation of Wollstonecraft similar to that in the *Memoirs*, in Mulford, *"Only for the Eye of a Friend,"* 305–6; Rosemarie Zagarri, "The Rights of Man and Woman in Post Revolutionary America," *WMQ* 55 (Apr. 1998): 203–30.

51. Ramsay, *Memoirs*, 104, 173, 200, 201, 198.

52. Ibid., 201.

53. Ibid., 198. Engraver (one of the earliest in America, who arrived in Charleston in 1779) and artist, benefactor of the Orphan House, active in the Circular Church, St. Andrew's Society and the Benevolent Society with the Ramsays, File #30–04, South Carolina Historical Society, Charleston.

54. Ramsay, *Memoirs*, 198.

55. Grey and Wood, *Come Shouting to Zion;* Milton C. Sernett, *Afro-American Religious History: A Documentary History* (Durham N.C.: Duke University Press, 1985); Mechal Sobel, *"Trabelin' On": The Slave Journey to an Afro Baptist Faith* (Westport, Conn.: Greenwood Press, 1979); Cynthia Lynn Lyerly, "Religion, Gender and Identity: Black Methodist Women in a Slave Society, 1770–1910," in *Discovering the Women in Slavery*, ed. Patricia Morton (Athens: University of Georgia Press, 1996), 202–26.

56. William B. Sprague, *Annals of the American Pulpit* (New York: Arno Reprints, 1969), 2:58–60. Rev. William States Lee wrote the 1853 supplemental letter about Hollinshead's ministry to slaves.

57. Ibid., 60.

58. For debate on the present-day construction of eighteenth-century race, see Robert E. Desrochers Jr., "Not Fade Away: The Narrative of Venture Smith, an African American in the Early Republic," *JAH* 84 (June 1997): 40–66; Joanne Melish, *Disowning Slavery: Gradual Emancipation and Race in New England, 1780–1860* (Ithaca: Cornell University Press, 1998); David Roediger, *Wages of Whiteness: Race and the Making of the American Working Class* (New York: Verso Publications, 1998); Dana Nelson, *The Word in Black and White* (New York: Oxford University Press, 1993); Martha's use of the word *race* in hymns, Ramsay, *Memoirs*, 28.

59. Quoted in Smith, *John Wesley and Slavery*, 44.

60. Ramsay, *Memoirs*, 159, 170.

61. Ibid., 163.

62. Ibid. See Fox-Genovese, *Within the Plantation Household*, 116–35, for a nuanced interpretation of the relationships between nineteenth-century white mistresses and their household slaves, balancing "chilling objectification" and "complicated affection" (132).

63. Ibid., 173.

64. Ibid.

65. HL to Abraham Schad, 23 Aug. 1765, Hamer, *Papers of Henry Laurens*, 4:665–66.

66. HL to James Laurens, 6 Aug. 1777, Hamer, *Papers of Henry Laurens*, 8:399. On 15 March 1777, to overseer Gambrell, HL wrote: "I will not . . . suffer Acts of Cruelty or unnecessary Rigour & severity to be exercised upon those Poor Wretches . . . There is a Medium which ought to be observed . . . which . . . would produce good . . . to your Plantation Crops, to the Health and preservation of the Negroes, & to your own health" (621).

67. J. F. Bosher, "Huguenot Merchants and the Protestant International in the Seventeenth Century," *WMQ* 52 (Jan. 1995): 77–102, Huguenot reputation for business acumen.

68. See Frank Klingberg, *The Carolina Chronicle of Dr. Francis Le Jau* (Berkeley: University of California Press, 1946), 102, for another Huguenot owner seeking pastoral answers about both religious and physical responsibility for slave property.

69. HL to Elias Ball, 1 Apr. 1765, Hamer, *Papers of Henry Laurens*, 4:595, against selling apart families; 4:645, HL to Joseph Brown, 28 June 1765, "I will not keep [Sampson], the first and only runaway, to be a bad example." Also 13:155, HL to John Gervaise, 19 Apr. 1778, "if they are catched, sell them."

70. HL to James Laurens, 26 Dec. 1771, Hamer, *Papers of Henry Laurens*, 8:123.

71. HL to John Laurens, 14 Aug. 1776, Hamer, *Papers of Henry Laurens*, 11:224–25.

72. Smith, *John Wesley and Slavery*, 79.

73. HL to John Laurens, 14 Aug. 1776, Hamer, *Papers of Henry Laurens*, 11:225.

74. Joyce E. Chaplin, *"An Anxious Pursuit": Agricultural Innovation and Modernity in the Lower South* (Chapel Hill: University of North Carolina Press, 1993), 363; Wallace, *Henry Laurens*, 451.

75. Joyce E. Chaplin, "Slavery and the Principle of Humanity: A Modern Idea in the Early Lower South," *JSocHist* 24 (winter 1990): 299–315.

76. Olwell, "Domestick Enemies," 21–48.

77. HL to George Appleby, 28 Feb. 1774, Hamer, *Papers of Henry Laurens*, 9:316–18.

78. Ibid.

79. Ibid. *Gust* carried the meaning of taste or proclivity.

80. Gretchen Holbrook Gerzina, *Black London: Life Before Emancipation* (New Brunswick: Rutgers University Press, 1995), 180, 179 (quoting *London Chronicle*, 1773).

81. HL to John Laurens, 14 Aug. 1776, Hamer, *Papers of Henry Laurens*, 11:223.

82. HL to John Loveday, 21 June 1777, Hamer, *Papers of Henry Laurens*, 11:386.

83. The cross-reference is Bell, *Major Butler's Legacy*, 158.

84. See Elaine Forman Crane, ed., *The Diary of Elizabeth Drinker, 1734–1807* (Boston: Northeastern University Press, 1994), 165–66, for the same cultural view of whipping as appropriate discipline of servants, indentured whites as well as slaves, in Quaker Philadelphia.

85. Catherine Clinton, "Caught in the Web of the Big House: Women and Slavery," in *The Web of Southern Social Relations*, ed. Walter J. Fraser Jr., R. Frank Saunders Jr., and Jon L. Wakelyn, 227–32 (Athens: University of Georgia Press, 1985); Elizabeth Fox-Genovese, *Within the Plantation Household: Black and White Women of the Old South* (Chapel Hill: University of North Carolina Press, 1988), 24, "Mistresses, even the kindest, commonly resorted to the whip."

86. HL to William Brisbane, 17 Oct. 1777, Hamer, *Papers of Henry Laurens*, 11:562; Wallace, *Henry Laurens*, 133 (23 Aug. 1765), instructions to his overseer for establishing authority over Laurens' slaves: "use gentle means mixed with easy authority first—if that does not succeed, make choice of the most stubborn one or two and chastise them severely but properly and with mercy, that they may be convinced that the end of correction is to be amendment."

87. Jones, "The 1780 Siege of Charleston," 72–73.

88. HL to John Gervaise, 5 Aug. 1777, Hamer, *Papers of Henry Laurens*, 11:430.

89. Ibid., 5 Sept. 1777, 11:487; Fox-Genovese, *Within the Plantation Household*, 188–89, slave mothers as rebellion inciters.

90. HL to John Gervais, 17 Oct. 1777, Hamer, *Papers of Henry Laurens*, 11:487; 11:492, HL to John Gervais, 5 Sept. 1777.

91. Benjamin West, Travel Notes: Life in the South, 1778–1779, Slavery Pamphlet Collection, John Carter Brown Library, Providence, R.I. A Northern-born tutor to the children of South Carolina planter Robert Gibbes cited him as "the Good Slavemaster for his humanity toward the most miserable of the human species," of whom he owned nearly a thousand (26). Bell, *Major Butler's Legacy*, 139, a slave-owner who ordered whippings but was disturbed by their frequency and severity; HL to William Brisbane, 17 Oct. 1777, Hamer, *Papers of Henry Laurens*, 11:562.

92. Chaplain, *An Anxious Pursuit*, 363.

93. John Laurens to HL, 14 Jan. 1778, Hamer, *Papers of Henry Laurens*, 12:305.

94. John Laurens to HL, 6 Feb. 1778, Hamer, *Papers of Henry Laurens*, 12:530.

95. Wallace, *Henry Laurens*, 447–91; also quoted in Bell, *Major Butler's Legacy*, 34.

96. HL to ML, 13 June 1784, Private Collection (copy).

97. HL to David Ramsay, 7 July 1790, Manuscript Collection, South Caroliniana Library, University of South Carolina, Columbia.

98. James Laurens to HL, 8 July 1773, Hamer, *Papers of Henry Laurens*, 9:92.

99. Ramsay, *Memoirs*, 171, reference to *Pamela*; Fiering, "Irresistible Compassion"; Marion B. Smith, "South Carolina and *The Gentleman's Magazine*," *SCHM* 95 (Apr. 1994): 102–29.

100. Maurice Jackson, "Anthony Benezet: America's Finest Eighteenth-Century Antislavery Advocate," in *The Human Tradition in the American Revolution*, ed. Nancy L. Rhoden and Ian K. Steele, 1–17 (Wilmington, Del.: Scholarly Resources, 2000).

101. Anthony Benezet, ed. (1713–1784), *Thoughts on Slavery (Collection of Religious Tracts)* (Philadelphia, 1778), 35, 47; also in "Empire without Slaves," by Christopher L. Brown, *WMQ* 56 (Apr. 1999): 288. Benezet's *Collection* included four tracts by Rev. James Ramsay, two by himself, and one by Thomas Clarkson, among others (John Carter Brown Library, Providence, R.I.); Crane, *Diary of Elizabeth Drinker,* cited his influence among Philadelphia Quakers in 1784 (68), and in petitioning Congress in 1797 to cease the slave trade (188).

102. Sheryl A. Kujawa, "The Great Awakening of Sarah Osborne and the Female Society of the First Congregational Church in Newport," *Newport History* 65 (spring 1998):132–53.

103. See Peter C. Hogg, *The African Slave Trade and Its Suppression* (London: Frank Cass, 1973), 140–83, for the vast literature appearing in Martha's era; and Ramsay, *Memoirs,* 211, for Ramsay relationship with Dr. Smith.

104. *The Columbian Magazine and Universal Repository* 1 (1787): 235–38.

105. Keith A. Sandiford, *Measure the Moment: Strategies of Protest in Eighteenth Century Afro-English Writing* (Selinsgrove, Penn.: Susquehanna University Press, 1988), 87; David Reynolds, *Faith in Fiction: The Emergence of Religious Literature in America* (Cambridge, Mass.: Harvard University Press, 1981).

106. James Walcott, *The New Pilgrim's Progress; or The Pious Indian Hattain Gelashmin Christened George James* (London, 1748), John Carter Brown Library, Providence, RI.

107. Phillip M. Richards, "Phillis Wheatley and Literary Americanization," in *Am Q* 44 (June 1992): 163–91; Michael Gilmore, "The Literature of the Revolution and Early National Period," in *The Cambridge History of American Literature, 1590–1820,* ed. Sacvan Bercovitch (New York: Cambridge University Press, 1994), 1:564; Rosemarie Zagarri, "The Rights of Man and Woman in Post-Revolutionary America," *WMQ* 55 (Apr. 1998): 203–30, emerging language of "natural rights."

108. Ramsay, *Memoirs,* 17; Sandiford, *Measure the Moment,* 34; Gerzina, *Black London,* 65, Wheatley's visit to England.

109. [Matilda], *New York Magazine or Literary Repository* 1 (Oct. 1796): 549–550.

110. "Letters from Mrs. Ralph Izard to Mrs. William Lee," *Virginia Magazine of History* 8, no. 20 (July 1900): 16–28. On Aug. 30, 1781, Mrs. Ralph Izard heard from her husband that "about sixty gentlemen who were sent to Augustine in violation of the Capitulation of Charles Town are exchanged [from British detention] and arrived in [Philadelphia]," mentioning David Ramsay among them.

111. Shaffer, *To Be an American,* 182–83; also chapter 11, "The Politics of Slavery," 165–87.

112. DR to BR, 3 Feb. 1779, Brunhouse, *Ramsay,* 58–59.

113. DR to BR, 3 June 1779, Brunhouse, *Ramsay,* 60.

114. DR to BR, 22 Aug. 1783, Brunhouse, *Ramsay,* 76.

115. Shaffer, *To Be an American,* 181, 183. In this preelection newspaper exchange, the first shot was an anonymous notice *denying* the rumor (against Dr. Ramsay), that his election would promote "an emancipation of the Negroes in this state." Speculators wondered if Dr. Ramsay himself initiated it.

116. Thomas Clarkson, *Essay on the Slavery and Commerce of the Human Species, Particularly the African. Translated from the Latin, 1st Prize* (London: University of Cambridge, 1786); he moved from a potential career in the church to investigative reporting, becoming "a detective for humanitarianism" in the slave trade centers of Bristol and Liverpool, England, and helping to lobby Parliament to abolish the trade. Clarkson also interviewed refugees from the Haitian revolution (Gerzina, *Black London,* 181–90).

117. James Ramsay, *Essay on the Treatment and Conversion of African Slaves in the British Sugar Colonies* (Dublin, 1784); Brown, "Empire without Slaves," 286–97; Tobin, an Antigua planter, published a rejoinder in 1788 to which Reverend Ramsay wrote a second pamphlet answering Tobin's "strictures" in question-and-answer form, concluding, "the *nature* of slavery, not the disposition of the master, is chargeable with the enormities of this debasing state." John A. Schutz, "James Ramsay, Essayist: Aggressive Humanitarian," in *British Humanitarianism* (Philadelphia: Church Historical Society, 1950), 145–65, credits Ramsay with the first convincing anecdotal evidence of brutality toward slaves in the production of sugar (145).

118. Mary Kelley, "Reading Women/Women Reading," *JAH* (Sept. 1996): 401–24, on "book culture"; Martha was fortunate to have a husband even further involved in it; see Hayes, *Colonial Woman's Bookshelf,* for the breadth of available reading materials.

119. Shaffer, *To Be an American,* 183.

120. Ibid.

121. *Columbian Magazine* 2 (Feb. 1788): 166, named antislavery writers Clarkson, Sharpe, and Benezet, among others, and reprinted excerpts from the Thomas Day poem "The Dying Negro."

122. Shaffer, *To Be an American,* 187.

123. DR to John Eliot, 26 Nov. 1788, Andrews-Eliot Correspondence, 1715–1814, Proceedings, 1864–65, vol. 81, Massachusetts Historical Society, Boston.

124. George C. Rogers, *Evolution of a Federalist: William Loughton Smith, 1758–1812* (Columbia: University of South Carolina Press, 1962), 166.

125. Fraser, *Charleston!,* 213.

126. Ramsay, *Memoirs,* 39 n: "In copying for him and tracing, through a variety of authors, any subject on which he . . . asked her aid, she shortened his literary labors."

127. Ramsay, *History of South Carolina,* 2:231.

128. Benjamin Trumbull to Roger Sherman, 28 Dec. 1791, citing Dr. Ramsay's reputation for data gathering: he was reputed to have "the best statistics available." Miscellaneous Bound Collection, Massachusetts Historical Society, Boston.

129. See Shaffer, *To Be an American*, 187; Shaffer, *The Politics of History* (Chicago: Precedent Publishing Co., 1975), 90–91, for Dr. Ramsay's prescience about the "amalgamation" of nonwhite racial groups.

130. Winthrop D. Jordan, *White over Black: American Attitudes toward the Negro, 1550–1812* (New York: W. W. Norton, 1977), 369.

131. Charles Bolton, *Southern Anglicanism*, 129, quoting Penuel Bowen.

132. See Barbara Lacey, "Visual Images of Blacks in Early American Imprints," *WMQ* 53 (Jan. 1996): 137–80, for newspaper image reinforcement of racial stereotypes; Shane White and Graham White, "Slave Hair and African American Culture in the Eighteenth and Nineteenth Centuries," *JSH* 61 (Feb. 1995): 45–75.

133. Elizabeth Fox-Genovese, *Within the Plantation Household*, 110.

134. Butterfield, *Letters of Benjamin Rush*, 1:441.

135. *Convention of Abolition Societies* (Philadelphia, 1794), 22 (Collection of Antislavery Pamphlets, John Carter Brown Library, Providence, R.I.).

136. George Buchanan, "Oration on Slavery," a verbatim copy separately bound and paginated in Poole, *Anti Slavery Opinion Before 1800*.

137. Ibid., 18; Winthrop Jordan, *White over Black*, 292.

138. Margaret Manigault to M. duPont, 24 Dec. 1790, Betty Bright-Low, "'Of Muslins and Merveilleuses': Excerpts from the Letters of Josephine du Pont (1770–1837) and Margaret Manigault (1768–1824)," *Winterthur Portfolio* 9 (1974): 29–75; see Kenneth Stampp, *The Peculiar Institution* (New York: A. A. Knopf, 1956), 135, for the Gabriel conspiracy in Henrico County.

139. See Stanley Kenneth Deaton, "Revolutionary Charleston, 1765–1800" (Ph.D. diss., University of Florida 1997), for the "intellectual blockade" erected against antislavery rhetoric after the Haitian revolution.

140. See *Columbian Magazine* 11 (Jan. 1792): 78; Tim Matthewson, "Jefferson and Haiti," *JSH* 61 (May 1995): 209–48, for cresting of antislavery opinion in 1791 and its sharp reversal the next year.

141. *The Providence Gazette*, 1 Sept. 1806, 16 (Rhode Island Historical Society, Reel 2122). A Charlestonian, then a child, recalled a benefit concert in January 1794 for the white refugees of this revolution. Fraser, *Reminiscences of Charleston*, 61.

142. *Columbian Magazine* 11 (Jan. 1792): 78; Philip D. Morgan, "Black Life in Eighteenth-Century Charleston," *Perspectives in American History*, n.s., 1 (1984): 187–222.

143. *Columbian Magazine* 11 (Feb. 1792): 147.

144. *Columbian Magazine* 11 (Mar. 1792): 179. Freetown in Sierra Leone was founded at this time by freed blacks from England (Gerzina, *Black London*, 171).

145. *Columbian Magazine* 11 (Mar. 1792): 179–80.

146. Edwards, "The Injustice," named the same fear in New England, though population ratios made it less probable there.

147. See *Columbian Magazine* 11 (Mar. 1792): 180; See *Yearbook of the City of Charleston, 1883*, 391–92, for the 1794 relief association and Charleston hospitality to French refugees; Thomas Petigru Lesesne, *Narrative and Biographical History of*

Charleston County, South Carolina (Charleston, S.C., 1931), 76, quoted David Ramsay's report of the refugee influx and the state legislature's vote of funds for the "unhappy sufferers from Saint Domingue"; Thomas O. Ott, *The Haitian Revolution, 1789–1804* (Knoxville: University of Tennessee Press, 1973), 52–55, quoted Gov. Charles S. Pinckney about fear of the same kind of insurrection in South Carolina and indicated that a chapter of the *Amis des Noirs* society might already have been founded in Charleston (54). Founded in 1781 by Condorcet, the *Amis des Noirs* supported the idea of making slaves into citizens (Laurent Dubois, "The Price of Liberty: Victor Hughes and the Administration of Freedom in Guadeloupe, 1794–1798," *WMQ*, 3d ser., 56 [Apr. 1999]: 363–92).

148. Fraser, *Charleston!*, 184.

149. Ramsay, *Memoirs*, 40.

150. Robert V. Remini, *Henry Clay: Statesman for the Union* (New York: Norton, 1991), 27; Herbert Aptheker, *Antiracism in U.S. History: The First 200 Years* (Westport, Conn.: Greenwood Press, 1992).

151. Dr. Benjamin Rush to Rev. Jeremy Belknap, 21 June 1792, Belknap Papers, 161.B.91, Massachusetts Historical Society, Boston; also printed in the Collections of the Massachusetts Historical Society, 6th ser., vol. 4, 527–29.

152. Ibid. See Emma Jones Lapsansky, "'Since They Got Those Separate Churches': Afro-Americans and Racism in Jacksonian Philadelphia," *AQ* 32 (spring 1980): 54–78, for white negative response to separate black institutions.

153. Tise, *Proslavery*, 201, argues that President Washington's national fast days in 1798 and 1799 signaled the end of revolutionary idealism, especially any hope that abolition could become a real political movement.

Chapter 8

1. Ramsay, *Memoirs*, iii. One-third of the diary's printed version is dated 1795.

2. Ramsay, *Memoirs*, 116, 102. I use this phrase for her psychic state as less anachronistic than a present-day psychological term such as *identity crisis;* Georgia Harkness, *The Dark Night of the Soul* (London: Andrew Melrose, 1944), the phrase originating from St. John of the Cross (1542–1591).

3. Ramsay, *Memoirs*, 111.

4. Doddridge, *Rise and Progress*.

5. Ramsay, *Memoirs*, vii, v, 165, 104.

6. See Ronald Paulson, *Representations of Revolution, 1789–1820* (New Haven: Yale University Press, 1983), for categorizing as "dark" everything that was considered unenlightened during the Enlightenment.

7. Ramsay, *Memoirs*, 104, 119, 147, 166; Dr. David Ramsay, Petition and Schedules of Insolvent Debt 1798, 16A, South Carolina Department of Archives and History, Columbia.

8. Ramsay, *Memoirs*, 193.

9. Ibid., 118.

10. Betsy Read, Charleston, to Betsy Ludlow, New York, 8 Dec. 1787, Jacob Read file, South Caroliniana Library, University of South Carolina, Columbia.

11. Ramsay, *Memoirs*, 124.

12. Ibid., 111.

13. Ruth Perry, introduction to *Memoirs of Several Ladies of Great Britain Who Have Been Celebrated for their Writings or Skill in the Learned Languages, Arts, and Sciences,* by George Ballard (1752; reprint, Detroit: Wayne State University Press, 1985), 29; Ramsay, *Memoirs,* 38 n.

14. See Brunhouse, *Ramsay,* 24, for a partial list of David's civic activities.

15. David had chosen the Independent Church (also called the Circular Church) in Charleston as the one least tainted by British heritage. He served on its board of trustees and published a *History of the Circular Church* (Charleston, S.C., 1814). Those clergy wrote the commendatory letters (Ramsay, *Memoirs,* iv–vii).

16. H. M. Bowdler, ed., *Fragments in Prose and Verse of Miss Elizabeth Smith,* 2 vols. (Bath, England, 1809), 228. Martha's obituary notice in the *Charleston Gazette* noted "a numerous and admiring acquaintance" and her knowledge of Latin and Greek (*SCHM* 36 [1935]: 136–37).

17. Ramsay, *Memoirs,* 111; Richardson, *Sentiments,* 112; Ramsay, *Memoirs,* 115.

18. Ramsay, *Memoirs,* 1 Mar. 1795, 113; 3 July 1795, 124; 3 Jan. 1796, 135; DR to John Eliot, 24 June 1795, carries a cryptic reference to Martha's depression amid his envy of the New England public school system (Proceedings, 1864–65, Massachusetts Historical Society, Boston).

19. Richard Price to Thomas Jefferson, 24 Oct. 1785, Boyd, *Papers of Thomas Jefferson,* 8:667–68.

20. Ibid., 8:163; Wallace, *Henry Laurens,* 451–52.

21. Ramsay, *Memoirs,* 99; Dye and Smith, "Mother Love and Infant Death," 329–53.

22. Hymns appended to Doddridge's *Rise and Progress* attributed to Dobell.

23. Doddridge, *Rise and Progress,* 241; Morey, "In Memory of Cassie," 87–104.

24. Ramsay, *Memoirs,* 100, 105; Jan Lewis, *The Pursuit of Happiness: Family and Values in Jefferson's Virginia* (New York: Cambridge University Press, 1983), 60.

25. Ramsay, *Memoirs,* 107, 109, 112 (emphasis added); Doddridge, *Rise and Progress,* 229.

26. Ramsay, *Memoirs,* 99, 105, 106.

27. Richardson, *Sentiments,* 73; Ramsay, *Memoirs,* 57.

28. Hamer, *Papers of Henry Laurens,* 4:295.

29. Ramsay, *Memoirs,* 146.

30. Johnson, *Traditions and Reminiscences,* 326.

31. Ramsay, *Memoirs,* 106.

32. Ibid., 41 n. The "unpropitious events [and] perplexing embarrassments" of their finances are addressed in a large editorial footnote.

33. Brunhouse, *Ramsay,* 136. In 1785 eighteen men formed the company to connect the Santee and Cooper Rivers for shipping goods through Charleston

from the upland region. In 1792 it reorganized and Ramsay became president. The *Charleston Daily Gazette and Advertiser,* 14 Nov. 1795, announced a Santee Canal lottery as an emergency fund-raiser.

34. DR to John Kean, 10 July 1794, David Ramsay, Letters, South Caroliniana Library, University of South Carolina, Columbia.

35. Robert L. Brunhouse, "David Ramsay's Publication Problems, 1784–1808," *Papers of the Bibliographical Society of America* 39 (1945): 51–67.

36. Ramsay, *Memoirs,* 127; Marylynn Salmon, "Women and Property in South Carolina: The Evidence from Marriage Settlements, 1730–1830," *WMQ* 39 (Oct. 1982): 655–85, on real estate as women's single note of power in a marriage settlement; Martha Laurens Ramsay, Renunciations of Dower, BIAE 017, District Court of Common Pleas, 1775–1887, Charleston County, South Carolina State Department of Archives and History, Columbia.

37. John Demos, *Past, Present and Personal: The Family and the Life Course in American History* (New York: Oxford University Press, 1986), quoting Anne Bradstreet's "The Four Ages of Man," 126.

38. John's child was baptized Frances Eleanor Laurens on 18 Feb. 1777 in St. Andrew's Undershaft, Register of Baptisms, 1771–1812, Guildhall Library, London. Hamer, *Papers of Henry Laurens,* 11:277 n.

39. "Mrs. Ramsay is . . . anxiously waiting for the publications of your lectures *[Thoughts upon Female Education] . . .* as she has charged herself with the education of a daughter the only child of her brother John Laurens" (DR to Benjamin Rush, 29 Sept. 1788, Brunhouse, *Ramsay,* 122–23).

40. A mid-nineteenth-century lawsuit against Fanny's inheritance from her grandfather Henry Laurens documents the short-lived marriage, the child it produced, and Fanny's divorce, remarriage, and death (*John Laurens et al. v. William C. Gatewood,* 1861, In Equity: Charleston District, Charleston, S. C.).

41. Joseph J. Ellis, *After the Revolution: Profiles of Early American Culture* (New York: W. W. Norton & Co., 1979), 38, on the "premodern" personality that survived the postrevolution upheavals.

42. Carol Ochs, *Women and Spirituality* (Lanham, Md.: Rowan and Littlefield Publishers, 1983), 10.

43. Ramsay, *Memoirs,* 114–15; David Jr.'s christening was not recorded. "Register of the Independent Congregational (Circular) Church of Charleston, S.C., 1784–1815," *SCHM* 33 (1932): 169.

44. Ramsay, *Memoirs,* 113, 114, 115.

45. Ibid., 115, 116, 117, 118, 120. Emphasis added.

46. Ibid., 118, 119, 124.

47. Gunn, *Autobiography.*

48. Ramsay, *Memoirs,* 121, 122.

49. Ibid., 124, 132. Emphasis added.

50. Ibid., 132–33; Brunhouse, *Ramsay,* 142 n. 2. The fossils were later sent to his brother-in-law's Peale's Museum in Philadelphia.

51. John Flavel, *A Saint Indeed* (London, 1673), later reissued as *On Keeping the Heart*. This version in Flavel's *Complete Works* 2 (London, 1691), 737–59.

52. Ramsay, *Memoirs*, 32–36 n. Emphasis added.

53. Flavel, 2:737, 738.

54. Ramsay, *Memoir*, 35–36 n.

55. Ibid., 133.

56. "Reminiscences of Abbeville (S.C.) by an ex-Abbevillian of Over Forty Years: Notable Persons—Marriage and Divorce in High Life/The Last Man Who Lost His Life in the Revolution" (unsigned), *Abbeville (S.C.) Press and Banner*, 19 Apr. 1876.

57. Richardson, *Pamela*, 2:62.

58. Ramsay, *Memoirs*, 58.

59. Ibid., 133. In 1798 DR petitioned for bankruptcy, and in 1803 her only surviving brother, Henry Laurens Jr., sued David for £94,205.40, the full amount of bonds owed him. Charleston District Judgement Rolls 1802, 413A, In Equity: *John Laurens et al. v. William C. Gatewood* (Charleston, S.C., 1861), Petition and Schedules of Insolvent Debt, 1798, 16A, for David Ramsay; 1803, *Henry Laurens Jr. v. David Ramsay*, South Carolina State Department of Archives and History, Columbia.

60. Ramsay, *Memoirs*, 126.

61. Ibid., 133–34.

62. DR to MLR, Brunhouse, *Ramsay*, 17 Dec. 1795, 142–43.

63. Ramsay, *Memoirs*, 135–36.

64. Ibid., 136.

65. Ibid., 136, 143, 187.

66. Ibid., 137.

67. Sonia Krause, unpublished diary no. 11 (10 Apr. 1832), cited in Barbara Wright, *"Pilgrim in Bethlehem: American Moravian Piety and the Identity Formation of a Nineteenth Century Woman"* (Ph.D. diss., Drew Theological Seminary, 1989); see also "Female Biography, the Life and Character of Twelve American Women" (unsigned), *American Sunday School Union Magazine* (1830): 49–50, naming *Memoirs of the Life of Martha Laurens Ramsay* "outstanding."

Chapter 9

1. Ramsay, *Memoirs*, 199–219, appendix 6, 199. "Extracts from Letters Written by Mrs. Ramsay, to her Son at Princeton College." An editor's note justifies including these "private confidential domestic letters" as useful "cautions to youth" and "models for parents corresponding with their absent sons." Their recipient, David Jr., had indeed "pursued knowledge and virtue" and assented to their publication in the *Memoirs*. Other parental-advice letters to collegiate children is in correspondence between Abigail Adam and her sisters (thanks to Edith Gelles). Robert Manson Myers, ed., *The Children of Pride* (New Haven: Yale University Press, 1972), preserves mid-nineteenth-century letters between a southern college boy and his parents.

2. Ramsay, *Memoirs*, 199, 200.

3. Ibid., 199 n. Dr. Ramsay's son by his second marriage, John Witherspoon Ramsay, a Princeton graduate in 1782, also received "many of the same kind" of letters from his stepmother, Martha, which were lost when the college burned that year.

4. Ibid., 201, 204.

5. See Fliegelman, *Prodigals and Pilgrims*, for filiopietism (267), the Lockean moment of independence, and parental grief as the new moral stop sign in novels (260). Geertz, "The Pinch of Destiny."

6. Ramsay, *Memoirs*, 203.

7. Mavis Gallant, review of Robert Darnton's *The Great Cat Massacre* (1985) in *New York Review of Books*, 12 Feb. 1984, 12, cites his phrase "epistemological exhilaration" for the mindset associated with the Revolutionary War experience, applicable to Dr. David Ramsay's rhetorical style. See Knapp, *American Cultural History*, for Dr. Ramsay as the progenitor of Fourth of July orations in 1778 and as being "well known to every child in the United States as a politician and historian" (104); Shaffer, *To Be an American*.

8. Ramsay, *The History of the American Revolution*, 2 vols. (Philadelphia, 1789), 2:316.

9. Shaffer, *To Be an American*, 4, 90.

10. If David Ramsay had been wealthy, Brown University in Providence, Rhode Island, might be named Ramsay University. A 1795 letter from the president of the College of Rhode Island suggested that the school would be honored to take the name of "Dr. Ramsay, a great patron of literature," if he could also provide the appropriate financial underpinnings. Manuscript Collection, file I-E, South Carolina Influence of Rhode Island College, John Hay Library, Brown University, Providence.

11. One other Southerner, Henry Middleton, was president of the Continental Congress for five days in October 1774.

12. Enos Hitchcock, *The Farmer's Friend; or the History of Mr. Charles Worthy* (Boston, 1793), 15, captured the social basis of self-esteem in a maxim about "the esteem of others": "to enjoy [it] is desirable, but to deserve it MUST GIVE exquisite pleasure." Abigail Adams also located individuals within larger circles—"families compose communities and individuals make up the sum total" (Abigail Adams to John Thaxter, 15 Feb. 1778, L. H. Butterfield et al., eds., *Adams Family Correspondence* (Cambridge, Mass.: Belknap Press of Harvard University Press, 1961), 2:391–92.

13. Ramsay, *Memoirs*, 22; Margaret W. Miles, *Practicing Christianity: Critical Perspectives for an Embodied Spirituality* (New York: Crossroads Publishing, 1988), 1.

14. Alexis de Tocqueville, *Democracy in America*, ed. J. P. Mayer (Garden City, N.Y.: Doubleday, 1969), 287; Bloch, "The Gendered Meaning of Virtue," 54. The phrase "habits of the heart" meant automatic patterns of response in family, religion, and political situations.

15. Linda Kerber, "History Can Do It No Justice: Women and the Reinterpretation of the American Revolution," in *Women in the Age of the American Revolution,* ed. Ronald Hoffman and Peter J. Albert (Charlottesville: University Press of Virginia, 1989), 3–42. Ramsay, *Memoirs,* 25. Dr. James Tilton's oration in *Universal Asylum and Columbian Magazine* 5 (Dec. 1790): 369–73 equating women's "citizenship" with legislative efforts; Bloch, "Gendered Meaning of Virtue," 54.

16. Ramsay, *Memoirs,* 47–54, letters from Henry Laurens to Martha Laurens, 1771–1776; Martha's first diary was burned in the 1770s lest it fall into the wrong hands during ocean crossings (14).

17. Ibid., 217.

18. Ramsay, *Memoirs,* 214; see Randolph Shipley Klein, *Portrait of an Early American Family: The Shippens of Pennsylvania across Five Generations* (Philadelphia: University of Pennsylvania Press, 1975), for similar financial disadvantage afflicting a similarly large family.

19. Ramsay, *Memoirs,* 41 n, 133; Brunhouse, *Ramsay,* 25; Petitions and Schedules of Insolvent Debt of 1798 (16A), and Charleston District Judgment Rolls 1801 (413A).

20. Ramsay, *Memoirs,* 205. Under the cloud of Ramsay penury, none of the daughters married but all kept school, cared for nieces and nephews, and were generous to family slaves.

21. *The Hapless Orphan; or Innocent Victim of Revenge: A Novel Founded on Incidents in Real Life,* 2 vols. (Boston, 1793), 2:39; Brunhouse, *Ramsay,* 138; Ramsay, *Memoirs,* 205.

22. Ibid., 200.

23. See Thomas Jefferson Wertenbaker, *Princeton 1746–1896* (Princeton: Princeton University Press, 1946), 136, for "jacobinic" tendencies; John Maclean, *The History of the College of New Jersey,* 2 vols. (Princeton: Princeton University, 1877), 2:15, 72.

24. Wertenbaker, *Princeton,* 136–37, 139.

25. Ibid., 136–37, 139, 141, 142.

26. Frederick Beasley, "Life of Dr. Smith," in *Sermons of Samuel Stanhope Smith: Life and Writings,* 2 vols. (Philadelphia, 1821), 1:50–51. The author of President Smith's *Life* was identified in Maclean's *History of the College of New Jersey,* 122.

27. Wertenbaker, *Princeton,* 143; Review of Enos Hitchcock's *Memoirs of the Bloomsgrove Family* (Boston, 1790) quoted in *Columbian Magazine* 5 (July 1790): 48.

28. Hitchcock, *Memoirs,* 48; Beasley, *Life of Dr. Smith,* 1:51.

29. *Columbian Magazine* 3 (September 1789): 553–54; David Paul Nord, "A Republican Literature: Magazine Reading and Readers in Late Eighteenth Century New York," 114–39, in *Reading in America: Literature and Social History,* ed. Cathy N. Davidson (Baltimore: Johns Hopkins University Press, 1989).

30. Wertenbaker, *Princeton,* 134, cites an 1804 Princeton student's schedule. "At six o'clock the bell rouses us to morning prayers. From this till breakfast, which is always at half past seven, I study the recitation. The time between breakfast and

nine I spend in conversation or reading. At nine the bell rings for the students to retire to their rooms, except the two lower classes which must attend in the recitation room where they are confined till twelve. From this till dinner at one I read. At two we go again to recitation and stay till five, when the bell rings for evening prayers. From this till supper at six I study or read, and also from supper till seven. Between seven and eight I take a walk and from eight to ten I read. At nine the tutor visits the rooms to see that all the students are in." Juniors at the College had scheduled time for recreation or letting off steam.

31. Ramsay, *Memoirs*, 210–12.

32. Maclean, *History of the College of New Jersey*, 15.

33. David Ramsay, *The History of the Independent or Congregational Church in Charleston* (Philadelphia, 1815). Wertenbaker, *Princeton*, 95; Rev. William Hollinshead's "The Gospel Preached to Every Creature," a sermon given on 21 Mar. 1798 in Charleston, cautioned against "reason" without "religion" that characterized the French Revolution: "a whole nation, dissolving the bands of religion . . . enthusiasts for liberty and equally enthusiasts for impiety," Box 3, 15, John Carter Brown Library, Providence, R.I.

34. Ramsay, *Memoirs*, 202; also Ramsay, "A Review of the Improvements, Progress, and State of Medicine in the XVIIIth Century," 1801, in Brunhouse, *Ramsay*, 196–217; Shaffer, *To Be an American*, Ramsay's honorary degree from Yale in 1803 (93); Wertenbaker, *Princeton*, 125; and Samuel Stanhope Smith to DR, 29 Sept. 1805, Brunhouse, *Ramsay*, 158. When fossils were found by the Santee Canal Company during the time he served as president, David Sr.'s loyalties were divided: he was related to the Peale "cabinet" (incipient museum) through his brother Nathaniel's marriage to Peale's sister, yet his own second wife had been the sister of Samuel Stanhope Smith's wife. He eventually sent them to Peale because the Princeton "cabinet" was not yet established. Brunhouse, *Ramsay*, 142 n. 2.

35. Ramsay, *Memoirs*, 202.

36. Ibid., 207; *Columbian Magazine* 3 (June 1789): 742; Ramsay, *Memoirs*, 207; see Nelson W. Aldrich, *Old Money: The Mythology of America's Upper Class* (New York: Vintage Books, 1989), 192, for twentieth-century dynastic wishes: the mother of Ned McLean, whose family owned the *Washington Post* in 1916, "wanted [her son] to have the admiration and acclaim that go with greatness. I wanted him to rule his father's fortune . . . and above all else I wanted our sons to be fit to play and work with the leaders of the nation."

37. DR to BR, 1 May 1787, Brunhouse, *Ramsay*, 112: "I long to see the day when an author will at least be on an equal footing with a taylor or shoemaker in getting his living"; Ramsay quoted in Review, *Columbian Magazine* 5 (July 1790): 43; David Ramsay, *The Life of George Washington* (New York, 1807).

38. Ramsay, *Memoirs*, 208, 207.

39. *Columbian Magazine* 3 (June 1789): 344; 1 (Oct. 1787): 698–702, essay welcoming all immigrants *except* the indolent. Ramsay, *Memoirs*, 27, 209, wasted opportunities and time; Warner, *The Letters of the Republic*. Richard D. Brown,

Knowledge Is Power: The Diffusion of Information in Early America, 1700–1865 (New York: Oxford University Press, 1989).

40. Ramsay, *Memoirs*, 209.

41. Ibid., 209–210.

42. See *Columbian Magazine* 3 (July 1789): 438 for image; Ramsay, *Memoirs*, 210–211.

43. Ibid., 213.

44. Ibid., 214, 215.

45. Maclean, *History of the College of New Jersey*, 2:66; Ramsay, *Memoirs*, 216, 217.

46. Maclean, *History of the College of New Jersey*, 41; Ramsay, *Memoirs*, 217.

47. Anonymous, *Hapless Orphan*, 2, 99.

48. Ramsay, *Memoirs*, 217. During Martha's youth, Charleston was "more European in its manners than any [city] in America," and French journalist Chastellux noted that "strangers abound [there] as at Marseilles and Amsterdam." *Columbian Magazine* 1 (June 1787): 478.

49. Ramsay, *Memoirs*, 217; 202, youths spoiling Princeton; 200, Carolinian indolence. Jonathan Edwards, *An Account of the Life of David Brainerd, 1718–1747, Chiefly Taken from His Own Diary and Other Private Writings* (Boston, 1755); Ramsay, *History of South Carolina*, 205–6, laudatory description of Waddel's school, curriculum, and physical context 190 miles distant from the "dissipations" of the city.

50. Ramsay, *Memoirs*, 218.

51. Review, *Columbian Magazine* 5 (Aug. 1790): 116.

52. Ramsay, *Memoirs*, 39.

53. Ibid., 21, 28 n.

54. Adrienne Rich, *Of Woman Born*, 1.

55. Shaffer, *To Be an American*, 173, 286 n. 30; 298 n. 4.

56. Daughter Martha Henry Laurens Ramsay raised and "highly educated" her great-niece Frances, the granddaughter of Martha's sister Frances Eleanor Pinckney, who had died in 1793. Another of Martha's daughters, Sabina Eliott Ramsay, made a pet of the other Pinckney niece, Mary Eleanor Pinckney Ramsay, who lived until 1841. (Mary Eleanor later became the second wife of Henry Laurens Pinckney, 1794–1863, the son of Martha's sister.) One of the misses Ramsay's pupils, Mary Palmer Shindler Dana (identified as a poet and hymnist in *Female Prose Writers in America*, 1852), paid tribute in 1840 to her "beloved teachers" Martha Jr. and Sabina as they mourned the death of David Ramsay Jr.'s wife (also his first cousin), who was also their beloved niece Mary Eleanor Laurens Pinckney. Mary Palmer Shindler Dana, *The Parted Family and Other Poems: An Offering to the Afflicted, and a Tribute of Love to Departed Friends* (New York: Dayton and Saxton, 1842), 206–7.

An interesting newspaper item from the *Carolina Gazette* reported that Martha H. L. Ramsay hosted the wedding of slave Charlotte, 9 October 1834, to

Jack, slave of Mrs. Campbell, in the Ramsay house on Broad St., "in the presence and consent of their owners" (*SCHM* 58 [1957]: 175).

An impression of the three Ramsay daughters (and their brother James and his wife, from Philadelphia, where he was studying medicine at the time) in the 1828 journal of Rev. Abiel Abbott praised their elevated conversation. "It was soon evident from what pedigree their minds sprang & under whose . . . tuition they had risen from infancy . . . [they used] a remarkable precision of thought & expression and manner," speaking in such "measured" prose as already "fit to be in type." He saw a "degree of formality" in them that might exert a little "chill on the flow of mind and soul," which he explained by their consciousness of being "regarded as models" by their pupils—and "that they are the offspring of illustrious ancestors & parents whose names are embalmed in the national history & their lives & writings & piety preserved among the choicest treasure of American biography." Their maternal grandsire's portrait was itself "indicative of the powerful mind & sterling integrity of Henry Lawrence [*sic*]," and their own father's portrait "a good painting . . . even said to be a flattering likeness," though in it the Rev. Abbott could not discern the "benignity" that he had anticipated seeing on Dr. Ramsay's countenance, from the time when Ramsay gave "his casting vote for the abolition of slavery." Abbott predicted that the "powerful & cultivated intellect" of the Ramsay children, because of their distinguished lines of inheritance, would provide him with rich, enjoyable social exchange (John Hammond Moore, ed., "The Abiel Abbott Journals," *SCHM* 68 [1967]: 65–66).

57. Robert Y. Hayne to Jedediah Morse, 25 May 1815, Jedediah Morse Papers, Box 3, Manuscripts and Archives Division, New York Public Library. Hayne became the executor of the Ramsay estate, valiantly attempting to sell DR's *History of the United States.* On 19 June 1812, Dr. Ramsay himself had written Morse that a third copy [edition] of Martha's *Memoirs* was now in "half binding," that his son David Jr. would be visiting the Morse family in Boston after graduating from the College of New Jersey in September, and that his daughters spent an hour and three-quarters hand coloring the maps and charts in each copy of his *History,* which were not selling well due to the economy and the war (Morse Papers, Box 2).

Chapter 10

1. The phrase quoted in the chapter title is from Ramsay, *Memoirs,* 43.

2. Mary Wollstonecraft, *Mary, a Fiction* (1788; reprint, New York: Schocken Books, 1977), 96.

3. Many of her documented readings made Providence a central theme; e.g., Flavel, *Complete Works;* Watt, *Divine and Moral Songs for Children;* Allestree, *The Whole Duty of Man;* Taylor, *Holy Living and Holy Dying;* and Law, *Serious Call to a Devout and Holy Life.*

4. Wollstonecraft, *Mary,* 19.

5. David Ramsay, *An Oration on the Cession of Louisiana to the United States* (Charleston, S.C.: W. P. Young, 1804), 19; John F. Berens, *Providence and Patriotism in Early America, 1640–1815* (Charlottesville: University of Virginia Press, 1978), 102, quoting "Oration for Delivery to the Inhabitants of Charleston," 1788, by David Ramsay.

6. Increase Mather, *An Essay for the Recording of Illustrious Providences*, 1684 (Delmar, N.Y.: Scholars Facsimiles & Reprints, 1977).

7. Patricia U. Bonomi, *Under the Cope of Heaven: Religion, Society, and Politics in Colonial America* (New York: Oxford Press, 1986).

8. Edwin S. Gaustad, *The Religious History of America* (San Francisco: Harper Collins, 1990).

9. Fliegelman, *Prodigals and Pilgrims.*

10. Ramsay, *History of South Carolina*, 2:204; The Female Charitable Association file, Rhode Island Historical Society, Providence.

11. See Jane H. Pease and William H. Pease, "Blood Thirsty Tigre: Charleston and the Psychology of Fire," *SCHM* 78 (1978): 281–95, for the role of slaves—"feared incendiaries" or "valued fire fighters"—in early Charleston fires. A slave, Will, owned by Maj. Charles Lining, was awarded his freedom for helping save Saint Philip's Church during the fire of 1796.

12. Ramsay, *Memoirs*, 166.

13. Ibid., 107.

14. Ibid., 109.

15. Ibid., 110; Charles Drelincourt, *The Christian's Defence against the Fears of Death, with Directions How to Dye Well* (Boston, 1744), 40; Ramsay, *Memoirs*, 43.

16. Ramsay, *Memoirs*, 157.

17. Ibid., 112; Stebbing, "Discourse Concerning the Governing Providence," 2–4.

18. Mossner, *Bishop Butler*, xiv.

19. Ramsay, *Memoirs*, 139, 142.

20. Ibid., 140; Wood, *American Republic*, 118.

21. Ramsay, *Memoirs*, 144, 145; Petition and Schedules of Insolvent Debt 1798 16A, David Ramsay, Charleston Court Records.

22. Michael E. Stevens, "The Vigilant Fire Company of Charleston," *SCHM* 87 (Apr. 1986): 130–35; Dr. Ramsay was president in 1791. *Providence Gazette*, 1 Sept. 1804, 41, Rhode Island Historical Society.

23. Ramsay, *Memoirs*, 148.

24. Lindley Murray, a Quaker born in New York who lived and wrote in England, produced eleven highly popular textbooks, which Martha prized; she chose his *English Reader* and *Grammar* for her children because "its pages were rendered subservient to piety and virtue." Review, *Panoplist* 1 (June 1807): 42; Charlotte Downey, "A Children's Text of the Eighteenth and Nineteenth Centuries: Abridgement of Murray's *English Grammar*," *Children's Literature Association Quarterly* 10 (fall 1985): 131–32.

25. Murray, *The Power of Religion on the Mind,* 11th ed. (York, England, 1802), 232–36.

26. Ibid., 235, for abolition energy; 236, funeral procession.

27. Ramsay, *Memoirs,* 41.

28. Ibid., 42.

29. Ibid., 43.

30. Ibid., 43–44.

31. Ibid., 42, 45.

32. Drelincourt, *The Christian's Defence,* 38, 91, 118.

33. Ramsay, *Memoirs,* 46.

34. Drelincourt, *The Christian's Defence,* 108.

35. Ramsay, *Memoirs,* 46.

36. Drelincourt,. *The Christian's Defence,* 45.

37. Pennington, *Memoirs of the Life of Mrs. Elizabeth Carter.*

38. Drelincourt, *The Christian's Defence,* 38.

39. Ramsay, *Memoirs,* 47; early vow, 83.

40. Ibid., 42, 43. Martha's dying remembrance may have echoed the perspective of her mentor Doddridge, who said of the countess, "I think I never saw so much of the image of God in any woman upon earth." Quoted in Barbeau, *Life and Letters at Bath,* 161 n. 3.

41. Ibid., *Memoirs,* iii.

42. Ibid., v, vi; James T. Kloppenberg, "The Virtue of Liberalism: Christianity, Republicanism, and Ethics in Early American Political Discourse," *JAH* 74 (June 1987): 9–33.

43. See Brunhouse, *Ramsay,* 229, for the publication history of *Memoirs.* A fourth edition was printed in 1814, in the 1820s, the 1840s, and the final one in 1895.

44. DR to James Rush, 5 May 1813, Brunhouse, *Ramsay,* 175.

45. *Portfolio,* 3d ser., 2 (1813): 587–99. *The Portfolio,* 1801–1827, edited by Joseph Dennie, believed itself a literary standard setter (Michael Gilmore, "The Literature of the Revolution and Early National Period," in *The Cambridge History of American Literature,* ed. Sacvan Bercovitch, 541–676 [New York: Cambridge University Press, 1994], 1:558, 660). Excerpts from Martha's letters to her son were reprinted in Sarah Josepha Hale's *Woman's Record: Sketches of All Distinguished Women . . . in Four Eras* (New York: Harper & Brothers, 1853): 484–86.

At least one female Charleston contemporary, reading *Memoirs* in 1812, speculated uncharitably in a family letter that Martha's "easily besetting sin" might well include secret despair over her husband's looks, since in this woman's view Dr. Ramsay's public appearance (blind in one eye and thinning hair) made him "one of the horridest looking objects in nature." The same person also noted acidly that "delicacy" and restraint in expressing her opinions were not Mrs. Ramsay's most obvious characteristics (Margaret Izard Manigault to Alice Izard, 5 Jan. 1812). Nevertheless, an earlier letter from the same neighbor reported that Dr. Ramsay's book about his wife was generally being well received and that at least some readers expressed admiration for Martha Ramsay's "piety and goodness." Although Margaret Manigault disapproved of Dr. Ramsay's public discussion of usually private matters such as family troubles, finances, and personal religious practices, she urged her collegiate son Charles to buy a copy of *Memoirs* and read carefully Martha's sound recommendations to son David Jr. (Margaret Manigault to Charles Manigault, 5 Jan. 1812, Manigault Papers, Box 6, South Caroliniana Library, University of South Carolina, Columbia).

46. Mossner, *Bishop Butler,* 236, paraphrased.

47. HL to Martha, 17 Aug. 1776, Hamer, *Papers of Henry Laurens,* 11:255.

Bibliography

Unpublished Manuscripts

Adams Papers. Letters and Other Loose Papers, June–Dec. 1781. Microfilm 355, Adams Manuscript Trust. Massachusetts Historical Society, Boston.

Belknap, Jeremy. Papers. Massachusetts Historical Society, Boston.

Charleston County District Court of Common Pleas, 1775–1887. Renunciations of Dower. BIAE 017. MLR. South Carolina State Department of Archives and History, Columbia.

Charleston District Judgement Rolls 1802, 413A. Petition for Benefit of Insolvent Debtors. Filed 11 May 1798. South Carolina State Department of Archives and History, Columbia.

Charleston District Judgement Rolls 1802, 413A. In Equity: *John Laurens et al. v. William C. Gatewood* (Charleston, S.C., 1861). Petition and Schedules of Insolvent Debt, 1798, 16A, for David Ramsay; 1803, *Henry Laurens Jr. v. David Ramsay.* South Carolina State Department of Archives and History, Columbia.

Circular Church. File 30–04. South Carolina Historical Society, Charleston.

Cleland, Ann. Commonplace Book, 1785. South Carolina Historical Society, Charleston.

Manigault Family Papers. South Caroliniana Library, University of South Carolina, Columbia.

Morse, Jedediah. Papers. New York Public Library, New York.

Read, Jacob. Read File. South Caroliniana Library, University of South Carolina, Columbia.

"South Carolina Influence of Rhode Island College." MS File I-E, John Hay Library, Brown University, Providence, R.I.

Stevens, John. Diary and Letterbooks, 1808–41. Henry Francis du Pont Winterthur Museum, Winterthur, Del.

Newspapers

Abbeville (S.C.) Press and Banner
Baltimore Weekly
Boston, Massachusetts, Centinel Extraordinary
Charleston Carolina Gazette
Charleston City Gazette
Charleston City Gazette and Advertiser
Charleston Daily Gazette and Advertiser

National Intelligencer and Washington Advertiser
New York Magazine or Literary Repository
Providence Gazette
Providence Phoenix

Contemporary Publications, Published Documents, Memoirs

An American Lady. *The Hapless Orphan; or Innocent Victim of Revenge: A Novel Founded on Incidents in Real Life.* 2 vols. Boston: Apollo Press, 1793. John Hay Library, Brown University, Providence, R.I.Andrews-Eliot Correspondence, 1715–1814. *Proceedings, 1864–65.* Vol. 81. Massachusetts Historical Society, Boston.

Axtell, James, ed. "Some Thoughts on Education." In *The Educational Writings of John Locke.* New York: Cambridge University Press, 1968.

Ballard, George. *Memoirs of Several Ladies of Great Britain Who Have Been Celebrated for Their Writings or Skill in the Learned Languages, Arts, and Sciences.* 1752. Detroit: Wayne State University Press, 1985.

Barbeau, Alfred. *Life and Letters at Bath in the Eighteenth Century.* London: William Heinemann, 1904.

Barlow, Joel. "Vision of Columbus." Excerpted in *Columbian Magazine* 2 (Jan. 1788): 47.

Barry, Richard. *Mr. Rutledge of South Carolina.* New York: Duell, Sloan & Pearce, 1942.

Batson, Whaley. "Thomas Coram, Charleston Artist." *Journal of Early Southern Decorative Arts* 1 (Nov. 1975), 38.

Belknap, Jeremy. *American Biography.* Boston, 1794.

Beasley, Frederick. "Life of Dr. Smith." In *Sermons of Samuel Stanhope Smith, Life and Writings.* 2 vols. Philadelphia, 1821.

Benezet, Anthony. "Thoughts on Slavery." In *Collection of Religious Tracts,* ed. Anthony Benezet. Philadelphia, 1778.

Boswell, James. *Journal of a Tour to the Hebrides with Samuel Johnson.* London, 1746.

Bowdler, H. M., ed. *Fragments in Prose and Verse of Miss Elizabeth Smith.* 2 vols. Bath, 1809.

Boyd, Julian Parks, et al., eds. *Papers of Thomas Jefferson.* Vol. 8. Princeton: Princeton University Press, 1953.

Boyle, Joseph Lee, ed. "The Revolutionary War Diaries of Captain Walter Finney." *South Carolina Historical Magazine* 98 (Apr. 1997): 126–52.

Bright-Low, Betty. "Of Muslins and Merveilleuses: Excerpts from the Letters of Josephine du Pont (1770–1837) and Margaret Manigault (1768–1824)." *Winterthur Portfolio* 9 (1974): 29–75.

Buchanan, George. "Oration on Slavery." In *Anti Slavery Opinion Before 1800,* ed. William Frederick Poole. 1873. Westport, Conn.: Negro University Press, 1970.

Burder, Samuel, ed. *Memoirs of Eminently Pious Women.* 1777. Philadelphia, 1835.

Burkitt, William. *An Help and Guide to Christian Families.* 33d ed. London: J. Rivington et al., 1767.

Butterfield, L. H., ed. *John Witherspoon Comes to America.* Princeton: Princeton Library, 1953.

Butterfield, Lyman Henry, et al., eds. *Adams Family Correspondence.* Vol. 2. 1961. Cambridge, Mass.: Belknap Press of Harvard University Press.

———. *Letters of Benjamin Rush.* 2 vols. Philadelphia: American Philosophical Society, and Princeton, N.J.: Princeton University Press, 1951.

Brunhouse, Robert L., ed. *David Ramsay, 1749–1815: Selections from His Writings.* Philadelphia: American Philosophical Society, 1965.

Clarkson, Thomas. *Essay on the Slavery and Commerce of the Human Species, Particularly the African.* London: University of Cambridge, 1785.

Convention of Abolition Societies. Philadelphia, 1794. In Antislavery Pamphlets Collection, John Carter Brown Library, Providence, R.I.

Cotton, Charles Caleb. "The Letters of Caleb Cotton, 1798–1802." *South Carolina Historical Magazine* 51 (July 1950): 17–25; (Oct. 1950): 132–44; 52 (Jan. 1951): 217–88.

Crane, Elaine Forman, ed. *The Diary of Elizabeth Drinker, 1734–1807.* Boston: Northeastern University Press, 1994.

d'Auborn [John McGowan]. *The French Convert, or A True Relation of the Happy Conversion of a Noble French Woman from the Errors and Superstitions of Popery to the Reformed Religion by Means of a Protestant Gardener, Her Servant.* Haverill, Mass., 1794.

d'Auvigny, Jean duCastre. *The Memoirs of Madame de Barneveldt.* 1796.

Davis, Matthew L., ed. *Memoirs of Aaron Burr.* 2 vols. New York: Da Capo Press, 1971.

de Tocqueville, Alexis. *Democracy in America.* Ed. J. P. Mayer. Garden City, N.Y.: Doubleday, 1969.

De Wolfe, Barbara. "Discoveries of America: Letters of British Emigrants to America, on the Eve of the Revolution." In *Perspectives in American History,* n.s., 1 (1984): 1–80.

Doctrina et Amicitia. 2 vols. Boston: Massachusetts Historical Society, 1864–65.

Doddridge, Philip. *The Rise and Progress of Religion in the Soul.* 1744. Philadelphia, 1810.

Donnan, Elizabeth. *Documents Illustrative of the History of the Slave Trade to America.* 4 vols. Washington, D.C.: Carnegie Institute of Washington, 1930–1935.

Drake, Francis S. *Memorials of the Society of the Cincinnati of Massachusetts* [Odijah Baylies], Boston, 1873.

Drelincourt, Charles. *The Christian's Defence against the Fears of Death. With Directions How to Dye Well.* Boston, 1744.

Edwards, Jonathan. *An Account of the Life of David Brainerd, 1718–1747, Chiefly Taken from His Own Diary and Other Private Writings.* Boston, 1755.

Edwards, Jonathan, Jr. "The Injustice and Impolicy of the Slave Trade and the Slavery of the Africans." Sermon preached at the Annual Meeting of the Connecticut Society for Promotion of Freedom and Relief of Persons Unlawfully Holden in Bondage, 17 Sept. 1791. Antislavery Pamphlets Collection, John Carter Brown Library, Providence, R.I.

"Essay on Women's Education." *American Periodical Guide* 1 (1 Apr. 1801): 241–42.

"Female Biography, the Life and Character of Twelve American Women." *American Sunday School Union Magazine* 7 (1830): 49–50.

Fenelon, Archbishop François de Salignac. *Spiritual Letters to Women.* London: Longmans, Green & Co., 1921.

Flavel, John. *A Saint Indeed.* 1673. Reprinted as *On Keeping the Heart* in *Complete Works,* ed. John Flavel. London, 1691, 2:737–59.

Ford, Timothy. "Diary of Timothy Ford, 1785–86." *South Carolina Historical and Genealogical Magazine* 13 (July 1912): 130–47; (Oct. 1912): 181–204.

Fraser, Charles. *Reminiscences of Charleston.* 1854. Charleston: South Carolina Historical Society, 1969.

Gardiner, John S. J. *Sermon for the African Society, 14 July 1810.* Boston: Munroe & Francis, 1810. In African Societies folder, Massachusetts Historical Society, Boston.

Gilman, Caroline, ed. *Letters of Eliza Wilkinson, Written 1776–1782.* New York: Samuel Colman, 1839.

Hale, Sarah Josepha. *Woman's Record; or Sketches of All Distinguished Women from "The Beginning" till* A.D. 1850. New York: Harper & Brothers, 1853.

Hamer, Philip M., George C. Rogers Jr., David R. Chesnutt, C. James Taylor, Peggy J. Clark, eds. *Papers of Henry Laurens.* 15 vols. to date. Columbia: University of South Carolina Press, 1968– .

Hennen, Sarah Jane, ed. *Sentiments and Experience and Other Remains of Lucy Cobham Hennen.* London, 1846.

Hitchcock, Enos. *The Farmer's Friend; or The History of Mr. Charles Worthy.* Boston, 1793.

———. *Memoirs of the Bloomsgrove Family.* Boston, 1790. Quoted in *Columbian Magazine* 5 (July 1790).

Hollinshead, William. "The Gospel Preached to Every Creature." Sermon, 21 March 1798. Box 3, file 15. John Carter Brown Library, Providence, R.I.

Hooker, Richard J., ed. *Carolina Backcountry on the Eve of Revolution, 1720–72, Based on the Journal of the Rev. Charles Woodmason, Anglican Itinerant.* Chapel Hill: University of North Carolina Press, 1953.

Hutson, William. *Living Christianity Delineated.* London, 1760, pt. 1; Boston, 1809, pt. 2.

Idzerda, Stanley J., and Robert R. Crout, eds. *Lafayette in the Age of the American Revolution: Selected Letters and Papers, 1776–1790.* Ithaca: Cornell University Press, 1977.

"Inducements for a Judicious Improvement of our National Privileges." *Columbian Magazine* 12 (July–Aug. 1806): 148–51.

Johnson, Joseph. *Traditions and Reminiscences of the American Revolution in the South.* Charleston, S.C.: Walker and James, 1851.

Jones, George Fenwick, ed. "The 1780 Siege of Charleston As Experienced by a Hessian Officer [Carl Bauer]." Pt. 2. *South Carolina Historical Magazine* 68 (Apr. 1987): 70–75.

Klingberg, Frank. *The Carolina Chronicle of Dr. Francis Le Jau.* Berkeley: University of California Press, 1946.

Knapp, Samuel Lorenzo. *American Cultural History, 1607–1829.* Delmar, N.Y.: Scholars Facsimiles and Reprints, 1997.

Krause, Sonia. Diary, no. 11, 10 Apr. 1821. Quoted in Barbara Wright, "Pilgrim in Bethlemen: American Moravian Piety and the Identity Formation of a Nineteenth Century Woman." Ph.D. diss., Drew Theological Seminary, Madison N.J., 1989.

Lathrop, Joseph. "The Constancy and Uniformity of the Divine Government." Sermon given in Springfield, Mass., 1803. Metcalf Collection, John Hay Library, Brown University, Providence, R.I.

"Laurens Lands." In *Streets of Charleston.* Charleston, S.C.: compiled for Charleston Museum, 1930.

Lesesne, Thomas Petigru. *Narrative and Biographical History of Charleston County, South Carolina.* Charleston, S.C.: privately printed, 1931.

"Letters from Mrs. Ralph Izard to Mrs. William Lee." *Virginia Magazine of History* 8 (July 1900): 16–28.

Marcou, Jane Belknap. *The Life of Jeremy, Historian of New Hampshire: Correspondence and Other Writings.* New York: Harper & Brothers, 1847.

Mather, Increase. *An Essay for the Recording of Illustrious Providences.* 1684. Delmar, N.Y.: Scholars' Facsimilies & Reprints, 1977.

Maclean, John. *The History of the College of New Jersey.* 2 vols. Princeton: Princeton University, 1877.

M'Calla, Daniel. *Works of The Rev. Daniel McCalla.* 2 vols. Charleston, S.C.: John Hoff, 1810.

More, Hannah. *The Complete Works of Hannah More.* New York: Harper & Brothers, 1839.

Moore, Caroline T. ed. *Abstract of Wills of Charleston County.* Columbia, S.C.: R. L. Bryan, 1974.

Moore, John Hammond, ed. "The Abiel Abbott Journals: A Yankee Preacher in Charleston Society, 1818–1827." *South Carolina Historical Magazine* 68 (Apr. 1967): 51–73.

Moore, Milcah. *Milcah Martha Moore's Commonplace Book.* Ed. Catherine L. Blecki and Karin A. Wulf. University Park: Penn State University Press, 1997.

Morris, Richard B., ed. *John Jay: Winning the Peace. Unpublished Papers, 1780–84.* New York: Harper & Row, 1980.

Mulford, Carla, ed. *Only for the Eye of a Friend: Annis Boudinot Stockton.* Charlottesville: University Press of Virginia, 1997.

Murray, Judith Sargent. *The Gleaner.* 3 vols. Boston, 1798.

Murray, Lindley. *The Power of Religion on the Mind.* 11th ed. York, England, 1802.

Oberg, Barbara, et al., eds. *Papers of Benjamin Franklin.* 35 vols. to date. New Haven: Yale University Press, 1959.

Panoplinst 2, no. 19 (1793), 429–30.

Pennington, Montague, ed. *Mrs. Elizabeth Carter.* Boston: Oliver C. Greenleaf, 1809.

Parrish, John. "Remarks on the Slavery of Black People." 1806. In *Anti-Slavery in America, 1619–1808,* ed. Mary Stoughton Locke. 1901. New York: Johnson Reprint, 1968.

Pease, Jane H., and William H. Pease. "Blood Thirsty Tigre: Charleston and the Psychology of Fire." *South Carolina Historical Magazine* 78 (1978): 281–95.

Pinckney, Elise, ed. *The Letterbook of Eliza Lucas Pinckney, 1739–1762.* Columbia: University of South Carolina Press, 1997.

Polewheale, Richard. "The Unsex'd Female." *Baltimore Weekly,* 5 July 1800, 82–83.

Poole, William Frederick. *Anti-Slavery Opinion Before 1800.* 1873. Westport, Conn.: Negro University Press, 1970.

"President Washington in South Carolina." *Columbian Magazine* 3 (May 1789): 288–90.

"Prolonging the Happiness of the Marriage Union." *Columbian Magazine* 1, 10, 473.

Ramsay, David. *An Oration on the Cession of Louisiana to the United States.* Charleston, S.C.: W. P. Young, 1804.

———. *An Oration, Prepared for Delivery Before the Inhabitants of Charleston, Assembled on 17 May 1788 to Celebrate the Adoption of the New Constitution by South Carolina.* Charleston, S.C., 1788.

———. *History of the Revolution of South Carolina, from a British Province to an Independent State.* 2 vols. Charleston, S.C., 1785.

———ed. *Memoirs of the Life of Martha Laurens Ramsay.* Charleston, S.C., 1811. 2d ed., Boston, 1814. 3d ed., Philadelphia: American Sunday School Union, 1814; 1845 ed. revised by ASSU Committee.

———. *History of the American Revolution, from a British Province to an Independent State.* 2 vols. Philadelphia, 1789.

———. "A Review of the Improvements, Progress and State of Medicine in the XVIIIth Century." 1801. In *David Ramsay, 1749–1815: Selections from His Writings,* ed. Robert L. Brunhouse, 196–217. Philadelphia: American Philosophical Society, 1965.

———. *The History of the Independent or Congregational Church in Charleston.* Philadelphia, 1815.

———. *The Life of George Washington.* New York, 1807.

Ramsay, James. *Essay on the Treatment and Conversion of African Slaves in the British Sugar Colonies.* Dublin, 1784. John Carter Brown Library, Providence, R.I.

Ramsay, Martha H. L. "Wedding of Slaves in Her House." *South Carolina Historical Magazine* 58 (1957): 175.

Ravenel, Harriott Horry. *Eliza Pinckney.* New York: C. Scribner's & Sons, 1896.

"Register of the Independent Congregational (Circular) Church of Charleston, S.C., 1784–1815." *South Carolina Historical and Genealogical Magazine* 33 (1932), 29–54, 154–74, 216–27, 306–16.

"Review: 'Memoirs of Martha Laurens Ramsay.'" *Portfolio,* 3d ser., no. 2 (1813).

Richardson, Samuel. *Pamela.* 2 vols. New York: W. W. Norton & Co., 1958.

———. *A Collection of the Moral and Instructive Sentiments, Maxims, Cautions, and Reflections.* 1755. Delmar: New York, 1980.

Richards, Phillip M. "Phillis Wheatley and Literary Americanization." *American Quarterly* 44 (June 1992): 163–91.

Rogal, Samuel J. "Watts' *Divine and Moral Songs for Children* and the Rhetoric of Religious Instruction." *Historical Magazine of the Episcopal Church* 40 (1971): 95–100.

Rowson, Susanna. *Reuben and Rachel: A Tale of Old Times.* New York, 1798.

"Rules and Maxims for Matrimonial Happiness." *Columbian Magazine* 4 (Jan. 1790): 24.

Rush, Benjamin. "The Paradise of Negro Slaves: A Dream." *Columbian Magazine and Universal Repository* 1 (January 1787): 235–38.

Showman, Richard, et al., eds. *Nathanael Greene Papers.* 11 vols. to date. Providence: Rhode Island Historical Society, 1976–.

Smith, D. E. Huger, and A. S. Salley Jr., eds. *Register of St. Philip's Parish, 1754–1810, Charles Town or Charleston, South Carolina.* Columbia: University of South Carolina Press, 1971.

Smith, Emily A. *Life and Letters of Nathan Smith.* New Haven: Yale University Press, 1914.

Smith, Josiah. Diary, 1780–1781. *South Carolina Historical Magazine* 34 (Apr. 1933): 1–79; (Oct. 1933): 197–281.

Smith, Marion B. "South Carolina and *The Gentleman's Magazine.*" *South Carolina Historical Magazine* 95 (Apr. 1994): 102–29.

Spalding, James A. *Dr. Lyman Spalding.* Boston, 1916.

Sprague, William B. *Annals of the American Pulpit.* 3 vols. 1866. New York: Arno Reprints, 1969.

Stebbing, Henry. "Discourse Concerning the Governing Providence of God." Sermon given 6 February 1756. Metcalf Collection, John Hay Library, Brown University, Providence, R.I.

Stevens, Michael E. "The Vigilant Fire Company of Charleston." *South Carolina Historical Magazine* 87 (Apr. 1986): 130–35.

———, ed. *Journal of the House of Representatives, 1792–1794.* Columbia: University of South Carolina Press, 1988. Clerk's notes filed with *Journals of House of Representatives,* South Carolina Archives, Columbia.

"Thoughts on Matrimony." *Royal American Magazine,* January 1774, 9.

Tilton, James. "Oration to the Delaware Society of the Cincinnati." *Universal Asylum and Columbian Magazine* 5 (Dec. 1790): 369–73.

Trimmer, Mrs. Sarah Kirby. *The Guardian of Education.* London, 1802–1806.

Twohig, Dorothy, ed. *Papers of George Washington.* Presidential Series. 7 vols. Charlottesville: University Press of Virginia, 1987–.

Wadsworth, Benjamin. "The Well-Ordered Family; or Relative Duties." 1712. In *The Colonial American Family: Collected Essays,* ed. David Rothman and Sheila Rothman. New York: Arno Press, 1972.

Walcott, James. *The New Pilgrim's Progress; or The Pious Indian Hattain Gelashmin Christened George James.* London, 1748. John Carter Brown Library, Providence, R.I.

Watts, Issac. *Divine Songs for Children.* 2 vols. London, 1715.

Wertenbaker, Thomas Jefferson. *Princeton, 1746–1896.* Princeton: Princeton University Press, 1946.

Wesley, John. *A Calm Address to Our American Colonies.* Philadelphia, 1775.

West, Benjamin. *Travel Notes: Life in the South, 1778–1779.* Antislavery Pamphlet Collection, John Carter Brown Library, Providence, R.I.

Wilson, James. "Introductory Law Lecture." *Universal Asylum and Columbian Magazine* 6 (Jan. 1791): 45.

Whitney, Janet Payne. *Elizabeth Fry, Quaker Heroine.* Boston: Little, Brown & Co., 1937.

Wollstonecraft, Mary. *Mary, a Fiction.* 1788. New York: Schocken Books, 1977.

Yeadon, Richard. *History of the Circular Church, Its Origin, Building, and Rebuilding.* Charleston, S.C.: J. B. Nixon, 1853.

Yearbook of the City of Charleston, 1883. Charleston: News & Courier Book Presses, 1884.

Young, Edward D. *The Complaint; or Night Thoughts on Life, Death, and Immortality.* 1745. Philadelphia: Prichard & Hall, 1787.

Books

Adams, Geoffrey. *The Huguenots and French Opinion, 1685–1787.* Waterloo, Ontario: Wilfred Laurier University Press, 1991.

Aldrich, Nelson W. *Old Money: The Mythology of America's Upper Class.* New York: Vintage Books, 1989.

Anne Norton. *Alternative Americas.* Chicago: University of Chicago Press, 1986

Appleby, Joyce. "Republicanism." *William and Mary Quarterly* 43 (Jan. 1986): 20–34.

Arnold, Edwin T., III. "Women Diarists and Letter Writers of Eighteenth Century South Carolina." In *South Carolina Women Writers,* ed. James B. Meriwether. Spartanburg, S.C.: Reprint Co. Publishers, 1897.

Atkinson, Clarissa W., Constance H. Buchanan, and Margaret R. Miles, eds. *Immaculate and Powerful: The Female in Sacred Image and Social Reality.* Boston: Beacon Press, 1985.

Ball, Edward. *Slaves in the Family.* New York: Farrar, Straus and Giroux, 1998.

Bell, Malcolm. *Major Butler's Legacy: Five Generations of a Slaveholding Family.* Athens: University of Georgia Press, 1987.

Bell, Susan Groag, and Karen Offen. *Women, the Family, and Freedom.* 2 vols. Stanford, Calif.: Stanford University Press, 1983.

Benson, Mary Sumner. *Women in Eighteenth-Century America: A Study of Opinion and Social Usage.* 1935. Port Washington, N.Y.: AMS Press, 1975.

Berens, John F. *Providence and Patriotism in Early America, 1640–1815.* Charlottesville: University Press of Virginia, 1978.

Bleser, Carol, ed. *In Joy and In Sorrow.* New York: Oxford University Press, 1991.

Bloch, Ruth H. *Visionary Republic: Millennial Themes in American Thought, 1756–1800.* New York: Cambridge University Press, 1985.

Bolton, Charles. *Southern Anglicanism: The Church of England in Colonial South Carolina.* Westport, Conn.: Greenwood Press, 1982.

Bonomi, Patricia. *Under the Cope of Heaven: Religion, Society and Politics in Colonial America.* New York: Oxford University Press, 1986.

Brewer, John, and Ray Porter, eds. *Consumption and the World of Goods.* New York: Routledge, 1993.

Bridenbaugh, Carl. *Myths and Realities: Societies of the Colonial South.* New York: Athanaeum, 1985.

Brown, Richard D. *Knowledge Is Power: The Diffusion of Information in Early America, 1700–1865.* New York: Oxford University Press, 1989.

Brown-Lawson, Albert. *John Wesley and the Anglican Evangelicals of the Eighteenth Century.* Durham, England: Pentland Press, 1994.

Chaplin, Joyce. *"An Anxious Pursuit": Agricultural Innovation and Modernity in the Lower South.* Chapel Hill: University of North Carolina Press, 1993.

Cohen, Hennig. *The South Carolina Gazette, 1732–75.* Columbia: University of South Carolina Press, 1953.

Coles, Edward. *A Virginia Family and Its Plantation Houses.* Ed. Elizabeth K. Langhorne, Edward Lay, and William D. Rieley. Charlottesville: University of Virginia Press, 1987.

Crane, Elaine Forman. *Ebb Tide in New England.* Boston: Northeastern University Press, 1998.

Davie, Jody Shapiro. *Women in the Presence: Constructing Community and Seeking Spirituality in Mainline Protestantism.* Philadelphia: University of Pennsylvania Press, 1995.

Demos, John. *Past, Present, and Personal: The Family and the Life Course in American History.* New York: Oxford University Press, 1986.

Edwards, George N. *A History of the Independent or Congregational Church of Charleston.* Boston: Pilgrim Press, 1947.

Ellis, Joseph J. *After the Revolution: Profiles of Early American Culture.* New York: W. W. Norton & Co., 1979.

Erickson, Victoria Lee. *Where Silence Speaks: Feminism, Social Theory and Religion.* Minneapolis: Fortress Press, 1993.

Fliegelman, Jay. *Prodigals and Pilgrims: The American Revolution against Patriarchal Authority, 1750–1800.* New York: Cambridge University Press, 1982.

Fox-Genovese, Elizabeth. *Within the Plantation Household: Black and White Women of the Old South.* Chapel Hill: University of North Carolina Press, 1988.

Fraser, Walter. *Charleston! Charleston! The History of a Southern City.* Columbia: University of South Carolina Press, 1989.

Fredrickson, George M. *The Black Image in the White Mind.* Middletown, Conn.: Wesleyan University Press, 1971, repr. 1987.

Free, William J. *The Columbian Magazine and American Literary Nationalism.* The Hague: Mouton, 1968.

Frey, Sylvia, and Betty Wood. *Come Shouting to Zion: African American Protestantism in the American South and British Caribbean to 1830.* Chapel Hill: University Press of North Carolina, 1998.

Davie, Jody Shapiro. *Women in the Presence: Constructing Community and Seeking Spirituality in Mainline Protestantism.* Philadelphia: University of Pennsylvania Press, 1995.

Gaustad, Edwin Scott. *The Religious History of America.* San Francisco: Harper Collins, 1990.

Gelles, Edith. *Portia: A Life of Abigail Adams.* Bloomington: Indiana University Press, 1992.

Gerzina, Gretchen Holbrook. *Black London: Life Before Emancipation.* New Brunswick: Rutgers University Press, 1995.

Gignilliat, George Warren, Jr. *The Author of Sandford and Merton: A Life of Thomas Day.* New York: Columbia University Press, 1932.

Ginzburg, Lydia. *On Psychological Prose.* Princeton, N.J.: Princeton University Press, 1991.

Golden, Richard, ed. *The Huguenot Connection: The Edict of Nantes, Its Revocation, and the French Migration to South Carolina.* Dordrecht: Kluver Academic Press, 1988.

Greene, Jack P. *Pursuits of Happiness: The Social Development of Early Modern British Colonies and the Formation of American Culture.* Chapel Hill: University of North Carolina Press, 1988.

Gunn, Janet Varner. *Autobiography: Toward a Poetics of Experience.* Philadelphia: University of Pennsylvania Press, 1982.

Hall, David D. *Worlds of Wonder, Days of Judgment: Popular Religious Belief in Early New England.* Cambridge, Mass.: Harvard University Press, 1990.

Hancock, David. *Citizens of the World.* New York: Cambridge University Press, 1998.

Hareven, Tamara K. *Family Time and Industrial Time: The Relationship between the Family and Work in a New England Industrial Community.* Lanham, Md.: University Press of America, 1982.

Harkness, Georgia. *The Dark Night of the Soul: A Modern Interpretation.* London: Andrew Melrose, 1944.

Hayes, Kevin. *Colonial Woman's Bookshelf.* Knoxville: University of Tennessee Press, 1996.

Heyward, Duncan Clinch. *Seed from Madagascar.* Columbia: University of South Carolina Press, 1993.

Hogg, Peter C. *The African Slave Trade and Its Suppression: Annotated Bibliography.* London: Frank Cass, 1973.

Holme, Charles Geoffrey. *Children's Toys of Yesterday.* London: Studio Ltd., 1932.

Hutchins, Catherine E., ed. *Everyday Life in the Early Republic.* Winterthur, Del.: Henry Francis duPont Winterthur Museum, 1994.

Huyler, Jerome. *Locke in America: The Moral Philosophy of the Founding Era:* Lawrence: University Press of Kansas, 1995.

Issac, Rhys. *The Transformation of Virginia.* Chapel Hill: University of North Carolina Press, 1982.

James, William. *The Varieties of Religious Experience: A Study in Human Nature.* New York: Modern Library, 1936.

Jedry, Christopher M. *The World of John Cleaveland, Family and Community in Eighteenth Century New England.* New York: W. W. Norton & Co., 1979.

Jeffrey, David Lyle. *A Burning and a Shining Light: English Spirituality in the Age of Wesley.* Grand Rapids: William B. Eerdmans Publishing, 1986.

Jones, Vivien, ed. *Women in the Eighteenth Century.* London: Routledge & Kegan Paul, 1990.

Jordan, Winthrop D. *White over Black: American Attitudes toward the Negro, 1550–1812.* New York: W. W. Norton, 1977.

Keller, Albert H. *A Brief History of the Circular Church, Charleston, South Carolina.* Contemporary pamphlet, undated.

Kerber, Linda. *Women of the Republic.* Chapel Hill: University of North Carolina Press, 1980.

Kierner, Cynthia A. *Southern Women in Revolution, 1776–1800: Personal and Political Narratives.* Columbia: University of South Carolina Press, 1998.

————. *Beyond the Household: Women of the Early South, 1776–1800.* Ithaca: Cornell University Press, 1998.

Klein, Randolph Shipley. *Portrait of an Early American Family: The Shippens of Pennsylvania Across Five Generations.* Philadelphia: University of Pennsylvania Press, 1975.

Lewis, Jan. *The Pursuit of Happiness: Family and Values in Jefferson's Virginia.* New York: Cambridge University Press, 1983.

Lutz, Donald S., and Jack D. Warren. *A Covenanted People.* Providence, R.I.: John Carter Brown Library, 1987.

Mallon, Thomas. *A Book of One's Own: People and Their Diaries.* New York: Ticknor & Fields, 1984.

Massey, Gregory D. *John Laurens and the American Revolution.* Columbia, S.C.: University of South Carolina Press, 2000.

May, Henry F. *The Enlightenment in America.* New York: Oxford University Press, 1976.

McDonald, Forrest. *Novus Ordo Seclorum: The Intellectual Origins of the Constitu-tion.* Lawrence: University Press of Kansas, 1985.

Melish, Joanne. *Disowning Slavery: Gradual Emancipation and Race in New Eng-land, 1780–1860.* Ithaca: Cornell University Press, 1998.

Middleton, Margaret Simons. *David and Martha Laurens Ramsay.* New York: Carl-ton Press, 1971.

Miles, Margaret W. *Practicing Christianity: Critical Perspectives for an Embodied Spirituality.* New York: Crossroads Publishing Co., 1988.

Morgan, Philip D. *Slave Counterpoint.* Chapel Hill: University of North Carolina Press, 1998.

Mossner, Ernest Campbell. *Bishop Butler and the Age of Reason.* New York: Macmillan & Co., 1936.

Myers, Robert Manson, ed. *The Children of Pride.* New Haven: Yale University Press, 1972.

Myers, Sylvia H. *The Bluestocking Circle: Women, Friendship and the Life of the Mind in Eighteenth Century England.* London: Clarendon Press, 1990.

Nelson, Dana. *The Word in Black and White.* New York: Oxford University Press, 1993.

Nussbaum, Felicity A. *The Autobiographical Subject: Gender and Ideology in Eigh-teenth Century England.* Baltimore: Johns Hopkins University Press, 1989.

Ochs, Carol. *Women and Spirituality.* Lanham, Md.: Rowman and Littlefield, 1983.

Ott, Thomas O. *The Haitian Revolution, 1789–1804.* Knoxville: University of Ten-nessee Press, 1973.

Paulson, Ronald. *Representations of Revolution (1789–1820).* New Haven: Yale Uni-versity Press, 1983.

Remini, Robert V. *Henry Clay: Statesman for the Union.* New York: W. W. Norton, 1991.

Reynolds, David. *Faith in Fiction: The Emergence of Religious Literature in America.* Cambridge, Mass.: Harvard University Press, 1981.

Rich, Adrienne. *Of Woman Born: Motherhood As Experience and Institution.* New York: W. W. Norton, 1976.

Roediger, David. *The Wages of Whiteness: Race and the Making of the American Working Class.* New York: Verso Publications, 1998.

Rogers, George C., Jr. *Charleston in the Age of the Pinckneys.* Norman: University of Oklahoma Press, 1969.

———. *Evolution of a Federalist: William Loughton Smith, 1758–1812.* Columbia: University of South Carolina Press, 1962.

Rose, Phyllis. *Parallel Lives.* New York: A. A. Knopf, 1983.

Rothman, David, and Sheila Rothman, eds. *The Colonial American Family: Col-lected Essays.* New York: Arno Press, 1972.

Ruether, Rosemary, and Rosemary Keller, eds. *Women and Religion in America.* 3 vols. San Francisco: Harper & Row, 1983.

Rutledge, Anna Wells. *Artists in the Life of Charleston.* Columbia: University of South Carolina Press, 1980.

Sandiford, Keith A. *Measure the Moment: Strategies of Protest in Eighteenth Century Afro-English Writing.* Selinsgrove, Pa.: Susquehanna University Press, 1988.

Schlent, Ernestine. *The Language of Silence: West German Literature and the Holocaust.* New York: Routledge, 1999.

Schulman, Lydia Dittler. *"Paradise Lost" and the Rise of the American Republic.* Boston: Northeastern University Press, 1992.

Sernett, Milton C. *Afro-American Religious History: A Documentary History.* Durham, N.C.: Duke University Press, 1985.

Shaffer, Arthur H. *To Be an American: David Ramsay and the Making of the American Consciousness.* Columbia: University of South Carolina Press, 1991.

―――. *The Politics of History.* Chicago: Precedent Publishing, 1975.

Shepherd, Massey. *The Oxford Prayer Book Commentary.* New York: Oxford University Press, 1950.

Skemp, Sheila. *Judith Sargent Murray: A Brief Biography with Documents.* New York: Bedford Books, 1998.

Slaughter, Thomas P. *The Natures of John and William Bartram.* New York: A. A. Knopf, 1996.

Smith, Warren Thomas. *John Wesley and Slavery.* Nashville: Abingdon Press, 1986.

Sobel, Mechal. *"Travelin' On": The Slave Journey to an Afro Baptist Faith.* Westport, Conn.: Greenwood Press, 1979.

Spruill, Julia Cherry. *Women's Life and Work in the Southern Colonies.* 1938. Chapel Hill: University of North Carolina Press, 1972.

Stampp, Kenneth. *The Peculiar Institution.* New York: A. A. Knopf, 1956.

Tise, Larry E. *Proslavery: A History of the Defense of Slavery in America, 1791–1840.* Athens: University of Georgia Press, 1987.

Ulrich, Laurel Thatcher. *A Midwife's Tale: The Life of Martha Ballard, Based on Her Diary, 1785–1812.* New York, A. A. Knopf, 1990.

Van Ruymbeke, Bertrand. Personal communication, 1988. See also *From New Babylon to Eden: The Huguenot Migration to Proprietary South Carolina* (Columbia: University of South Carolina Press, forthcoming).

Voelz, Peter M. *Slave and Soldier: The Military Impact of Blacks on the Colonial Americas.* New York: Garland Publishing, 1993.

Wagner-Martin, Linda. *Telling Women's Lives: The New Biography.* New Brunswick, N.J.: Rutgers University Press, 1994.

Wallace, David Duncan. *The Life of Henry Laurens.* New York: G. P. Putnam's Sons, 1915.

Warner, Michael. *The Letters of the Republic: Publication and the Public Sphere in Eighteenth Century America.* Cambridge, Mass.: Harvard University Press, 1990.

Weir, Robert M. *Colonial South Carolina: A History.* Millwood, N.Y.: Kraus-Thomson Organization, 1983.

Welch, D'Alte A. *American Children's Books Printed Prior to 1820*. New Haven: American Antiquarian Society, 1972.

Winslow, Donald J. *Life Writing*. Honolulu: University of Hawaii Press, 1980.

Wood, Gordon. *The Creation of the American Republic, 1776–1778*. New York: W. W. Norton & Co., 1972.

Woody, Thomas. (1929) *A History of Women's Education in the U.S.* 2 vols. Reprinted New York: Octagon Books Reprint, 1974.

Woolverton, John. *Colonial Anglicanism*. Detroit: Wayne State University Press, 1984.

Articles, Conference Papers, Essays, and Theses

Bloch, Ruth H. "The Gendered Meanings of Virtue in Revolutionary America." *Signs* 13 (autumn 1987): 37–58.

Bosher, J. F. "Huguenot Merchants and the Protestant International in the Seventeenth Century." *William and Mary Quarterly* 52 (Jan. 1995): 77–102.

Boyd, Stanley Schlenther. "'To Convert the Poor People in America': The Bethesda Orphanage and the Thwarted Zeal of the Countess of Huntingdon." *Georgia Historical Quarterly* 72 (summer 1994): 225–56.

Braude, Benjamin. "The Sons of Noah and Construction of Ethnic and Geographic Identities in Medieval and Early Modern Periods." *William and Mary Quarterly* 54 (Jan. 1997): 103–42.

Breen, T. H. "The Meaning of Things: Interpreting the Consumer Economy in the 18th Century." In *Consumption and the World of Goods*, ed. John Brewer and Roy Porter. London: Routledge, 1993, 249–60.

Brown, Christopher L. "Empire without Slaves." *William and Mary Quarterly* 56 (Apr. 1999): 288.

Brown, Irene Quenzeler. "Domesticity, Feminism, and Friendship: Women, Aristocratic Culture and Marriage in England, 1660–1760." *Journal of Family History* 4 (1982): 406–24.

———. "Death, Friendship and Female Identity during New England's Second Great Awakening." *Journal of Family History* 4 (1987): 368–72.

———. "Leisure, Prayer, and Inclusive Friendship from Bunyan and Law to the Lowell Girls." Paper presented at the American Academy of Religion, Boston, 1987.

Brown, Richard D. "Modernization and Modern Personality in Early America, 1600–1865: A Sketch of a Synthesis." *Journal of Interdisciplinary History* 2 , no. 4 (1972): 201–28.

Chaplin, Joyce E. "Slavery and the Principle of Humanity: A Modern Idea in the Early Lower South." *Journal of Social History* 24 (winter 1990): 299–315.

Clark, Elizabeth B. "'The Sacred Rights of the Weak': Pain, Sympathy, and the Culture of Individual Rights in Antebellum America." *Journal of American History* 82 (Sept. 1995): 463–93.

Clinton, Catherine. "Caught in the Web of the Big House: Women and Slavery." In *The Web of Southern Social Relations,* ed. Walter J. Fraser Jr., R. Frank Saunders Jr., and Jon L. Wakelyn, 227–32. Athens: University of Georgia Press, 1985.

Cody, Cheryll Ann. "There Was No 'Absalom' on the Ball Plantations: Slave Naming Practices in the South Carolina Low Country, 1720–1865." *American Historical Review* 92 (June 1997): 563–96.

Cohen, Patricia Cline. "Reckoning with Commerce: Eighteenth Century Numeracy." In *Consumption and the World of Goods,* ed. John Brewer and Ray Porter, 329. New York: Routledge, 1993.

Davis, David Brion. "At the Heart of Slavery." *New York Review of Books* 43 (Oct. 1996): 51–53.

———. "Constructing Race: A Reflection." *William and Mary Quarterly* 54 (Jan. 1997): 7–18.

Deaton, Stanley Kenneth. "Revolutionary Charleston, 1765–1800." Ph.D. diss., University of Florida, 1997.

Demos, John. "The Changing Faces of Fatherhood: A New Exploration in Family History." In *Father and Child: Developmental and Clinical Perspectives,* ed. Stanley Cath, Alan Gurwitt, and John M. Ross. Hillsdale, N.J.: Analytic Press, 1982.

Desrochers, Robert E., Jr. "'Not Fade Away': The Narrative of Venture Smith, an African American in the Early Republic." *Journal of American History* 84 (June 1997): 40–66.

Downey, Charlotte. "A Children's Text of the Eighteenth and Nineteenth Centuries: Abridgement of Murray's *English Grammar.*" *Children's Literature Association Quarterly* 10 (fall 1985): 131–32.

Dubois, Laurent. "'The Price of Liberty': Victor Hughes and the Administration of Freedom in Guadeloupe, 1794–1798." *William and Mary Quarterly* 56 (Apr. 1999): 363–92.

Dye, Nancy Schrom, and Daniel Blake Smith. "Mother Love and Infant Death, 1750–1920." *Journal of American History* 73 (Sept. 1986): 329–53.

Ezell, J. M. "John Locke's Images of Childhood." *Eighteenth-Century Studies* 17 (winter 1983–84): 139–55.

Fiering, Norman. "Irresistible Compassion: An Aspect of Eighteenth Century Sympathy and Humanitarianism." *Journal of the History of Ideas* 37 (Apr.–June 1976): 195–218.

Fryer, Darcy R. "The Mind of Eliza Pinckney." *South Carolina Historical Magazine* 99 (July 1998): 215–37.

Gallant, Mavis. Review, *The Great Cat Massacre* by Robert Darnton. *New York Review of Books,* 12 February 1984, 12.

Genovese, Eugene. "'Our Family, White and Black': Family and Household in Southern Slaveholders' World View." In *In Joy and in Sorrow,* ed. Carol Bleser, 69–87 (New York: Oxford University Press, 1991).

Geertz, Clifford. "'The Pinch of Destiny'—Religion As Experience, Meaning, Identity, Power." *Harvard Divinity School Bulletin* 27, no. 4 (1998): 7–12.

Gilmore, Michael. "Eulogy As Symbolic Biography." In *Harvard English Studies* 8, ed. Daniel Aaron, 131. Cambridge, Mass.: Harvard University Press, 1978.

———. "The Literature of the Revolution and Early National Period." In *The Cambridge History of American Literature.* Vol. 1, *1590–1820,* ed. Sacvan Bercovitch, 541–676. New York: Cambridge University Press, 1994.

Gillespie, Joanna B. "'The Clear Leadings of Providence': Pious Memoirs and the Problems of Self-Realization for Women in the Early Nineteenth Century." *Journal of the Early Republic* 5 (summer 1985): 197–221.

———. "1795: Martha Laurens Ramsay's 'Dark Night of the Soul.'" *William and Mary Quarterly* 48 (Jan. 1991): 68–92.

Greenberg, Kenneth S. "The Nose, the Lie and the Duel in the Antebellum South." *American Historical Review* 95 (Feb. 1990): 57–74, 68.

Gunderson, Joan. "Independence, Citizenship, and the American Revolution." *Signs* 13 (autumn 1987): 59–77.

Hall, David D. "The Uses of Literacy in New England, 1600–1850." In *Printing and Society in Early America,* ed. William L. Joyce, David D. Hall, Richard D. Brown, and John B. Hench, 1–47. Worcester, Mass.: American Antiquarian Society, 1983.

———. "On Common Ground: The Coherence of American Puritan Studies." *William and Mary Quarterly* 44 (Apr. 1987): 193–229.

Hargrove, Richard J. "Portrait of a Southern Patriot: Life and Death of John Laurens." 182–202 in *The Revolutionary War in the South: Power, Conflict, and Leadership,* ed. W. Robert Higgins. Durham, N.C.: Duke University Press, 1979.

Hoover, Cynthia Adams. "Music and Theater in the Lives of Eighteenth Century Americans." In *Of Consuming Interests,* ed. Cary Carson, Ronald Hoffman, Peter J. Albert. Charlottesville: University Press of Virginia, 1994.

Jackson, Maurice. "Anthony Benezet: America's Finest Eighteenth-Century Antislavery Advocate." In *The Human Tradition in the American Revolution.,* ed. Nancy L. Rhoden and Ian K. Steele, 1–17. Wilmington, Del.: Scholarly Resources, 2000.

Kouffman, Avra. "The Cultural Work of Stuart Women's Diaries." Ph.D. diss., University of Arizona, 2000.

Kelley, Mary: "Reading Women/Women Reading: The Making of Learned Women in Antebellum America." *Journal of American History* 83 (Sept. 1996): 401–24.

Kerber, Linda: "'History Can Do It No Justice': Women and the Reinterpretation of the American Revolution." In *Women in the Age of the American Revolution,* ed. Ronald Hoffman and Peter J. Albert, 3–42. Charlottesville: University Press of Virginia, 1989.

Kloppenberg, James T. "The Virtue of Liberalism: Christianity, Republicanism and Ethics in Early American Political Discourse." *Journal of American History* 74 (June 1987): 9–33.

Kramnick, Issac. "'The Great National Discussion': The Discourse of Politics, 1788. *William and Mary Quarterly* 45 (Jan. 1988): 3–32.

Kujawa, Sheryl. "Religion, Education, and Gender in Eighteenth-Century Rhode Island: Sarah Haggar Wheaten Osborn, 1714–1796." *Rhode Island History* 52 (May 1994): 35–47.

———. "The Great Awakening of Sarah Osborn and the Female Society of the First Congregational Church in Newport." *Newport History* 65 (spring 1998): 132–53.

Lacey, Barbara. "Visual Images of Blacks in Early American Imprints." *William and Mary Quarterly* 53 (Jan. 1996): 137–80.

Lapsansky, Emma Jones. "'Since They Got Those Separate Churches': Afro-Americans and Racism in Jacksonian Philadelphia." *American Quarterly* 32 (spring 1980): 54–78.

Lewis, Jan. "The Republican Wife; Virtue and Seduction in the Early Republic." *William and Mary Quarterly* 44 (Oct. 1987): 689–721.

———. "Motherhood and the Construction of the Male Citizen." In *Constructions of the Self,* ed. George Levine, 143–63. New Brunswick: Rutgers University Press, 1992.

Little, Thomas J. "A Quantitative Analysis of Churches and Ministers in Colonial South Carolina, 1681–1780." Seminar Paper presented September 1997 at Omohundro Institute of Early American History and Culture, Williamsburg, Va.

Lyerly, Cynthia Lynn. "Religion, Gender and Identity: Black Methodist Women in a Slave Society, 1770–1910." In *Discovering the Women in Slavery,* ed. Patricia Morton, 202–26. Athens: University of Georgia Press, 1996.

Masur, Louis P. "'Age of the First Person Singular': The Vocabulary of the Self in New England, 1780–1850." *Journal of American Studies* 25 (Aug. 1991): 189–211.

Matthews, Jean. "Race, Sex and the Dimensions of Liberty in Antebellum America." *Journal of the Early American Republic* 6 (fall 1986): 275–92.

Matthewson, Tim. "Jefferson and Haiti." *Journal of Southern History* 61 (May 1995): 209–48.

Morey, Ann Janine. "In Memory of Cassie: Child Death and Religious Vision in American Women's Novels." *Religion and American Culture* 6 (winter 1996): 87–104.

Morgan, Philip D. "Black Life in Eighteenth-Century Charleston." *Perspectives in American History,* n.s., 1 (1984): 187–222.

———. "Three Planters and Their Slaves: Perspectives on Slavery in Virginia, South Carolina, and Jamaica, 1750–1790." In *Race and Family in the Colonial South,* ed. Winthrop D. Jordan and Sheila L. Skemp, 37–80. Jackson: University Press of Mississippi, 1987.

Nash, Gary B. "The Hidden History of Mestizo America." *Journal of American History* 82 (Dec. 1995): 941–64.

Nord, David Paul. "A Republican Literature: Magazine Reading and Readers in Late Eighteenth Century New York." In *Reading in America: Literature and*

Social History, ed. Cathy N. Davidson, 114–39. Baltimore: Johns Hopkins University Press, 1989.

Offen, Karen A. "Was Mary Wollstonecraft a Feminist? A Contextual Re-Reading of *A Vindication of the Rights of Woman, 1792–1992.*" In *Quilting a New Canon: Stitching Women's Words*, ed. Uma Parameswaran, 3–24. Toronto: Sister Vision Press, 1993.

Olwell, Robert A. "'Domestick Enemies': Slavery and Political Independence in South Carolina, May 1775–March 1776." *Journal of Southern History* 55 (Feb. 1989): 21–48.

Ott, Joseph K. "Rhode Islanders in Charleston." *South Carolina Historical Magazine* 75 (July 1974): 180–83.

Porterfield, Amanda. Review of Ann Taves' *Fits, Trances, and Visions: Experiencing Religion and Explaining Experience, from Wesley to James.* Princeton: Princeton University Press, 1999. In *William and Mary Quarterly* 57 (Apr. 2000): 432–34.

Ruttenberg, Nancy. "George Whitefield, Spectacular Conversion and the Rise of Democratic Personality." *American Literary History* 5 (fall 1963): 429–58.

Salmon, Marylynn. "Women and Property in South Carolina: The Evidence from Marriage Settlements, 1730–1830." *William and Mary Quarterly* 39 (Oct. 1982): 655–85.

Savage, Thomas. "Material Culture in the Low Country." In *Southern Furniture, 1680–1830*, ed. Ronald Hurst and Jonathan Prown. New York: Abrams, 1997.

Schaffer, Arthur H. "Between Two Worlds: David Ramsay and the Politics of Slavery." *Journal of Southern History* 50 (May 1984): 175–96.

Schutz, John A. "James Ramsay, Essayist: Aggressive Humanitarian." In *British Humanitarianism*, ed. Samuel Clyde McCulloch, 145–65 (Philadelphia: Church Historical Society, 1950).

Scott, Joan W. "Deconstructing Equality-Versus-Difference: Or, The Uses of Poststructuralist Theory for Feminism." *Feminist Studies* 14 (spring 1988): 33–50.

Shalhope, Robert. "Republicanism and Early American Historiography." *William and Mary Quarterly* 39 (Apr. 1982): 334–56.

Shuffleton, Frank. "Endangered History: Character and Narrative in Early American Historical Writing." *Eighteenth Century: Theory and Interpretation* 34 (1993): 221–41.

Sioli, Marco. "Huguenot Traditions in the Mountains of Kentucky: Daniel Trabue's Memories." *Journal of American History* 84 (Mar. 1998): 1313–33.

Smith, Samuel C. "'Through the Eye of a Needle': The Role of Pietistic and Mystical Thought among the Anglican Elite in the Eighteenth Century Lowcountry South." Ph.D. diss., University of South Carolina, 2000.

Smith, Mark M. "Old South Time in Comparative Perspective." *American Historical Review* 101 (Dec. 1996): 1432–69.

Smith-Rosenberg, Carroll. "Misprisoning Pamela: Representations of Gender and Class in Nineteenth Century America." *Michigan Quarterly Review* 36 (winter 1987): 9–28.

————. "Subject Female: Authorizing American Identity." *American Literary History* 5 (fall 1993): 481–511.

Sweet, James H. "The Iberian Roots of American Racist Thought." *William and Mary Quarterly* 54 (Jan. 1997): 143–66.

Thompson, C. Bradley. "Young John Adams and the New Philosophic Rationalism." *William and Mary Quarterly* 55 (Apr. 1998): 259–80.

Toews, John E. "Intellectual History After the Linguistic Turn: The Autonomy of Meaning and the Irreducibility of Experience." *American Historical Review* 92 (Oct. 1987): 879–907.

Wates, Wylma. "Precursor to the Victorian Age: The Concept of Marriage and Family in the Correspondence of the Izard Family of South Carolina." In *In Joy and In Sorrow*, ed. Carol Bleser, 3–14. New York: Oxford University Press, 1991.

White, Shane, and Graham White. "Slave Hair and African American Culture in the Eighteenth and Nineteenth Centuries." *Journal of Southern History* 61 (Feb. 1995): 45–75.

Wright, Barbara. "Pilgrim in Bethlehem: American Moravian Piety and the Identity Formation of a Nineteenth Century Woman." Ph.D. diss., Drew Theological Seminary, Madison, N.J., 1989.

Wyatt-Brown, Bertram. "God and Honor in the Old South." *Southern Review* 25 (spring 1989): 283–96.

Zagarri, Rosemarie. "The Rights of Man and Woman in Post-Revolutionary America." *William and Mary Quarterly* 55 (Apr. 1998): 203–30.

Zuckerman, Michael. "Penmanship Exercises for Saucy Sons: Some Thoughts on the Colonial Southern Family." *South Carolina Historical Magazine* 84 (July 1983): 152–66.

Index

Episcopal Church. *See* Anglican
Church

federalist political stance: factions pro
and con, 140; supporting strong
national government, 118
filiopietism, 202; appropriate for Lau-
rens/Ramsay heir, 204; ideal plan of
self-discipline for David Jr., 203
Franklin, Benjamin, xxi, 16; lobbying
to intervene for HL in Tower of
London 88, 90
Fry, Elizabeth, 59; steps to establish a
school, 86

Garden, the Rev. Alexander, xvi;
farewell sermon, 29; refusing hospitality to the Rev. George Whitefield in Charles Town, 154
gout, 55, 90, 105

Haitian revolution 1792, 13; *Columbian*
news articles on, 181–83
Hale, Sarah Josepha, xxii, 285n. 45
heart, heartwork (code for personal
religiosity), 10–11, 198, 239n. 20;
"culture of the heart," parental
reliance on suasion rather than
force, 221
Himeli, the Rev. Henry B., 56
Hollinshead, the Rev. William, 161–62;
officiant at Martha's funeral, 233;
supporting DR's creation of *Memoirs,* 235
Huguenot heritage of Laurens family,
xv; 7, 19–20, 24, 34, 57; international
network of merchants, 164; Martha's
Huguenot temperament, 59

intemperance, 158–59; Martha's
responsibility to protect young
slaves from, 160

intention (psychological essential in
actions) 130–31; elevating women's
friendship, 132; essential for instill-
ing wide "social affections" in the
young, expanding mothering to
include education, 132–37; idealizing humility, 142; key element in
new American identity, 127; transformed into principle, 132

kinkeeping (Hareven's phrase for relative duties), 128; guarding family
honor, 130; metaphor for "social
affections," 136; Martha's version of,
145; to the nation, 139; transformed
by intention, 131; visible in naming
pattern, 131

language, religious, 2; agonies over
"easily besetting sin," 192–93, 216;
appropriate for diaries, 110–11; of
citizenship for women, 126; of
compassion, altering view of "reasonableness," "right," 171; diary of
marital submission, 120; discourse
giving gravity to correspondence,
206; DR's Protestant Calvinist, for
marriage, 108; "errors" as human
perversity (original sin), 216; of
"race," 162; of slavery, avoiding
word "slave," 151, 163
Laurens, Eleanor (Nelly), 1755–1763,
HL's oldest daughter, 22; death of,
25, 35, 37; excuse for young
Martha's tears at dame school, 37
Laurens, Eleanor Ball, wife of HL, 21;
cited as model, 100; concern for
relatives, 23; hysteria during Stamp
Act invasion of household, 41–43;
predicted Laurens brothers' competition, 97; prolonged dying after
birth of youngest child, 43–45